Familicidal Hearts

INTERPERSONAL VIOLENCE

Series Editors

Claire Renzetti, Ph.D.
Jeffrey L. Edleson, Ph.D.

Parenting by Men Who Batter: New Directions for Assessment and Intervention
Edited by Jeffrey L. Edleson and Oliver J. Williams

Coercive Control: How Men Entrap Women in Personal Life
Evan Stark

Childhood Victimization: Violence, Crime, and Abuse in the Lives of Young People
David Finkelhor

Restorative Justice and Violence Against Women
Edited by James Ptacek

Familicidal Hearts: The Emotional Styles of 211 Killers
Neil Websdale

FAMILICIDAL HEARTS

The Emotional Styles of 211 Killers

Neil Websdale

OXFORD
UNIVERSITY PRESS

2010

OXFORD

UNIVERSITY PRESS

Oxford University Press, Inc., publishes works that further
Oxford University's objective of excellence
in research, scholarship, and education.

Oxford   New York
Auckland   Cape Town   Dar es Salaam   Hong Kong   Karachi
Kuala Lumpur   Madrid   Melbourne   Mexico City   Nairobi
New Delhi   Shanghai   Taipei   Toronto

With offices in
Argentina   Austria   Brazil   Chile   Czech Republic   France   Greece
Guatemala   Hungary   Italy   Japan   Poland   Portugal   Singapore
South Korea   Switzerland   Thailand   Turkey   Ukraine   Vietnam

Copyright © 2010 by Oxford University Press, Inc.

Published by Oxford University Press, Inc.
198 Madison Avenue, New York, New York 10016
www.oup.com

Oxford is a registered trademark of Oxford University Press

Library of Congress Cataloging-in-Publication Data
Websdale, Neil.
Familicidal hearts: the emotional styles of 211 killers/Neil Websdale.
p. cm.—(Interpersonal violence; 5)
Includes bibliographical references and index.
ISBN 978–0–19–531541–7
1. Family violence—Sociological & Psychological aspects. 2. Homicide—Sociological & Psychological
aspects. 3. Uxoricide—Sociological & Psychological aspects.
4. Infanticide—Sociological & Psychological aspects. I. Title.
HV6626.W43 2010
364.152—dc22
2009030185

1 3 5 7 9 8 6 4 2

Printed in the United States of America
on acid-free paper

In memory of John Arthur Websdale.
And in memory of Julia and William Pemberton.

One cannot understand the breakdown of civilized behavior
and feeling as long as one cannot understand and
explain how civilized behavior and feeling came
to be constructed and developed.

Norbert Elias

I will show you fear in a handful of dust.

T. S. Eliot

ACKNOWLEDGMENTS

I have benefited enormously from working with a large number of people connected with the domestic violence fatality-review movement and the movement to end domestic violence in general. These people include: David Adams, Tom Andrew, Michael Bauer, Libby Bissa, Linda Blozie, Nica Boback, Allie Bones, Pam Booth, Larry and Shirley Bostrum, Jerry Bowles, Alana Bowman, Mike Brigner, Craig Broughton, Jackie Campbell, Tiffany Carr, Nancy Cline, Cameron Crandall, Sherrie Currens, Chic Dabby, Shamita Das-Gupta, Gabby Davis, Myrna Dawson, Joanne Del-Colle, Billie Lee Dunford-Jackson, Mike and Deanne Durfee, Mary Ann Dutton, Julie Field, John Fileu, Amy Fitgerald, Dale Fox, Loretta Frederick, Denise Gamache, Ed Gondolph, Susan Gottschalk, Norm Gregorish, Linda Griebsch, Nancy Grigsby, Roberta Hacker, Margaret Hobart, Peter Jaffe, Amy Karan, Kelly Starr, Marylouise Kelly, Maureen Kiehm, Nikki Kight, Helen Kinton, Andy Kline, Lauren Lazarus, Vicki Lutz, Jim Malouf, Rhonda Martinson, Jerry Monahan, Mark Moran, Shelia Moser, Frank Mullane, Nancy O'Malley, Janet Napolitano, Sue Ostoff, Alison Paul, Marcia Petchers, Pete McDonald, Ellen Pence, Rolanda Pierre-Dixon, Pat Pirkle, Bridget Poule, Rod Reeder, the late Susan Schecter, Robert Stephan, Chiquita Rollins, Lynn Rosenthal, Cynthia Rubenstein, Maureen Sheeran, Connie Sponsler-Garcia, Anita St. Onge, Betsy Stanko, Gail Straeck, Nancy Tanner, Taylor Thompson, Angelo Trimble, Debby Tucker, Pat West, Freda Widera, Janet Wilson, Linda Wong-Kerberg, Nina Zollo and Joan Zorza. Particular thanks to Matthew Dale for his support, friendship, and impressive insights into and commitment to his work.

I especially want to thank Sue Carbon, Barbara Hart, Merry Hofford, Byron Johnson, Catherine Pierce, Robin Thompson, and Mike Town for help, encouragement, and support from the very inception of the national movement to review domestic violence-related deaths. Many thanks to Leah Gatlin and Sarah Saville.

Thanks to the staff at Oxford University Press for their professionalism, support, and kindness. Special thanks to Maura Roessner. I am very grateful to the five anonymous reviewers who provided insightful and detailed feedback on the first draft of the manuscript. Claire Renzetti and Jeff Edleson gave me the opportunity to publish in this Oxford University Press series and have always encouraged and supported my work in a very classy way. I cannot thank them enough.

I also benefited from my working relationships with many colleagues at Northern Arizona University, including Steven Barger, Ray Michalowski, Rich Fernandez, Sumner Sydenum, Lynn Jones, Cyndi Banks, Ann Moore, Valerie Hanneman, Kooros Mamhoudi, Doug Degher, Mark Beeman, Warren Lucas, Yvonne Luna, Dave McKell, Dick Skeen, Geeta Chowdhry, Sheila Nair, Steve Wright, Eric Otenyo, David Schlosberg, and Ann Medill. Particular thanks to Jim Wilce for warm friendship and for numerous conversations about emotion and social life. In my own department, special thanks to Michael Costelloe for his wit and methodological insights and for carrying Federal Express boxes; to Robert Schehr for his passion for his work and his acting ability; and to Alex Alvarez for his abiding friendship and for having a heart that will not retreat.

On a more personal note, I have a number of people to thank. I owe a debt of gratitude to my long-time running partner, Jim Novak, for listening to far too much of this book as it took shape, fell apart, and finally saw the light of day. I thank Andrew Bush for lifelong friendship and for his graveside etiquette at my father's recent burial. A number of years ago, my father, John Arthur Websdale, suggested that I write a book that paid serious attention to men's lives and perspectives. Among other things, *Familicidal Hearts* attempts to do that. As always, thanks to my mother, Molly Websdale, and my sisters, Jill and Judy, for their love over the years.

Finally, I am lucky enough to live a life intertwined with those of two remarkable women, my daughter, Mia Websdale, and my partner, Kathleen Ferraro. Muses both, I owe them, albeit in different ways.

CONTENTS

1. Situating Familicide   1

2. Figurations of Feeling, Haunted Hearts,
    and Uncanny Acts   60

3. Familicide: A History   87

4. Livid Coercive Hearts   125

5. Civil Reputable Hearts   176

6. Familicide as a Consequence of Modern
    Emotional Formations   216

7. Some Implications: A Few Closing Thoughts   258

    Appendix I: The Occupational Backgrounds of the
                  Livid Coercive and Civil Reputable Hearts   285

    Appendix II: The Racial/Ethnic Backgrounds of the
                  Livid Coercive and Civil Reputable Hearts   286

Appendix III: Rates of Familicide   287

Appendix IV: Survey Instrument: Male Perpetrators   290

References   301

Index   313

Familicidal Hearts

1

SITUATING FAMILICIDE

"Familicide" refers to the deliberate killing within a relatively short period of time of a current or former spouse or intimate partner and one or more of their children, perhaps followed by the suicide of the perpetrator. The word *familicide* therefore refers to a killing event, a strange and disturbing, albeit relatively rare, episode that punctuates social life in the modern era. The term "*familicidal hearts*" refers to the emotional styles of those who commit familicide. These styles manifest within familial atmospheres of feeling and wider-ranging social and historical currents of feeling. In what follows, I explore the lives of a sample of familicidal hearts, situating them amidst the social networks and interdependencies of which they were a part.

In this opening chapter, I introduce a social-historical approach to the study of familicide. The chapter commences with a personal statement outlining the origins of my interest in this strange form of multiple murder or "multicide." The personal statement segues into a discussion of the systematic approach used to gather information on 211 cases of familicide. Throughout I refer to these 211 cases and the files and information they contain as the "familicide archive." My analysis identifies familicide as consequence of modern era emotional life. I carefully examine modern life before exploring the historical emergence of familicide. Since my arguments draw upon the work of other researchers, I discuss the research into familicide, family killing, and homicide, paying particular attention to the relationship between intimate partner violence, control, and emotional capital. Departing somewhat from this insightful research literature, I discuss the importance of focusing on emotions as a way of making sense of familicide. In particular, I develop the idea of an emotional continuum as a means of understanding the range of perpetrators' emotional styles, especially in relation to their management of anger, rage, hostility, and aggression. My substantive and conceptual groundwork enables me to introduce the argument of the book and the outline of the chapters.

PERSONAL STATEMENT

In the mid 1990s, under the leadership of Robin Hassler, the Florida Governor's Task Force on Domestic and Sexual Violence funded Dr. Byron Johnson and me to study domestic violence homicides. The project called for us to visit criminal justice agencies to gather files and learn in depth about the microdynamics of these cases. In conducting this work we met many different agency professionals, particularly police officers, advocates, judges, prosecutors, and medical examiners. In some instances these professionals helped us iron out some of the inconsistencies in cases and to fill in some of the missing information. On rare occasions I met family members who had lost loved ones. Eventually, I drew upon all these experiences and a plethora of case files and documents to write my second book, *Understanding Domestic Homicide*.

During the Florida study of domestic violence-related killings, I wrote a couple of grants in conjunction with the Florida Task Force to seek funds from the newly formed Violence Against Women Office (U.S. Department of Justice) to create the first fatality review teams in Florida. At that time only a handful of states had fatality review teams, most of them local or regional.[1] In Hawaii, for example, Judge Michael Town had pioneered fatality reviews within the family courthouse system. Mike and I became friends, and I learned much from him about reviewing cases in the spirit of prevention rather than with a punitive energy directed at blaming and shaming various parties involved or not involved in the cases.[2]

The handful of fatality review teams active in the mid-1990s worked to identify homicides and suicides caused by, related to, or somehow traceable to domestic violence. They reviewed cases in an attempt to prevent similar deaths in the future and to reduce domestic violence in general. In some states, statute law enabled the creation of the teams, guaranteed the confidentiality of their deliberations and findings, recommended team members, and informed the nature and form of review work. In others, review teams operated more casually, expressing concerns about the dangers inherent in prescribing the process of death review and housing it within state agencies and organizations.[3]

Either way, review teams worked mostly without the benefit of learning from others doing similar work. A group of us, including Barbara Hart, Merry Hofford, Judge Susan Carbon, and Judge Michael Town, discussed the possibility of setting up a national initiative to act as a clearinghouse for information about fatality review, to provide technical assistance to the emerging network of teams, and to put on national training conferences. In 1999, I wrote a pilot grant seeking funds from the Violence Against Women Office (VAWO) to establish the National Domestic Violence Fatality Review Initiative (NDVFRI). VAWO funded the grant, and we held our first national summit on fatality review in the beautiful setting of Key West, Florida, in late October 1999.

The renamed Office on Violence Against Women still funds NDVFRI, and at time of writing this book, I direct the project. Providing technical assistance to communities and engaging in social policy discussions brought me into close contact with a vast array of service professionals; battered women; policymakers at local, state, and federal levels; and, to a much lesser extent, fellow researchers. As an ethnographer, I shared many of the concerns of grassroots advocates and others that reviews might become too formal, too impersonal, excessively bureaucratic, and overly professional in orientation. We wrestled for years with how to involve family members, friends, neighbors, and those who knew victims. In the early years, teams expressed suspicions about learning from these non-agency professionals. Would community members close to the case tell the truth? Have an ax to grind? Want statutorily protected information from the team? Or simply break down emotionally?

Many review teams started by examining homicide-suicides; always selecting cases with no pending civil litigation or criminal prosecutions. Reviews occurred in private, and those teams operated under protective confidentiality statutes that shielded their deliberations from the prying eyes of the media and others. Death review was a "safe" activity for the agencies at the table. Teams reported aggregate data to units of central government charged with gathering and publishing it. In some cases, data in these reports encouraged reform and social change.

In my opinion, the early reluctance of agencies to solicit community input into death reviews reflected prevailing ways of seeing cases of domestic violence. It was supposedly the experts who made sense of these cases. These experts included police, judges, prosecutors, advocates, emergency medical room personnel, social workers, batterer treatment specialists, attorneys, and so on. Each had their story to tell. At times, these players had their own turf to protect and their own understandings of what lay at the root of domestic violence.

Feminist scholars and advocates often explained that men's intimate violence and murder stemmed from their power, their attempts to control women, their sense of entitlement to exert power and control, or their sense that their power and control were somehow ebbing. Some examples illustrate these positions. Constance Bean wrote, "Murder is the final irrevocable step, the ultimate expression of men's control over women. For some men, the need for control is not satisfied until this irrevocable step is taken."[4] Anne Campbell observed that men's aggression stems from threats to their masculine pride. Such aggression comprised "a means of instilling fear and gaining power."[5] Christine Alder opined, "male violence against women in male dominated society is an expression of male power which is used by men to reproduce and maintain their status and authority over women."[6] According to Ann Goetting, battering was something engaged in exclusively by men in intimate relationships. She defined it as "an obsessive campaign of coercion and intimidation designed by a man to dominate and control a woman, which occurs in the personal context of intimacy and thrives in the sociopolitical climate of patriarchy."[7] Finally, in her exploration of male-perpetrated spousal homicide in New South Wales, Alison Wallace identified the central importance of women's exiting or attempting to exit these relationships and the male jealousy that accompanied such developments. In particular, Wallace stressed, the killings were the ultimate attempt by men to exert "their power and control over their wives."[8]

Psychologists and therapists brave enough to speak up identified men's sense of shame, humiliation, dependency, vulnerability, and relative powerlessness at the heart of the killings. At one conference, Native American Indians explained that domestic violence and domestic homicide arose from the spiritual imbalances in Indian communities brought about by the profoundly debilitating effects of colonization.

Those attached to these seemingly conflicting interpretations often shared a strong sense that the public; the community; and, more specifically, families, friends, workplace peers, and neighbors of the decedents could not know of the technical complications involved in working these perplexing cases and perhaps did not fully appreciate the complexities of domestic violence cases. To the extent that state service providers often shielded their inner workings from the general public, this concern was perhaps well placed.

Fortunately, these somewhat condescending sentiments began to change, and fatality review teams began to become more permeable to community influence and input. First, review teams learned that, in a significant number of domestic violence–related killings, victims did not have contact with agencies. Even in cases where there was contact, it was often limited to a particular agency. It was a rare case where agencies worked in concert with a battered woman prior to her demise. Second, researchers such as Jacqueline Campbell began to publish important data showing that those closest to decedents knew the most about their lives and the compromises they faced.[9] Campbell showed that family members such as sisters and close friends knew much more about battered women's plight than agencies charged with supportin   . Third, surviving family members begar   . On one occasion I was confronted by a   r to intimate partner homicide. This ang   y a death review team would not autom   - tions. In some cases I talked at great le   d ones. They wanted to tell their story a   r tragedies in the future. Since these earl   e talked with about their involvement wi   e experience was more often than not cathartic.

Shirley and Larry Bostrum, whose son-in-law murdered their daughter, Margie, contributed enormously to the formation of the Connecticut Fatality Review Team Initiative.[10] This team reserves a place for family members. At time of writing, the Bostrums currently work on the team.

In an attempt to widen the interpretative lens, the Montana Death Review Initiative welcomed the stepmother of a perpetrator to the table.[11] This unfortunate stepmother had attracted the opprobrium of many because she had supposedly "spawned a monster," as one member of the team told me. The stepmother was relieved the team treated her as a human being. She testified for four hours, providing many insights.

Similar community and familial involvement in death review occurred in other liberal democracies. From 2002, the Ontario, Canada, fatality review team invited family members and others close to the decedents to testify. In Great Britain, Frank Mullane, who lost his sister, Julie Pemberton, and his nephew, Will Pemberton, to domestic violence-related familicide, challenged the British Home Office in the courts and through the press to include families in homicide review.[12] Mr. Mullane's efforts to have his family members heard at the homicide review contributed greatly to the publication of the extremely detailed landmark death review concerning the now-infamous Pemberton familicide.[13]

Open, comprehensive, permeable, and what I call *wide-angled lens death review* brings the complexities of intimate partner homicide and other domestic violence-related deaths into sharp focus. Domestic violence deaths are not merely a *piecemeal processional*, to echo British historian Edward Thompson's ringing phrase, of unrelated incidents and violent episodes. Rather, they build over time. Tensions accumulate, fear intensifies, women's physical and emotional options diminish, isolation often increases, and many abusers seemingly strive to micro-regulate women's lives. Women struggle against and negotiate this pressure and violence. Sometimes they make choices that system players cannot discern as either rational or useful.

Looking at the review process from the outside, I sensed that the invisible and intangible aspects of abuse, those emotionally intense shifts in intimate relationships, offered important insights into these tragic acts of killing. Often these emotional realignments emerged over relatively long periods of time. As providers of national technical assistance to death review teams, a number of us encouraged review teams to examine the cases in the long term. At a practical level, we recommended the construction of timelines dating as far back as team members thought useful. In some cases teams worked back into the childhoods of perpetrators and victims alike. What emerged was both telling and disconcerting. Fear, tension, isolation, entrapment, and attempts to closely control the eventual homicide victims intensified greatly before the killing. Agencies looking in from the outside usually concentrated upon violent incidents and breaches of the criminal code. Often agencies worked without talking with each other. Battered women often sensed the danger, frequently interpreting their options differently than did the professionals. The latter often talked of an array of available options. Where we learned of their perceptions, battered women often talked of confronting a confusing maze rather than an array of choices.

We met and still meet considerable resistance to trying to recreate intimate partner homicides through the eyes of decedents. One obvious objection is that "she is now dead, so how can we possibly recreate the case through her eyes?" A good point, indeed, and one that draws support from the fact that battered women probably take much important information to the grave. A different objection came from a number of advocates who asked, "Why waste money reviewing cases where women died?" Rather, they contended, it is better to spend that money on women who are alive and in need of services; another valid concern. Nevertheless, the research was compelling; battered women and those closest to them often knew the most about victims' compromises. If we wanted to improve service delivery and reconsider how best to support, protect, and serve, we needed to know more about battered women's knowledge, maneuverability, and choices. It became clear that meticulous and humane fatality review work ought recreate the victim's experiences and discern her perception of her options rather than superimposing a multi-agency/ professional interpretation of her maneuverability and compromises as she confronted, negotiated, and lived them.

Some team members have also been reluctant to acknowledge just how perceptive battered women are about their own situations. In my community presentations and trainings, I suggest to audiences that battered women can read their abusive partners with the sensitivity of a seismograph needle. This does not mean battered women do not operate in the dark sometimes in terms of knowing some of the strategies abusers may deploy. Neither does it mean that battered women will not have significant cognitive deficits in terms of knowing precisely what an abuser is capable of or what resources are available to that abuser.

As fatality review teams take on new members, the struggle over how to review continues. Team data-gathering instruments sometimes chop battered women's lives up into countable parts, variables if you will, rather than capture an essence, a trajectory, and a mélange of feelings, tensions, fears, ambiguities, and nuances. Clearly, we need aggregate data about these cases, especially if we are to influence legislators and the press. We especially need empirical findings regarding age, income, sex, the issuance of protection orders, police attendance at the home, and so forth, so that we can compare across cases, regions, states and so on. However, that search for standardized information ought accompany rather than eclipse the acquisition of personal, highly complex idiosyncrasies. Wide-angled lens fatality review involves much more than collecting statistical data and identifying trends and patterns across cases. Every life is different, and it is important to capture highly idiosyncratic and nuanced information. Incident-based data gathering tends to catalogue people's lives through the organizational schema and analytical filters and interests of authorities, experts, professionals, and social science researchers. Conducting death reviews that rely solely on the bureaucratic criteria of the criminal justice apparatus or various service providers runs the risk of failing to capture the chilling themes and continuities in abuse that far transcend either the immediacies of violence or the at-times clumsy, mismatched official responses to that violence.

It was through my extensive involvement in domestic violence fatality review that I developed a keen interest in familicide. Over the years, a number of teams reviewed these cases, and other teams at least pointed out the phenomenon, logging incidents and providing important summary data. The familicides they alluded to and occasionally reviewed shocked the communities where they occurred. Familicides also presented fatality review teams with enormous challenges. The number of victims exceeded those found in intimate partner homicides and homicide-suicides. Teams found themselves reviewing an array of killings including intimate-partner homicide, the murder of a child or children and often the suicide of the perpetrator. In addition, perpetrators of familicide often killed unexpectedly and with considerable planning. In some cases, teams accustomed to finding a long history of escalating domestic violence found no violence or tyranny at all.

At the same time as I was rather haphazardly accumulating information about familicide through my role in NDVFRI, I also set about developing a more systematic way of identifying and researching familicides. These two parallel approaches that I will loosely refer to as the *haphazard* and the *systematic* warrant scrutiny because they speak to different ways of knowing about familicide and alternative methods of studying it.

APPROACH

My working definition of familicide draws upon the important insights of a number of researchers. Wilson, Daly, and Daniele use the word *familicide* to refer to the killing of a former or current spouse or intimate partner and one or more children.[14] Dwight Duwe employs the word *familicide* to refer to the killing of four or more family members, within a 24-hour period, by another family member.[15] My definition excludes cases where the perpetrator does not kill a current or former spouse or partner. Neither do I include cases of parricide (where children kill parents). I also exclude cases where a single parent kills his or her children.

Clearly, one might argue for the inclusion of the killing of parents and relatives, or the killing of children, among the ranks of familicide cases. After all, we describe kinship arrangements without intimate partners as families. Neither do I examine cases of intimate partner killing where no children were killed. In some cases, perpetrators took the lives of other people as well, extended family, friends, workplace peers, or bystanders. These cases I included because they still involved acts of familicide, albeit familicide augmented by further killing. My principal focus therefore concerns the annihilation of the nuclear family as we have come to know it; a historical phenomenon of fairly recent origin and highly idiosyncratic emotional intensity. It is this emotional intensity and its links with broader social and historical landscapes that concern me as I proffer an explanation of familicide.

Over the years a number of graduate students working with me explored newspaper search indexes, keying in words such as *familicide, family murder, family killing, mass killing, mass murder, mass shooting, arson, kill family, kill wife, kill children, poisoning,* and numerous other words and phrases to identify familicides. Our list of search indexes included the following: Google, Early American Imprints (especially for the older cases), Academic Search Complete, New York Times, New York Times Archives, Access World News, ArticleFirst, Early American Newspapers, and various Coroner's Rolls from the United Kingdom.

Our newspaper search was global in scope. We combined our findings with the cases I already knew of through my involvement with fatality review teams. Under the Freedom of Information Act, I requested whatever files authorities possessed on the cases of familicide handled within their jurisdictions. I requested police files, court data, probation reports, psychological evaluations, medical examiner and coroner's reports, and newspaper clippings. In some cases I called advocacy agencies and state coalitions against domestic violence to try to find out if the deceased had any contact with shelters or outreach services for battered women. Sometimes authorities refused my requests for information. Other times I received an abundance of information, literally hundreds of pages per case. In some of the older cases, I found local histories that referenced familicides. In a couple of these cases, I talked with surviving family members or other community members close to the case.

Many of these sources come from agencies of the state, including police, medical examiners, courts, advocacy agencies, social services, and counseling services.[16] Clearly, we ought not just accept these "state-mediated" ethnographies as pure expressions of truth. Nevertheless, when detectives conduct field interviews, stenographers transcribe sworn testimony, medical examiners meticulously examine corpses, and advocates for battered women listen with their hearts, they enact and simultaneously remake culture and history. The socially situated remains of their activities call for our most careful attention. Needless to say, much is lost as the corpses find their way back into the soil. However, this harsh reality ought not dissuade us from piecing together the evidence of a life and the latticework of emotional styles and meanings haunting that life.

My approach therefore relies on the richness of the archival files and the multiple interpretations associated with them and available through them. These files include the accounts of journalists, homicide detectives, perpetrators, witnesses, advocates for victims of domestic violence, neighbors, bystanders, surviving family members, and those who worked with perpetrators and victims, to name just a few. In general, the available information is much greater in cases where the state pursued a prosecution of the offender. Here we find considerable information on early childhood socialization of perpetrators, for example. Where the case materials provided early childhood data, I was nearly always able to identify some combination of the physical, emotional, and sexual abuse of perpetrators. Obviously, we cannot conclude that early childhood trauma among all the familicidal hearts correlates with the commission of familicide. However, in cases where we do find examples of such trauma, I try to trace links between the trauma and the future emotional styles of perpetrators.

On many occasions these sources are several orders removed from the perpetrators or victims themselves. Many of these files provide ethnographic snapshots, selective renderings of sometimes highly charged episodes, mediated memories filtered through the innumerable screens and prescriptive formulae of criminal justice agencies. In its selective renderings, the archive is not as comprehensive as I would wish, but it reflects the state of the various investigative arts, and we must live with that and augment it wherever possible and ethical.

At other points, we see a starker interaction with a corpse. Medical examiners write in meticulous detail about organ systems and provide at least partial histories of broken bones. Their toxicological screens and medical histories offer rich insights into the use of medications and what conditions those medications sought to alleviate or contain. In a sense, the report of the medical examiner constitutes a terminal scientific scrutiny. We ought not think less of it for this. Amidst the science and the aura of detachment and objectivity, we obtain a haunting sense of the person's physiology, health habits, drug use, surgical history, emotional torments, and their final demise.

My approach, of course, relies on much more than these sources. As a man, a writer, a father, and a member of familial networks, I bring my own heart to these pages. I select what I write about and project into what I hear and see.[17] My own family upbringing, not a violent or despairing one I might add, clearly informs my work. My writing reflects my own interpretative matrices; my political filters, if you will. I do not merely observe these cases from a distance. The words I write reflect my own engagement in and negotiation of late-modern life. My own fascination with the archive caused me to wonder about the voluminous popular writings on mass killing and their seemingly enthusiastic consumption. Do readers somehow share in the thoughts, feelings, or impulses of perpetrators? In a related vein, David Garland observes, "The fact that criminals sometimes act out wishes which are present in the unconscious of law-abiding citizens may account for the deep fascination which crime holds for many, and for the widespread appeal of crime literature, crime news, and the gruesome interest provoked by figures such as Jack the Ripper."[18]

Like perpetrators of familicide, we all experience the emotional climate of modern life. Indeed, as we map lives and explore compromises, we might imagine what it must have felt like to commit these killings. It is not that in our analyses we are trying to walk in the shoes of those who committed familicide or those perpetrators killed. Clifford Geertz addresses these matters rather nicely: "We are not, or at least I am not, seeking either to become natives (a compromised word in any case) or to mimic them. Only romantics or spies would seem to find point in that. We are seeking, in the widened sense of the term in which it encompasses very much more than talk, to converse with them, a matter a great deal more difficult, and not only with strangers, than is commonly recognized."[19]

Nevertheless, to pursue what I will call *familicidal hearts* is to chase social and historical extremes. Given the rarity of familicides, I suggest some perpetrators assume notoriety because of the remote human possibilities they realize. In some ways these possibilities seem bleak and depressing, perhaps symptomatic of the way many of us feel, at least at times. However, because of their rarity we might see familicidal hearts as the exceptions that point out the fact that modern era intimacy has great potential and is for many people rife with emotional opportunities.

In many ways my approach, especially to the case studies in chapters 4 and 5, comports with what Clifford Geertz calls *thick description*. Geertz contends that the ethnographic appreciation of a culture involves accessing these thick layers of interpretation. These layers might include the many ways members of that culture make sense of their lives and living arrangements, the manner in which key informants comment on what they see, and the interpretive work of ethnographers who spin the tales in yet other ways.

I also used my personal contacts in the field of domestic violence and fatality review to acquire information. In a relatively small number of cases, I gained access to the deliberations of fatality review teams that reviewed the familicide. Such access included seeing statutorily protected notes, interview transcripts, and sensitive personal information.[20] The need to protect the confidentiality of the parties involved in these cases was paramount, and it is for this reason that I cannot list the 211 cases or provide precise dates and locations of the killings. It is neither ethical nor legal to write about sensitive matters such as the sexual abuse of surviving family members in such a manner that someone might be able to trace their identity.

The depth of material I collected in each of the 211 cases varied enormously, creating what I refer to as my *familicide archive*. Historians are usually more comfortable than sociologists and criminologists with piecing together cultural life, family life, and personal life through the use of documents such as diaries, letters, oral histories, court transcripts, minutes of meetings from political bodies such as city councils and units of government, and other sources such as photographs or film. Indeed, Harriet Bradley talks of the allure of the archive and its potential to enlighten us about lives and events.[21] Others have examined the virtues of the case-study approach to unravel the phenomenon of attempted multiple murder.[22]

Ninety percent of the cases I settled upon as meeting the criteria for constituting a familicide came from the United States. Specifically, 21 of the 211 familicides (10 percent) came from outside the United States.

Like the United States, all these societies are modern in character. These included cases from: Canada, 8; France, 2; New Zealand, 2; United Kingdom, 2; Germany, 1; Poland, 1; Holland, 1; Austria, 1; Ireland, 1; Australia, 1; South Africa, 1. These 211 cases of familicide date from 1755 to 2007. Appendix III shows the rates of familicide per 100,000 people for ten-year intervals. Appendix IV shows the 112 questions we asked in each case of male-perpetrated familicide. My analysis of the 15 female-perpetrated cases was entirely qualitative. Although my approach is primarily qualitative, at various points I use quantitative data to illustrate trends among cases.

Critics might contend that my approach to creating the familicide archive is haphazard and that the variation in the depth of case material makes comparisons across the entire 211 cases difficult. It is certainly true that in some cases, especially the older ones, I had perhaps a newspaper article or two to work with, and in others a plethora of documentary materials that included police files, court documents, social histories from probation officers, a filmed confession, private letters, interviews with surviving family members, newspaper articles, child abuse and neglect reports, and so on. I do not see such variation as anything other than a reflection of the realities of historical and sociological research. It seems to me that the historical record is haphazard, and that historians take what they can from the past. It is also the case that authorities investigate familicides with varying degrees of enthusiasm and rigor, depending at least in part upon the resources available to them.[23] We would therefore expect to find some aspects of cases explored in great depth in one jurisdiction and not in others.

The variability in the depth of the case material does not mean we cannot compare cases and search for themes and commonalities. Rather, the varying detail limits the degree of comparability and cautions us to be wary about trends and patterns. Neither does the fact that the cases are drawn from different time periods or centuries render them incomparable. A familicide that occurred in 1800 may have many of the characteristics of a 2000 case. For example, both may contain evidence of shame and rage. Is it inappropriate to compare the shame and rage of a case from 1800 with those emotions evident in a case from 2000? No. Is it important to realize that emotions such as shame and rage probably manifest differently and perhaps mean different things in 1800 than in 2000? Yes. We must be alive to the fact that the emotional characteristics of the cases may mean different things at different junctures in history. Such a realization does not mean that comparing the cases is unreliable or invalid. If this were the case, we would either have no history or only a history of scientifically verifiable or countable variables. Rather, the caveats about historical time remind us of the importance of carefully specifying historical context and socially situated meaning as a way of interpreting seemingly similar or dissimilar discoveries. It also reminds us that history is complex, subjective, and contested.

In some cases the insights of those very close to the killings added another layer of interpretive complexity. Through my work with the NDV-FRI, I met a number of family members who had lost loved ones to familicide. Some talked with me at great length about their experiences. Others conversed with me and provided rich documentary material about the cases involving their loved ones. Their generous insights provided information often not available through police files, court documents, autopsy reports, medical examiner reports, and newspaper accounts.

In some cases I interviewed investigators or other professionals who worked the case. Many files contained rich and detailed interviews with family members and evinced a wealth of information about the emotional lives of families. In one case I interviewed the perpetrator. A few perpetrators refused my requests for interviews. Lack of time and money prevented me from interviewing more perpetrators. In just over a hundred of the 211 cases, I either conducted interviews with various involved parties or had access to a wealth of personal information through the case files. In the remaining cases, the files offered more limited information; for example, a newspaper article or two. My interviews and content analyses of case files enabled me to recreate a sense of the emotional atmospheres in the families that experienced familicide: the complex constellation of relationships and feelings among family members. Most of the cases I present in the subsequent chapters were those where I did some interviewing work or those that contained rich information about the emotional atmosphere of family life. In cases where I interviewed family members, the interviews typically took the form of broad-ranging life histories of the victims or perpetrators. I was not interested in the gory details of the violence or the killings, although surviving family members often ended up raising these matters. In nearly all conversations with family members I began with open-ended questions such as, "Can you tell me about X's life? Your own life?"

My emotionally charged contact with surviving family members began to alter the way I made sense of the cases. Family members provided an emotional connection to the biographies of those murdered. We talked of decedents' experiences, of hurt, of pain, of abuse and emotional scars. These links to the emotional lives of victims and perpetrators augmented related evidence present in the documents. The emotional landscapes accessed through interviews and case files enriched and extended the trends and patterns discovered through a statistical analysis of the 211 cases. Piecing together these various sources of information, I began to use the biographies of the parties to craft the notion of what I identify in Chapter 2 as the *familicidal heart*. As readers will see, I essentially argue that familicidal hearts emerge in modern times being shaped by the emotional conditions of modern life. In order to introduce these ideas we must first examine modern life.

MODERN LIFE: LINKING EMOTIONAL, SOCIAL, AND HISTORICAL LANDSCAPES

One means of exploring familicide is to use what C. Wright Mills once called a *sociological imagination*. This entails grappling with people's biographies and the social and historical contexts within which they take shape. Mills expresses the adventure rather nicely, "The sociological imagination enables its possessor to understand the larger historical scene in terms of its meaning for the inner life and the external career of a variety of individuals."[24] The emphasis on "meaning for the inner life" is crucial to my approach. For Mills, "*Troubles* occur within the character of the individual and within the range of his immediate relations with others."[25] As the evidence will demonstrate, familicidal hearts are deeply troubled hearts, and, to employ Avery Gordon's language of haunting, hearts *haunted* by modern patterns and atmospheres of feeling.[26] The sociological imagination offers an understanding of the social world and, to a degree, an explanation of familicide. However, the sociological imagination is just that, an imagination. As such, it furnishes us with an appreciation of the social, historical, and emotional milieu *apparently necessary* for the rise of the familicidal heart, without ever specifying the *sufficient* conditions for such a spawning.

Modern societies began to emerge from the later eighteenth century in Western Europe, although we trace their roots as far back as the later fifteenth century. At the heart of modernization was the massive increase in productive capacity that attended the rise of capitalist industrialization. The relative pacification of large regions of Western Europe and America enabled the spread of market forces and encouraged the rise of capitalism. It also provided the possibility of a safer, more secure life in public settings, a gradual development that created conditions conducive to the growth of various self-controls.[27] As Norbert Elias contends, it was not until the state assumed a monopoly over the use of violence and the rights of taxation that we witness conditions conducive to the rapid spread of mass capitalist production. For sure, capitalism had been tried in agriculture and trade well before the eighteenth century but never assumed the pride of place it did from the beginnings of the nineteenth century. The commencement of the factory manufacture of commodities changed ways of life in unprecedented ways. These changes marked a swift and radical shift away from traditional ways of living. People flocked to the growing towns and cities in search of work, spurring urbanization and unprecedented population growth.[28] Working in these towns and cities, people lived in close physical proximity. This crowding among strangers spelled a different kind of community life than that experienced in rural settings. Uprooted from long-established traditions and customs, new generations of city dwellers experienced alienation or estrangement, anomie or normlessness, competition with each other, anonymity, and much closer discipline and surveillance at work and in public spaces.

Modern people also had to develop new ways of relating to each other, moderating their strong emotions toward each other; in particular, their aggressiveness. In some ways, the rise of capitalism created new sensibilities, novel senses of what others needed. As Norbert Elias argues, the expanding network of modern interconnections and interdependencies gradually altered the way people behaved toward one another. Haskell makes the point that modern market relations instilled a new sense of morality. He comments, "The market altered character by heaping tangible rewards on people who displayed a certain calculating, moderately assertive style of conduct, while humbling others whose manner was more unbuttoned or who pitched their affairs at a level of aggressiveness either higher or lower than the prevailing standard."[29]

In premodern societies, the home was the center of production. In this setting people produced what they needed and traded with those in their communities. Men and women both made valued yet different economic contributions to premodern production. In bringing workers under one roof, industrial capitalism undermined the productive function of the home. Families increasingly became consumers of mass factory-produced commodities. Some argued families became havens in a heartless world.[30] Others contended that much of the image of families as a respite from the rational, impersonal rigors of capitalist production was ideological, serving to mask the internal oppression and exploitation of wives and the violence that served as the ultimate resort of heads of household, and the external oppression and exploitation of poor and racially disadvantaged families.[31] The argument that families were havens in a heartless world also obscures the manner in which some families were torn apart. For example, slaves were subject to sale and colonized Indians were forced to send their children to boarding schools.

Notwithstanding these reservations about the role of the family in history, I agree with Van Krieken who complains Elias's theory of modernization devotes insufficient space to the changing role of the family in increasing psychological restraints. It is important, as Van Krieken contends, "to examine what is probably the primary arena of interpersonal obligation, family life, and the ways in which it mediated wider social changes."[32] It is because of criticisms such as these that I attempt to weave together an analysis of familicide that addresses the links between emotional styles, family atmospheres of feeling, and broader-ranging figurations of feeling.

Suffice it to say that the differences between private and public spheres became more intense in the modern era, with romantic love gradually becoming the basis of marriage, and what Lawrence Stone refers to as *affective individualism* emerging as increasingly important.[33] Stone uses the term *affective individualism* to describe a complex mélange of sociohistorical forces affecting familial, economic, and political life. In particular, we might note the growing tendency of spouses to select each another for reasons of romantic love and emotional compatibility, the rise of more affectionate and permissive parenting, the increasing importance of market forces, and the rise of individual political rights. In short, the notion of affective individualism provides an important link between modern era patterns of feeling and the social, economic, and political forces of modern life. I return to these matters in Chapter 3. These modern era changes occurred unevenly among social groups, reflecting groups' historic experiences in the new world. A few of these developments warrant mention.

From the time of first settlement of the American colonies, authorities encouraged women of European descent to settle and reproduce. Bonnie Thornton Dill reminds us that the "groundwork for public support of women's family roles was laid during the colonial period."[34] The London Company, for example, encouraged single women to settle in the colonies as a means of encouraging men and women to put down roots in the form of a nuclear family system. This strategy continued until the closing of the Western frontier toward the end of the nineteenth century.[35] In colonial America, "white women were seen as vital contributors to the stabilization and growth of society."[36] With urbanization and the rise of the middle class, one sure sign of the successful self-made man was his ability to keep his wife at home to care and nurture children. Working-class families did not follow this pattern, with wives and children working in the expanding factories, before eventually being replaced as machines slowly displaced these weaker, non-unionized workers. White middle-class women often hired domestic labor to perform more menial tasks, such as laundry and cleaning, although many still complained bitterly about the drudgery of their life in the increasingly separate sphere of the nuclear family. The hiring of domestic labor freed some white middle- and upper-class women to contribute to the moral development of the family and society.

Although wives of European descent were increasingly confined to the nuclear family, legal codes recognized their important reproductive contributions, bestowing upon them various legal protections within the family even as they remained under the legal authority of husbands. The same cannot be said for women from other races and ethnic groups. Slave owners recognized the reproductive potential of black women for producing new laborers, and to a degree encouraged slave family life. Nevertheless, slave-owning whites had ultimate authority over the bodies of black men and women. These privileges included slave owners' having sexual access to black females, an entitlement that mediated the intimacy between black intimate partners. The slaves built enduring yet nevertheless compromised and vulnerable kin networks because family members were subject to sale, breakup, and early death. The black family had a permeable relationship with community and extended kin, differing markedly from its Western European counterpart. Black women continued to labor outside the home, rarely becoming sole nurturers of their own children in the way many middle-class women of European descent did. As Herbert Gutman observes, the evidence from Mississippi and northern

Louisiana reveals that "about one in six (or seven) slave marriages were ended by force or sale."[37] Most sales involved teenagers or young children, something most adult slaves knew. Living with this "probably served as reason to socialize one's children to prepare for possible sale, a damaging and unenviable task for any parent."[38] As Gutman notes, "all masters poisoned the relationship between slave parents and their children."[39]

The social organization of the black family before and after slavery reveals the profound importance of extended kinship networks. According to Sudarkasa, the extended kinship networks trace a lineage back to Africa.[40] These flexible and historically enduring kin networks militated against the black nuclear family becoming overly isolated and insular.

Latinos do not evidence the development of isolated, nuclear families with the companionate bond between spouses as the fulcrum of family life to anything like the degree we see in Caucasian families. With the American colonization of Mexico in the nineteenth century, Dill notes Chicanos earned a subsistence living off the land. She points out, "Patriarchal families were important instruments of community life, and nuclear family units were linked together through an elaborate system of kinship and godparenting."[41] Chicano and African-American families both evidenced a sexual division of labor, with wives assuming prime responsibility for household labor and child care, as well as working outside of the home to augment the often-low wages of the patriarch. Importantly, in both groups, the permeability between family and community was significantly higher than it was among Caucasians, providing these poorer minority groups with collective solutions to common problems. In all likelihood, the greater permeability between family and community enhanced cohesion and values, and created an important sense of belonging, albeit in the midst of acute poverty.

As Karin Wang points out, "Asian cultures are group-oriented. A person's identity and worth are not measured individually, but are instead reflected by the group as a whole. Consequently, the family is the most important social unit."[42] This means that Asian-Americans were effectively seen as extensions of their families rather than as individuals in their own right in the sense intended in Caucasian households. Historically, most Asian-American families have differed greatly from the middle-class family of European origin where the wife served as a decorative symbol of her husband's success. These observations apply to Asian cultures from the time they migrated to the United States in the nineteenth century.

Space precludes a more detailed exploration of the numerous forms of the American family. Suffice it to say that the insulated nuclear family form, imbued with a growing sense of affective individualism, became the model the majority of Caucasian families aspired to or adopted. This model differed from that among minority groups such as African-Americans, Hispanics, or Asians, all of which retained stronger ties with their respective communities and placed much less emphasis on the value of the individual. Later, I suggest that the insulated nuclear family and its attendant celebration of individualism might, in some cases, have created an atmosphere of feeling conducive to the insurgent array of negative emotions that drives familicide.

As noted, affective individualism was part of a more general cultivation of individuality. The diversity of job types and social roles expanded dramatically in urban industrial societies, rendering individuals more aware of their identity and individuality. Growing social differentiation and individuation was accompanied by the gradual spread of political rights. Representative democracies formed out of upheavals such as the French and American revolutions. In modern societies, feelings of detachment increased as state apparatuses became ever more bureaucratic and impersonal, mirroring much broader historical shifts toward the rationalization of social life in general. Enlightenment thinking from the eighteenth century influenced the way people saw the world. Scientific and technological advances called into question more traditional religious and spiritual perspectives. Notions of time and space changed. The discipline of the clock regulated factory life just as the rhythms of the seasons had governed traditional agrarian production.

From the end of the fifteenth century, Western explorers began to travel the globe, paving the way for new trade and colonization. In short, the world shrank, becoming more accessible through modern communication channels such as the telegraph, the telephone, television, and the Internet. Standardized time zones permitted greater coordination between vastly different global regions. The management of time and space sometimes merged, producing (for example) ever more sophisticated timetables. Anthony Giddens captures nicely this combined coordination of time and space when he describes the train timetable as a "time-space ordering device" that "permits the complex coordination of trains and their passengers and freight across large tracts of time-space."[43]

The rational planning of the movement of passengers and freight on trains epitomizes one of the central features of modernity, its forward-looking nature. Certainly the rationalization of capitalist industrial production made available many more commodities to a large range of people. At the same time as they generated enormous profits for successful capitalists and caused considerable class conflict, many of these products made life easier and more enjoyable. However, the forward-looking nature of modernity also yielded new uncertainties as tradition and social solidarity diminished. The modern individual was gradually faced with what Emile Durkheim described as *anomie* or "normlessness," a condition of being increasingly cut adrift from the collective conscience, common interests, and shared values, with ever fewer informal and community norms to guide his behavior.[44] Karl Marx pointed out that under capitalism, workers increasingly became commodities, cut off from the products of the their labor, competing with their peers for jobs. In place of premodern communally organized labor, embedded in the ebb and flow of social life, politics, and religion, the logic of the market assumed pride of place, turning work-ers into the extrinsically motivated objects of the capitalist wage.[45]

As modernity dawned, people began to experience the world a little differently. The expression of strong emotion was increasingly frowned upon. Over the centuries, people slowly internalized feelings such as rage and shame. Public violence diminished, as did spectacular punishments such as torture, branding, and public executions. Gradually, over several centuries, people increasingly monitored themselves, internalizing social strictures, and thereby gaining some control over and insight into their emotions. These changes in the modern era expression of strong feelings began in the ascendant social classes, little by little making their way to the vast majority of the population in relatively recent times. Generally, we witnessed a gradual diminution in fears of public violence and murder over a period of five centuries or so. Social life has become more peaceful. However, with the rise of the cult of the self, the lessening of community ties, the increasing insularity of the nuclear family, and the weakening of the collective conscience, we find that people feel increasing frustration and anxiety about their personal direction and the meaning of life.

Crudely put, we might say that physical safety in modern public space increased as ontological security, or our confidence in the nature and meaning of our existence, decreased. This divergence between physical and emotional security attended the decline of the emotional sureties of community life and the predictable rhythms that tradition and ritual fur-nished. These modern emotional transformations provide us with a win-dow into the emergence of familicide. In the chapters that follow, I explore these changes in the emotional landscape, taking care to map them against the idiosyncrasies of feeling and sensibility evident through the familicide archive. As readers will see, certain permutations and combinations of emotions loom larger in some types of cases than others.

THE HISTORICAL EMERGENCE OF FAMILICIDE

As we will see in much more detail in Chapter 3, familicide appeared for the first time in the early American republic. A substantial discourse devel-oped regarding what the arrival of this new offence might signify.[46] Writ-ers wondered if fast-changing ways of life caused these atrocities. Such reflection on the meaning of familicide continues to this day, as these rare yet highly publicized killings shock communities, generating exten-sive media coverage.[47] As Fox and Levin emphasize, "We like to think of the family as a crucible of love and affection. Hence, murder by the hands of a family member can be too much for the mind to fathom."[48] However, the notion of the family as a crucible of love and affection is itself historically and socially situated. As we have seen, romantic love and affection did not serve as the basis for marriage and family life in pre-modern times and only slowly infused the multitude of forms of family life possible or realizable among groups such as slaves subject to sale and colonized Indians forced to re-socialize their children in boarding school systems.

Familicide first appeared in colonial America in the 1750s. The historical record documents only one familicide during that decade, a 1755 case in Pennsylvania that I discuss at some length in Chapter 3 ("Familicide: A History"). We find no other recorded examples of familicide until the 1780s, a decade that witnessed three cases. Although the actual number of cases increased significantly over the next two centuries, with the 1990s witnessing 39 and the period from 2000 to 2007 seeing 67, the rates per 100,000 population remained low.[49] Given the unreliable estimates of population in colonial America and the early days of the American republic, we cannot make too much of these early rates of familicide. For example, it would be inappropriate to suggest that the rates have gone down during the last two hundred and fifty years because the early rates are likely to be overestimates. My central point is that familicide emerged slowly but created grave concerns about what was happening in society to generate such implosive forces within families. Appendix III suggests the rate of familicide increased considerably over the last five decades, a period of time with more reliable population estimates and homicide statistics.[50] Such an upward trend is consistent with the general increase in the rate of "multicide," the killing of more than one person. However, I do not want to exaggerate the extent of familicidal killing or multicide. Indeed, as Alex Alvarez and Ronet Bachman point out, multicides compose only around five percent of murders as a whole.[51]

RESEARCH INTO FAMILICIDE, FAMILY KILLING, AND HOMICIDE

The preliminary research into familicide helps set the stage.[52] Men commit nearly all these mass interpersonal killings. In their analysis of 109 cases of familicide in Canada and Britain, Wilson, Daly, and Daniele note, "Men were responsible for 95 percent of all familicidal killings."[53] As we will see, men comprised 196 of the perpetrators (92.9 percent) in my familicide archive. This glaring under-representation of women as perpetrators mirrors their infrequent roles as serial, mass, and spree killers. As I will go to demonstrate, the overwhelming preponderance of men also mirrors the gendered emotional formations of modernity and the way they inform familicidal thought, feeling, and action.

The extant research also offers important insights into the motives and emotions of perpetrators. The work of Wilson, Daly, and Daniele (1995) and Wilson and Daly (1998) posits two types of perpetrators, although they concede that the usefulness and validity of this taxonomy "have yet to be established."[54] The *angry* and *accusatory* perpetrator has various grievances against his female partner, many apparently associated with his perception of her sexual infidelity or her desire to exit their intimate partnership.[55]

He may have battered his partner before committing familicide. Indeed, Wilson, Daly, and Daniele acknowledge the utility of "accusatory anger and non-lethal violence" as "effective means of coercive control," serving to deter some women from exiting intimate relationships.[56]

The *despondent* offender is more likely to suffer from depression, much less likely to have battered his partner, and much more likely to commit suicide as part of the familicide. In both types of cases, these researchers note the common strand of male entitlement in taking the lives of family members. Specifically, they point out, "The killer's professed rationale for his actions invokes a proprietary conception of wife and children."[57] Similarly, they contend, "the killer feels entitled to decide his victims' fates,"[58] although it is not clear how they know this, other than inferring it from his act of killing.

Forensic psychiatrist Charles Ewing's insightful book chapter on familicide draws almost entirely from a limited number of newspaper accounts.[59] Ewing focuses on the notion of control or control that is ebbing. At one point he notes, "The typical family killer is more likely to have been concerned about losing control over more than just his wife and/or family. His concern is more often with losing control over all aspects of his life, or at least those that he most values. He is a man who, in his own eyes, is, or is about to become, a failure."[60] This sense of failure the eventual perpetrator experiences reflects how ashamed they feel of themselves or how fearful they are of being unmasked or exposed as failures.

Ewing goes on to identify certain personality characteristics that appear to predispose men to acts of familicide. He states, "They are men who expect to be—and usually have been—in control. They appear to have been over-controlling and yet overly dependent on family members. They are men who have always perceived themselves as being at the center of the family and have viewed their families as extensions of themselves."[61] This language of control suggests killers are often highly narcissistic, primarily thinking of themselves before others, even to the extent perhaps of failing to recognize the individuality of their intimate partners and their children. However, there is also a sense of perpetrators' being out of control, that their sense of self is threatened and greatly diminished. We find these observations in the psychiatric literature that occasionally addresses cases of familicide. These psychiatric case reports enlighten us further and are well worth considering.

Marc Nesca and Rudolph Kincel report the case of a 43-year-old Caucasian man, Mr. X., who used an ax to murder his common-law wife and his two children he had with his first wife, before unsuccessfully attempting to commit suicide. The familicide occurred in January of 1998. Mr. X had no criminal history, substance-abuse problems, or prior violent behavior. By all accounts, Mr. X. "was deeply devoted to his children and a contributing member of society."[62] Interviewed in the penitentiary, Mr. X. sought to understand his behavior and consented to the publication of his case history. Mr. X. appears to be what I will later refer to as a *civil reputable* perpetrator of familicide.

Mr. X. lost his father at age three and was raised by his mother, a single parent. He reported no history of childhood maltreatment, although interviews with other family members revealed "the presence of substantial family dysfunction, including maternal unavailability and emotional lability."[63] Mr. X's sister reported that he had a history of depression and episodes of suicidality. He did well in mathematics and science and graduated from a prestigious Canadian university, going on to become a successful computer programmer. Mr. X's second intimate relationship took the form of a long marriage that resulted in the birth of his two children. This first wife reported Mr. X. to be "emotionally over-controlled."[64] According to his first wife, their marriage began to deteriorate, as Mr. X. felt neglected by her, whom he saw as devoting too much emotional energy to their two children and not enough to him. The relationship completely broke down when Mr. X. sired a child with their family's nanny. Apparently Mr. X. had little involvement with his child born of the nanny.

Mr. X. entered the relationship with his common-law wife in the summer of 1996. In his interview, Mr. X. reported having concerns that his common-law wife had been unfaithful. Indeed, on the day of the familicide, Mr. X. arrived home to find her packing her things and getting ready to go to a friend's house. When she told him she would return to collect her furniture, he killed her with the ax. He then wrote a suicide note to his children.

Mr. X. then collected his oldest daughter from school, engaging in a perfectly civil conversation with her teacher and helping one of the other students with a challenging computing task. A little later, as his daughter sat at her computer desk, he attacked her with the ax. He recalls her asking him after he had delivered the first blow, "What are you doing, Dad?"[65] Mr. X. recalled that at this point in the proceedings he felt "extreme detachment" and "he apparently turned to see who his daughter was referring to when she uttered the word 'Dad.' "[66]

He reported the same feeling of detachment as he killed his second daughter as she sat reading on her bedroom floor after he had collected her from school later that afternoon. Indeed, Mr. X. reported amnesia after delivering the first blow to his second daughter.

Psychological testing suggested Mr. X. had a "narcissistic personality structure, with evidence of entitlement, dependency, and mild depression."[67] Curiously, in the immediate aftermath of the familicide, Mr. X. agreed with a psychological test item that stated, "I have never felt better in my life than I do now."[68] Further clinical assessments identified Mr. X. as "a generally passive individual, prone to suppress anger."[69] He also had a high need for social approval, indicative of a vulnerability to attacks on the self. Mr. X. was highly sensitive to shame. Using the language of psychiatry, Nesca and Kincel suggest these kinds of traits render offenders like Mr. X. hypersensitive to "narcissistic injury conducive to the rapid loss of ego control."[70] They identify offenders such as Mr. X. as suffering from low ego-strength and being in need of constant approval from others, rendering them highly dependent on others, a dependency seen among many perpetrators of domestic violence.

Mr. X's feelings of inadequacy and shame echo psychiatric findings in other case reports of familicide. Louis Schlesinger reports the case of F.C., who committed familicide. He lived with his wife and three children in their own home. F.C. worked for a local utility company. The family attended church. His employer described F.C. as "industrious, quiet, and even-tempered."[71] Neighbors described F.C. as friendly and as a man who lived for his family. About a month before the familicide, F.C. plunged into a deep depression, apparently triggered by his continued inability to get the heating system working in a room he and friends had added to his house. Schlesinger describes how F.C. began to sleep poorly, to wake up early and pace the floor, obsessing about what those who knew him deemed to be a relatively unimportant mechanical problem. F.C. began to experience "overwhelming feelings of failure and the humiliation of explaining the problem to his family."[72] Subsequent psychological test-ing suggested "feelings of inadequacy that run quite deep, to the core of F.C.'s personality."[73] Other tests revealed poor self-image, feelings of inferiority, and low self-esteem.

F.C.'s shame about his inability to fix the heating system mirrored much deeper feelings of shame regarding his intellectual shortcomings and his lack of a college education. Schlesinger reports F.C.'s making com-ments such as, "I made as much money or more money than a lot of guys who finished college." He told people, "college didn't teach you how to solve commonsense problems of life."[74] Although Schlesinger does not make this point, F.C. experienced shame that he did not recognize. F.C. moved quickly toward the rut-like fixation that familicide was the solution to the growing humiliation he was feeling.

These reports by Nesca and Kincel and Schlesinger highlight the threats to the self-identity of perpetrators in the lead-up to the familicide. These threats reflect the fact that perpetrators see themselves as failures, as worthless and unloved, as inadequate in various areas of their lives, such as their intimate relationships or their ability to succeed in their work. At this point the self is struggling for its very survival, and to employ the language of psychiatry, sometimes faces disintegration into acute states such as psychotic depression and schizophrenia. The findings from these cases echo themes in much earlier psychiatric studies of homicide. For example, Suzanne Reichard and Carl Tillman's study of a number of hitherto inexplicable homicides suggests that perpetrators may have killed to protect against the ego-disintegrating effects of schizophrenia.[75]

The extant research into familicide pays insufficient attention to the social and historical contexts within which these tragic mass killings take place. It is not my argument that a thoroughgoing analysis of such contexts will provide all the answers about familicide. Rather, such scrutiny only takes us so far, leaving inexplicable forces that both invite and defy explanation. Later, I will develop the "language of haunting" as a metaphorical device for addressing these inexplicable forces. My use of the language of haunting is not a direct challenge to the language of empirical criminology, but rather a frank recognition of the limits of our understanding. Nevertheless, it is clear that researchers have learned a considerable amount about the role of social and historical forces in various forms of killing. This literature warrants our attention, not because such killings exhibit common causal roots, but rather because close scrutiny of one form of killing offers rich insights into the possible mechanisms at work in other forms.

In his classic popular book *The Mainspring of Murder*, Philip Lindsay argues that mass murder "begins its great career in the late eighteenth century, growing stronger during the nineteenth century until it arrives in full red horror in the twentieth century."[76] For Lindsay, we find the conditions conducive to mass murder in the rise of industrial life. He observes, "Today is a forcing-ground for murderers because it is both an age of security and of insecurity, of economic security but of physical and spiritual insecurity. When the world is insecure, the family becomes insecure, and children feel intensely any emotional stresses in the home. Such conditions will breed criminals, although not necessarily mass murderers."[77] Lindsay situates the etiology of mass murder at the confluence of psychological forces, particularly the failure of children to thrive in emotionally secure families, and social pressures, especially the loss of community and its attendant sense of morality and seeming concern for others.

Elliot Leyton's thoughtful analysis of multiple murder also reminds us of the importance of welcoming historical and biographical forces into our interpretive matrix. Leyton comments, "It is incumbent upon us to look much more deeply into the historical process and its impact upon the lives of individuals."[78] According to Leyton, the multiple murderer differs from the property offender, the rapist, or the murderer, because these offences "tend to be little more than a demonstration of individual power and a cathartic release of rage."[79] Rather, the destructiveness of the multiple murderer reveals something more ambitious, in Leyton's words, "a kind of sustained sub-political campaign directed toward 'the timelessness of oppression and the order of power.' "[80] Leyton is well aware that most individuals with what he refers to as "tainted origins" or "thwarted ambitions" do not become multiple killers. The goal, he contends, is to identify the processes whereby individuals build the identity of multiple killer, and the varied interventions and societal supports that subvert these processes for nearly all other similarly situated individuals. For Leyton, the multiple murderer "is in many senses an embodiment of the central themes in his civilization as well as a reflection of that civilization's critical tensions."[81] In particular, the poverty, humiliation, insecurity, and inequality of modern capitalism contributed significantly to the rise of the multiple murderer.

In their important book *Crime and the American Dream*, Steven
Messner and Richard Rosenfeld argue that crimes, especially serious
crime such as robbery and homicide, are so disproportionately high in
the United States because of the pressures of the American dream to succeed in a material sense. A consequence of this widely agreed-upon cultural goal to achieve material success is that those who are economically
unequal are seen as unsuccessful and, as Messner and Rosenfeld note,
"by extension, 'unworthy.'"[82] Messner and Rosenfeld, drawing upon the
strain theory of Robert Merton and the insights of Karl Marx, identify an
important connection between serious crime and the feeling of unworthiness, humiliation, or shame. This feeling of unworthiness arises out
of the social and economic realities of American life, not from individual
character flaws, personality problems, laziness, or immorality. The intensity of these negative feelings is particularly acute because the materialist
ethos of the American dream and its emphasis on achievement orientation
and competitive individualism dominates other social institutions such
the political system, the family, and the education system to a far greater
extent than among other capitalist nations. For Messner and Rosenfeld,
serious crime is so prevalent in the United States because of the extent to
which economic pressures hold sway over every other social institution. As
readers will see, like Messner and Rosenfeld, I draw connections between
the rise of modern life in America and the appearance of familicide. Like
these authors, I suggest the internalization of a sense of failure is socially
patterned, infusing the souls of some more than others, men much more
so than women.

Research into certain forms of killing within families contains rich
insights that also warrant our attention. Unlike familicide that is almost
exclusively male-perpetrated, men and women kill the children they parent, although the participation of the genders varies with the form of child
killing. As Fiona Brookman points out, it is almost exclusively mothers
that commit neonaticide, the killing of a child in the first 24 hours of that
child's life.[83] There is more than a hint of shame at the center of many
neonaticide cases. Brookman notes their pregnancies are often unplanned,
the birth unexpected. The birth of the illegitimate child causes the mother
to fear rejection from significant others such as parents, husbands, or boy-
friends. We witness similar elements in cases of infanticide, the killing of
a child during the first 12 months of life. For example, Motz notes that
infanticide is "a tragic act of violence which can result from a *tremendous fear of social stigma*, feelings of total helplessness in relation to an
unplanned baby, or a range of complex psychological factors, which result
in an almost psychotic panic, in which killing seems the only solution."[84]

As a number of researchers indicate, male and female parents and step-
parents commit fatal child abuse in comparable numbers.[85] Alder and Polk
identify two broad categories of parental filicide: fatal child abuse and filicide-suicide. In the former cases, we are more likely to see prior child abuse
and domestic violence. In the latter, we are much more likely to encounter

some kind of mental illness, delusional behavior, and acute depression. In some fatal child abuse cases, we witness the role of shame, evidenced, for example, in some perpetrators' feelings that children had undermined their (tenuous) sense of parental authority, humiliating them. According to Alder and Polk, the filicide-suicide killings sometimes occur within the context of the breakup of the parental partnership and the resulting devastation, depression, and hopelessness that such events often bring.

Given the complexities of parental filicide, we would do well to note Brookman's caution that there are cases that "fall somewhere in between these two broad categories of parental filicide."[86] Brookman identifies one such case that falls between "the more usual cases of fatal abuse (where there is not generally any evidence of psychiatric illness, though the perpetrators may have been suffering from some form of depression) and filicide-suicides, where, according to Alder and Polk (2001: 78) there is rarely evidence of previous violence."[87]

Ken Polk's seminal work, *When Men Kill: Scenarios of Masculine Violence*, raises a number of issues central to the focus of my book.[88] Polk identifies the role of masculine pride, honor, and competitiveness at the heart of many different scenarios of male-perpetrated homicide. One such category of killings is what Polk refers to as "the use of lethal violence as a feature of the control over the behaviour of sexual partners."[89] Male perpetrators view their intimate or former intimate partners as their possessions. Such killings include the murder of male sexual rivals. They also include cases where "depressed males take the lives of their sexual partners as part of their suicide plan."[90] Polk's data set contained no examples of women killing male partners out of sexual jealousy.[91] Neither did it contain cases of women murdering their husbands as part of their own suicide plan. Put simply, the commission of these offences was profoundly gendered. In addition, regardless of the degree of planning or premeditation, these killings stemmed from the wounding of masculine pride and the various attempts to restore authority, control, and honor.

Many of Polk's points are consonant with the arguments of Martin Daly and Margo Wilson that the central driving force underlying male intimate partner homicide is men's sexual proprietariness over women. Daly and Wilson contend that "men the world around think and talk about women and marriage in proprietary terms. Men *strive* to control women and to traffic in their reproductive capacities, with varying degrees of success."[92] Citing numerous studies of intimate partner homicide, Daly and Wilson conclude that sexual jealousy is the most important reason that men kill their spouses and partners.[93] They also identify the adultery, jealousy, and sexual proprietariness at the root of wife-battering.[94]

Daly and Wilson explain sexual proprietariness as an outcome of natural selection. Men evolved a sense of sexual proprietariness, with only a very small number going to the extreme of killing spouses and partners to enforce their proprietary rights. Specifically they contend, "What men are competing for—whether immediately or more ultimately—is control over the reproductive capacities of women."[95] At a later point they note, "violence against wives is a product of aggressive masculine inclinations to coerce and control wives," and "these inclinations evolved and assumed their present forms in order to deter infidelity and autonomy."[96] Put simply, men and women have evolved different thought processes, emotional styles, and behaviors in relation to sexual proprietariness. Their argument is therefore steeped in evolutionary theory, contending that the men who killed, brutalized, or coerced their spouses/partners to enforce their sexual entitlement went on to reproduce, thus passing these tendencies on to subsequent generations.

My own approach to the study of familicide attaches great importance to historical forces, although it does not have the evolutionary scope of Daly and Wilson. In a very real sense, their emphasis on human evolution far transcends what we can learn from the annals of recorded history. Given the difficulties of interpreting written and oral history, the process of discerning evolving sexual proprietariness and homicidal jealousy from bone residues and the stuff of archaeology strikes me as daunting. Daly and Wilson recognize some of the difficulties with their approach. They candidly note, "We do not pretend to have solved the mystery of why homicidal violence is so variable in its occurrence between times and places, but we argue that a satisfactory answer will have to include some consideration of the evolved motives of the individual protagonists of violence."[97]

As Polk points out, the arguments of Daly and Wilson need considerable elaboration and refinement if we are to make sense of the fact that homicide varies not only by gender but also by social class. Polk also observes that lower class, underclass, or marginal men perpetrate the vast majority of these killings of female intimates and male sexual rivals, a finding that echoes Marvin Wolfgang's classic study of homicide.[98] Wolfgang's analysis of 588 cases of homicide in Philadelphia identified a subculture of violence "which does not define personal assaults as wrong or antisocial; in which quick resort to physical aggression is a socially approved and expected concomitant of certain stimuli; and in which violence has become a familiar but often deadly partner in life's struggles."[99] Amidst this sub-cultural milieu, "the collective id dominates social consciousness" and "basic urges, drives, and impulses" are less well regulated.[100] Some violence-prone lower-class men respond aggressively to various threats and insults, whereas their middle- and upper-class peers see such slights as trivial or at least as not warranting a violent response.

Drawing upon the anthropological work of David Gilmore, Polk contends that middle- and upper-class men have much less reason to commit intimate partner homicide or to kill a sexual rival. Rather, these more privileged men compete successfully in other ways, accruing more wealth, prestige, and power than their less fortunate peers.

Daly and Wilson's point that biological forces have a major role to play in explaining intimate partner homicide and indeed familicide provides an important touchstone. Indeed, there is much merit in their argument that there is "no more mischievous false dichotomy than 'social' versus 'biological.'"[101] For them, "sociality has no meaning outside of the biological world."[102]The detailed criticisms of Daly and Wilson's theoretical approach lie well beyond the scope of my current project or understanding.[103] However, as Fiona Brookman argues, it is difficult to prove or disprove the role of natural selection in the evolution of homicidal behavior.[104] I return to some of these matters when I discuss the visceral and emotional dimensions of familicide.

INTIMATE PARTNER VIOLENCE, CONTROL, AND EMOTIONAL CAPITAL

Intimate partner violence precedes a significant number of familicides. Consequently, we find many of the themes evident in the research literature on intimate partner and domestic violence in the familicide cases. As we have seen, many researchers allude to the central role of control, attempts to control, and the seeming or actual loss of control by batterers as central to our understanding of intimate partner violence, intimate-partner homicide, and familicide. I concur with these researchers but caution against presuming that the batterer's control is fully realized or that acts of killing necessarily reflect some realization of control. Rather, I suggest we remember that coercive violence is complex and concerned with much more than physical action or the expression of naked power. Erving Goffman puts it nicely, "Thus the most objective form of naked power, i.e., physical coercion, is often neither objective nor naked but rather functions as a display for persuading the audience; it is often a means of communication, not merely a means of action."[105]

Evan Stark highlights the centrality of coercive control in the lives of battered women and usefully stresses the importance of batterers' nonviolent attempts to regulate their partners. He defines *coercive control* as "a malevolent course of conduct that subordinates women to an alien will by violating their physical integrity (domestic violence), denying them respect and autonomy (intimidation), depriving them of social connectedness (isolation), and appropriating or denying them access to the resources required for personhood and citizenship (control)."[106]

For me, coercive control implies the existence of a normative order of compulsion and compliance between former or current spouses/partners that comes dangerously close to absolute control. At one point Stark notes, "it is inconceivable to most Americans that millions of modern women in our midst could be suffering under regimes of intolerance that are no less totalitarian than those imposed by fundamentalist cultures."[107] My reservation here is that coercive control, when conceptualized in such a way, runs the risk of minimizing women's agency and paying insufficient regard to battered women's roles in the arenas of work, education, and cultural life. Paradoxically, at other points, Stark observes how women's resistance has increased as a result of recent gains. He comments, "Women have been greatly emboldened by formal equality, dramatically increasing their capacity and willingness to initiate violence or to retaliate violently against oppression in personal life."[108]

Stark suggests coercive control is a relatively recent historical phenomenon. He is uncertain when coercive control emerges, although he does note feminist psychologists began to document "hostage-like" experiences as women entered the first shelters that opened in the early 1970s. Women entering these shelters also talked about the regime of controls in their lives. Stark notes that nineteenth-century reformers did not mention "a similar despotic regime."[109] He suggests this is because "Women's daily regimen of obedience was fully regulated by religion, and custom or sexism was codified in the law."[110] Phrases like *fully regulated* are troubling. It is as if battered women were automatons. In a very real sense, phrases like *fully regulated* deny women's negotiation of social life and their complex personhood.

I borrow the term *complex personhood* from Avery Gordon's beautiful book, *Ghostly Matters*. She reminds us, "those who live in the most dire circumstances possess a complex and oftentimes contradictory humanity and subjectivity that is never adequately glimpsed by viewing them as victims or, on the other hand, as superhuman agents."[111] She continues, "At the very least, complex personhood is about conferring the respect on others that comes from presuming that life and people's lives are simultaneously straightforward and full of enormously subtle meaning."[112]

I use Gordon's notion of complex personhood as a means of exploring the multifarious ways battered women who end up dying in familicides *negotiate* their abusive intimate relationships. I prefer not to use the words "coercive" and "control" in combination because of the danger of presuming or implying a certain response from battered women. I want to avoid assuming that a batterer coerces and control automatically follows. Fortunately, a number of other researchers enlighten us about these tricky nuances.

Drawing upon the work of Raven,[113] Mary Ann Dutton and Lisa Goodman offer a dynamic appreciation of the workings of power in intimate relationships.[114] They distinguish between what they refer to as the *ability* or *potential* to control, *attempts* to control, and the *outcomes* of power (e.g., compliance or resistance).[115] Importantly, Goodman et al. found that a community sample of victims of intimate partner violence displayed increasing levels of both resistance and placating strategies as violence increased in intensity.[116] As Dutton and Goodman remark, "these findings suggest that seemingly opposite responses to coercion co-occur as the level of threat increases."[117] Findings such as these point to the complexity of responses to intimate partner violence and intimidation and call into question the very idea that the complex personhood of a woman subject to battering is simply "controlled."

Dutton and Goodman note victims of violence resist the coercion of their partners in a variety of ways. Noncompliance can be oblique and

involve a victim's not directly confronting the partner with a refusal. In
other situations, women become worn down by endless demands. Nevertheless, even worn-down victims can strategically comply with demands,
perhaps as a means of ensuring their own safety or that of their children.
Dutton and Goodman suggest that compliance can eventually become
internalized or routinely incorporated into behavior. Here the victim's
actions take "on the appearance of being 'voluntary.' "[118]

In another scenario, Dutton and Goodman note, "In some cases, the
failure to comply is about 'giving up'—feeling desperation and lack of
energy to respond to a partner's incessant demands and abuse, such as
when a woman says, 'go ahead and kill me, just get it over with—I'm
not going to do what you want.'"[119] Of course one might interpret such
a statement as "giving up" or nearing the end of one's capacity to resist.
The statement, as Dutton and Goodman point out, still constitutes a form
of noncompliance. Kathleen Ferraro reports hearing battered women who
have killed abusers making similar statements. Given these women eventually kill, they are not so emotionally exhausted or lacking in agency that
they are unable to strike back.[120]

One can imagine a range of possible and competing interpretations
of these kinds of statements that do not necessarily involve seeing them
as "giving up." One possible interpretation of Ferraro's record of hearing
such statements is that they might constitute a form of emotional defiance,
a way of asserting her willpower in the face of his coercion and seeming
omnipotence. She reaches an emotional precipice where she is willing to
tell him that he can take her life but he cannot take her soul or her personhood. Seen in this way, a statement like "just get it over with," rather
than constituting an acute form of resignation or giving up, may evidence
a summoning of emotional resources. Clearly, there is a danger here that
we might either romanticize or somehow exaggerate a battered woman's
resistance. However, we ought not rule out the possibility that saying,
"go ahead and kill" is a calculated strategy or visceral survival skill in
the resistive arsenal of battered women. Clearly, we need more research
into the ways victims of intimate partner violence respond to coercion.
Dutton and Goodman put it nicely, "The role of a woman's own behavioral compliance and the extent to which she believes her own actions can
control whether threats can be averted, is also an important line of research
to consider."[121] We might add that it would also be helpful to learn more
about how abusers interpret women's statements like "go ahead and kill."
Do they see this as a final victory? A terminal act of resignation? The triumph of his will? Or alternatively, a threatening statement that speaks to a
renewed energy on her part or at least a dangerous position she has moved
to that presents him with the prospect of losing his love interest? Finally,
it is possible to see such statements as ultimatums that present the abuser
with the choice of ceding some power or losing his love interest.

The findings from the familicide archive paint a complex picture of
the way men attempt to control women, especially after couples separate.

The evidence from the archive cautions against the automatic coupling of the words "coercion" and "control." As we will see, in familicides evidencing a prior history of domestic violence, 44 percent of victims had exited the family home. Some women displayed enormous levels of fear during these periods. At the same time, many also got on with their lives, working, caring for children, and, in some instances, dating other men. Put simply, the agency and courage of these women was remarkable. The archive suggests women negotiated these changes very carefully and thoughtfully. Again we ought not romanticize women's perceptiveness in this regard; in the end, many simply did not appreciate the intensification of their estranged husband/partner's desperation and destructiveness. At times their abusers stalked them, assaulted them, and otherwise harassed them. A number of abusers reacted venomously to their estranged partners' dating other men. In some cases men apparently killed their estranged partners and children at least in part because of what they perceived as women's betrayal and abandonment. Nevertheless, many women avoided this male surveillance, at least partially.

The term *coercive control* also implies that attempts to control tend to be unidirectional. The evidence from the familicide archive does not comport with such an interpretation. Former and current spouses/partners make sense of and act upon attempts to control them in different ways. To suggest, even in cases where men are clearly the sole perpetrators of severe violence, that only men control or attempt to control their intimate partners, minimizes women's agency, resistance, and complex personhood and presents an image of men and women in essentialist and universalizing ways. For example, the complexities of class, racial, and ethnic differences among women disappear in the face of the overwhelming determining power of gender. There is more than a hint of condescension in gendered formulations such as coercive control and also an ironic denial of women's power. Avery Gordon makes a related point: "It has always baffled me why those most interested in understanding and changing the barbaric domination that characterizes our modernity often—not always—withhold from the very people they are most concerned with the right to complex personhood."[122]

Canadian psychologist Donald Dutton offers us another perspective on control in abusive intimate relationships. Dutton challenges what he describes as a tenet of feminist thought "that male violence is part of a wider repertoire of control tactics by which men dominate women."[123] Citing survey data, Dutton claims that women are at least as controlling as men. He cites the Canadian General Social Survey, where male and female partners report controlling behaviors by the other. Dutton opines the "Use of controlling behaviors and verbal abuse appears to be bidirectional in intimate relationships."[124] Furthermore, Dutton contends that in intimate relationships women enjoy more power than men because of their differential ability to "introspect, analyze, and describe feelings and processes."[125] Dutton claims that some men's emotional deficiencies are belied by their seeming social and political domination in intimate relationships.

The work of sociologist Helga Nowotny resonates with Dutton's observations concerning women's greater facility in the world of emotions. Developing some of Pierre Bourdieu's ideas, Nowotny identifies what she calls *emotional capital*. According to Nowotny, emotional capital comprises "knowledge, contacts and relations as well as access to emotionally valued skills and assets, which hold within any social network characterized at least partly by affective ties."[126] Patricia Allatt's study of private schooling and the perpetuation of privilege situates emotional capital amidst other forms of capital, all of which contribute to the reproduction of social advantage.[127] Allatt recognizes "emotional capital" as valued assets and skills, including the ability to love, devote time to others, and to develop caring and nurturing skills. Put simply, women's emotional capital can serve as a resource and a form of power that batterers must contend with in their intimate partnerships.

According to Dutton and a plethora of other researchers, many men who batter women experienced a number of traumas and emotional difficulties growing up.[128] They have problems bonding with parents. Some parents died. Other men experienced a disruption in their attachment to parents, resulting in serious emotional insecurity. For Dutton, a sizeable majority of these batterers have personality disorders. This is especially true for men who chronically deploy severe violence in their relationships with spouses and partners. He defines personality disorders as "chronic, dysfunctional ways of seeing the world, ways of feeling and behaving that are atypical within the ambient culture."[129]

Drawing upon John Bowlby's work on attachment and emotional health, Dutton points out that "anger follows unmet attachment needs. Anger's first objective is to get a missing attachment object to return."[130] Applying these observations to his therapeutic work with male batterers, Dutton conceptualizes battering as an immature and misguided attempt to maintain intimacy. He comments, "With adult males, the realization that a wife or lover is leaving or has left produces deep depression and suicidal ideation (or threats/actions) where previously anger and violence were used to control the female's emotional proximity to the male."[131] Dutton's linking of anger and violence to unmet attachment needs among some men raises the question of why it is more often men than women who resort to intimate partner violence in the face of seeming abandonment. Linda Mills provides indirect insight into these matters when she notes, "Men's shame has been most often identified with aggression and women's shame most likely to manifest in depression."[132]

I return to these matters when I explore familicide as one of the consequences of modern era emotional formations, a transgression clearly associated with the different ways men and women construct their identities (individuate) and the way this happens among different class, racial, and ethnic groups. Drawing upon history, sociology, and psychology helps us grasp the gendered nature of familicide, and doing so provides an interdisciplinary approach that offers new insights into intimate-partner violence in general.

The differences of opinion between Stark and Dutton are instructive. However, both researchers are wedded to the language of power as a possession or thing, the idea of control, and the linear notion of directionality. Stark prioritizes the voices and perspective of female victims. Dutton pays considerable attention to the input of batterers. Both, in their own ways, pay homage to the language and logic of modern science. The tensions between these authors and others of their ilk mirror much deeper tensions between sociology and psychology. The psychological and psychiatric research into the roots of violence and murder is extensive. To the extent that it incorporates actors' meanings in social settings, this research can be valuable.[133] However, this is usually not the case. The profession of psychology often relies on experimental approaches and statistical methods, with the atomized and seemingly asocial individual as its primary unit of analysis. One recalls Jean Paul Sartre's critique of psychologists: "The psychologist's first precaution consists, in effect, of considering the psychic state in such a way that it removes from it all *signification*. The psychic state is for him always a *fact* and, as such, always accidental."[134] For Sartre, emotion is socially situated, reflecting "an organized form of human existence."[135] Sartre's critique is on point. Mainstream psychology often ignores social context and socially situated meaning. In the arena of interpersonal violence, it is crucial to grasp context and meaning. Without them, violence dissolves into mere human action, a flailing of a fist, or the firing of gun. We know not what such flailing or firing is directed at, designed to achieve, or how others perceive it.

From the standpoint of female victims of domestic violence, it is easy to see how victims (and those who advocate on their behalf) might perceive a male abuser as powerful and themselves as having limited options or as relatively powerless. Indeed, the sociological literature persistently identifies gender as one of the principal axes of power in modern societies, variously referring to these unequal structures or patterns in terms of the language of patriarchy, the social organization of gender, the gender regime, the gender order, and so on. Clearly, in the modern era, or in other eras for that matter, men enjoy more power, wealth, and status than women. However, we ought not presume that these power differentials hold the key to explaining familicide.

The familicide archive demonstrates that male perpetrators exercised power over women and children as husbands/partners and fathers, respectively. This observation applies to familicides preceded by a history of domestic violence and tyranny and those not evidencing these abusive phenomena. However, in all these cases men's power was not monolithic. Nor was it exercised without giving rise to potent resistance. Neither were women powerless. They exercised power within their own families, often in ways different from those of their male partners.

The preponderance of evidence from the archive does not justify reaching the conclusion that men's power over women either explains their familicidal behavior or provides the motive force behind it. Neither does the evidence support the rather facile conclusion that the power men enjoyed in these families was seamlessly continuous with the social and political power of men in general. Rather, the social standing of many male perpetrators, regardless of whether they had tyrannized their families, was in many ways unraveling. As we will see, most of these men faced humiliation in one form or another. Put simply, there is no easy correspondence or simple articulation between men's overall social and political power vis-à-vis women and their commission of familicide. Rather, the relationship between men and women's social/political power and the commission of familicide is indirect and complex. Indeed, my interpretation of the familicide archive is that it is dangerous to read the workings of power from one vantage point only, from one actor (such as a victim), or from one form of its alleged manifestations (violence, coercive control), and at one juncture in a person's life. We miss an awful lot when we stop at the point that we recognize perpetrators of familicide stand in a relation of power to those they eventually kill. It is incumbent upon us to ask, within what context is his seeming supremacy embedded? Modern patriarchy may appear to be deeply rooted in the social structure. However, this does not mean that the power relationships evident at a macro- or society-wide level manifest themselves smoothly, neatly and un-problematically within each nuclear family unit or between spouses and intimate heterosexual partners.

As I pored over case after case, it became clear that male perpetrators were powerful in some ways and not in others, and that the relationship between this power and their violence/tyranny was complex. Their violence and tyranny seemed simultaneously associated with feelings of power over their partners/families and their feelings of losing that power. It is helpful here to distinguish between perpetrators' own *feelings* of being powerful or powerless, their partners' *perceptions* of that power or lack of power, and the *social power* accruing to perpetrators. Perpetrator power or lack thereof is socially situated, shifting according to who assesses that power and the context within which it operates.

My sense that perpetrator power does not simply drive violence and tyranny recalls Hannah Arendt's observation that "Power and violence are opposites; where the one rules absolutely, the other is absent. Violence appears where power is in jeopardy, but left to its own course it ends in power's disappearance."[136] In a related vein, Chairman Mao, the Chinese revolutionary, famously remarked that power grows out of the barrel of a gun. Simply put, the revolutionary Communists needed to deploy violence in order to seize power. In both these examples, violence is not an expression of power; rather it signifies an absence of it and an attempt to obtain it.

Psychiatrist James Gilligan makes a related point when asking why men want to control their wives. He notes, "I can only conclude that their desire for omnipotence is in direct proportion to their feeling of impotence."[137] Likewise, Dutton observes, "While batterers may appear powerful in terms of their physical or sociopolitical resources, they are distinctly impotent in terms of their psychic and emotional resources, even to the point of depending on their female partners to maintain their sense of identity."[138] Power manifests in a number of different ways. Men who batter women may be powerful in some of those ways, especially perhaps in terms of their immediate physical domination of their spouses/partners. However, they are not powerful in other ways, and it is those aspects of the social location of batterers and perpetrators of familicide I am keen to explore.

A number of authors have already pointed to the problems with arguing that men's intimate-partner violence is rooted in their power and control over women. A decade ago Ellen Pence wrote, "We have developed some of our own truisms that also reduce complex social relationships to slogans. One was the notion that batterers use violence, coercion, and intimidation to control their partners. *He does it for power, he does it for control, he does it because he can*—these were advocacy jingles that, in our opinion, said just about all there was to say."[139] As Pence notes, in the setting of women's groups, battered women developed the "Power and Control Wheel" and its detailed descriptions of men's violence. Power and control resided at the center of the wheel, violence at its periphery, the different sectors evidencing various abusive strategies men deployed as part of their privilege in a patriarchal society. Pence comments that the original wheel effectively argued that, "When he is violent, he gets power and he gets control."[140] However, early on, this mantra changed to the message, "he is violent *in order* to get control or power."[141] She then goes on to note, "we created a conceptual framework that, in fact, did not fit the lived experience of many of the men and women we were working with. Like those we were criticizing, we reduced our analysis to a psychological universal truism. . . . Speaking for myself, I found that many of the men I interviewed did not seem to articulate a desire for power over their partner."[142]

Insofar as models such as the Power and Control Wheel dwelt on the ways men wield power over women, controlling them in various ways, they tended to downplay women's own power and ability to resist men's efforts to control them. Also, in situating men's intimate power and control over women within the broader framework of the power relations of gender, these accounts tended to homogenize the experiences of men from different class, racial, and ethnic groups and minimize the importance of men's own feelings of being powerless and out of control in their intimate relationships and in the world in general.

Susan Faludi's experiences with men at a batterer's intervention program illustrates the way men's own feelings of powerlessness tend to get submerged in the rhetoric of the Power and Control Wheel. An engineer participating in a batterer intervention program told Faludi that the Power and Control Wheel was "misnamed."[143] He argued, "It should be called the Powerlessness and Out-of-Control Wheel."[144] In the course of conducting research for her book, *Stiffed: The Betrayal of the American Man*, Faludi got to know some of these batterers. Her reflections on the links between their power and control and their intimate-partner violence are worth quoting. She opines, "There was something almost absurd about these men struggling, week after week, to recognize themselves as dominators when they were so clearly dominated, done in by the world. . . . The men had probably felt in control when they beat their wives, but their everyday experience was of feeling controlled—a feeling they had no way of expressing because to reveal it was less than masculine, would make each of them, in fact, 'no man at all.'"[145]

Clearly, just because some batterers report feeling out of control or appear powerless in many areas of their life, particularly perhaps in terms their emotional literacy and expressiveness, it does not negate the fact they exercise power over their intimate female partners. To the extent the Power and Control Wheel implies that men wield unfettered or unmediated power over their female intimates, that such power lies at the root of their violence and is continuous with and an expression of men's social and political supremacy, I find the Wheel less than compelling. Certainly, the familicide archive does not support the argument that men's use of familicidal violence flows from their power as patriarchs in a patriarchal society. Rather, the archive suggests something more complex.

Limited as the familicide archive is, it nevertheless offers an opportunity to explore intimate relationships through a different language, one that examines issues of power and control through the lens of human emotion. In a very real sense, such an analysis allows us to scrutinize power at the point that it is exercised. This requires an appreciation of power as complex, contested, haunting, relational, and socially and historically situated. Such an approach involves sidestepping some psychiatric and feminist perspectives on power that tend to see power as a thing that is possessed, procured, or wielded. There is no doubt that such concrete psychiatric and feminist appreciations of power have their virtues and their appeal. My point is not that these perspectives are incorrect as much as it is that they do not take us far enough. They train our attention upon the ostentatious workings of power, the gun, the blood, the scar, and the corpse. However, there are other aspects about the workings of power that are more relational and covert. Indeed, as Steven Lukes puts it, "power is at its most effective when least observable."[146] Exploring the ebb and flow of emotion in those intimate relationships that end in familicide casts light on both the relational and covert workings of power. Such an approach identifies the hidden workings of shame and humiliation and the central role these emotions play in these mass interpersonal killings. By focusing on emotion we also witness the frailties of power, its contested deployment, and its historically and socially contingent nature. It requires us to dispense with the easy notion that power flows almost unimpeded from the overall socio-political privilege of the group to which nearly all perpetrators belong (men) to the various knifings, shootings, and acts of incineration that characterize familicidal killings.

FOCUSING ON EMOTIONS

Although I gathered large amounts of quantitative data about cases of familicide, asking 112 closed-ended questions about each of the 211 cases, my focus is principally qualitative, concentrating in particular on the interconnectedness of emotional, social, and historical landscapes. Emotion courses through bodies and between people and consists of experiential, behavioral, and physiological components that allow people to deal with situations, problems, and other phenomena. In a very real sense, emotion is the juice of human interaction. Randall Collins puts it well: "Humans are hard-wired to get caught in a mutual focus of inter-subjective attention, and to resonate emotions from one body to another in common rhythms."[147] He continues, "We have evolved to be hyper-attuned to each other emotionally."[148]

Perpetrators of familicide *viscerally experience* and alarmingly amplify destructive and inhibitory emotional energies that ebb and flow through modern society. My use of the word *visceral* is deliberate. Following Connell, I do not picture the body as the passive recipient of cultural forces. Bodies have a definite and highly significant physicality and physiology, and these aspects of bodily life are continuous with rather than distinct from social life. As Connell puts it, "bodies are addressed by social process and drawn into history. They do not turn into symbols, signs or positions in discourse. Their materiality is not erased, it continues to matter."[149] I attach considerable importance to the way bodies appear to discharge those emotions we find so frequently among perpetrators of familicide. These age-old emotions, including fear, shame, and anger, have served human beings well for most of their history. Modernity alters the handling of these emotions, and it does so selectively and in a socially patterned manner.

Emotions are universal, although their expression varies considerably by culture. Jonathon Turner and Jan Stets see emotions bringing people together. They remark, "emotions are the 'glue' binding people together and generating commitments to large-scale and cultural structures; in fact, emotions are what make social structures and systems of cultural symbols viable."[150] However, emotions can also map social and historical fault lines. Rage, shame, jealousy, and fear can separate and divide people. We see evidence of these disintegrative aspects of emotion in the familicide cases. Nevertheless, at yet another level, observers' descriptions of these killings as immoral, misguided, evil, or inexplicable reflect their own commitment to moral codes that rule out killing one's family.

At the same time as people decry familicide, we often find nagging doubts about the way we live our modern lives, almost as if the angst of perpetrators and their families resonated with the lives of those consuming these atrocity tales. For some, these atrocities and the emotions that precipitated them have a haunting effect, inviting questions about the meaning of their own lives, the divisions between people even amidst familial relations, and their sense of belonging to something greater than themselves.

It is not easy to study emotion. Feelings come and go. Human memory stirs emotion. Indeed, strong feelings can reshape memory, alter it, and obscure it. The chapters that follow are therefore not intended as a scientific rendition of the peculiar swirls of intense feeling that constitute the emotional milieu of familicide. Rather, the chapters represent attempts to understand familicide from a different angle than has hitherto been the case. My thinking here was influenced by C. Wright Mills, who, in talking of the sociological imagination recommended, "You try to think in terms of a variety of viewpoints and in this way to let your mind become a moving prism catching the light from as many angles as possible."[151]

Wherever possible, I situate the feelings and vulnerabilities of the parties, especially perpetrators, within their emotional biographies and the increasing repression of strong feelings emblematic of modern life. For some sociologists, such an approach may appear to cede too much ground to disciplines such as history, psychology, and psychiatry. For others, my concern with the visceral aspects of the killings may appear to cede too much ground to biology. Notwithstanding these possible objections, it seems to me that the familicidal heart is no respecter of subject disciplines and that familicidal energy is perhaps best appreciated using not only a multidisciplinary but also an interdisciplinary approach.

Exploring intimate-partner violence through the lens of human emotion is not new. Norman Denzin's phenomenological analysis assumes that "domestic violence is situated, interpersonal, emotional, and cognitive activity involving negative symbolic interaction between intimates."[152] He contends that such violence "must be examined from within; that although structural processes (economic, legal, religious, cultural, ideological) influence and shape family violence, their meanings are filtered and woven through the lives of interacting individuals, each of whom is understood to be a universal singular, embodying in his or her lifetime the forces, contradictions, and ideologies of a particular historical moment."[153] For Denzin, "emotionality lies at the core of violent conduct."[154] He defines violence "as the attempt to regain, through the use of emotional and physical force, something that has been lost."[155] In the batterer's own mind, some of those things "lost" include his sense of control over himself and others and his own pride.

For Denzin, the world of social interaction "haunts" the violent subject.[156] Denzin believes this violent self might seek to control his spouse or children, and he may succeed in effecting various degrees of physical compliance. However, he never succeeds in controlling the will of his victims, in spite of his wish to do so. Put simply, by his violence, the abuser changes the emotional configuration of the relationship and the authenticity

of human interaction. His partner may recoil, she may fight back, but
she also regroups. Denzin opines, "In this sense his violent actions are
doomed to failure, yet his very failure destroys the relationship with the
one he wishes to control."[157] Control then is never fully realized. Talking
of husbands' violence toward wives he comments, "After the violence has
appeared the husband may initially achieve some measure of control and
pleasure over his spouse through his use of violence."[158] Nevertheless, as
the violent atmosphere intensifies and as "the violence increases and per-
sists, hostility on the wife's part increases and the husband becomes hostile
toward her in response to her hostility. A loss of affection for the violent
spouse begins to appear."[159]

Others who have written about violence and murder in general note
the pivotal importance of emotions. From his ethnographic work, Elijah
Anderson comments, "Among young people, whose sense of self esteem
is particularly vulnerable, there is an especially heightened concern about
being disrespected. Many inner-city young men in particular crave respect
to such a degree that they will risk their lives to attain it and maintain
it."[160] Using a micro-sociological approach, Randall Collins sees violence
as a situational process that is "shaped by an emotional field of tension and
fear."[161] For Collins, background conditions such as race, poverty, and
childhood experiences "are a long way from what is crucial to the dynamics of the violent situation."[162]

In his important pioneering work, James Gilligan identifies shame and
humiliation as the root of the rage and hatred that lead to violence and
murder. For Gilligan, violence functions to "replace shame with pride."[163]
He continues, "The emotion of shame is the primary or ultimate cause of
all violence, whether toward others or toward the self. Shame is a necessary
but not a sufficient cause of violence."[164] Many others agree, although as
criminologist Jack Katz helpfully points out, "we should not err by treating rage as an escape from humiliation. There is an essential link between
rage and humiliation. As a lived experience, rage is livid with the awareness
of humiliation."[165] For these authors and others, humiliating someone can
elicit violence or even homicide. Those disrespected who respond in such
a violent way often have biographies steeped in humiliation. The prisoners
Gilligan worked with over the years described how they had been "humiliated repeatedly throughout their childhoods."[166] This humiliation took
the form of "violent physical abuse, sexual abuse, and life-threatening
degrees of neglect."[167]

Thomas Scheff and Suzanne Retzinger contend that unacknowledged
or unconfronted alienation and shame can lead to conflict and violence in
intimate relationships. These researchers straddle the fields of sociology,
psychology, history, and politics to come up with a theory that is at once
individualistic and social. They observe, "Alienation and shame lead to
violence only when they are repressed or disguised—that is, when they
are not acknowledged."[168] For these authors, shame is particularly important as the *master emotion* in modern societies, because these societies

actively deny shame. Under these repressive conditions, shame constitutes the individual visceral and emotional recognition of social disconnection. Alienation constitutes the social aspect of social disconnection.

Scheff and Retzinger's ideas about alienation and shame resonate with the important work of Foucault and others in attempting to unravel a family killing in post-revolutionary France. Michel Foucault's edited collection, *I, Pierre Riviere: Having Slaughtered My Mother, My Sister, and My Brother*, contains numerous references to the shame and humiliation of the perpetrator, although these emotional states merely provide a backdrop for the authors to wax lyrical about the discursive struggles between law and medicine. The contributors situate the debate about the Riviere parricide amidst the increasing tendency to deploy psychiatric concepts in the arena of criminal justice, and, during the 1830s, the reluctance of lawyers and doctors alike to accept the notion of *monomania*, a term that referred to an abnormal obsession or preoccupation with one particular phenomenon by a person who was otherwise deemed normal. The edited collection assembles numerous documents regarding the case, central among which is Riviere's own lengthy, detailed, and perceptive memoir.[169] These documents contain rich information about Pierre Riviere's emotional condition and are well worth revisiting as a means of illustrating the central role of shame and humiliation in family killings.

On June 3, 1835, Pierre used a pruning fork to kill his mother, Victoire Brion; his 18-year-old sister, Victoire Riviere; and his seven-year-old brother, Jules Riviere. His mother was six months' pregnant at the time of the killings. In the wake of the parricide, Pierre feigned madness, thereby confusing authorities and creating a major stir about the veracity of psychiatric interpretations of criminal behavior. The prosecutor described Pierre as "an affliction to his family, he was obstinate and taciturn."[170] In addition, the prosecutor notes Pierre's social disconnection, "He was solitary, wild and cruel, a being apart, a savage not subject to the ordinary laws of sympathy and sociability."[171] And later, "he constantly keeps his head down, and his furtive glances seem to shun meeting the gaze of others, as if for fear of betraying his secret thoughts."[172]

One newspaper account informs readers Pierre showed "no sign of emotion or repentance at the recollection of his crime" and that "he keeps his eyes on the ground, furtively, and seems to be afraid to look those who speak to him in the face."[173] Michel Harson, 57, a property owner and mayor of the village of Aunay, told authorities, "The young man had no friend, according to what I have heard about him, he did not go to the inn three times in his life."[174]

In his memoir, Pierre notes his increasing anger at what he perceived as his mother's ongoing mistreatment of his father. He comments, "My father thus became the butt of people's mockery."[175] Pierre notes his own nominal sense of belonging; he comments, "I displayed singularities. My schoolmates noticed this and laughed at me."[176] He found it particularly difficult to relate to girls and women. Pierre continues, "I saw quite well however how people looked upon me, most of them laughed at me. I applied myself diligently to find out what I should do to stop this and live in society, but I did not have tact enough to do that, I could not find the words to say, and I could not appear sociable with the young people of my own age, it was above all when I met girls in company that I lacked words to address them, so some of them by way of jest ran after me to kiss me."[177] He then acknowledges, "I despised in my heart those who despised me."[178]

Mixed with these feelings of not fitting in with his peers, Pierre also demonstrates strong feelings of superiority, seeing others as inferior to him. He comments, "I knew the rules of man and the rules of ordered society, but I deemed myself wiser than they, I regarded them as ignoble and shameful. I had read in Roman history and I had found that the Romans' laws gave the husband the right of life and death over his wife and his children."[179] Clearly, Pierre was deeply disturbed by what he saw as the emasculation of his father and was resisting the wave of ideas that promoted men as softer patriarchs, kinder fathers, and loving husbands.[180]

Pierre's shame is evident throughout his confession and the commentaries on his life. We learn he casts his eyes down, he is mocked, he is isolated, he is shy with girls, and he lacks the words to address them. As in Pierre's case, acute shame permeates the vast majority of the familicides I examine, regardless of the presence or absence of battering behavior or what I will call *livid coercion*. The intensity of unacknowledged, bypassed, repressed, or disguised shame immediately prior to the killings suggests a pivotal role for this emotion. Given that modernity drives shame underground and that familicide constitutes a modern transgression, I explore the connections between familicide and the subterranean circulation of shame.

My concern with the history of emotion and its seeming correspondences with the emergence of familicide may strike some readers as odd; others as reactionary. Clearly it is difficult to identify or measure the precise manifestations of emotion, or, perhaps for some critics, to do anything more than infer the working of emotion from the empirical observation of actual behavior. Whatever one's reservations, emotion is central to sociology, not a peripheral concept best left to the psychologists and psychiatrists. As Eva Illouz reminds us, emotion lies at the heart of Max Weber's writing about the relationship between Protestantism and the spirit of capitalism, Karl Marx's formulation of alienation as a process of estrangement, and Emile Durkheim's understanding of social solidarity as a "bundle of emotions binding social actors to the central symbols of society."[181] For Illouz, emotion energizes social action. The inner life looms large in her discussion, just as it does in my exploration of familicide. She comments, "Emotions are deeply internalized and unreflexive aspects of action, but not because they do not contain enough culture and society in them, but rather because they have too much."[182]

Approaching familicide through the history, sociology, and psychology of emotional life not only recognizes the emotional intricacies of intimate relationships but also the complex personhood of social actors.

This complex personhood is at once continuous with the everyday interdependencies of social life and a range of biographical experiences and historical changes. To explain familicide, a modern phenomenon *par excellence*, we need to explore the emotional formations of modernity in their historical, social, and psychological guises.

To this end, I draw upon Norbert Elias's work on the gradual historical emergence of social constraints on the expression of strong emotions such as aggression, and public displays of violence and rage. For Elias, the civilizing process results in the social inculcation of psychic restraint. More and more behavior became the target of shame and repugnance (disgust). Over half a millennium, Western peoples increasingly repressed and sublimated their basic emotional drives, particularly their sex drives and urges toward violence. They became more mannerly and more respectable, less overtly violent, especially in publicly visible space. At first this happened in response to social pressures emanating especially from ascendant classes. Slowly, people considered, negotiated, and finally internalized many of these constraints, thus monitoring their own levels of compliance.[183]

In the original German version of *The Civilizing Process*, Elias took great care to write about drives as socially and historically situated, as malleable, and as inextricably interwoven into the overall pattern of social drives evident in the networks of relationships and interdependencies within which the individual lives. As Jonathan Fletcher points out, the word "instinct" did not appear in the original publication. However, the word "instinct" appears often in the English translation, giving the impression, especially to English readers, that Elias is positing a theory of drives rooted in biological forces. Fletcher comments, "This does not mean that he is unaware of the biological *capacity* for humans to behave aggressively, believing that humans, like other animals, have a nervous system which prepares them for the classic 'fight or flight' reaction in threatening situations. But he suggests that this inbuilt tendency is necessarily developed in different ways via social learning."[184]

Historicizing Freud, Elias sees the regulation of people's emotional drives as central to the process of modernization. Like Weber, Elias also recognizes the importance of increasingly rational calculation in human affairs. Dating from the sixteenth century in Western societies, these two historical tendencies constitute principal developmental axes. As Elias points out, "the strong spurt of rationalization and the no less strong advance of the threshold of shame and repugnance . . . are different sides of the same transformation of the social personality structure."[185]

THE IDEA OF AN EMOTIONAL CONTINUUM

I situate perpetrators with respect to how they appear to have controlled their emotional drives. *Emotional drives* refers to internal sources of motivation that force or pressure a person to act. As noted, these drives are often conceived of as either innate, physiological urges, sometimes referred to as instincts, or as more socially induced passions. The former, more physiological or organic, drives include the need for sex, food, and water, and the need for physical survival as evidenced in the fight or flight response. The latter concern the social and historically molded passions rooted in character, such as the desire for love, freedom, achievement, and a sense of social belonging. It is the latter that mostly concern me in this book, although, as readers will see, the dividing line between instincts and drives is not always easy to recognize.

Psychoanalytical approaches identify three components of the human mentality, the id, the ego (a largely conscious element colloquially understood as the sense of self or self esteem), and the superego (colloquially, the conscience and its self-monitoring action). Freud used the word *id* to refer to that reservoir of energy derived from instincts, an "unconscious mental entity."[186] He talks of the "instinctual strength of the id,"[187] seeing it as a primal essence that continually struggles with the ego and the superego.[188] The id is not synonymous with the unconscious, because, as Andrew Colman observes, "the repressive functions of the ego and many of the functions of the superego are also unconscious."[189]

As Eli Zaretsky notes, the idea of the unconscious was alive and well at the end of the nineteenth century and was "understood, before Freud, to be anonymous and transpersonal. Frequently likened to the ocean, it aimed to leave the 'petty' concerns of the ego behind."[190] One of Freud's important contributions was to discern an "internal, idiosyncratic source of motivations peculiar to the individual. In his conception, contingent circumstances, especially in childhood, forge links between desires and impulses, on one hand, and experiences and memories on the other. The result was a *personal unconscious*, unique, idiosyncratic, and contingent."[191]

Elias took a number of Freud's important ideas and put them into a broader social and historical context. Specifically, Elias argues that modernity involves the gradual and uneven repression and sublimation of emotional drives, urges, and passions. Unlike Freud and the psychoanalysts, Elias strongly situates these changes amidst the increasing differentiation of Western societies and the growing interdependencies that accompanied the rise of modern capitalism, urbanization, and population growth. Elias is critical of theories that break the psyche up into different parts that exist independently of each other. He also challenges the branches of the humanities and the sociology of knowledge that dwell excessively on knowledge and thought. Elias remarks, "Thoughts and ideas appear in these studies as it were as that which is the most important and potent aspect of the way men steer themselves. And the unconscious impulses, the whole field of drive and affect structures, remains more or less in the dark."[192] These investigations that consider only "the consciousness of men, their 'reason' or 'ideas,' while disregarding the structure of drives, the direction and form of human affects and passions, can be from the outset of only limited value."[193]

Elias is also critical of psychoanalytic approaches that "extract some-thing 'unconscious,' conceived of as an 'id' without history, as the most important thing in the whole psychological structure."[194] The problem with such approaches, he says, is that the steering of individuals by drives such as unconscious libidinal impulses appears to assume "a form and structure of its own," in curious isolation from social and historical rela-tionships among individuals and the groups they belong to, interact with, cooperate with, and compete against. It is worth quoting Elias at length here to capture precisely his argument.

> Decisive for a person as he appears before us is neither the "id" alone, nor the "ego" or "superego" alone, but always *the relationship* between these various sets of psychological functions, partly conflict-ing and partly cooperating in the way an individual steers himself. It is they, these relationships *within* man between the drives and affects controlled and the built-in controlling agencies, whose structure changes in the course of a civilizing process, in accordance with the changing structure of relationships *between* individual human beings, in society at large. In the course of this process, to put it briefly and all too simply, "consciousness" becomes less permeable by drives, and drives become less permeable by "consciousness."[195]

I will return to elements of Elias's argument in subsequent chap-ters. Suffice it to say at this point that the civilizing process moderates aggressive and hostile drives, tempering them, thus liberating people from their sway. This happens more rapidly, in a historical sense, among the ascendant classes in Western societies. For my purposes, the range of ways perpetrators of familicide express aggression, rage, anger, and hostility provides one means of understanding their behavior. It is in that direction I turn.

Schematically speaking, at the left-hand end of this continuum, we find perpetrators who frequently resorted to coercive violence in their intimate relationships. At the right-hand end we see perpetrators who exhibited enormous emotional restraint, decorum, and outward confor-mity with mainstream social values, rarely behaving in a hostile, aggressive manner, especially in public. An emotional thread of unacknowledged or bypassed shame, humiliation, and repugnance runs along this continuum of socially regulated drives. The familicidal hearts, to a much greater degree than the general population, failed to acknowledge their shame, often repressing it or masking it with anger. This modern-era thread of shame links the cases empirically, conceptually, and historically. To use Erving Goffman's language, the perpetrators at either ends of the con-tinuum engage in very different presentations of self, especially to their spouses and partners.[196] One deploys varying degrees of violence and intimidation, the other provides for his family with civility, decency, and a sense of rectitude.

The violent and intimidating husbands and partners who commit familicide have, in many ways, not fully internalized these modern era psychic restraints. Many of these men possess what I call *livid coercive hearts*, remaining significantly unaffected by the state policing of domestic violence and the modern cultural imperatives that eschew violent paternal discipline and punishment. In this sense, the livid coercion found at the left-hand end of the continuum is increasingly at odds with progressive husbandly and fatherly behavior. Their final act of mass interpersonal killing comports with their prior livid behavior, appearing in some cases as a logical, albeit extreme and shocking, extension of their earlier violence.

At the right-hand end of the continuum, the male and female *civil reputable hearts* who commit familicide do so as a seemingly abrupt departure from their everyday routines as respectable, well-disciplined social actors, often known for their outward adherence to mainstream values and gender roles. Unlike the livid coercive hearts, the civil reputable hearts shock communities, not because they take violence to a new level like their livid coercive peers, but because they use violence in the first place, let alone familicidal violence.

Situating perpetrators on an emotional continuum is an arbitrary way of understanding familicide.[197] Given the complexity of these cases, it would be perfectly appropriate to argue that the cases defy any kind of conceptual analysis. If we accept such an argument, we might end up arraying the cases as multidimensional points in space, strewn like stars against the night sky. Having immersed myself in the minutiae of these cases for the last several years, I find that such a chaotic appreciation has considerable appeal. Nevertheless, it strikes me that positing a continuum is a good way of inviting future debate and, indeed, refutation. Given my aforementioned reservations about linearity and directionality, especially regarding research debates about notions of control, it is with some irony I acknowledge the linearity and directionality embedded in the notion of a continuum. Nevertheless, I contend that while emotion is difficult to explore using the language of linearity and directionality, the display or socially situated manifestation of emotion lends itself more readily to representation on a continuum.

While part of the appeal of using the notion of a continuum might lie in its simplicity and accessibility to readers, it is important to distinguish between this and a typology. I do not propose that livid coercive hearts and civil reputable hearts are distinctive types. Rather, in using these terms, I am identifying emotional tendencies and polarities in modern life. Less sociologically informed language might describe these extremes as positions between relatively under-controlled or selectively emotionally expressive (*livid coercive*) and relatively over-controlled or emotionally inexpressive (*civil reputable*) hearts. Either way, it is also the case that there are *contradictory/intermediate* cases that fall somewhere between these two extremes. These contradictory/intermediate cases evidence much lower levels of livid coercion, if any at all, with perpetrators also tending to have a somewhat tarnished reputation, as opposed to enjoying the kind of social esteem that the civil reputable hearts do.

Christian Longo serves as an example of a perpetrator occupying a contradictory/intermediate location on the emotional continuum of familicide cases.[198] Longo murdered his wife, Mary Jane, and their three children, Zachary, four; Sadie Ann, three; and two-year-old Madison in December 2001, "because he was tired of them and they were preventing him from living a wilder lifestyle," a prosecutor argued. Longo confessed to the familicide. After the killings he fled to Mexico to indulge his philandering lifestyle. These killings, apparently for personal gain, showed no evidence of the altruism or caring we sometimes find among the civil reputable hearts. Longo strangled and asphyxiated his victims. Like other contradictory/intermediate hearts he had no known history of using livid coercion or domestic violence in his family. His father-in-law, Jim Baker, told reporters, "I never heard him raise his voice once to her."[199] According to Baker, "There was no history of him beating on her, being abusive verbally or physically. . . . Something snapped."[200]

By all accounts, Christian Longo wanted a lavish lifestyle. He craved luxury items. Providing for his family did not enable him to indulge his acquisitiveness. Longo was therefore not like the civil reputable hearts in the data set insofar as he was a self-acknowledged forger, liar, conman, and thief. He therefore belongs neither at the livid coercive nor at the civil reputable end of the emotional continuum. But, like his livid coercive and civil reputable peers, we discern the presence of significant shame. Of especial importance was the fact that the Jehovah's Witnesses church shunned him for passing bad checks. He was also facing financial ruin due to the failure of his business. Also like the livid coercive and civil reputable hearts, Longo was socially isolated, suffering from a nominal or minimal sense of social belonging.

For the most part, I focus on the livid coercive and civil reputable hearts, although in Chapter 2, I closely examine the familicide committed by Mrs. Emma Cooper, who, like Christian Longo, occupies a contradictory/intermediate location. Out of the 211 cases, I have coded 77 as evincing livid coercion (76 male, one female) although as I go on to explain, not all of these are what I call fully blown livid coercive hearts. I identify 47 civil reputable hearts (40 male, 7 female). Thirty-nine perpetrators (33 male, 6 female) occupy contradictory/intermediate locations. A further 48 cases (47 male, one female) contained insufficient information to situate them on the emotional continuum or otherwise defied coding. The cases with insufficient information are usually the older cases about which I located a newspaper article with only the barest data. Those that defy the grammar and logic of the emotional continuum usually involved perpetrators suffering from severe mental illness of long–standing, involving what the psychiatrists called "breaks with reality"; for example, some form of schizophrenia. These cases account for no more than five percent of the data set.

Although the archive is not amenable to rigorous statistical analyses, two other impressions regarding social patterns warrant mention. First, livid coercive hearts tended to have blue collar, manual, or service jobs and often struggled to earn a living. In contrast, their civil reputable peers tended to be white-collar or technical workers, professionals, public servants such as teachers and guidance counselors, and small independent businessmen (see Appendix I). Female perpetrators worked mostly as middle-class or, in a couple of cases, working-class homemakers. Simply put, most livid coercive hearts were working class and most civil reputable hearts middle class. Second, the racial and ethnic backgrounds of perpetrators appear to mirror offenders' presence in the population. With familicide we do not see the startling overrepresentation of historically disadvantaged groups such as African-Americans, Latinos, or American Indians that we see with the commission of homicide in general or intimate-partner homicide in particular.[201]

Table 1.1 classifies the 211 cases by location on the emotional continuum and sex of offender and Figure 1 represents this diagrammatically.

THE ARGUMENT

In the chapters that follow, I argue familicide constitutes one of the undesirable consequences of modern era emotional formations. Drawing upon Raymond Williams's notion of a structure of feeling and Norbert Elias's figurational sociology (see Chapter 2), I contend those who commit familicide experience overwhelmingly intense feelings of shame, fear, anxiety, and aggression that literally drive their acts of mass killing. Perpetrators' emotional styles reflect their simultaneous contribution to and negotiation of what I refer to as *modern era figurations of feeling*. These figurations tend to inhibit the expression of anger, invite anxieties about the future, and, in particular, inculcate shame. Indeed, the single most important and consistent theme among the familicide cases is the presence of intense shame in the lives of perpetrators, much of it unacknowledged or bypassed. The livid coercive hearts tend to disguise or mask their shame, deploying violence, hostility, and intimidation to do so. Their civil reputable peers are more likely to repress these painful feelings, submerging or sublimating them to the point they assume menacing forms of deep depression and hopelessness.

The primarily working class livid coercive hearts temporarily dissipate their shame through their humiliated fury and the act of familicide, perhaps realizing a fleeting sense of control and pride. In these cases the familicide is the end point in a violent, sometimes tyrannical relationship where the eventual perpetrator engages in frantic and obsessive attempts to control a spouse or partner. The sources of their shame vary, but the threatened or actual loss of their love object assumes center stage, producing great anxiety, fear, and rage among men typically vulnerable, dependent, and often relatively powerless. The mostly middle class civil reputable hearts were

Table 1.1   Classification of the 211 Familicidal Hearts by Location on the Continuum and by Sex

Perpetrator location on continuum	Male	Female	Totals
Livid coercive	76	1	77
Civil reputable	40	7	47
Contradictory/intermediate	33	6	39
Insufficient data/Defies coding	47	1	48
Totals	196	15	211

quiet, subdued, respectable, upstanding citizens who had not used violence and intimidation in an attempt to control their intimate partners. These perpetrators killed because their lives were spinning out of control and they perceived they faced the threat of bankruptcy, destitution, familial dissolution, or some other calamity. For most perpetrators, shame stemmed in large part from their sense they failed to live up to the dominant modern ideas about masculinity, and, in a very small number of cases, femininity. It is also the case that livid coercive and civil reputable hearts have a skewed relationship with the expression of anger, having significant problems managing the emotion.

Like many mass killers and serial killers, perpetrators of familicide are socially disconnected, displaying a nominal sense of self. This ought not surprise us, given that shame functions to isolate and, at times, to ostracize. Drawing upon the work of psychoanalytic feminists, among others, I suggest that men are more vulnerable than women to social disconnection, a fact that partly explains their vast overrepresentation among perpetrators of familicide. Men's differential vulnerability to these isolating and alienating forces also reflects their economic roles in modern American capitalism. Another element of my argument is that women seem to be under less pressure to individuate than men, although this is clearly changing. It is also the case that women are not socialized to use violence to solve problems to anything like the same degree as men. Importantly, although the bulk of male perpetrators enjoyed some form of power over their spouses or partners and their families, I argue the power relations of

Livid coercive			Contradictory/intermediate			Civil reputable		
Males	Females	Total	Males	Females	Total	Males	Females	Total
76	1	77	33	6	39	40	7	47

Figure 1.1   Classification of the 163 of the 211 Familicidal Hearts by Location on the Continuum and by Sex

(Figure does not include the 47 male and 1 female [48 total] cases either lacking enough information to be placed on the continuum or who simply defy such placement.)

modern gender regimes appear to exert a contextual and indirect influence on the commission of familicide and that power is best seen as relational, contested, and contingent. However, the fact that women do commit familicide reminds us these gendered differences are questions of degree, not kind. All of this is rather different than saying that men's power over women is the causal root of the vast majority of familicides.

It is important to remember that women's emotional capital is a source of power in their intimate relationships with men, offering them problem-solving options other than committing familicide. Men and women's access to emotional capital, their emotional expressivities and acumen, exist within the framework of their relationships. It is not my point that women are emotionally expressive and men are not, or that women have feelings and men do not. Clearly, the emotional expressiveness of men and women differs by class, race, ethnicity, and sexual orientation.

At the same time as noting women's emotional expressiveness vis-à-vis their male partners, battered women who end up the victims of familicide or female perpetrators of familicide who are not battered can also have little control over their feelings and suffer serious cognitive deficits compared with their non-battered peers. Nevertheless, these same battered women may still have an emotional edge over their husbands and male partners. Notwithstanding these caveats, the adult female victims and perpetrators of familicide tended to have more emotional skills, a greater fluency with feelings, and more of a willingness to express these feelings in words than their male partners.

My argument therefore connects the visceral and emotional immediacies of the act of familicide with broad-ranging social and historical developments. As such, it differs from many theories of homicide that implicate social structural forces such as unemployment or poverty, or point to subcultures of violence as the breeding ground for murderers. Put simply, I explore the small-scale, interpersonal context, particularly the familial and interpersonal ebb and flow of emotion, in combination with larger social and historical forces. I fully recognize the caveats of those who research these problems: many people experience what appear to be the necessary conditions for the spawning of a homicidal or familicidal offender, but very few commit these offenses. Bearing these caveats in mind, a central element of my argument is that we must take into account our inability to fully explain familicidal behavior. It is for this reason that I develop the metaphoric language of *haunting* and write of the *ghostly presence of modern era figurations of feeling*, as a means of grappling with the inexplicability of the killings and the very real limits of our understanding. In a sense, my argument for recognizing the haunting and powerful presence of the inexplicable helps us move from the seemingly necessary emotional milieu for familicide to the seemingly sufficient conditions for such forms of annihilation. My logic here is akin to that of the mathematician who uses the symbol i to talk of the square root of a negative number, an otherwise unknowable quantity.

It is important not to confuse my argument with a wholesale rejection of quantitative or qualitative methods or construe it simply as a form of skepticism. I choose to focus on emotion because it offers us a fresh view of a particularly harrowing form of mass murder that continues to shock communities. My argument may privilege subjective ways of knowing but it certainly does not make any special claims for their veracity. In fact, my contention that we must recognize the importance of the inexplicable in cases of familicide challenges research that tends to imply that, one day, if only we can get close enough to the phenomenon under test, or if only we can control for every possible confounding variable, then we can precisely identify why familicides occur. It is not my lack of optimism about the potential of either quantitative or qualitative approaches that causes me to argue for the importance of the inexplicable. Rather, it is my desire to emphasize the complex personhood of the parties in these atrocities and to invite circumspection when it comes to explaining the killings.

It is equally important to state what my argument is not. Merely because I identify the seeds of familicide in the midst of the growing psychological restraint of the modern era does not mean that modern era intimate relationships are somehow suspect, pathological, or doomed. As I go on to show, modernity is a period of emotional experimentation, holding great potential in terms of building identities and crafting relationships.

Finally, my focus on emotional styles, familial atmosphere of feeling, and socially and historically situated figurations of feeling enables us to develop an appreciation of homicide and familicide in terms of continuities rather than as abrupt breaks or distinctive episodes. Often, popular accounts of familicide talk in terms of the offender finally "snapping." Indeed, Mary Jane Longo's father (cited above) used that very language to describe Christian Longo's descent to familicide. The anti-violence against women movement is critical of explanations that dwell on acts of "snapping," arguing that intimate killings involve a building of abuse and often an amplification of tyranny, intimidation, and violence.[202] However, it seems to me that both the final act of killing and what appears as the buildup to it both warrant our careful attention. Focusing on emotion and the lived, visceral immediacy of the familicide provides clues in terms of making sense of what came before. In fact, I argue we not only find shame, fear, anxiety, or repressed or sublimated rage running the length of many of these cases, we also sense their remains at crime scenes. I contend the language of cumulative processes and the final snapping is a little misleading and belies the continuities of emotion up until the end.

THE OUTLINE

Familicidal Hearts is set out as follows. For chapters 2 through 5, I include tables that provide summary notes on the principal cases I discuss in the chapter. These notes name perpetrators and victims. They also include key facts that highlight distinctive aspects of the cases, or cues, thereby helping readers recall cases or at least refer to the summaries as they read. The tables only include the dates of cases that I explored solely through the public record. In cases where I had access to confidential files and information, I do not list dates because of the need to protect the privacy of the parties. The tables therefore offer readers a quick reference guide, a touchstone to familiarize them with the cases and to keep them straight.

Chapter 2 ("Figurations of Feeling and Haunted Hearts") explores the mysteries of familicide as an intensely emotional process rather than an isolated, discrete event or violent episode. Through case excerpts, I frame familicide as a moving rather than stationary target. I contend that, to make sense of familicide as an emotional phenomenon that reflects the confluence of emotional, social, and historical forces, we must fuse our quantitative grasp of the archive with an appreciation of the subjective complexities of these cases. As another way of thinking about familicide, I develop the notion of "haunted hearts"; hearts haunted by socially and historically situated figurations and atmospheres of emotion and feeling.

Chapter 3 ("Familicide: A History") traces familicide back to its origins in the early American republic. I explore various aspects of what I call *modern emotional formations* for clues about the historical elaboration of emotional styles that harbor within their recesses the drive to commit familicide. In particular, I scrutinize changes in political, economic, and social life, especially shifting conceptions of family, masculinity, and gender relationships. Mapping familicide in terms of a socially and historically situated continuum of emotions sets the scene for a detailed analysis of what appear at the extreme left- and right-hand ends of this continuum of sensibilities: livid coercive hearts and civil reputable hearts.

Chapter 4 ("Livid Coercive Hearts") focuses particularly on violence, anger, coercion, intimidation, sexual jealousy, and attempts to control spouses and partners. Given the richness of information in some cases and the paucity in others, it is difficult to map precisely the nature, form, and extent of the violent behavior and intimidation that preceded the famili-cide. Seventy-seven cases contain clear and convincing evidence of varying degrees of livid coercion. I selected what appear to be some of the most extreme examples of livid coercion from among these 77 cases (76 male and one female perpetrator). As we will see, in these cases, violence and intimidation regularly punctuate the intimate or formerly intimate rela-tionship. In these examples, we also witness the perpetrator attacking the personhood of his current or former partner. In addition, I include the case of a female perpetrator who used domestic violence and livid coercion against her husband but who cannot be described as a fully blown livid coercive heart.

My intent is not to present a thoroughgoing statistical analysis of the precise nature, form, and extent of domestic violence in these cases but rather to convey a sense of the range of violence and emotional turmoil in a handful of cases for which rich data exist. Chapter 4 therefore explores that end of the emotional continuum evincing a lack of regulation of strong emotions such as anger and rage. My discussion includes consideration of the emotional plight of perpetrators, their anxieties, shame, narcissism, vulnerability, and seeming dependency.

Forty-seven cases of familicide exhibited no signs of domestic violence until the terminal act of mass interpersonal killing. In these cases, social and economic pressures deeply disturbed hitherto proud and seemingly successful spouses and parents, creating an acute sense of shame. The emotional styles of these 47 perpetrators (40 male; seven female) evinced considerable self-control and restraint. These men and women were of good social standing in their communities. Chapter 5 ("Civil Reputable Hearts") explores the lives and final acts of some of these perpetrators. As in Chapter 4, the differential richness of the archive guides my selection of cases. As we will see, the roots of shame and humiliation in these cases differ from those found at the livid coercive end of the continuum. However, among livid coercive and civil reputable hearts, shame and humiliation consistently derive from a failure to meet the restrictive and punishing standards of the gender regime and the socially and historically situated imperatives of masculinities and femininities.

Superficially, the labyrinthine emotional conflicts and tensions the familicidal hearts navigate span a range of sensibilities, attitudes, behaviors, and affects. In Chapter 6 ("Familicide as a Consequence of Modern Era Emotional Formations"), I explore these microcircuits of emotion and their continuities with social patterns of feeling and familial atmospheres of feeling. I conclude that, although many aspects of gender relationships are moving toward equality, the profoundly gendered nature of familicide suggests the durability of subtle and deeply gendered modern emotional formations seamlessly interwoven with the sometimes ordered and sometime conflict-ridden interdependencies of modern life.

In Chapter 7 ("Some Implications: A Few Closing Thoughts"), I explore the implications of some of my observations. In particular, I suggest the anti–domestic violence movement has more than lost its way. It pays far too much attention to violence and the criminal justice response to domestic violence. One of the things that is lost, I contend, is an appreciation of the deep-seated changes in the emotional formations of modernity. These shifts, and particularly notions about appropriate and desirable forms of masculinities, provide the backdrop for regimes of violence, tyranny, and intimidation in intimate relationships and familial networks. Those same shifts also contribute significantly to the precipitation of disappointment, depression, shame, and anxiety often associated with aspects of nuclear family life and civil reputable forms of familicide.

In summation, my approach is interdisciplinary, subjective, and concerned more with processes than with cause and effect. I therefore remain cognizant of the utter inexplicability of many of these sad and bizarre mass interpersonal killings. Perpetrators experience, in a highly concentrated way, the emotional consequences of modernity. We might say these men and a few women act as conduits, or, more melodramatically, lightning rods for these highly charged emotional energies that drive their acts of killing.

NOTES

1. For details of these early developments see ndvfri.org a website funded by the Office on Violence Against Women, US Department of Justice.

2. See Websdale, Town, and Johnson, 1999.

3. See Websdale, 2003; Websdale, Moss, and Johnson, 2001; Websdale, Town, and Johnson, 1999.

4. Bean, 1992: 43.

5. Campbell, A., 1993: 72.

6. Alder, 1991: 168.

7. Goetting, 1999: 4.

8. Wallace, 1986: 123.

9. Campbell, J., 2003a, b.

10. See Bostrum, 2002.

11. See Matthew Dale, 2005, "Fatality Reviews in a Rural Setting: The Case of Montana," Fatality Review Bulletin, Spring, 2005: 3–4.

12. See, for example, the discussion of the Pemberton case in Westminster Hall Debates, March 16, 2005. Published in *Hansard: House of Commons Daily Debates*, London: Parliament. See also *BBC News*, April 20, 2005: "Police Face Family Murder Probe"; *The Guardian,* June 7, 2005: "The Family No One Could Save"; *The Swindon Advertiser,* April 26, 2005: "Family's Murder to Be Reviewed"; *The Irish Examiner*, September 29, 2004: "Inquest Hears Last Words of Woman Killed by Husband". By John Bingham, *The Observer*, March 11, 2007: "My Sister Was Killed While the Police Did Nothing."

13. West Berkshire Safer Communities Partnership, 2008.

14. Wilson, Daly, and Daniele, 1995: 275.

15. Duwe, 2000, 2004, 2005.

16. My reliance might concern those worried about the surveillance capabilities of the late modern state. It is likely that the rather punitive ethic at the heart of this criminal justice juggernaut shapes the information that the police, courts, and others seek. But information is always socially situated and historically contingent. In a sense, we take these state-mediated cultural remains as we find them and work with the materials as best we can. The aggressive, institutionally bound, perhaps somewhat jaundiced homicide detective who investigates killings and contributes to the American prison system has just as much to tell the world as the critical criminologist who attacks the state at the same time as picking up a paycheck from it.

17. As Bourdieu puts it, "other human beings are not objects but alter-egos" (2005: 49).

18. Garland, 1990: 239.

19. Geertz, 1973: 13.

20. The research received Institutional Review Board approval for the protection of human subjects through my own university. In addition, my practical policy work through NDVFRI has always been subject to the human subjects rules of the U.S. Department of Justice Grant Programs, even though NDVFRI provides technical assistance and does not conduct research.

21. Bradley, 1999.

22. Cresswell and Hollin, 1992.

23. See for example Howard Taylor's (1998) questioning of the efficacy of using homicide statistics as a means of measuring the manifestation of homicidal behavior. Taylor argues that police chiefs might have used considerable discretion to reclassify some cases of killing as manslaughter, suicide, or accidental death to preserve vital resources. For a discussion of the implications of Taylor's work, see Archer, J. E., 2003.

24. Mills, 1959: 11–12.

25. Mills, 1959: 14–15.

26. Gordon, 1997.

27. My comments regarding Elias's arguments about the links between the state monopolization of legitimate public-sphere violence and the rise of psychological restraint apply to Western cultures. I am aware of the critiques of Elias's position on the relationship between internal psychological restraint and its predication upon the rise of an increasingly strong state apparatus. See, for example, Van Krieken, 1989.

28. See, for example, Kumar (1978), who notes that as birth rates increased and death rates fell, the population of Europe grew from 120 million in 1750 to 468 million in 1913. He observes that in 1810, one-fifth of the British population lived in urban areas. By, 1910, the proportion of urban dwellers had increased to four-fifths.

29. Haskell, 1985: 550.

30. Lasch, 1979.

31. Barrett and McIntosh, 1982.

32. Van Krieken, 1989: 197–198.

33. Stone, 1977.

34. Dill, 1988: 416.

35. For a discussion of the extension of landowning rights to settlers in Oregon, see Chused, 1984.

36. Dill, 1988: 416.

37. Gutman, 1976: 318.

38. Gutman, 1976: 318.

39. Gutman, 1976: 319.

40. Sudarkasa, 1981.

41. Dill, 1988: 424–425.

42. Wang, 1996: 168.

43. Giddens, 1990: 20.

44. Durkheim, 1952.

45. See Marx, 1964. See also Karl Polanyi (2001), who argued that one of the hallmarks of modernity was the domineering logic of the capitalist marketplace. This logic pushed for the disembedding of the economic sphere from that of social life, religion, and politics.

46. See, for example, Cohen, 1995; Barnes, 2002. I return to this discourse in considerable detail in Chapter 3.

47. Nevertheless, this coverage of familicide pales in comparison to that usually devoted to the mass killings strangers perpetrate. As Duwe reminds us, the news media disproportionately report mass killings involving stranger victims, public locations, assault weapons, workplace violence, and interracial victim–offender relationships. He observes that 55 percent of media examples of mass killings

and 63 percent of academic examples use cases with stranger victims (2005: Table 1). He stresses that only 24 percent of U.S. mass killings from 1900–1999 involve stranger victims. In a related vein, only 18 percent of media and academic examples used cases with family members as victims. This contrasts with the 44 percent of actual mass killings between 1900 and 1999 involving family victims.

48. Fox and Levin, 1985: 98.

49. The rate of familicide per 100,000 population is given by multiplying the number of familicides by 100,000 and dividing that outcome by the average population in the country for that period.

50. Readers will see that the one familicide in 1755 produces a rate of 0.071 per 100,000 for the decade of the 1750s. The rate drops to zero in 1760s and 1770s, only to climb to 0.089 in the 1780s and fall again to zero during the 1790s. The overall increase over the last five decades seems steadier, with an apparently sharp increase in the last two decades: 1960s (0.003); 1970s (0.005); 1980s (0.004); 1990s (0.015); 2000–2007 (0.029).

51. See Alvarez and Bachman, 2008: 100. For precise details of the rates of multicide, see Fox and Zawitz, 2006, "Homicide Trends in the United States: Multiple Victims and Offenders." Available at www.ojp.usdoj.gov/bjs/homicide/tables/multipletab.htm (downloaded March 3, 2009).

52. Wilson, Daly, and Daniele note, "Their epidemiology remains virtually unstudied" (1995: 275). Carolyn Johnson's brief study of familicide in Australia focused on custody disputes or access to children. She, too, points to the "dearth of research dealing specifically with familicide" (2005: 105).

53. Wilson, Daly, and Daniele, 1995: 286.

54. Wilson and Daly, 1998: 225.

55. I use the word *intimate* to connote emotional communication and sharing.

56. Wilson, Daly, and Daniele, 1995: 287.

57. Wilson and Daly, 1998: 225.

58. Wilson and Daly, 1998: 226.

59. Ewing, 1997: Chapter 10, "Familicide."

60. Ewing, 1997: 135.

61. Ewing, 1997: 134.

62. Nesca and Kincel, 2000: 44.

63. Nesca and Kincel, 2000: 45.

64. Nesca and Kincel, 2000: 46.

65. Nesca and Kincel, 2000: 47.

66. Nesca and Kincel, 2000: 47.

67. Nesca and Kincel, 2000: 48.

68. Nesca and Kincel, 2000: 48.

69. Nesca and Kincel, 2000: 48.

70. Nesca and Kincel, 2000: 50.

71. Schlesinger, 2000: 200.

72. Schlesinger, 2000: 201.

73. Schlesinger, 2000: 201.

74. Schlesinger, 2000: 202.

75. Reichard and Tillman, 1950.

76. Lindsay, 1958: 194.

77. Lindsay, 1958: 195.

78. Leyton, 2005: 321–322.

79. Leyton, 2005: 322.
80. Leyton, 2005: 322.
81. Leyton, 2005: 331.
82. Messner and Rosenfeld, 1993: 9.
83. Brookman, 2005, 189–191.
84. Motz, 2001: 131–132, cited in Brookman, 2005: 192. Italics are mine and are designed to emphasize the central role of the tremendous fear of social stigma in these cases, another way of talking of the importance of shame.
85. See, for example, Alder and Polk, 2001, Chapter 1, especially pp. 3–4, for a useful summary of the studies of male- and female-perpetrated fatal child abuse.
86. Brookman, 2005: 197.
87. Brookman, 2005: 197; citing case B.08/94.
88. Polk, 1994.
89. Polk, 1994: 189.
90. Polk, 1994: 189.
91. In his classic analysis of homicide-suicide, Marvin Wolfgang notes that "in only one of the 47 cases in which a wife killed her husband did she later commit suicide; but that in 10 of the 53 cases in which a husband killed his wife did he commit suicide" (1958: 282). Wolfgang infers that this gender disparity is due to the "greater feelings of guilt and remorse on the part of husbands" (1958: 282). In their classic work, Daly and Wilson argue "unplanned suicide out of remorse for having killed appears to be an extremely rare event" (1988: 217).
92. Daly and Wilson, 1988: 189. Their use of the phrase "strive to control" informed the formulation of question 53a (see Appendix IV) of the survey of familicide cases; namely, "Was the perpetrator striving to control the victim?" Italics in the original.
93. See especially Daly and Wilson, 1988: Chapter 9.
94. Daly and Wilson, 1988: 207.
95. Daly and Wilson, 1988: 295.
96. Wilson and Daly, 1998: 299.
97. Daly and Wilson, 1988: 296.
98. Wolfgang, 1958.
99. Wolfgang, 1958: 329.
100. Wolfgang, 1958: 329.
101. Daly and Wilson, 1988: 296.
102. Daly and Wilson, 1988: 296.
103. For a critique of Daly and Wilson, see Gould (1997) and Polk (1998).
104. Brookman, 2005: 82.
105. Goffman, 1959: 241.
106. Stark, 2007: 15. Stark contends, "Nothing men experience in the normal course of their everyday lives resembles this conspicuous form of subjugation" (2007: 15). Notice Stark is not saying women are incapable of coercive control. Stark's notion of coercive control recalls Michael Johnson's concept of *intimate terrorism* (see Johnson: 1995, 2006). Johnson first used the term *patriarchal terrorism* to describe that brand of controlling, terrifying, fear-inducing violence evident in battering relationships, particularly those identified through agency samples as opposed to population surveys. He replaced patriarchal terrorism with intimate terrorism because patriarchal terrorism implied "that all such intimate terrorism was somehow rooted in patriarchal structures, traditions, or attitudes." Johnson goes on to note that "most intimate terrorism is perpetrated by men in

heterosexual relationships and that in such cases the violence is indeed rooted in patriarchal traditions." However, as Johnson points out, "it is clear that that there are women intimate terrorists in heterosexual and same-sex relationships. Furthermore, it is not clear that all intimate terrorism, even men's, is rooted in patriarchal ideas or structures" (see Johnson, 2006, footnote 2, page 1015). In addition to the fact that the notion of coercive control was well established in the domestic violence literature well before Johnson began writing, Stark prefers the term *coercive control* to *intimate terrorism* for two principal reasons (2007: 104–105). First he contends that most of the escalating violence, intimidation, stalking, and isolation occur when couples are not living "intimately." Rather, the couples are often separated or in the process of separating. Second, the actual tactics men deploy bear little resemblance to those terrorists use.

107. Stark, 2007: 197.
108. Stark, 2007: 195–196.
109. Stark, 2007: 193.
110. Stark, 2007: 194. Italics are mine.
111. Gordon, 1997: 4.
112. Gordon, 1997: 5.
113. Raven, 1992, 1993.
114. Dutton and Goodman, 2005: 745.
115. My italics.
116. Goodman et al., 2003.
117. Dutton and Goodman, 2005: 746.
118. Dutton and Goodman, 2005: 752.
119. Dutton and Goodman, 2005: 752.
120. Personal communication, December 11, 2007.
121. Dutton and Goodman, 2005: 753.
122. Gordon, 1997: 4.
123. Dutton, 2006: 126.
124. Dutton, 2006: 127.
125. Dutton, 2006: 127.
126. Nowotny, 1981: 148.
127. Allatt, 1993.
128. Dutton, 2006. See also Mills, 2008.
129. Dutton, 2006: 67.
130. Dutton, 2006: 81.
131. Dutton, 2006: 82.
132. Mills, 2008: 632.
133. For a good summary, see Gilligan, 2003. For a specific reference to shame as a precursor to violence, see Thomas, 1995.
134. Sartre, 1939: 15. Italics in the original.
135. Sartre, 1939: 18.
136. Arendt, 1970: 56.
137. Gilligan, 1996: 132.
138. Dutton, 2006: 128.
139. Pence, 1999: 28. Italics in the original.
140. Pence, 1999: 28.
141. Pence, 1999: 28–29. Italics in the original.
142. Pence, 1999: 29.
143. Faludi, 1999: 9.

144. Faludi, 1999: 9.
145. Faludi, 1999: 9.
146. Lukes, 2005: 1.
147. Collins, 2008: 26.
148. Collins, 2008: 27.
149. Connell, 1995: 64–65.
150. Turner and Stets, 2005: 1.
151. Mills, 1959: 235–236.
152. Denzin, 1984: 483–484.
153. Denzin, 1984: 487.
154. Denzin, 1984: 488.
155. Denzin, 1984: 488.
156. Denzin, 1984: 489.
157. Denzin, 1984: 489.
158. Denzin, 1984: 491.
159. Denzin, 1984: 491.
160. Anderson, 1999: 75–76.
161. Collins, 2008: 19.
162. Collins, 2008: 2.
163. Gilligan, 1996: 111.
164. Gilligan, 1996: 110.
165. Katz, 1988: 23.
166. Gilligan, 2003: 1153.
167. Gilligan, 2003: 1153.
168. Scheff and Retzinger, 2001: xviii.
169. Foucault, 1975: 53–121.
170. Foucault, 1975: 9.
171. Foucault, 1975: 10–11.
172. Foucault, 1975: 11.
173. Foucault, 1975: 18.
174. Foucault, 1975: 14.
175. Foucault, 1975: 80.
176. Foucault, 1975: 101.
177. Foucault, 1975: 103.
178. Foucault, 1975: 103.
179. Foucault, 1975: 105.
180. At one point he remarks, "It is the women who are in command now in this fine age which calls itself the age of enlightenment, this nation which seems so avid for liberty and glory obeys women, the Romans were far more civilized, the Hurons and Hottentots, the Algonquins, these peoples who are said to be idiots are even more civilized, never have they debased strength, it has always been the stronger in body who have laid down the law among themselves" (Foucault, 1975: 108).
181. Illouz, 2007: 1–2.
182. Illouz, 2007: 3.
183. Elias, 1994.
184. Fletcher, 1997: 24. Italics in the original.
185. Elias, 1994: 492.
186. Freud, 2005: 38.
187. Freud, 2005: 150.

188. See also Sigmund Freud, *The Ego and the Id* (1923).

189. Colman, 2006: 362.

190. Zaretsky, 2004: 16.

191. Zaretsky, 2004: 16; italics in the original. As Zaretsky points out, Freud's appreciation of the personal unconscious was a response to two strands of alternating thought emblematic of late–nineteenth century psychiatry. He notes, "On one side, the tradition of psychiatry that descended from the Enlightenment sought to restore control by strengthening the will and ordering the reasoning processes of 'disordered' individuals. On the other side, a later generation of 'dynamic' psychiatrists and neurologists sought to facilitate 'release' through hypnotism and meditation. Freud's idea of the personal unconscious represented an alternative to both positions. Treating neither self-control nor release as a primary value, it encouraged a new, nonjudgmental or 'analytic' attitude toward the self. The result was a major modification of the Enlightenment idea of the human subject. No longer the locus of universal reason and morality, the modern individual would henceforth be a contingent, idiosyncratic, and unique person, one whose highly charged and dynamic interiority would be the object of psychoanalytic thought and practice" (2004: 17–18).

192. Elias, 1994: 486.

193. Elias, 1994: 486.

194. Elias, 1994: 486.

195. Elias, 1994: 487. Italics in the original.

196. Goffman, 1959.

197. Other researchers employ the notion of a "continuum" to study interpersonal violence. See, for example, Stanko (1990) and Kelly (1988).

198. For more information see, Joseph B. Frazier, "Family Murder: It Happens in the Nicest Homes." *The Shawnee News-Star*, May 18, 2003; Andrew Kramer, "Officials: Ex-Iowan Killed Family for Wild Lifestyle." *The Daily Iowan*, March 12, 2003.

199. *Eugene Register-Guard*, January 15, 2002.

200. *Eugene Register-Guard*, January 15, 2002.

201. As a glance at Appendix II reveals, Caucasians compose the majority of familicide offenders, accounting for 60 percent of the livid coercive hearts and 85 percent of the civil reputable hearts. African-Americans account for 16 percent of the livid coercive hearts; Latinos, another 16 percent. African-Americans account for none of the 47 civil reputable hearts; Latinos, just one. American Indians accounted for one of the 77 livid coercive offenders and none of the civil reputable hearts. Compared with their presence in the population, Caucasians are slightly over-represented among civil reputable hearts and somewhat under-represented among livid coercive hearts. African-American, Latino, American Indian, Middle Eastern and Asian-American livid coercive hearts feature roughly in proportion to their presence in the population. African-American, Latino, Middle Eastern, and American Indian civil reputable hearts are under-represented in the archive compared with their presence in the general population. Asian-American civil reputable hearts are over-represented among the civil reputable hearts. Research into intimate-partner homicide clearly indicates that we find the highest rates among African-Americans, followed by American Indians and Alaska Natives, then Caucasians and Asian or Pacific Islanders, in that order. See, for example, Paulozzi et al., 2001: 4.

202. The tensions between interpretations that focus on the act of homicide and the social factors that appear to distally inform, influence, or drive it and the interactive character of the exchange between perpetrators and victims is one of the dichotomies that Luckenbill addresses in his classic characterization of homicide as an interactive process. See Luckenbill, 1977.

2

FIGURATIONS OF FEELING, HAUNTED HEARTS, AND UNCANNY ACTS

Time and again in the aftermath of a familicide, community members and others wondered why perpetrators killed. People discern the perpetrators' distress: a pending bankruptcy, illness, or some form of grand humiliation. Nevertheless, an air of mystery pervades the social post mortems into these tragedies. Simply put, we sense the ghoulish presence of *inexplicable* forces, which seem, sometimes, as if they come from beyond the grave or are at least not of this world. In many ways, this sense of mystery, this aura of the unknown, haunts communities in the wake of a familicide. In rare cases where perpetrators survive to reflect on their acts of mass interpersonal killing, their transgressions haunt them as well. Perhaps the most infamous perpetrator of familicide in late modernity, John List, who killed his wife, mother, and three children before fleeing to Denver and starting a new life as "Bob Clark," put it as follows, "The memory of what I did on that pivotal day in my life has ever since haunted me, filled me with remorse."[1]

In what follows, I employ Avery Gordon's language of ghosts and haunting as one point of entry into exploring these deaths. I commence with the recognition, based on extensive time with the familicide archive, that these mass killings are saturated with emotion. It is, of course, useful to map patterns of abstract factors concerning economic stressors, triggers, timing, weaponry, and the other usual suspects: the things that we can supposedly code, count, and compare. Yet in order to explore the emotional styles of the perpetrators who paced around with hammer, axe, knife, or gun, we need a rather different epistemological gestalt, an alternative opening, one that is at once descriptive, interpretive, and processual and at the same time one that links emotional styles with what I will refer to as "figurations of feeling."

Chapter 2 develops the concepts of *emotional styles* and *figurations of feeling* as theoretical tools for interpreting familicide. These concepts lay the groundwork for an analysis of two of what I call *haunted hearts* (Lonnie Shell and Emma Cooper) and the *uncanny acts* of familicide they end up committing.

EMOTIONAL STYLES: THE MÉLANGE OF VISCERAL, PSYCHOLOGICAL, SOCIAL, AND HISTORICAL ENERGIES

In the preceding chapter, I noted some of the competing explanations of intimate-partner violence and homicide. I traced these explanations to the various turf wars between so-called experts who have a political axe to grind. Specifically, I alluded to the tensions between those who saw intimate-partner violence and homicide in terms of men's power and control over women and those who interpret them in terms of shame. At a more general level we see similar interpretive struggles about how to explain human behavior. Both sets of ideological struggles are relevant to our study of familicide because, if we let them, they will define our horizons and limit our maneuverability.

Drawing upon the work of authors such as Antonio Damasio, Norbert Elias, Erving Goffman, Charles Horton Cooley, George Herbert Mead, and Raymond Williams, I develop the notion of *emotional styles* as a flexible analytical concept that addresses the continuities between the visceral, the psychological, the social, and the historical. The idea of emotional styles also enables us to appreciate the *momentary realization* or *instantiation* of these seemingly disparate and conceptually incompatible energies. My use of the language of emotional styles sidesteps the often fruitless pontificating about macro and micro forces in the social sciences. Rather, I follow Giddens, who contends that as people engage in social action, they contribute to the reproduction and transformation of what sociologists and historians often refer to as structures or social patterns.[2] Much human action is routine, occurring without a lot of thought. Emotions play an important part in these actions, steering and steadying them, producing a sense of consistency and direction compatible with the survival of the physical body.

We cannot see the reasoning powers of those who commit familicide as somehow distinct from their emotional style. In his book *Descartes Error: Emotion, Reason, and the Human Brain*, Antonio Damasio, a leading neurologist, contends, "emotion could assist the reasoning process rather than necessarily disturb it, as was commonly assumed."[3] He goes on: "Certain aspects of the process of emotion and feeling are indispensable for rationality." Damasio's insights are consistent with the importance

I attach to the emotional styles of perpetrators and the crucial role these styles play in the commission of familicide. At one point he notes, "Emotion and feeling, along with the covert physiological machinery underlying them, assist us with the daunting task of predicting an uncertain future and planning our actions accordingly."[4]

At another level, the body is the medium through which feeling finds expression. Damasio puts it nicely, "Feelings form the base for what humans have described for millennia as the human soul or spirit."[5] He continues, "The soul breathes through the body, and suffering, whether it starts in the skin or in a mental image, happens in the flesh."[6]

Just as it is inappropriate to separate reason and emotion, feelings and the flesh, so, too, is it unacceptable to make sense of human behavior as a product of isolated, atomized, inner selves, cut off in time and space. Human beings are social. They survive collectively, through interdependencies that are in a constant state of flux. We cannot freeze this flux and examine it as one might a photograph, pointing out all the distinctive parts of a scene, a line here, an edge there, a structure weighing heavily above, a foundation below, and so on. The interdependencies between people involve what Norbert Elias calls a multitude of figurations, some tense and conflict-ridden, others more harmonious and ordered. Elias prefers the word *figurations* to "structure" because *figuration* conveys an active sense of the historical engagement among people, whereas *structure* might be misconstrued as an entity "apart from the people who form it."[7] Elias notes, "What we call 'structure' is, in fact, nothing but the pattern or figuration of interdependent individual people who form the group or, in a wider sense, the society. What we term 'structures' when we look at people as societies, are 'figurations' when we look at them as individuals."[8]

Elias is critical of economic, psychiatric, psychoanalytic, and sociological approaches that see certain atomized individuals (*Homo economicus, Homo psychiatricus, Homo psychoanalyticus,* or *Homo sociologicus*) in the foreground and their "social background" or "environment" as a vague and rather distant context. He opines, "The terminology itself implies the existence of a wall between the highly structured person in the foreground and the seemingly unstructured network of relations and communication in the background."[9] For Elias, for example, the theoretical notion of *Homo psychiatricus* assumes "a fairly radical division between what goes on 'inside' and what goes on 'outside' the individual human being."[10] The person who becomes the focus of the psychiatrist's gaze "is a human being stripped of most attributes which one might call 'social.'"[11] Most important for our analysis of familicide, the atomized perception of human beings Elias is criticizing is a powerful viewpoint in the human sciences. For Elias it is the "perspective of a human being who experiences himself alone at the centre of things, while everything else lies outside, separated from him by an invisible wall, and who imputes as a matter of course the same experience to all other individuals."[12]

Using emotional styles to make sense of the predicaments of perpetrators of familicide first requires consideration of a body of thought that identifies the importance of some of the emotions that manifest in these perplexing cases. Thomas Scheff indicates that, in *Studies in Hysteria* (1895), Freud and Breuer linked repression to shame. They comment, "The ideas that were being repressed were all of a distressing nature, calculated to arouse the affects of shame, self-reproach and psychological pain and the feeling of being harmed."[13] Freud never returned to explicitly examine the regulatory effects of shame on human psychological development. His later studies focused much more on the role of the regulation of libidinal forces. However, as Scheff notes, in his early work on hysteria, Freud identified the key role of shame as the principal vehicle of repression and emotional illness.[14] The fact that Freud never returned to posit a central role for shame in the inculcation of social restraint need not concern us. For our purposes, it is enough to note that Freud saw repression at the heart of modern-era life. In *Civilization and Its Discontents* Freud is emphatic: "It is impossible to overlook the extent to which civilization is built upon a renunciation of instinct, how much it presupposes precisely the non-satisfaction (by suppression, repression or some other means?) of powerful instincts. This 'cultural frustration' dominates the large field of social relationships between human beings."[15]

Seeing social life as analogous to a theatrical performance, Erving Goffman writes eloquently in *The Presentation of Self in Everyday Life* of the way people interact with each other and act out social rules and norms. One of his central concepts is *impression management*, the notion that in their everyday lives, people act in order to appear favorably to others and in a manner that comports with various role expectations and social situations. Social life is a precarious achievement, and social actors live at the edge of possible embarrassment or some more onerous consequence. In a very important sense, the threat of Goffman's social actors' experiencing feelings of shame, humiliation, and particularly embarrassment is one of the organizing principles of human interaction. As Goffman remarks, "It seems that there is no interaction in which the participants do not take an appreciable chance of being slightly embarrassed or a slight chance of being deeply humiliated."[16] At another point he remarks on the fragility of the individual as performer:

> He is given to having fantasies and dreams, some that pleasurably unfold a triumphant performance, to others full of anxiety and dread that nervously deal with vital discreditings in a public front region. He often manifests a gregarious desire for teammates and audiences, a tactful considerateness for their concerns; and he has a *capacity for deeply felt shame*, leading him to minimize the chances he takes of exposure.[17]

Other social theorists saw social life in terms of the negotiation of shared roles and the building of identities honed through social interaction.

In a manner consonant with Elias's figurational sociology, George Herbert Mead situated the *self* amidst the ebb and flow of social life. Specifically, Mead comments, "The self is not something that exists first and then enters into relationship with others, but it is, so to speak, an eddy in the social current and so still a part of the current. It is a process in which the individual is continually adjusting himself in advance to the situation to which he belongs, and reacting back on it."[18]

In his discussion of the social aspects of "I," Charles Horton Cooley comments, "Since "I" is known to our experience primarily as a feeling, or as a feeling-ingredient in our ideas, it cannot be described or defined without suggesting that feeling."[19] Like the aforementioned authors, Cooley sees no sense of self in isolation from the sentiments and judgments of others. Cooley's identification of pride and shame as the generative emotional juice of social life resonates strongly with Elias's understanding of the vital importance of emotions such as shame and repugnance (disgust) in modern era psychological and social restraint. For Cooley, "There is no sense of 'I,' as in pride or shame, without its correlative sense of you, or he, or they."[20] Individuals constantly interpret what other people think about them. Cooley refers to this social self as the "reflected" or "looking-glass self." He comments:

> Each to each a looking-glass
> Reflects the other that doth pass.[21.]

In particular, Cooley emphasizes that our sense of self derives from "the imagination of our appearance to the other person; the imagination of his judgment of that appearance, and some sort of self-feeling, such as pride or mortification."[22] As we will see in our analysis of familicide, these feelings of pride and shame are socially situated. Cooley points out, "We are ashamed to seem evasive in the presence of a straightforward man, cowardly in the presence of a brave one, gross in the eyes of a refined one, and so on. We always imagine, and in imagining share, the judgments of the other mind. A man will boast to one person of an action—say some sharp transaction in trade—which he would be ashamed to own to another."[23]

The above-mentioned observations suggest social actors experience considerable anxiety, fear, shame, humiliation, and embarrassment about how others judge them, their performance in social situations, and their performances as fathers, mothers, spouses, lovers, workers, and so on. These observations also provide a means of understanding how a perpetrator of familicide presents one face to some people and another to those within his or her family. As we will see in Chapter 5, this variability of the self emerges particularly powerfully with the civil reputable hearts that often appear as quiet, peaceful, and easy going, yet who nevertheless manage to kill their families.

These socially situated concerns about how one is seen by others gradually come to plague the lives and emotional styles of perpetrators of familicide. Put simply, prior to acts of familicide we witness the exhaustion of pride, the eclipse of self-respect, and the triumph of shame and humiliation among most of the familicidal hearts. Like all of us, these perpetrators and victims of familicide live in the midst of various chains of human interaction and interdependence, particularly within their families, at work, and among their faith communities and churches, schools, and communities. The archive, with its rich detail about the everyday lives of the parties involved in familicides, lends itself well to the inferring of emotional suffering and turmoil; in short, to the exploration of the life of the heart. Indeed, my approach situates these killings in the midst of the ebb and flow of emotion and feeling associated with these networks of interaction and interdependence. It is in the pursuit of a language to capture these networks of emotion, feeling, and human interrelationships that I now turn.

FIGURATIONS OF FEELING

Raymond Williams wrote about the meaning of culture in a variety of ways; one such way was to see culture in terms of a *structure of feeling*.[24] He observes, "The most difficult thing to get hold of, in studying any past period, is this felt sense of the quality of life at a particular place and time: a sense of the ways in which the particular activities combined into a way of thinking and living."[25] In talking of a structure of feeling, he comments, "it is as firm and definite as 'structure' suggests, yet it operates in the most delicate and least tangible parts of our activity. In one sense, this structure of feeling is the culture of a period: it is the particular living result of all the elements in the general organization."[26] People stand in complex relationship to this structure of feeling; nevertheless, Williams contends people's possession of it runs deep and wide in all communities, forming the basis for human communication. Such acquisition is not merely a matter of learning or formal socialization. Rather, it is as if the structure of feeling were one of the great phantoms of social life, infusing everyday life with a spirit and energy.

Through the notion of the structure of feeling, Williams attempts to fuse everyday material reality with lived experience. His emphasis is clearly on *process*. He is at pains to distinguish a structure of feeling "from more formal concepts of 'world view' or 'ideology.'"[27] Structures of feeling speak to "meanings and values as they are actively lived and felt."[28] He prefers *structure of feeling* to *structure of experience*, because the latter still has elements of that past sense, of something that informs the present from behind, from a point of detachment. Williams goes on, "We are talking about characteristic elements of impulse, restraint, and tone; specifically affective elements of consciousness and relationships: not feeling against thought, but thought as felt and feeling as thought: practical consciousness of a present kind, in a living and interrelating continuity."[29]

At a practical level, Williams acknowledges the difficulties involved in describing or explaining the character of structures of feeling. He understands we are dealing with etherealities, essences that are difficult to put into words. Williams notes how a structure of feeling "can fail to be fully understood even by living people in close contact with it, with ample material at their disposal, including the contemporary arts."[30] It is for this reason, he comments "we shall not suppose that we can ever do more than make an approach, an approximation, using any channels."[31]

Intuitively, the phrase *structure of feeling* is paradoxical and therefore somewhat problematic. Terry Eagleton describes it as a "quasi-oxymoronic notion that captures the sense that culture is at once definite and impalpable."[32] Insofar as a structure of feeling can convey a sense of an almost ghostly phenomenon that surrounds and envelops people as much as it informs and infuses their lives and constitutes them, it is indeed useful. However, as Bernard Sharratt points out, at times Williams's notion of a structure of feeling "acts simultaneously as both a mediating term and a formulation of the totality."[33] The effect of this is to present a "certain polar relationship between the individual and a whole society."[34] This is an unfortunate effect, partly due, I think, to the use of the word *structure* that Williams uses alongside other generic language such as "all the elements in the general organization."[35]

Instead of the word *structure*, I prefer to use Elias's term *figuration*, and employ the phrase *figuration of feeling*. A "figuration of feeling" refers to the articulation and circulation of feelings among, between, and within complex networks of interrelationships connecting people, groups, and institutions. Figurations of feelings are social processes emergent and evident in everyday lives, in which, over time, people create webs of mutual dependencies.[36] It is worth noting Elias's understanding of the term *figuration*.

Elias proposed the notion of figurations to counter the tendency to see individuals as atomized, self-contained, and, in extreme renditions, virtually asocial. He uses the example of the social dance to illustrate the concept.

> The image of the mobile figurations of interdependent people on a dance floor perhaps makes it easier to imagine states, cities, families, and also capitalist, communist, and feudal systems as figurations. . . . No one will imagine a dance as a *structure outside* the individual or as a mere abstraction. The same dance figurations can certainly be danced by different people; but without a plurality of reciprocally oriented and dependent individuals, there is no dance. Like every other social figuration, a dance figuration is relatively independent of the specific individuals forming it here and now, but not of individuals as such.[37]

Figurations therefore compose sets of continually shifting interdependencies between people and the groups, institutions, and organizations they make up. As in social dance performances, figurations evidence a dynamic process that transcends the motives and intentions of individual social actors, although the motives and intentions of participants clearly influence outcomes. It is also the case that dances have a preexisting pattern and a set of rules to guide performance. These existing formations mean that dancers cannot dance as they please.

Like the figurations of feeling of which they form a part, familicides also assume the form of a social process. It is therefore difficult to pin them down with the language of abstract, contextual notions such as factors, variables, social background, or the environment, although, as we will see in the two cases I explore in this chapter, authorities certainly attempt to make sense of cases in these quasi-scientific ways.

We can return to Raymond Williams for thoughtful assistance in grasping the essence of familicidal behavior as lived practice or a social process. In his commentaries on society, history, and culture, Williams identifies the "reduction of the social to fixed forms" as "the basic error."[38] He goes on to suggest that "the mistake . . . is in taking terms of analysis as terms of substance."[39] In regard to the lives of those now dead, he comments, "Perhaps the dead can be reduced to fixed forms, though their surviving records are against it."[40] The surviving records in the familicide archive support Williams's observations and warrant an interpretation that transcends statistical analysis alone. We may bury the dead and use abstract factors to explain their transgressions. However, the emotions that drove their murderous acts continue to course their way through the social body, requiring us to pause carefully before dispatching the dead with their mere burial. Put simply, the emotional electricity of these cases remains long after the scientific judgments of coroners, journalists, psychiatrists, and others who traffic in fixity and abstraction. This electricity remains and is passed on through surviving family members, something I sensed as I conversed with them, observed family photographs, and so on. It is for this reason that I analyze the everyday life of those involved in familicide.

HAUNTED HEARTS AND UNCANNY ACTS

As a symbol of the epicenter of feeling, the heart serves as a literary device for conveying the emotional nature of familicide. My hope is that this notion resonates with readers, for at some level, I would contend, we all live the life of the heart. The heart has assumed a place of prominence among human symbols, variously used to refer to things spiritual, emotional, moral, pertaining to love and the soul, and, in the more distant past, intellectual and cognitive matters. To argue that perpetrators had familicidal hearts is not to ignore the heinous nature of their acts. These offenders lived lives amidst various swirls of anxiety, shame, rage, and desperation; they, too, lived the life of the heart, navigating, absorbing, and themselves contributing to modern era figurations of feeling.

I discuss three cases in this chapter. Table 2.1 summarizes these cases, acting as a touchstone for readers as they engage the case material.

(Note: I only disclose date and location in cases where I relied solely upon public-record information.)

The word "heart" also has a certain gravitas. When we know something in our hearts, we know it deeply, with intuition, certainty, faith, and conviction. The language of hearts is therefore compatible with this intuitive knowledge and sensibility. I found many illustrations of intuitive knowledge and heartfelt sensibilities among perpetrators and victims of familicide. For example, among the women subjected to the domestic violence and tyranny of livid coercive hearts, a number intuitively sensed they would die. Often they shared their terrible fears with loved ones. One such case involved a man named Norman Keane, who lost his sister, Nancy Mason, and nephew, Peter Mason, to familicide. Over the last few years, Norman and I have communicated regularly. On one occasion, Norman recalled a chilling conversation with Nancy. The two siblings conversed about a year or so before Nancy was murdered. Norman's brother-in-law, Owen Mason, eventually murdered Nancy and their son, Peter, before committing suicide. Nancy had told Norman many times that Owen would "come for her." Owen had moved out of the Mason family home,

Table 2.1   Summaries of the Cases Discussed in Chapter 2
(PS = Perpetrator Suicide)

Perpetrator	Victims	Summary Notes
Cooper, Emma	Daniel (husband) and six children. PS	Emma treated her children to candy and peanuts at a theater. She then chloroformed her family before shooting them all. Her husband was unable to work because of illness and the family was facing poverty. Emma made several attempts to kill their youngest child, Florence, in the year preceding the familicide. 1908: Cadillac, Michigan.
Mason, Owen	Nancy (estranged wife) and Peter Mason (son). PS	Owen was living with a new partner but threatened Nancy's life on numerous occasions. He was enraged by what he perceived as Nancy's allegation that he'd raped her. The family home was a mansion. Owen's financial planning business was threatened with a lawsuit. He visited websites to learn how to commit murder.
Shell, Lonnie	Sybil (wife) and three children. Eventual PS	Lonnie axed to death his wife and three children before attempting his own suicide. He had recently been convicted as a Peeping Tom and feared his family and others would find out about his sexual deviancy. He was also facing significant debts and the bankruptcy of his business. The night of the familicide, Lonnie and his family entertained at their house, singing Christmas carols. Lonnie later committed suicide in prison. The subsequent owners of the house where the killings occurred reported paranormal phenomena.

a mansion in a well-to-do neighborhood. In fact, Owen was living with another woman. Yet as Norman told me, Nancy "knew in her heart" that Owen would make good on his promise to kill her.

Norman and Nancy had this particularly ominous conversation in Nancy's kitchen. Norman recalled he was eating shredded wheat cereal and reading the newspaper as they began to converse. Nancy had told Owen she wanted a divorce. Originally she had planned to wait until their son moved out of the home, perhaps to attend university. However, Owen's intimidation and cruelty intensified. He had threatened to kill her on a number of occasions. On one occasion he put his hands around her neck as she was lying in bed. She arose terrified, saying she needed to use the bathroom. Owen told her he was just measuring her neck size. Owen had also denied her money and food and belittled her job as a health visitor, telling her he would not get out of bed for the pittance she earned. He had also mocked her religious beliefs and her closely knit extended family. On the one occasion when Nancy requested an injunction against Owen, she filed an affidavit saying Owen expected her to have sex when she did not want to do so. Nancy's statement about Owen's sexual expectations further enraged Owen.

Nancy told Norman of a recent conversation she'd had with Owen during which he warned her, "I will take my life and I will take your life." Owen then walked away, only to return to make a seemingly innocuous comment about what a nice day it was. Norman told me he was not sure if Owen deliberately vacillated between the chilling and the mundane, hoping to scare Nancy. Sadly and poetically, Norman then told me, "I saw it in Nancy's eyes. She told me, 'Norman, I know he is going to kill me.' At that point, I knew what she was telling me, I knew it in my blood. There was no doubt about what she was telling me."

I suspect that part of what Norman sensed and felt in his blood was what I will call Owen's haunted heart; a heart haunted by an unusual coalescence of fear, anger, sorrow, despair, shame, and a profoundly diminished sense of belonging. Nancy was proposing to sever a number of the interdependencies that comprised important parts of Owen's life. For Norman it was a matter of faith, something he just knew, felt unconsciously. Nancy knew it too, perhaps in similar ways. Her vantage point was different. Her motherhood, her love of her extended family, her work, her life, and, of course, her terrible fear shaped her strategies and her horizons.

As we will see in Chapter 4, Nancy Mason's emotional capital was a source of power in her tense relationship with Owen. Her emotional capital, her awareness, and her expressiveness enabled her to continue with her life, her work, her parenting. We discount her emotional capital, her feelings and grave misgivings at our collective peril. Her sensitivity to these matters is not accessible through the language of abstract factors. Rather, her sensitivity emerges in the midst of the complex human networks and interrelationships and the figurations of feeling that constituted her life. These figurations of feeling haunted Nancy and Owen's emotional styles.

Although simultaneously drawing upon, reproducing and transforming modern era figurations of feeling, each heart evinces its own personal life, emblematic of an inner self.[41] As a vital organ the heart is shielded, protected by the ribs and hidden from view. Symbolically, then, the word *heart* serves well as a literary device for exploring people's individuality, their privacy, their secrecy; in short, their personal life. I use the term *personal life* in the sense described by Eli Zaretsky, "the experience of having an identity distinct from one's place in the family, in society, and the social division of labor."[42] At another level, the heart is an important metaphor for modern life, a life that cultivates the individual, complex personhood, and in later modernity, the unconscious.[43] In many ways, personal lives, just like familicides, are modern products.

As readers will infer from my discussion of Damasio's account of the links between rationality and emotion, I do not use the word *heart* as a way of ruling out logic and reason. We ought not see the seemingly "rational" aspects of familicide as somehow distinct from the emotional elements of these cases. Indeed, the archive clearly points to the simultaneous feats of emotion and rationality in a way that renders these twin conceptual pillars of modernity indistinguishable. Readers will recall Raymond Williams, quoted above talking about "not feeling against thought, but thought as felt and feeling as thought."[44] The notion of the heart enables us to access both of these themes simultaneously, thus avoiding the pervasive modern tendency to dichotomize emotion and reason, value and fact, subjective and objective. Indeed, as Blaise Pascal once famously put it, "The heart has its reasons of which reason itself does not know."[45]

The haunting feelings that leave their mark on the familicides continue to course through society long after loved ones bury their dead. There is durability to emotion, a chronic character reminding us that society continues long after individuals perish. As a metaphor, the heart and its autonomic beat symbolizes the chronic, the habitual, and the everyday conscious and unconscious actions that make the world go round.

Two cases of familicide (Shell, Cooper) illustrate the ghostly importance of emotional styles and figurations of feeling and the fact such killings take the form of social processes that cannot be distilled down to the logic of abstract factors; in spite, as we shall see, of authorities' attempts to the contrary. Indeed, there are elements of both cases that speak to the workings of ethereal, sinister, uncanny, even ghostly forces. Ultimately, perpetrators reach a point of no return, a place where they can no longer participate in the social interdependencies that characterize everyday life.

As I will argue, in the lead-up to the kill, the familicidal hearts have little or no sense of place and a heavily circumscribed emotional *habitus*.[46] By *emotional habitus*, I simply refer to a person's sense of emotional place, one's socially acquired emotional and behavioral leanings or dispositions. Emotional habitus is interwoven into the networks of feelings and interdependencies in which the individual participates.

As we will see through the case studies in the chapters that follow, the emotional styles of the familicidal hearts vary considerably. The livid coercive hearts enter the darkness kicking and screaming. The civil reputable hearts go quietly into the unknown.

Lonnie Shell: The End of Repression

The Shell familicide introduces the language of haunting in a very direct and practical manner.[47] A crime analyst, Jack Graham, and I conversed about the possibility of swapping information in the familicide case involving a perpetrator by the name of Lonnie Shell.[48] I had copies of the autopsy report and court report. Jack knew about other things, including the fact that Lonnie Shell later committed suicide while in prison. The autopsy report interested Jack much less than the court report, since the latter contained psychiatric information on Lonnie. In fact, as he told me, the case had become somewhat of a curiosity for him. Jack and his wife had visited the house where Lonnie Shell committed familicide. The home where the Shells had once lived came up for sale recently. Living in the neighborhood, Jack knew the history of the house. The seller apparently did not know of the familicide, although she did mention strange sounds and the presence of paranormal forces.

According to Jack, the house was essentially as it had been in the mid-1950s, when Lonnie murdered his wife and three children. Jack told me that since the time of the familicide, many people had owned the house. Owners stayed only a year or two and moved on. Such flux, according to Jack, was not merely a reflection of the vicissitudes of the housing market. Rather, a succession of owners had reported paranormal disturbances at the house. Not wanting to spook the seller or inform the seller's realtor of the apparent links between the energy in the house and the familicide, Jack kept his knowledge to himself.[49]

Briefly, the details of the Shell case are these. At a party one mid-December night in a quaint, well-to-do town, Lonnie Shell and his family entertained several friends, enjoying refreshments and singing Christmas carols at the home Jack Graham and his wife would visit more than half a century later. As midnight approached, Lonnie commenced his act of familicide. He told a psychiatrist, "I struck my wife six times with a tomahawk ax in the head, two times quite hard. The ax was sharp and new. I bought it at a clearance sale about a year before this happened." He continued, "I started about 11:30 p.m. and the whole thing, I guess, lasted until 2:00 or 3:00 a.m. I struck my son in the back of his neck four times, and two times again. I waited just a little while. Then the oldest daughter, two times on the back of the neck and two times on the side of the neck. Then my younger daughter, in the head, very hard, and then possibly in the back of the neck. I dealt a severe blow to my wife. I realized there was no turning back, that the whole thing never could be rectified. I knew it was wrong all along, but it seemed the only way out and I intended to kill myself." Sharp ax, sharp memories.

The court report offers information to assist the interpretation of these disturbing events. Like many of the civil reputable hearts, Lonnie was facing financial ruin. By 1940, he had his own business. It started as a little furniture store but morphed into a rug and carpet business. Lonnie told investigators, "I always hated the business." He continued, "My business has been going behind for the past four years, that is, it was not adequate to operate or profitable enough to continue operation and take care of the needs of the family." By 1948, then, Lonnie's business was in trouble. He observed, "I more or less operated the business on borrowed money. I sold out in 1948 and then borrowed money from my uncle and from banks and started again. We also owed for the car that Sybil (Lonnie's wife) wanted." With some sadness, Lonnie comments, "I couldn't say no to the desires of the family and I didn't know what hard times were because I started about the time the war boom began." Assuming responsibility for these misfortunes himself, Lonnie did not attempt to lay the blame for their financial distress at Sybil's feet. He went on, "I was playing the role of a good provider on borrowed money which was embezzlement in a way." At the time of the familicide, Lonnie owed his father $11,000 and his uncle $6,000. At this point in his interview with the psychiatrist, Lonnie's shame is almost palpable.

Nevertheless, his reflexivity remains clear and acute. He goes on to talk about his social isolation. "I have always considered myself a misfit and I should have written or taught instead." Reflecting on his familial upbringing, Lonnie shared, "I was an only child and I have always regretted that." His family's move from Ohio when he was 12 perhaps compounded his sense of social isolation. At age 17, Lonnie attended a Bible institute for three years, with members of his church picking up some of the costs. However, he did not pursue the ministry. He explains, "I thought of studying for the ministry but I gave this up. I quit as I could not justify or parallel the theology taught by the institute with other reading I did. They had a very narrow concept, or I might say a reactionary view. This situation was very frustrating as it cost a lot of money and time." In regard to his failure to pursue the ministry, Lonnie laments the fact that his three years of Bible study "cost a lot of money and time." We might speculate that Lonnie's failure to pursue the ministry caused him considerable embarrassment in the eyes of the church members who provided financial support for his Bible studies. Lonnie's early disappointments and his highly idiosyncratic grasp of Scripture seem to have kept him from bonding with some members of his church in later life. He comments, "My family has been active in the church but our church is practicing nineteenth-century theology. This has caused me conflicts."

Lonnie and Sybil married at the Tiny Church of the Angels in 1940. His psychiatrist describes Lonnie's sexual relations with Sybil as "satisfactory." We learn the couple had tried oral sex but had not continued to practice it. Lonnie saw his "sexual deviancy" contributing to the familicide, sharing with his psychiatrist details of his sexual repression and sublimation.[50] Lonnie talked of his early sexual experimentation. We learn he masturbated from around 12. The psychiatrist's report notes Lonnie "was introduced to masturbation by a boy friend slightly older than he. There was some mutual masturbation for three or four times. Then he says he came to California and he did not mutually masturbate any more. He says he and the other boys would masturbate each other, then they stopped that and only masturbated before each other." One wonders if Lonnie's parents relocated after discovering Lonnie's sexual experimentation.

In short, Lonnie saw his failure to regulate his sexual urges as central to the commission of familicide. He comments, "My great desire in sex was to see and touch. I have remained juvenile and almost puerile. I know I have not been like other men this way. I started Peeping Tom activities at six or seven and continued. I would peep and masturbate. It got to be about one or two times weekly that I would try to peep. Sometimes seeing a pretty girl was enough; that is just walking on the street; then I would masturbate. Then after marriage I was getting better but had peeped some but was not caught. A psychiatrist examined me in 1953, after I was arrested for being a Peeping Tom.[51] My spirit went down when I found out what his report was. He said I was a constitutional sex deviant with neurotic symptoms. I took it as something from birth and that made me feel that I was bringing children into the world that would be like me. My boy was timid, artistic and afraid." At one point Lonnie comments, "I am neurotic and I guess a sex degenerate." Put simply, Lonnie worried he had passed what he and others saw as his troubled sexuality on to his vulnerable son. At the same time, the psychiatrist notes that Lonnie was ashamed his family was about to find out about his sexual antics, his voyeurism. Probably the fact that Lonnie tells us his family enjoyed "the highest respect of the community" added to his shame.

The social history also tells us Lonnie's mother died a year before the familicide. She had spent the last three years of her life as an invalid as a result of a stroke. We learn nothing of Lonnie's relationship with his parents. Yet we do get an almost poetic sense of Lonnie's emotional decline from his reports of his wife's description of his condition. Lonnie tells the psychiatrist that in the month before the familicide he suffered something akin to a nervous breakdown. Lonnie reports "crying like a baby." He asked his wife to "stay with him" during this time. As Lonnie tells his psychiatrist, it was during this period that Sybil told him that watching his decline "was like seeing a ship at sea go down."

Lonnie was deeply disturbed at the time of the familicide and tells us, "I was not rational, I suppose, for a few days after this happened." Nevertheless, he insists it was his attorney who concocted the insanity plea introduced as a defense, not himself. Lonnie tells us, "I don't think I am insane." The psychiatrist noted Lonnie experienced no hallucinations or delusions indicative of "a settled insanity." However, the deterioration of Lonnie's emotional style goes back further. From around 1951,

Lonnie found it increasingly difficult to sleep. He began taking sleeping pills: Nembutal and Seconal. Two different doctors prescribed these drugs, but neither doctor knew of the other's role in treating Lonnie. Lonnie reported he took these for his nervousness and to enable him to sleep. Indeed, Lonnie told the court-appointed psychiatrist that he always considered himself neurotic but never psychotic.[52]

Finally, the detailed court report also addresses hereditary factors. We learn Lonnie denied any history of mental illness, convulsive disorders or fits, alcoholism, drug addiction, or mental defectiveness among his blood relatives. For authorities, Lonnie's lineage was not predictive of his committing familicide.

The Lonnie Shell case illustrates a number of themes that recur among the civil reputable hearts. The Shell case files are peppered with factors that vie with each other to explain his familicide (for example: depression, drug addiction, sexual deviancy, pending bankruptcy, profound social isolation). Lonnie is emotionally isolated, depressed, out of step with his business, his church, and, it seems, his family. Yet, people surround him and perhaps engulf him. He was one of many of the familicidal hearts who experienced loneliness without being physically isolated from others. Lonnie was ashamed of his failures, his arrests, his drug use, and his sexuality, although we have no record of his acknowledging that shame prior to meeting with the court-appointed psychiatrist in the wake of the familicide. Yet through all this, Lonnie holds back more than a little from everyone. He secretly plans. He organizes. He even sings Christmas carols before the big kill. One wonders what he was thinking and feeling as he sang that fateful night.

Taken on their own or in some ominous statistical formation, these factors lurk somewhere outside of Lonnie's life. Proximal factors such as Lonnie's mother's death, his nervous breakdown, and his pending bankruptcy surface fleetingly or intermittently in the relatively short time prior to the killings. Criminologists sometimes see these as triggering mechanisms: incendiary sparks that ignite the world; or the parts of the iceberg, to echo Sybil Shell's phrase, that cause "a ship at sea to go down." Distal factors such as his enduring social disconnectedness, his sexual troubles, his internalization of the onerous rights and responsibilities of a mid–twentieth century patriarch, and his failures in the arenas of divinity and business assume a seemingly weightier and deeper significance. These are Lonnie's lifelong demons.

Whatever array of explanatory variables we find in the psychiatrist's report, the court report, and the social history, there is still a sense that the factors, Lonnie's background, his environment, and so on are not really a part of his lived experience, his life, for better or for worse, the interdependencies of which he is an important hub. Rather, the abstract explanatory factors are frozen units of analysis, influences, or frames of reference, as isolated as Lonnie himself. In Lonnie's case, as in others, we need a sense of the way Lonnie's emotional style and his socially and historically situated steering mechanisms failed him. Quite simply, modern psychological restraints failed to regulate various aspects of Lonnie's libido, and, more important, his eventual urge to kill his family. Lonnie moved to a remote location, somewhere beyond the reach of these powerful restraints.

Lonnie lived during the mid-twentieth century when successful middle class men provided for their families, ran their businesses, exhibited religious pride, and exercised great restraint regarding their sexual and aggressive urges. We must understand his repression and sublimation as his way of negotiating the numerous interdependencies involving his family members, including his father, his uncle, his wife, and his children. Lonnie had failed to uphold his part of the numerous bargains that typically characterize these interrelated networks of obligation. He didn't pursue the ministry after church members contributed to three years of Bible school. Neither could he repay his father or uncle the money they loaned him to keep his failing business afloat. All of these failings bespoke social relationships gone awry; obligations to his father, uncle, wife, church, and children unfulfilled.

The concept of *haunting* provides a mediating mechanism, a means of explaining, albeit in metaphorical terms, the articulation between the figurations of feeling of which Lonnie formed a part, and his emotional style. Avery Gordon's work on haunting enables us to explore this perplexing juncture between figurations of feeling and emotional styles. For Gordon, haunting "is an animated state of existence and perception in which a repressed or unresolved social violence makes itself known to you, sometimes very directly, sometimes more obliquely. Haunting is a vivid, sensual or embodied way of being made aware that what's been contained or repressed or blocked is very alive and present, messing with our various ways of keeping the troublesome and disturbing at bay."[53] Gordon's eloquence is particularly apt when thinking through Lonnie Shell's act of mass killing. Indeed, she might as well have been talking about Lonnie when she observes, "Ghosts arise when repression fails, and thus they are not silent, dead, or invisible, but animated with the return or the uprising of what's been repressed. The modus operandi of haunting, why it unsettles and defies detached reasoning, is the recognition that a ghost is present, demanding its due, demanding attention."[54]

Lonnie's case provides a segue into the phenomenon of haunted hearts; an alternative, if you will, to explanations couched in terms of what Elias refers to as *Homo psychiatricus, Homo psychoanalyticus*, or *Homo sociologicus*. For some, my approach may appear to rely too heavily on irrational forces, energies that cannot be verified, and so on. However, such approaches are not unprecedented in the study of familicide. Indeed, the use of the insanity defense in a handful of familicide cases relies on the existence of behavior beyond the bounds of reason. We see such reliance in a disproportionate number of the very few cases in which women commit familicide. Although I address some of these cases in more detail in Chapter 5, I introduce one of them at this stage to expand upon the points I have made about figurations of feeling, emotional styles, and haunted hearts.

Emma Cooper: The Suspension of Reason

On Sunday June 14, 1908, in Cadillac, Michigan, people peered apprehensively through the windows of a house on East Chapin Street. Crowds milled around the house all day, anxiously awaiting an opportunity to enter. No one entered. It was as if the crowd wanted to absorb or experience the strange ambience of the house. Two days earlier in that house, Mrs. Emma Cooper, 45, shot and killed her ailing husband, Daniel, 48, and six of their seven children.[55] She then committed suicide.

Denied entry, throngs of people made their way to the undertakers who had laid out the dead Coopers for the world to see. The viewing at the undertakers commenced at 8:00 a.m. At that hour a large crowd had already assembled. Until 2:00 p.m., an unbroken line of viewers filed past the eight corpses. The undertaker, Mr. Dunham, estimated that between nine and ten thousand people viewed the bodies, some driving up to 20 miles from the surrounding villages to do so.[56]

Like the Sunday viewings, the Monday burial gripped the region. A funeral procession carried the Coopers to the Sherman cemetery, close to the farm they formerly occupied.[57] We learn, "Two hearses and two undertaker's wagons were used to convey the seven bodies to their last resting place. The bodies of Mr. and Mrs. Cooper were placed in the hearses and the five children were placed in the two wagons."[58] Reverend J. B. McGinness preached the funeral sermon, emphasizing as his theme, "Right choosing and right living because of the immanence of death."[59] The *Cadillac Evening News* reassured readers the seven victims of the "deed of a frenzied wife and mother" had been "laid away in a quiet country cemetery."[60]

The press account noted Mrs. Cooper had been "mentally unsound" for more than a year and was "insane" at the time of the killings.[61] In spite of her supposed insanity, Emma Cooper apparently planned the familicide. The evening before the mass killings she took all her children to the theater. There she negotiated with the ticket-seller to admit the whole family for a total of fifty cents. The seller, Mrs. Campbell, indicated to Mrs. Cooper that she should not consider the bargain a precedent. Eerily, Mrs. Cooper replied, "You will never need to again because none of us will ever come here after this."[62]

The suggestion that Emma Cooper was at least temporarily insane comes from various people's interpretations of an encounter she had with Mr. Campbell, the ticket-seller's husband. He was standing in the lobby of the theater with his back to Emma Cooper. According to the press report, he had not looked at Emma Cooper or made any contact with her. Nevertheless, Emma tapped Mr. Campbell on the shoulder and said, "Did you address me?"[63] She continued to "insist for sometime that he wished to speak with her."[64] A number of people who witnessed her insistence later reflected on what it meant, reaching the conclusion "that she was at that moment insane."[65] We have no knowledge of Emma's understanding of the meaning of her interaction with Mr. Campbell.

However, the newspaper article goes on to note that Emma proceeded to the show and acted "perfectly natural."[66] After the show, Emma treated her children to candy and peanuts. In fact, she appeared especially cheerful. We will never know how Emma felt at the show. Her outward appearance suggests she was calm, and this may have signified she had decided to commit familicide, leaving behind her worries about pending poverty and the care of her children. One thing is clear, once those children fell asleep that night she chloroformed them and then shot them.

Coroner Ralston felt sure that Emma Cooper planned the killings several weeks earlier. She had apparently taken out an insurance policy worth $1,500 on May 4, 1908. Emma duly inquired as to whether her beneficiaries could collect on the policy in the event of her suicide. It is noteworthy Emma named her husband, Daniel, as the beneficiary, suggesting that at the time of taking out the policy she might not have intended to kill him.

Daniel Cooper had been in poor health for several months and unable to work and provide for his family. Although the eldest son, Fred, worked the family farm, the newspaper notes the family was "not in the best of circumstances financially."[67] The press described Emma as "morbid and excitable."[68] It appears the birth of her youngest child, Florence, taxed her emotional strength to the limit. Florence was a year and a half old at the time of the familicide. The newspaper reported Emma being "out of her mind for a time"[69] in the period following the birth of Florence. Indeed, Emma attributed much of her sorrow to the arrival of her youngest daughter. On a number of occasions she had threatened to kill Florence and herself. In fact, Ira Cooper, Mr. Daniel Cooper's brother, told the coroner's inquest Emma had made several attempts to kill Florence since the child was a month old.

Dr. A. W. Johnstone, the pastor of the Presbyterian church Emma attended, "often remonstrated with her for disliking her baby."[70] According to the press, after these conversations Emma "always seemed soothed and quieted and was perfectly rational."[71] Notwithstanding the good pastor's sterling attempts at intervention, Emma's emotional distress worsened quickly. The press reported her saying on the day of the familicide that she "would put herself and her family out of their troubles."[72]

It was Emma's mother, Mrs. Esther Heady, who found the bodies. Like other witnesses, Mrs. Heady testified to the coroner's inquiry that on many occasions her daughter had indeed threatened to kill herself. However, Emma's mother was also quick to point out that Emma had never indicated she was capable of killing her entire family.[73] Mrs. Heady went to her daughter's house to make bread. She entered at around 8:30 a.m. and saw her daughter lying on the bed. Mrs. Heady assumed Emma was sleeping. She commenced to make bread. Fred Cooper, the only survivor, staggered into the kitchen some time later, covered in blood. Mrs. Heady asked him if he had been fighting. He answered, "No."[74]

Fred Cooper then drank some water and lay down on the couch. At
this point Mrs. Heady called her daughter. When Emma did not awaken,
Mrs. Heady soon realized she was dead. She then found Mr. Cooper's
corpse. Disturbed and confused, Mrs. Heady turned to Fred and asked
if all the children were dead. He replied, "No."[75] At this juncture Fred
told Mrs. Heady his father and mother had quarreled the night before.
We have no way of knowing what "quarreling" meant, whether it had
happened before, and whether it was indicative of some kind of violence
or tyranny in their marriage.

The *Cadillac Evening News* opined, "Her insane condition and the
knowledge that harmony was an unknown quantity in the family circle
seem to be sufficient incentive in the minds of most people, for the woman
committing the murders."[76] Did the newspaper use these words euphe-
mistically to refer to what some readers might have understood to be a
violent home? A home in which Daniel Cooper beat his wife? A home
in which Emma assaulted Daniel? Or does the reference to the absence
of harmony refer to some kind of chronic emotional disturbance or shift
in Emma's emotional style? Unfortunately, the historical record does not
allow us to answer these important questions.

One thing is for sure: the Cooper familicide sent shock waves out
across the region. The *New York Times* picked up the story. The curious
spectacle of the Cooper corpses captured the public imagination. It is possible the mourners and gazers were merely lamenting the loss of fellow
community members. However, we ought be alive to the possibility that
the throngs of people also sensed a shift in prevailing figurations of feeling, perhaps linking these changing figurations to the Cooper familicide.
Indeed, the Cooper's transition to a more urban lifestyle is an important
focal point in the newspaper reporting on the case.

The day Emma's mother discovered the carnage, the *Cadillac Evening News* told readers the family "came to the city because of the illness
of Mrs. Cooper and because in her moments of derangement she would
insist they leave the farm and come to the city."[77] We do not know the
reasons for Emma's insistence on moving into town. Perhaps she sensed
a new way of life was possible, a life where she managed to escape from
the pressures of the extended kin networks that surrounded her. In the
Sherman Township where Daniel and Emma Cooper worked their family
farm, Daniel Cooper's two brothers, Will and Ira, also worked farms. Two
of Daniel's sisters, married at the time of the familicide, also lived in the
same township.

Emma Cooper was clearly disturbed and troubled by the birth of her
youngest child, Florence. In today's world she would probably be diagnosed as suffering from post partum depression and/or psychosis. However, Emma also displayed considerable caring toward her children. She
treated them to the theater and bought them candy and peanuts. Emma
also rendered the children unconscious with chloroform before shooting
them to death, presumably to minimize any suffering. Her conversation at

the theater with Mr. Campbell was interpreted by a number of people as a sign that she had broken with reality, whatever that is. However, could she also have been reaching out to Mr. Campbell in some way? Establishing some kind of possible connection, however strangely she might have done so?

The coroner concluded Emma had been of unsound mind for some time and that she was insane at the time of the familicide. It is possible to see the insanity label a way of explaining the inexplicable, lessening the stigma attached to this poor mother and her tragic family, and enabling the community to dispatch the tragedy to the ashes of history. The insanity label served as a form of catharsis for the community, perhaps lessening the community trauma at this profoundly disturbing transgression. Clearly, for a mother to do such damage in a thoughtful, calculating way, was beyond the comprehension of many of those who knew the Coopers. As the local press put it, "It seems so difficult to believe that a wife and mother could commit such a deed."[78]

Like the court report in the Lonnie Shell case, the coroner's verdict in the Cooper familicide lists the causal or contributing factors. Emma's temporary insanity, itself linked to the birth of Florence, family poverty, and Daniel's ill health and inability to work, is given as the principal reason for her committing familicide. It is tempting to let the analysis rest with the coroner's assessment and accept the temporary insanity verdict as a proxy for what appeared at the time as an utterly inexplicable act. However, I want to suggest another interpretation, one that relies on the haunting links between shifting figurations of feeling and Emma's deeply distressed emotional style. Indeed, I propose that the use of the insanity label in the Cooper case is akin to the logic of explaining Emma's familicidal emotional style in terms of her being haunted by shifts in modern era figurations of feeling. The insanity label and talk of the haunting distillation of modern era figurations of feeling both attempt to find a language to explain the inexplicable. The former relies on recognizing a break with rational behavior. The latter does not require such a break but rather acknowledges the inseparability of emotion and reason.

I emphasize the importance of historically and socially situated figurations of feeling because familicidal hearts like Emma Cooper are products of their time and their society. In other epochs it would have been more acceptable for Emma to commit infanticide, thus removing the threat she may have felt Florence posed to the survivability of the family. In their summary of cross-cultural ethnographic research on infanticide, Daly and Wilson point out that the killing of children, particularly young ones, reflects a number of choices, strategies, and decisions on the part of parents; often, but not always mothers. Important predictors of infanticide might include "the size of one's larder, or one's present mate's skills as a hunter."[79] On this last point they note specifically that mothers are also influenced by a "lack of paternal support that is characteristic of the society."[80] In a brief cross-cultural history of infanticide, Cheryl Meyer and Michelle Oberman note its widespread acceptance as a means of population control. They reason that mothers commit infanticide because "they cannot parent their child under the circumstances dictated by their unique position in place and time."[81] In cases where mothers purposefully killed multiple children, Meyer and Oberman's scrutiny of suicide notes points to suicidal and depressed mothers not wanting their children to grow up without them or mothers burdened by overwhelming financial pressures, often associated with current or former spouses' or partners' not providing financial support. These authors contend most of these mothers who kill multiple children have not abused or neglected their children. On the contrary, many show much love and devotion.

Daniel Cooper was ill to the point he could not work on the farm. Emma was overwhelmed by her seven children and now had to assume responsibility for providing for the family. Had she lived at a time when those around her supported her killing of Florence, she may never have become a familicidal heart. Did the failure of her extended kin, Daniel's siblings, the reverend, and others to understand the way her speeded-up mothering plagued her contribute to the maturation of her familicidal heart? We will probably never know what went through Emma's mind as she plotted her course and decided to kill her family. One thing is for sure: the networks of interdependencies in which she played a pivotal role underwent a profound change. It is this profound change in patterns of interdependencies and the haunting effects of shifting figurations of feeling on Emma's emotional style that I suggest offers an important alternative to explaining the Cooper familicide in terms of Emma's break with reason.

However we make sense of the Cooper familicide, the language of abstract factors denies its social complexity. What we see in the Shell and Cooper familicides is the profound undermining of social interdependencies, chains of obligation, agreements, reciprocities, conflicts, and raw human engagements. These are active, moving aspects of social life that the local newspaper captured far more ably than did the coroner and other authorities. For example, in its coverage of the funeral, the newspaper account is vivid, alive with movement, human interaction, ritual, and collective angst. We read of the milling of the crowds, the shuffling of feet past the coffins in the mortuary, the clatter of the undertakers' wagons, and Emma's curious exchange with the ticket-seller's husband, Mr. Campbell. Amidst this sensuous ebb and flow of life, the explanatory factors authorities offer such as temporary insanity and the specter of poverty seem flat, fixed, abstract, and ill equipped for the task of conjuring up the emotional atmosphere in the Cooper home.

Recognizing the haunting presence of inexplicable forces in the Cooper and Shell cases is another way of saying that some social phenomena defy analysis. In fact, the logic of haunting—and it is a form of logic—flies in the face of the sureties of human sciences such as forms of criminology that rely upon the explanatory power of various

permutations and combinations of abstract factors. Avery Gordon tells us that
haunting is:

> . . . a paradigmatic way in which life is more complicated than those
> of us who study it have usually granted. Haunting is a constituent
> element of modern social life. It is neither premodern superstition nor
> individual psychosis; it is a generalizable social phenomenon of great
> import. To study social life one must confront ghostly aspects of it.[82]

For our time, the familicidal behavior of Emma Cooper appears almost
uncanny, unnerving, eerie, and perhaps supernatural. We might make a similar point about famously "subversive" mothers such as Andrea Yates, who
drowned her five children in a Texas bathtub.[83] When the uncanny presents
itself in the behavior of women like Emma Cooper and Andrea Yates, the
response of the human sciences is often to re-situate the behavior in terms
of a break with reason. Instead of interpreting the heinous acts of Emma
Cooper, Andrea Yates, or, indeed, Lonnie Shell in terms of a break with
reason, I have suggested an explanation in terms of the unraveling of the
interdependencies of which the individual and their inner self form a part.

Freud himself addressed the uncanny and, as Gordon points out, was
troubled by "the presence of uncanny experiences that are not reduc-
ible to the acting out of an individual's psychic state."[84] For Freud, "the
uncanny is that class of the frightening which leads back to the old and the
familiar."[85] In discussing the work of Jentsch on the topic of the uncanny,
Freud notes the writer's attention to phenomena such as epileptic fits
and manifestations of insanity "because these excite in the spectator the
impression of automatic, mechanical processes at work behind the 'ordinary' appearance of mental activity."[86] Freud uses an everyday example to
flesh out the meaning of the uncanny:

> We naturally attach no importance to the event when we hand in an
> overcoat and get a cloakroom ticket with the number, let us say, 62;
> or when we find that our cabin on a ship bears that number. But the
> impression is altered if two such events, each in itself indifferent,
> happen close together—if we come across the number 62 several
> times in a single day, or if we begin to notice that everything which
> has a number—addresses, hotel rooms, compartments in railway
> trains—invariably has the same one, or at all events one which
> contains the same figures. We do feel this to be uncanny. And unless
> a man is utterly hardened and proof against the lure of superstition,
> he will be tempted to ascribe a secret meaning to this obstinate
> recurrence of a number; he will take it, perhaps, as an indication of
> the span of life allotted to him.[87]

Freud's discomfort is evident in his pejorative reference to the "lure of
superstition." He goes on to note that many people experience uncanny
feelings "in relation to death and dead bodies, to the return of the dead,
and to spirits and ghosts."[88] He traces people's sense of the uncanny

back to what he calls "the animistic conception of the universe"[89] and the "subject's narcissistic overvaluation of his own mental processes."[90] The belief in the uncanny reflects residues of more primitive thoughts and beliefs. Freud assures readers that, "All supposedly educated people have ceased to believe officially that the dead can become visible as spirits."[91] His use of the word "officially" speaks to his sense that these beliefs linger as recessive elements among the emotional styles of many modern people. Modern thinkers who have purged themselves of animistic beliefs have surmounted these primitive understandings of the uncanny, dismissing them through "reality testing." For these advanced modern thinkers, the issue of the uncanny "is purely an affair of 'reality-testing,' a question of the material reality of the phenomena."[92]

It is my position that we witness the workings of the uncanny in the highly charged emotional acts of the familicidal hearts. As we will see in the case studies to follow, the everyday lives of the familicidal hearts evidence a profound erosion of their sense of place in the social order; a progressive, often depressing and shameful unraveling of the ties that bind them to something greater than themselves. Another way of stating this is in terms of the profound undermining of the emotional habitus of the familicidal hearts. Put simply, in the lead-up to the killings, many have no sense of place, fast developing a self-referential and narcissistically remote emotional style simultaneously infused with deadly doses of alienation and anomie. It is this "no sense of place" that characterizes the uncanny nature of familicide. We must once again emphasize the socially situated nature of the familicidal heart. Indeed, Avery Gordon might just as well be talking about familicide when she notes:

> The social is ultimately what the uncanny is about: being haunted in the *world of common reality*. To be haunted is not a contest between animism and a discrediting reality test, nor a contest between the unconscious and the conscious faculties. It is an enchanted encounter in a disenchanted world between familiarity and strangeness. The uncanny is the return, in psychoanalytic terms, of what the concept of the unconscious represses: the reality of being haunted by worldly contacts.[93]

The familicidal hearts do strange and frightening things; in short, uncanny things. Their acts require a focus on the inexplicable. The phenomenon of haunting provides a metaphorical device for exploring the mysteries of familicide. For some readers, my use of the language of ghosts might be off-putting, irritating, or even, as Freud suggests, a remnant of primitive or infantile thought patterns, or, perhaps, heaven forbid, a narcissistic overvaluation of one's own mental processes. Notwithstanding these possible objections, I see ghostly analyses as part of a rich tradition in the field of sociology, one that values the imaginative, the speculative, and the imponderable. As Avery Gordon observes, "the 'reality testing' that we might want to perform in the face of hauntings must first of all admit those hauntings as real."[94] Insofar as familicides defy abstract explanation, the heart provides the perfect symbol for their ghoulish inexplicability. That familicidal hearts are haunted hearts takes us to the epicenter of modernity—for want of a better phrase, to the heart of the matter.

NOTES

1. List, 2006: 99.
2. See Giddens, 1979, for a discussion of the relationship between structure and action.
3. Damasio, 1994: xi.
4. Damasio, 1994: xvii.
5. Damasio, 1994: xx.
6. Damasio, 1994: xxi.
7. Goudsblom and Mennell, 1998: 101.
8. Goudsblom and Mennell, 1998: 101.
9. Goudsblom and Mennell, 1998: 79.
10. Goudsblom and Mennell, 1998: 79.
11. Goudsblom and Mennell, 1998: 79.
12. Goudsblom and Mennell, 1998: 80.
13. Freud and Breuer, 1895; cited in Scheff, 2004: 230. As Zaretsky points out, both Freud and Breuer saw trauma as the cause of hysteria. However, the two authors disagreed about what made the hysteric vulnerable to the "splitting of consciousness or breakdown of synthesis that followed trauma. Breuer believed that if an event did not reach consciousness, that was because the hysteric had been in a susceptible or hypnoid state (a fugue state) when the event occurred. A predisposition toward a state of lessened psychological tension, he maintained, was hereditary. Freud, by contrast, believed the splitting occurred because the hysteric *defended* against awareness of the traumatic event; he believed, in other words, that the splitting was motivated" (Zaretsky, 2004: 29).
14. Scheff, 2004: 231.
15. Freud, 2005: 84.
16. Goffman, 1959: 243.
17. Goffman, 1959: 253. Italics added.
18. Mead, 1967: 182.
19. Cooley, 2006: 172.
20. Cooley, 2006: 182.
21. Cooley, 2006: 184.
22. Cooley, 2006: 184.
23. Cooley, 2006: 184–185.
24. Williams, 1977.
25. Williams, 1961: 60.
26. Williams, 1961: 61.
27. Williams, 1977: 132.
28. Williams, 1977: 132.
29. Williams, 1977: 132.
30. Williams, 1961: 61.
31. Williams, 1961: 61.
32. Eagleton, 2000: 36.
33. Sharratt, 1989: 134.
34. Sharratt, 1989: 134.

35. Williams, 1961: 61.

36. Zygmunt Bauman contends that "making sense of the human condition through analyzing the manifold webs of human interdependency" is one of the central tasks of the sociologist. See Bauman, 1990: 14.

37. Goudsblom and Mennell, 1998: 131. My italics.

38. Williams, 1977: 129.

39. Williams, 1977: 129.

40. Williams, 1977: 129.

41. It is my argument that we cannot understand familicide without an appreciation of an inner self. In this sense my approach is akin to that of Arlie Hochschild (1983) and Nancy Chodorow (1999).

42. Zaretsky, 2004: 5.

43. See, for example, Zaretsky's discussion of the relationship between modern art and psychoanalysis in what he refers to as the second modernity of the 1920s. He notes, "In a great variety of guises, *some* conception of the unconscious was at the center of every modern innovation" (2004: 157; italics in the original).

44. Williams, 1977: 132.

45. Pascal, 1995: 158. In *Habits of the Heart*, Robert Bellah points out that Old and New Testament usage of the word *heart* involves "intellect, will, and intention as well as feeling." He notes a "somewhat comparable" notion of the heart in both Confucianism and Buddhism. See Bellah, 1996: 312, footnote 28.

46. For a discussion of emotional habitus, see Kane, 2001; Illouz, 2007. The notion of habitus has its origins in the work of Elias and was later used by French sociologist Pierre Bourdieu.

47. We find the language of ghosts in other cases, too. For example, James Gray killed his wife and four children. Gray, a successful farmer and businessman, had recently gone deaf (see Armstrong, 1996). He later told authorities one of his cows had died from an infection and others were similarly infected. Mr. Gray feared his family hurtling toward poverty. After the familicide, authorities found no dead or infected cows at the Gray farm. The bloody killings stunned Oakdale Township, Minnesota, where the Grays had been an influential and much-respected pioneer family. Subsequent generations not only talked of the case but also shared a sense of Gray's ghost, roaming the fields with the ax he used to commit familicide.

48. I employ pseudonyms in cases where I report information not on the public record.

49. Jack knew that if he told the Realtor of the familicide, real estate law required the communication of that information to prospective buyers. Information of this kind would almost certainly lower the value of the property, something that caused Jack concern.

50. The psychiatrist's report contains the language of sexual deviancy and neurosis. Today the psychiatric term used to describe behavior like Lonnie's is *paraphilia*. The paraphilias consist of mental disorders "characterized by recurrent sexually arousing fantasies, sexual urges, or behavior involving non-human objects, children or other non-consenting sexual partners, or suffering or humiliation of oneself or a sexual partner" (Colman, 2006: 549).

51. Lonnie was arrested twice on Peeping Tom charges. The first arrest was in 1938. He was found guilty, spent four or five days in jail, and received a year's probation. His second arrest was in 1953, although he claims he was not peeping at this time but was merely drunk. Nevertheless, he was fined $100 and received a year's probation.

52. In the language of contemporary psychology, *neurosis* refers to significant anxiety or other distressing emotional symptoms. These might include "persistent or irrational fears, obsessive thoughts, compulsive acts, dissociative states, and somatic and depressive reactions" (APA, 2007: 622). These symptoms "do not involve gross personality disorganization, total lack of insight, or loss of contact with reality" (APA, 2007: 622). Most emotional states that used to be referred to as neuroses are now classified as "anxiety disorders." *Psychosis* refers to abnormal mental states evidencing "serious impairments or disruptions in the most fundamental higher brain functions—perception, cognition and cognitive processing, and emotions or affect—as manifested in behavioral phenomena, such as delusions, hallucinations, and significantly disorganized speech" (APA, 2007: 756).

53. Gordon, 2006: page 9.

54. Gordon, 2006: page 9.

55. The seventh child, the oldest son, Fred Cooper, was shot in the head but survived.

56. *Cadillac Evening News*, Cadillac, Michigan, Monday, June 15, 1908. "Verdict of the Jury: Relative To the Tragedy through Which Cooper Family Lost Their Lives."

57. *Cadillac Evening News*, Cadillac, Michigan, Monday, June 15, 1908. "Verdict of the Jury: Relative to the Tragedy through Which Cooper Family Lost Their Lives."

58. *Cadillac Evening News*, Cadillac, Michigan, Monday, June 15, 1908. "Verdict of the Jury: Relative to the Tragedy through Which Cooper Family Lost Their Lives."

59. *Cadillac Evening News*, Cadillac, Michigan, Monday, June 16, 1908. "Victims at Rest."

60. *Cadillac Evening News*, Cadillac, Michigan, Monday, June 16, 1908. "Victims at Rest."

61. See *Cadillac Evening News*, Cadillac, Michigan, Saturday, June 13, 1908. Front page. "Mrs. Daniel Cooper Shoots Husband, Six Children and Herself."

62. *New York Times*, June 14, 1908, p.16. "Insane Mother Kills Seven."

63. *Cadillac Evening News*, Cadillac, Michigan, Saturday, June 13, 1908. Front page. "Mrs. Daniel Cooper Shoots Husband, Six Children and Herself."

64. *Cadillac Evening News*, Cadillac, Michigan, Saturday, June 13, 1908. Front page. "Mrs. Daniel Cooper Shoots Husband, Six Children and Herself."

65. See *Cadillac Evening News*, Cadillac, Michigan, Saturday, June 13, 1908. Front page. "Mrs. Daniel Cooper Shoots Husband, Six Children and Herself."

66. *Cadillac Evening News*, Cadillac, Michigan, Saturday, June 13, 1908. Front page. "Mrs. Daniel Cooper Shoots Husband, Six Children and Herself."

67. *Cadillac Evening News*, Cadillac, Michigan, Saturday, June 13, 1908. Front page. "Mrs. Daniel Cooper Shoots Husband, Six Children and Herself."

68. *Cadillac Evening News*, Cadillac, Michigan, Saturday, June 13, 1908. Front page. "Mrs. Daniel Cooper Shoots Husband, Six Children and Herself."

69. *Cadillac Evening News*, Cadillac, Michigan, Saturday, June 13, 1908. Front page. "Mrs. Daniel Cooper Shoots Husband, Six Children and Herself."

70. *Cadillac Evening News*, Cadillac, Michigan, Saturday, June 13, 1908. Front page. "Mrs. Daniel Cooper Shoots Husband, Six Children and Herself." Dr. Johnstone's intervention is the only official one noted in the newspaper accounts.

71. *Cadillac Evening News*, Cadillac, Michigan, Saturday, June 13, 1908. Front page. "Mrs. Daniel Cooper Shoots Husband, Six Children and Herself."

72. *Cadillac Evening News*, Cadillac, Michigan, Saturday, June 13, 1908. Front page. "Mrs. Daniel Cooper Shoots Husband, Six Children and Herself."

73. *Cadillac Evening News*, Cadillac, Michigan, Saturday, June 13, 1908. Front page. "Mrs. Daniel Cooper Shoots Husband, Six Children and Herself."

74. *Cadillac Evening News*, Cadillac, Michigan, Monday, June 15, 1908. "Verdict of the Jury: Relative to the Tragedy through Which Cooper Family Lost Their Lives."

75. *Cadillac Evening News*, Cadillac, Michigan, Monday, June 15, 1908. "Verdict of the Jury: Relative to the Tragedy through Which Cooper Family Lost Their Lives."

76. My italics. *Cadillac Evening News*, Cadillac, Michigan, Wednesday, June 24, 1908. "Theories Have Died Out: Nothing Remains to the Cooper Tragedy Except the Most Reasonable Theory That Mrs. Cooper Was the Murderer."

77. *Cadillac Evening News*, Cadillac, Michigan, Saturday, June 13, 1908. Front page. "Mrs. Daniel Cooper Shoots Husband, Six Children and Herself." The newspaper's choice of the words *farm, township* and *city* is striking. By today's standards the Cadillac, Michigan, of 1908 was a very small town. We might even question the appropriateness of using the word *city* to describe it. However, a century ago, the contrast between farming and town and city living was stark and potentially ominous.

78. *Cadillac Evening News*, Cadillac, Michigan, Monday, June 16, 1908. "Victims at Rest."

79. Daly and Wilson, 1988: 43.

80. Daly and Wilson, 1988: 52.

81. Meyer and Oberman, 2001: 2.

82. Gordon, 1997: 7.

83. For a discussion of the Andrea Yates case that affirms her insanity, see McClellan, 2006.

84. Gordon, 1997: 52.

85. Freud, 1899 (1953–1974): 220.

86. Freud, 1899: 226.

87. Freud, 1899: 237–238.

88. Freud, 1899: 241.

89. Freud, 1899: 240.

90. Freud, 1899: 240.

91. Freud, 1899: 242.

92. Freud, 1899: 248.

93. Gordon, 1997: 54–55. Italics in the original.

94. Gordon, 1997: 53.

3

FAMILICIDE: A HISTORY

In this chapter, I chart the historical contours of familicide, providing wherever possible a tentative sense of the emotional milieu within which these tragic killings take place. The extant historical research strongly suggests familicide first appeared in the United States from the middle of the eighteenth century, a time when the formal infrastructure of modern life emerged in earnest. This does not mean people did not kill family members in premodern times. Indeed, as we will see, a variety of forms of family murder punctuated the histories of premodern and modern societies. However, the killing of the entire nuclear family unit—spouse, children, oftentimes followed by the suicide of the perpetrator—appears confined to modern times, or more precisely the period from 1755 in the United States, the principal focus of this book. If I am correct, the historically and socially situated nature of familicide has important implications not only for the study of interpersonal violence but also for the history of emotional life in general.

Table 3.1 provides a synopsis of the principal cases discussed in Chapter 3, offering readers a quick reference guide as they encounter each case. I organize the chapter around three historical periods: *medieval, early modern* and *modern*. The modern era receives the bulk of my attention because it is here we find a detailed research literature on the early familicides. The familicide cases from the early Republic included in this chapter feature among the 211 cases composing the archive. I devote considerable space to these cases because they take place within the shifting modern era figurations of feeling that haunt the lives and emotional styles of perpetrators. In short, I use these cases from the early American Republic to illustrate historical points, particularly concerning the nature of family life, gender relationships, and emotional formations.

Table 3.1 Summaries of the Cases Discussed in Chapter 3
(PS = Perpetrator Suicide)

Perpetrator	Victims	Summary Notes
Beadle, William	Lydia (wife) and four children. PS	A well-thought-of businessman and a soft patriarch, Beadle was facing poverty. He toyed with idea of familicide for several years. Weeks before the killings he began carrying a knife and ax to bed. Lydia had dreams of her children being killed. William drugged his family before axing them to death and slitting their throats. Deist religious beliefs implicated. Wethersfield, Connecticut, 1782.
Burland, William	Agnes (wife)	He tried to conceal her body in a cesspit. Oxford, England, 1391.
Kannon, Daniel	Wife and child	Earliest African-American familicide in the archive. Daniel axed his wife and child, fleeing. He had previously killed another of his children. Tennessee, 1870.
Cowan, John	Mary (wife) and two young children	Cowan was a drunkard, a batterer, and a highly jealous husband. Prior attempts to kill, one by arsenic poisoning. Cowan was abandoned by his parents, something he lamented deeply and said contributed to his brutish behavior. Cincinnati, 1835.
Le Bere, Emma	Four children. PS	Emma axed her children to death. Authorities concluded she suffered from "frenesye." Bedfordshire, England, 1316.
Myrack, John	Wife, two children, and a third child being nursed by his wife	Myrack burned his wife's face beyond recognition and crushed his children's' skulls. First documented familicide in the archive. Pennsylvania, 1755.
Purrinton, James	Betsy (wife) and six of their seven children. PS	James worried about the effects of a drought. A shy, taciturn man who would not look people in the eye. A former militia captain. His daughter caught him preparing a butcher knife for his throat prior to the killings. James had unorthodox religious beliefs. Hallowell, Maine, 1806.
Talbie, Dorothy	Daughter	Dorothy broke her daughter's neck. Talbie was melancholic and had previously attempted to kill other family members. Case was reported in 1638.
Womble, Matthew	Wife and two of their children	Matthew had chastised a man for visiting his wife, threatening him with an ax. His wife criticized him for his behavior and this apparently enraged him. Virginia, 1784.
Yates, James	Wife and four children	Yates saw a light shining into the room and heard voices telling him to "kill all idols." Yates jailed as a lunatic. Tomhannick, New York, 1781.

THE MEDIEVAL PERIOD

Elizabeth Pleck provides a thoughtful synopsis of the prevalence of family murder from medieval times until 1984.[1] Most of the cases she references involve the murder of one spouse by another or the killing of children by parents. She acknowledges that relying on crime and population statistics is somewhat hazardous for drawing conclusions about long-term trends.[2] Historians and criminologists agree that homicide statistics are more reliable than data on lesser offences such as assaults. Over the historical long term, family members, neighbors, and friends probably reported most spousal killings. Community members and authorities may have turned a blind eye to excessive disciplining of wives and some forms of violence and conflict within families, but they widely condemned homicide. As a result, spousal murder was well known and often prosecuted, therefore reliably entering the historical record.[3]

Historians, like the communities they study, consistently report the murder of multiple family members. These multiple killings, perhaps more so than the murder of only one spouse or relative, attracted considerable community attention, as they do today. In locales where historical records of murder survive, it seems unlikely that authorities would fail to record acts of familicide.

Much of the discussion of the history of murder focuses on England. This discussion warrants consideration for two reasons. First, it is in England that we find surviving records covering relatively long periods of time. Second, the history of English social life exerted a powerful influence on the development of the early American colonies and rise of the American Republic.

Using the Bedfordshire, England, coroner's rolls, Barbara Hanawalt reports a mass family murder in 1316. The explanation for it is uncannily similar to the one that authorities used in the Cooper familicide nearly six centuries later. The perpetrator was Emma le Bere, who apparently suffered from an illness known as "frenesye" (frenzy). On June 15, 1316, Emma rose from her bed, seized a large axe, and cut the throats of her four children, killing them all. She then used two cords of hemp, attached them to a beam, and hanged herself.[4]

As Hanawalt tells us, the jurors of the day explained these killings in terms of what they called *frenesye* or frenzy, a form of what today some might call psychological illness or psychosis. According to Hanawalt, the psychological ailment was the only interpretive device open to jurors to make sense of cases involving suicide.[5] It is probably significant this multiple killing occurred during the Great Famine of 1315–1317, a period when crime rates in general rose significantly, in tandem with the price of grain.[6] The similarities between Emma le Bere's killing of her children and then herself resonate profoundly with similar killings some five, six and seven centuries later, attesting to the powerful contextual framework of acute poverty and maternal distress at the heart of many child killings. Nevertheless, as seemingly shocking and frenzied as Emma's killings must have appeared at the time, they did not constitute familicide. Her husband seems to have either escaped the family or, at least, the axe. Nevertheless, the appearance in the Bedfordshire coroner's rolls of rare cases such as the le Bere family slaying is noteworthy.[7] It is likely that cases such as this created an enormous stir in medieval communities, finding their way into the historical record.

Coroners in medieval England performed their tasks with diligence, and it is unlikely they would have either ignored or somehow missed a case of familicide. Even in cases where people found bones with no flesh and identification of the body was impossible, coroners still held inquests. In medieval society, community members had to raise the hue and cry if they found a dead body. As high-ranking local officials, coroners examined dead bodies carefully. Members of townships guarded dead bodies until the coroner arrived. However, it is clear that community members occasionally removed and buried dead bodies without coroners' knowing.[8]

It seems much less likely communities would have removed and buried all the bodies in the case of a familicide. In such an instance, concealment of the deaths might prove extremely difficult and result in substantial fines. As Hunnisett observes, the first task of the coroner was to determine whether a person died during the commission of a felony, by misadventure, or from natural causes. If a person died feloniously, then the coroner had to ascertain whether the death was a homicide or suicide. Hunnisett notes, "All homicides, whether felonious, accidental or in self-defence, and all misadventures had to be investigated."[9]

Given these considerations, the small size of communities, the financial penalties incurred for not reporting deaths or for concealing them, and the widespread prohibitions and penalties for committing suicide levied in the form of fines against surviving family members, it is unlikely that familicides escaped inclusion in the historical record.

Carl Hammer's meticulous study of homicide in fourteenth-century Oxford also suggests familicides would have found their way into the historical record. He notes the high levels of homicide in the medieval town, averaging 110 per 100,000 people.[10] In examining 36 cases of homicide between 1342 and 1348 in some detail, Hammer stresses that all but one of the victims were adult males. Over the entire century, Hammer found only one case of a man murdering his wife. His coverage of this case and related matters is illustrative of just how difficult it would have been to conceal a familicide, or indeed, for a familicide not to enter the historical record. Hammer tells us that in September of 1391, William Burland killed his wife, Agnes, and tried to conceal her body in a cesspit. He notes, "Moreover, the scarcity of such incidents is certainly not due to disinterest by the coroners in this sort of crime; for example, when Mathild Pouk died a natural death in May 1342, her body was nevertheless viewed because 'there was much talk that her husband beat her unduly.'"[11] Incidentally, this is another good example, like Burland's, of the difficulty of concealing a serious crime, particularly intrafamilial homicide, in a community as small as fourteenth-century Oxford. If concealing a single act of intrafamilial homicide was unlikely, difficult, or both, then concealment of familicide would have been much less likely still.

Like other historians of crime, Hammer makes the point that "most homicides were not premeditated but were, rather, spontaneous, arising on the spot."[12] His observation is not insignificant and comports with Hunnisett's sense that "most medieval homicides were committed during sudden fits of angry violence with whatever weapon the felon might happen to have in his hand."[13]

The medieval homicide data show family murders comprise an even lower proportion of total murders than they did in early modern times. For example, James Given, reporting eyre court data from thirteenth-century England, found that 159 (6.5 percent) out of 2,434 murder victims died at the hands of a relative.[14] Of these 159 family murders, 96 were intimate-partner killings, with 64 men killing women, and 32 women slaying men. The lower proportion of family murders as a fraction of total murders ought not obscure the fact that the actual medieval rates of family murder per 100,000 people appear to have surpassed those of early modern England.[15] These relatively higher rates of family murder in medieval England reflect the much higher homicide rates in that society compared with its early modern equivalent.

Barbara Hanawalt reports similar patterns from fourteenth-century England, noting, "The medieval family appears to be remarkably free from murder."[16] Among 10,456 criminal cases listed in Norfolk, Yorkshire, and Northamptonshire jail deliveries from 1300–1348, Hanawalt notes that only 75, or 0.7 percent, consisted of one family member committing a felony against another. Sixty-nine of these 75 felony cases consisted of family homicides where one relative killed another. Using coroners' rolls from Bedfordshire and Northamptonshire, Hanawalt found twenty intrafamilial murders out of a total of 237 homicides (8.4 percent).[17] She goes on to note that the absence of intrafamilial crime, including homicide, constitutes "one of the most striking differences between medieval and modern criminal behavior."[18]

It appears the proportion of family murders, as a fraction of all murderous activity, declines significantly as we move back in historical time. More specifically, the rate of family murder declines from the medieval period to the early modern period and then increases significantly as modernity unfolds. Possibly this U-shaped rate distribution from medieval to modern times is an artifact of the underestimations of medieval populations. The historians who work this terrain are well aware of these difficulties. Ted Gurr puts it succinctly: "The estimates of rates of offenses, or indictments, are subject to substantial error because population data for premodern English towns and counties were considerably less accurate than records of violent deaths."[19]

James Given's work on homicide in thirteenth-century England is replete with caveats. Noting how difficult it is to even estimate the number of settlements in England during this period, he adds, "Estimating the actual number of people in these areas in the thirteenth century is even more fraught with difficulty."[20] He admits the population estimates are "very crude" and that the "unreliability of the estimated figures for the thirteenth century should be obvious."[21] Nevertheless, in spite of the difficulties estimating population, he defends the study of homicide across different parts of England in the thirteenth century. Such study "reveals with a clarity that few other phenomena can match many of the aspects of medieval life that are at once the most interesting and the *most mysterious*."[22] The point here is that the precise rates of homicide are difficult to determine accurately. However, the debate about the validity of the population figures does not detract from the fact that familicides would have been reported during medieval times.

EARLY MODERN PERIOD

Working with 431 cases of homicide in Essex between 1560 and 1709, Sharpe concludes domestic homicides comprised a smaller proportion of murders than in contemporary England and Wales. He comments, "Some 14 percent of the homicides in the Essex sample involved family members. . . . In modern England and Wales, by contrast, just over half the homicide cases recorded between 1957 and the early sixties involved domestic killing."[23]

For Sharpe, the typical early modern homicide involved a "fight between two men or two groups of men which went too far, and differed from assault only in that a fatality occurred."[24] Sharpe contends it is possible the rising proportion of family murders amongst murders in general might stem from changes in other forms of public behavior, such as the more rigorous policing of modern communities that results in a lowering of homicides in more public settings.[25] He suggests the emerging constable system may have exerted a more powerful regulatory effect than hitherto recognized.[26]

The same trajectory appeared in the New England colonies, where low rates prevailed until a gradual increase began in the nineteenth century. For example, Roth observes that the post-Revolutionary gross marital homicide rate in New Hampshire and Vermont was only 0.03 per 100,000 persons per year between 1776 and 1827, rising to 0.39 (1828–1847) and 0.47 (1848–1865). He attributes the more than tenfold increase to a variety of factors including the emerging tendency to *appear honorable and successful in a fast-changing society* that valued both prosperity and temperance.[27] Randolph Roth comments, "Abusers may have sensed that they had failed in society's eyes, in their spouse's, and in their own. . . . Murderous men were failures."[28] From the cases he examines, Roth suggests, "Failed husbands were dangerous when challenged in any way."[29] I suggest that what we see in Roth's observations is the increased effect of shame and humiliated fury as modernity unfolds and as some men fall short of the prescriptions of the fast-changing gender regime, new ideas, and imperatives that recommended certain things successful men ought do, have, and become.

Other work identifies changes in the emotional expectations between spouses as a possible reason for changes in family murder and suicide. Sharpe emphasizes the "virtual absence of murder followed by suicide from sixteenth- and seventeenth-century England."[30] Indeed, the 431 cases of murder from the Essex assizes (circuit courts) between 1560 and 1709 revealed only one homicide followed by the suicide of the perpetrator, and no familicides. Armed with these empirical observations about the absence of homicide-suicide, Sharpe is willing to entertain the possibility that the "emotional demands" made by the modern family somehow contributed to elevated rates of homicide(s) followed by suicide.[31] As he notes, the absence of acts of suicide following homicide(s) points to a very significant difference between early modern and modern English society.

I found only one example from the early colonial period in America of what might have been an attempted familicide. Brenda McDonald reports the case of Dorothy Talbie, an apparently melancholic woman, who on various occasions, had attempted "to kill her husband, her children, and herself."[32] We do not learn if she attempted these killings in one episode, thus committing what would have amounted to an attempted familicide. Nor do we learn anything about her. What McDonald does tells us is that Talbie "was executed after breaking the neck of her three-year-old daughter."[33] Talbie's case was reported in 1638.

In premodern times, suicide was widely condemned and penalized. It is probably for this reason that premodern murderers were far less likely than their modern peers to take their own lives. Indeed, West's classic mid–twentieth century English study of murder followed by suicide points out that in roughly one third of all homicides the perpetrator then commits suicide, a proportion that rises in cases of spousal killings.[34] However, these premodern attitudes to suicide began to change as Enlightenment thinking gained ground. Writers increasingly began to portray suicide as the outcome of either mental illness or rational choice, rather than an affront to God. Michael MacDonald and Terence Murphy explain that the lessening of disapproval of suicide from around 1660 in England had complex causes: "They included local hostility to the forfeiture of self-murderers' goods, the abolition of the prerogative courts during the English revolution, the governing elite's intensified reverence for private property, the reaction against religious enthusiasm, the rise of the new science, Enlightenment philosophy, the increase in literacy among the middling classes, the vast expansion of the periodical press, and the gradual absorption of empirical epistemology into the mentality of the upper and middle classes."[35]

MacDonald and Murphy describe these changes in the social meaning of suicide as the *secularization of suicide*. By this they mean the increasingly widespread belief that the supernatural does not intrude into the natural world. Put simply, suicide began to lose its connection with the supernatural. Throughout Europe, elites began to reject religious zealotry and became more tolerant of suicide. These cultural shifts included the rise of deist beliefs, identified by some orthodox religious commentators as contributing to the familicides in the early American Republic.[36] *Deism* refers to a belief in God based on reason rather than revelation. Under this way of thinking, God created the universe but does not interfere in its day-to-day operation.

In the early Republic, increasingly liberal attitudes toward suicide may have made it easier for the perpetrators of familicide to kill their families, then themselves. The American colonies adopted most of the English punishments of suicide.[37] However, growing tolerance was evident among the colonies. Pennsylvania and Delaware eliminated forfeiture in 1701. After the American Revolution, MacDonald and Murphy point out that, in their first state constitutions, Maryland and New Jersey decriminalized suicide.[38] Indeed, one of the founding fathers, Thomas Jefferson, argued for the abolition of the laws punishing suicide. None of this should be taken to mean that actual rates of suicide increased during the early Republic since the statistical data from this period do not enable us to reach such a conclusion.

The invention of the printing press is one of the hallmarks of early modernity. Among other things, the presses produced crime narratives for mass circulation. This crime literature constitutes a principal source of our understanding of phenomena such as family murder. In no way ought we see this source as an objective account of events, however. As is the case today, early modern accounts were products of their time, conveying popular understandings of why people committed murder. Ultimately, as Karen Halttunen thoughtfully points out, at some level these accounts are fictional. She notes, "Any story of murder involves a fictive process, which reveals much about the mental and emotional strategies employed within a given historical culture for responding to serious transgressions in its midst."[39]

The mass circulation of crime literature in the form of pamphlets, broadsides, and newspaper reports began in the late seventeenth century. Religious explanations of crime, largely in the form of published execution sermons, dominated this literature. Halttunen describes these published sermons as "sacred narratives" focusing on the "spiritual condition of the condemned criminal."[40] It is no surprise that the first early modern accounts of familicide accentuated the religious dissension of many of the perpetrators, although, as we will see, this began to change by the middle of the nineteenth century.[41]

THE MODERN ERA

The early modern preeminence of religious explanations of crime and murder gave way to gothic accounts of violence and mayhem that emphasized the inexplicability and horror of such transgressions. Halttunen argues the depictions of horror were not gratuitous. Rather, vividly bloody narratives functioned "to shock the reader into an emotional state that mingled fear with hatred and disgust."[42] Ironically perhaps, the gothic genre conveyed a sense of the innate goodness of human beings. Such approaches contrasted sharply with earlier religious explanations that emphasized the threat of universal human depravity lurking just beneath the surface of a tenuous social order.

Domestic murders provided fertile ground for the elaboration of gothic accounts. These horrific and mysterious killings emerged as particularly troubling because they appeared in startling contrast to the image of the companionate, affectionate family. Halttunen puts it nicely: "Popular accounts of domestic murder may be read as cultural nightmares of the new sentimental domesticity, terrible tales of transgression against the emerging norms of companionate marriage, 'true womanhood,' and loving child nurture. As such, these stories of deviance reinforced the new domestic ideal with their didactically sensationalistic depictions of patriarchal violence, female depravity, and child abuse."[43]

With advancing modernity, the gothic genre portrayed offenders as profoundly deviant outliers in an otherwise normal population. In addition to conveying the horror of events such as familicide, the gothic narratives also captured their mystery. The notion of mystery was alluring because in many ways it invited a solution or answer to why perpetrators strayed from the path of innate human goodness.[44] Consequently, one important modern theme in the first decade of the nineteenth century was the idea of motive. Because people possessed reason, they therefore killed for a reason. As we will see, these discursive developments happened well in advance of the invention of detective fiction by writers such as Edgar Allen Poe in 1841 and Sir Arthur Conan Doyle in the later nineteenth century.

That domestic murders proved particularly amenable to gothic elaboration made it much more likely that they would enter the historical record. The limited historical analyses of these murders reach a similar conclusion. In his study of spousal murder in northern New England from 1776–1865, Randolph Roth notes, "Murders, however, were difficult to conceal and left more traces in historical records than other violent assaults. Once suspected, murders attracted the attention of relatives, neighbors, coroners, reporters, and magistrates."[45] He argues these records "yield a fairly complete count"[46] of the homicides in the region. With familicide, the horror and allure increased dramatically, making it unlikely these cases could elude the historical record.

According to historian Daniel Cohen, perpetrators of familicide were "profoundly traumatized" by a growing religious pluralism, a market economy, geographic expansion and mobility, and progressive shifts away from more traditional forms of patriarchy toward more freedom regarding the selection of marital partners, the timing of marriage, the rise of loving, companionate partnerships, and less authoritarian styles of parenting.[47] To put it differently, we might say the emotional styles of perpetrators proved particularly vulnerable to the reconfigurations of feeling that attended these momentous historical shifts in the early Republic. However, the developments that Cohen references did not have the same impact on the entire population. As I mentioned earlier, modern life offers numerous emotional and material opportunities for vast numbers of people. It also involves a general extension of political rights. Nevertheless, Cohen's point is well taken and entirely in line with my own interpretation that social and historical changes are constitutive of and further transformed by reconfigurations in emotional fields. As we will see in the case studies (chapters 4 and 5), the familicidal hearts proved exceptionally sensitive to failure in various competitive arenas, whether these arenas concerned the accumulation of wealth, possessions, status, or especially the successful performance of masculine roles or, in rarer cases, feminine ones.

The first familicide in the archive occurred in Pennsylvania in 1755, a colony that Marietta and Rowe describe as the "first liberal society in the Western world."[48] In this fomenting political milieu, John Myrack murdered his wife and two children in the East Caln Township of Chester County, Pennsylvania.[49] The *New York Mercury* described the familicide as follows:

> We hear from Chester County, that on Tuesday last, one John Myrack of East Caln, murdered his wife, two of his own children, and a child of Mr. John Gilliland's that was nursing at his house, in a most barbarous manner; after he had murdered his wife, he burnt her face to such a degree that no person could know her. His children's skulls he beat to pieces against a rock that was before his door. Mr. Gilliland's he carried a little way into the woods, and there killed and left it.[50]

We learn nothing else of the Myrack case.[51] It would be especially helpful to know if he had beaten his wife previously, if he was sexually jealous of her, or if he envied her nursing the infant of Mr. Gilliland.[52] Clearly, we need to know more about Myrack before we situate it *vis-à-vis* the other cases of familicide. Nevertheless, John Myrack's brutal killing displays not even a smidgeon of altruism, civility, or restraint, and it is more likely the work of a livid coercive heart than a civil reputable one.

In their discussion of violence and murder in Pennsylvania from 1682 to 1800, Marietta and Rowe note the rise of notions of individual freedom and the increasing importance of commitment to self and immediate family, as opposed to allegiance to community or government. During the period prior to and after the American Revolution, we witness changes in the organization of society. Families became more privatized units, and individuals, particularly men, increasingly sought personal satisfaction and economic independence. The growing freedoms received much positive press, but, as Marietta and Rowe point out, increased rates of violence and murder accompanied them.[53]

Chester County, where John Myrack committed familicide, experienced huge increases in both violent and homicidal behavior between 1682 and 1754. Indictments for homicide increased from 0.9 per 100,000 people from 1682 to 1717, to 9.0 (1718–1732), falling to 2.2 (1733–1754).[54] From 1700 to 1709, Chester County witnessed 75 indictments for assault per 100,000 people. This rate gradually increased to 101 (1750–1759).[55] These changes suggest that the county in which Myrack committed familicide in 1755 was unusually violent.

News of the Myrack case seems to have circulated rather narrowly compared with the small number of cases that occurred several decades later. Two familicides stand out from the early Republic: Yates (1781) and Beadle (1782). It soon surfaced that both perpetrators, James Yates and William Beadle, held unorthodox religious beliefs, particularly deistic ones.[56] Deism involves a belief in God based on rational principles rather than revelation. Deism recognizes God set the universe in motion but considers that God does not interfere with how it runs. The widely circulating newspapers, magazines, broadsides, pamphlets and published sermons of the day seized upon this fact and quickly made connections with a number of other momentous historical changes, particularly growing individualism and religious dissension.[57]

James Yates killed his wife and four children in Tomhannick, New York, in mid-December 1781. He was jailed as a lunatic. Newspapers reported that up until the day of the killing, neighbors saw James Yates as a "sane and pedestrian cottager."[58] However, their impressions changed as they learned Yates had bludgeoned his family to death and axed his dog, two horses, and two cows to death.

Cohen informs us that Yates's neighbors came over to the Yates' residence the afternoon prior to the familicide. These neighbors included his sister and brother-in-law. The group read scripture and sang psalms. According to witnesses, Yates used "endearing expressions toward his wife" and displayed a caring affect toward his children.[59] By Yates's own account, a "light shone into the room" and he saw "two spirits," as Cohen describes, "one at his right hand and the other at his left."[60] The spirit to the left directed Yates to destroy all his idols, starting with his Bible. He threw his Bible into the fire. His wife apparently retrieved it. Yates then threw it in again, restraining his wife from once again retrieving it. He then exited the house, took an axe to a sleigh and eventually killed one of his horses. When he reentered the house he again heard the spirit telling him he had yet more idols, including his wife and children. It was at this point he commenced his carnage.

Authorities held Yates for two days at the home of a Mrs. Bleeker. There a Lutheran minister recommended that he pray and repent. Cohen informs us that Yates "rejected the pious man's admonitions with contempt and ridicule, 'refusing to confess his error' or join in the prayers of his captors."[61] Rather, Yates addressed God directly, saying, "My father, thou knowest that it was in obedience to thy commands, and for thy glory that I have done this deed."[62]

What Yates considered as visions of a light or the presence of spirits, modern-day psychiatry might interpret in terms of hallucinations and delusions. Among the familicide archive there are few records of such visions, hallucinations, delusions, or what some might call mental or emotional distortions of reality. However, on the rare occasions where we find evidence of such phenomena, I prefer to talk of them in the language of haunting. In particular, I suggest that in a small number of familicides, less than five percent, we find evidence of especially intense disturbances in emotional styles that are likely linked to exceptionally strong reconfigurations of feeling and peculiar realignments in sociohistorical steering mechanisms.

Yates was not alone among the early perpetrators of familicide in expressing unorthodox Christian beliefs. However, although news of the Yates case circulated widely in the newspapers,[63] it did not form the basis for an extensive pamphlet literature.

This was not true of the second case involving the deist William Beadle, aged 52. Indeed, Halttunen describes the Beadle familicide as "the first full-blown horror account in American murder literature."[64]

Fearing the fall of his family into poverty and despair due to his business failures and not wanting people to ridicule him, Beadle axed his wife, Lydia, 32, and his four children to death and then committed suicide. The killings occurred in Wethersfield, Connecticut, in December 1782. The subsequent publicity was both extensive and remarkable, contributing a gothic tale to American cultural history.[65]

One of the first people to enter the house after the familicide, Stephen Mix Mitchell, was a local lawyer, a judge, and a friend of Beadle. Mitchell wrote an account not only of the killings but also of Beadle's life and beliefs. In what follows, I draw upon Mitchell's account.

William Beadle was born in a small village in Essex, not far from London, England, around 1730. He became familiar with unorthodox Christian beliefs at a deist club. William migrated to America in 1762, eventually settling in Wethersfield some ten years later. Beadle was a man of small physical stature. He enjoyed considerable esteem in the community as an honorable and ethical businessman, a loving husband, and an indulgent parent. In his unorthodox religious beliefs, his affection for his wife, and his caring parenting, William Beadle's emotional style was emblematic of a kinder, gentler patriarch, a civil reputable heart.

Having migrated to America, Beadle established himself as a pillar of the community. He was an erudite and successful businessman. Yet amidst the economic uncertainties and vicissitudes of the American Revolution, his business began to fail. In spite of his diminishing income, he proudly maintained the appearance of wealth. According to Mitchell, "he adopted a plan of the most rigid family economy, but still kept up the outward appearance of his former affluence."[66] Referring to Beadle's writings, Mitchell observes, "he was determined not to bear the mortification of being thought by his friends poor and dependent."[67] Mitchell quotes

Beadle's own words on these matters, "If a man who has once lived well, meant well and done well, falls by unavoidable accident into poverty, and then submits to be laughed at, despised and trampled on by a set of mean wretches, as far below him as the moon is below the sun; I say, if such a man submits he must become meaner than meanness itself."[68]

Beadle's writings suggest he had been brooding over the decision to kill for as long as three years. Apparently, he came close to committing familicide on several occasions. One such occasion happened just a month before the actual familicide. On November 13, 1782, and in a manner that is reminiscent of Emma Cooper's treating her impoverished family to the theater, candies, and peanuts, William Beadle prepared a treat for his family. We learn from Mitchell that on this date William "procured a supper of oysters, of which the family ate plentifully."[69] A citation from Beadle's own writing clarifies his intention that night, "I have prepared a noble supper of oysters, that my flock and I may eat and drink together, thank God and die."[70] He dispatched his maid to take a note to a friend's house. However, the maid returned, perhaps disrupting his murderous plans.

Note Beadle's proud reference to the Last Supper, a final gesture of paternal authority as his world, in his eyes, was collapsing around him. Observe also his use of the word "flock." Beadle was the patriarch, albeit a seemingly soft, affectionate one, with a profound responsibility to lead those under his care. What we find in the Beadle case is the coming home to roost of reconfigurations of feeling *vis-à-vis* the new roles of husbands and wives, parents and children. In a sense Beadle was the embodiment of the newer, softer, patriarch, a product of shifting interdependencies between men and women, a rebalancing of the power between them. Beadle internalized these vicissitudes with alarming intensity, and his family paid a dear price for his inability to deal with his problems by seeking help from his community and peers.

Other evidence tells us William brooded over his decision for some time. The intensity of his brooding seems to have increased in the weeks prior to the familicide. We learn he began carrying to bed the ax and the carving knife later used in the killings. It is not clear if Lydia Beadle was aware of the presence of these objects. The evidence suggests she had a grave sense of foreboding, although it does not appear related to William's terrorizing her behind closed doors or in a secretive manner. Beadle himself addressed his wife's sense of foreboding in his own writings. He comments, "I have mentioned before that my wife had a dream concerning this affair, she has since had two more, one of them, that she was suddenly seized and liable to great punishment, that it created great confusion, but she afterwards got free and was happy."[71] Beadle continues, "On the Thanksgiving night she dreamed that her three daughters all lay dead, and that they even froze in that situation."[72]

William Beadle reported being "little affected" by his wife's dreams and premonitions, at one point writing that they constituted messages from God that Beadle's intentions were perfectly appropriate.[73] Such was his resolve and sense of righteous certainty in the path he had chosen. His writings sought to rationalize his acts of killing, to explain to the world that he had taken his family to a better place. We see such rectitude in a number of familicides involving righteous men, pillars of their communities, once successful but somehow crestfallen, overcome by the events of their lives, the fluctuations in the economy, or the prospect of the undoing of their social esteem. At their core, these men seem to have sensed they had failed as providers, as heads of household, and as men in a fast-changing patriarchal order. If they had any allegiances left, any meaningful connections to what they saw as real entities, it was to their God and the otherworldly. Their sense of having no place in this world, coupled with their firm belief in their ties to another world beyond their material life, left them only one option in their own minds. In short, what we witness in Beadle and other cases like his is the tension between everyday interdependencies that offer little solace or hope and otherworldly ties that increasingly present another way out, a permanent hiding place from the shame of the present.

The afternoon before the familicide, Mrs. Beadle visited an acquaintance, a lady who lived nearby. The lady, unnamed by Mitchell, reported later that Mrs. Beadle was "uncommonly pensive."[74] She asked the reason for Mrs. Beadle's pensiveness. The lady reported Mrs. Beadle saying that for months "she had been troubled with uncommon and frightful dreams and that very morning she dreamed that violence had been offered her family, and her children destroyed."[75] Was Mrs. Beadle somehow sensing a change in the atmosphere of feeling in her own home? Was she reading the haunting shifts in her husband's emotional style? I suggest she was and that her consistent pattern of troubling dreams reflected her growing inability to make sense of these reconfigurations of feeling. There is a fine line here between her instinct for survival and her socially induced drives. Was Mrs. Beadle deeply disturbed, rather like the hackles of a dog or cat rise in the face of threat? Was it the case that Lydia Beadle sensed the emotional tension in her home with the sensitivity of a seismograph needle, or are we reading too much into things? From the evidence it seems likely she lived with fear and trepidation for some time. Her dreams reflected the depths of this haunting sense of foreboding, and her recollection of them probably added to that sense.

Mitchell suggests that William Beadle probably interpreted her dreams as a premonition, as a sign from his God "his purpose was right."[76] If this was his interpretation, it is just one more sign of just how far out of touch he had become from the interpersonal interdependencies that had made up his life as a loving husband, a father, a man of prestige in the community.

On the evening of December 10, 1782, he entertained guests at his house. Like Lonnie Shell, he entertained friends and sang Christmas carols just before he committed familicide. In fact, we learn William Beadle "appeared cheerful and serene as usual."[77] Like many perpetrators of familicide who have not brutalized family members in the lead-up to the killings, William seems to have gone through a period of calm and cheer, an emotional hiatus if you will. The guests left at 9:00 p.m., although Mitchell makes it clear that "he was urgent as usual for their stay."[78] That night and in a manner reminiscent of the way Emma Cooper chloroformed her children, William gave his family laudanum to ensure sleep.[79] The couple retired to their bedroom. The maid slept with the children in a separate chamber. In the early hours of the morning, William woke the maid and sent her off to the house of the family physician with a note. He then killed his wife and children. He axed each in the skull, then slit their throats from ear to ear. Mitchell attended the crime scene, and informs us that "The woman and little boy were partly drawn over the side of their beds, as if to prevent the bedding from being besmeared with blood; the three daughters were taken from their beds and laid upon the floor side by side, like three lambs, before their throats were cut; they were covered with a blanket and the woman's face with a handkerchief."[80]

William Beadle drained the blood of his dead wife into a vessel so it did not stain the sheets. It appears he was anxious to present an orderly mausoleum. The placement of the handkerchief and blanket suggests protectiveness. These concerns with a sense of dressage, even in death, appear in the killing work of a small proportion of other civil reputable hearts.[81] Perhaps his gestures reflect the proprietary sense of the respectable and civil patriarch, a sense of entitlement, reminding us of the curious blending of perceived altruism, tenderness, mercy, and terminal violence. It is indeed possible to situate William Beadle's act of familicide amidst changing patriarchal sensibilities, a blending if you will, of the onerous historic responsibilities of the patriarch with the affectionate dispositions of a loving husband and a caring, indulgent father. Perhaps his axing and knifing bespoke the former; his administering of laudanum, draining of the blood, and covering with handkerchief and sheets, the latter. This tense dissonance between the bloody mass killing and the seemingly caring treatment of the corpses perhaps reflects the gender role strains of the day and the pervasive influence of new ideas about masculinities, ideas as we will see that attached greater significance to the personal responsibility of heads of household for their own families.

Later writers, particularly orthodox religious ministers, would use Beadle's deism as an example of free-thinkers trying to steer their own course, eschewing the imperatives of biblical doctrine and traditional Christianity. In short, for some orthodox Christian pundits, deists rejected the notions of hell and sin, thus leaving them vulnerable to transgressions of all kinds, including familicide.[82]

The publications generated by the Beadle case fed the expanding popular coverage of familicide. The most intense popular coverage of familicides in the early Republic corresponded precisely with the period of most militant or aggressive deism (circa 1781–1807). It was no accident that defenders of orthodox Christianity emphasized the deistic, freethinking qualities of the murderers. The rationality of these heinous killers and their willingness to play fast and loose with established religious doctrine and principles helped explain their unfathomable acts of violence.

As Williams notes, there is a precise correspondence between the publication of the Beadle texts in 1794, 1795, and 1796, and the first appearance of Thomas Paine's *The Age of Reason*.[83] The familicide texts, especially those pertaining to Beadle, found themselves at the center of a storm of controversy over the relationship between authority and freedom, and society and self. It perhaps appeared at a time when perpetrators of familicide proved exceptionally susceptible to the haunting effects of increased individuation, alienation, and anomie, aspects of life that others, perhaps with more orthodox religious values, were better able to negotiate.

According to Williams, the Beadle case provided much of the factual and ideological grounding for Charles Brockden Brown's infamous gothic novel, *Wieland or The Transformation: An American Tale* (1798).[84] Like Beadle, the fictional Theodore Wieland committed familicide. Wieland was a child of the Enlightenment and an endearing father and husband. He was called by his God to sacrifice his wife and then his children, and, in the wake was "gruesomely happy" to have served his Lord so well.[85] Brockden Brown, through Wieland, lucidly articulates the tensions between various religious and spiritual sensibilities. The accused Wieland informs the court:

> It is true, they were slain by me. . . Your memory has forsaken you; your eyes are not shut; your reason is still vigorous. You know whom it is that you thus charge. The habits of his life are known to you; his treatment of his wife and his offspring is known to you; the soundness of his integrity, and the unchangeableness of his principles, are familiar to your apprehension; yet you persist in this charge. . . .[86]

Having communicated his good standing as a father and husband, Wieland explains how his familicidal act was simply the performance of his religious duty. His (familicidal) heart remained untainted and honorable in the eyes of his God. Wieland comments: "It is needless to say that God is the object of my supreme passion. I have cherished in his presence a single and upright heart. I have thirsted for the knowledge of his will. I have burnt with ardor to approve my faith and obedience."[87]

A differentiation between perpetrators with civil reputable hearts and livid coercive hearts slowly emerges between the War of Independence and the Civil War. The civil reputable hearts belonging to men like William Beadle seemed unduly threatened by what they perceived to be impending poverty, a loss of social status, and the prospect of their wives and children suffering.[88] This threat and the shame it induced seem inextricably tied up with Beadle's failure to fulfill his religious duties as a patriarch. It is likely the small number of civil reputable hearts discerned, with considerable sensitivity perhaps, the economic and cultural changes of their day.

As at least superficially proud yet emotionally labile men, they appear to have enjoyed considerable social esteem in their communities. Nevertheless, the record suggests they interpreted their social standing as tenuous, provisional, and, especially as the familicide approached, precarious.

The unorthodox religious beliefs of these men perhaps reflected their emotionally labile nature. Their attempts to renegotiate and refine their unorthodox religiosity seem to have further marginalized them. Often they seemed shy or taciturn, perhaps painfully respectable, even repressed. Those close to them regarded them as loving husbands and nurturing fathers. There is no evidence these men behaved as violent or brutal husbands and fathers. Rather, they appear to have performed their patriarchal rights and responsibilities with care and diligence. For these men and perhaps many others, modern masculinities came with both privileges and burdens.

We find another example of civil, restrained, respectable masculinity in the case of Captain James Purrinton. Like William Beadle, Purrinton was older, 46, when he killed his wife, six of his seven children, and himself on July 9, 1806. Purrinton was a wealthy and successful independent farmer. As a well-respected citizen of Bowdoinham, Maine, Captain Purrinton had commanded the local militia for several years. Prior to 1803, he purchased 100 acres of undeveloped land near Hallowell, Maine, just south of Augusta on the Kennebec River. The Purrinton holding was just above the farm owned by the Ballard family. In her diary entry of April 13, 1803, the midwife and healer Martha Ballard first noted James Purrinton's arrival.[89] We do not know the reason he purchased the land or eventually moved his family upriver. On May 6, 1803, Martha notes making brown bread for Mr. Purrinton. Laurel Thatcher Ulrich notes James Purrinton appearing ten times in Martha's diary during the summer of 1803. During that time he cleared the land for a house and garden. Later that autumn, James Purrinton paid Martha for her baking on his behalf.

Within two years, Purrinton had built a house and barn on the cleared land. In August 1805, his family moved from Bowdoinham up to the Hallowell farm. During that first full year of residence, Ulrich informs us that James Purrinton "had cleared six acres-two of tillage, four of pasture—a respectable ratio in this part of the world."[90] Ulrich described him as "a sober and industrious man, if a bit taciturn."[91] In a broadside entitled "Horrid Murder," the author, probably Peter Edes, depicts Purrinton's habits as "steady and correct."[92] He was "also not a little avaricious, and therefore a diminution of his property or prospects, was a disappointment he seemed to want fortitude to support."[93] Purrinton was a man of "grave countenance, and reserved in company."[94] Significantly, Edes tells of people remarking that Purrinton "never looked the person in the face he was addressing."[95] As psychologists remind us, this inability to engage in facial gazing is a sign of shyness or shame. Kaufman puts it as follows, "Shyness, or shame in the presence of strangers, will influence an individual's capacity for sustaining eye contact."[96]

Edes opines that Purrinton's attachment to his wife and children "was uniformly tender and affectionate."[97] However, James Purrinton, like many parents of his generation, had experienced considerable losses. He and Betsy had produced twelve children, only eight of whom survived infancy. He was clearly a disciplined provider who took his patriarchal responsibilities very seriously.

Purrinton was "rapidly improving his estate, and was apparently contented and happy, until within a few weeks of his death."[98] Edes's impression comports with Ulrich's observations from Martha Ballard's diary entries. Mrs. Betsy Purrinton visited Martha Ballard for the first time on December 13, 1805. The Purrinton children visited Martha on a number of occasions. On May 7, 1806, Betsy Purrinton visited the Ballards for tea. Two days later, the neighborly James Purrinton transported Martha to and from a birthing. Ulrich notes the Purrinton family was gradually "taking its place in the neighborhood, weaving in and out of Martha's diary with near neighbors."[99] Perhaps the increasing integration of the Purrinton family was something Martha sensed because of the behavior of Betsy Purrinton and the children. Perhaps Martha was engaging in wishful thinking by recording these observations in her diary. Whatever Martha may have been alluding to by referencing the Purrintons' increasing integration seems not to have been substantial enough to either reassure James Purrinton about the drought or provide him with a sense he might be able to call on his neighbors to help his family in a crisis. Within two months of these neighborly interactions, Captain Purrinton committed familicide.

In the weeks preceding the familicide, James became increasingly anxious about what he perceived as a serious threat from a worsening drought.[100] He told his neighbors he worried about his family's not having enough bread to eat. Purrinton fretted that his cattle would starve and that his crops would fail. In the aftermath of the familicide, Martha Ballard and other neighbors searched their souls for clues about James's worsening emotional condition. They did not know the extent of his ups and downs. Edes tells us James Purrinton was "obstinately tenacious of his opinion, and it was very difficult to convince him he was in an error."[101] What James steadfastly saw as the threat posed by the worsening drought conditions may have been the straw that broke the camel's back.

It seems Betsy Purrinton suspected her husband was suicidal. The one daughter to temporarily survive the familicide, Martha, 15, reported seeing her father writing a letter on Sunday, July 6, 1806. She sensed he felt he had been overseen and made an attempt to conceal his letter. When Martha Purrinton asked what he was writing, he replied, "Nothing."[102] He then asked for his butcher knife. Once he obtained it, he proceeded to sharpen it. Edes tells us, "After making it very sharp, he stood before the looking glass, and with his left hand seemed to be preparing his throat for the knife."[103] Edes reports Martha being terrified by his behavior. She apparently cried out, "Dada, what are you doing?"[104] He again replied, "Nothing,"[105] laying the knife aside.

Martha told her mother of her father's strange and frightening behavior. Betsy Purrinton found the note her husband had written and confronted him about his intention to commit suicide. He denied any such intention. According to Edes, Betsy Purrinton became inconsolable. Edes surmises that it was at the point of witnessing his wife's deep distress that James Purrinton decided to commit familicide rather than suicide. For Edes, James Purrinton's act of familicide contained elements of misguided altruism. Edes' interpretation drew strength from Purrinton's own letter to his brother in which he comments, "I cannot see the distress of my family—God only knows my distress."[106]

Ulrich asks us to consider whether James Purrinton "deliberately terrorized his daughter by asking her to bring him the knife, that he wanted his wife to find the letter, that he deliberately used the threat of suicide to manipulate her."[107] Ulrich acknowledges we have no way of knowing the perpetrator's intentions. Her reasoning does require us to think again about the presumption that Purrinton acted out of benevolence. It also introduces the possibility that Betsy Purrinton's inconsolable emotional state reflected her terror in the face of an intimidating rather than a depressed and suicidal husband.

Within a couple of days, James Purrinton killed his family members with an ax and razor. His eldest son, James Jr., 17, escaped. Daughter Martha died later of her injuries. The killings stunned the communities around. At the bloody crime scene, authorities found James Purrinton's Bible. The book was open at the ninth chapter of Ezekiel. Authorities, including Edes, homed in on the language of Ezekiel 9:6, 11, "Slay utterly old and young, both maids, and little children, and women. . . . And, behold, the man . . . reported the matter, saying, I have done as thou hast commanded me."[108] It is not clear whether Purrinton himself had somehow marked this particular verse or whether authorities, including those who wrote the pamphlets on the case, selected it because it fit with their theory that Purrinton's religious unorthodoxy, particularly his belief in universal salvation and fatalism, underlay the killings.

Purrinton's belief in universal salvation was embedded, as we have already seen, in a fast-changing religious and spiritual milieu that included increasing denominationalism. As Ulrich reminds us, in 1780 in Lincoln County, Maine, where the Purrinton familicide occurred, all the churches had been Congregationalist. Within two decades, she notes, "In the by-then two counties of Lincoln and Kennebec, sectarian churches—Separate Baptist, Free-Will Baptist, Methodist, and Universalist—outnumbered orthodox congregations by almost three to one."[109] Ulrich continues, "James Purrinton, it was said, had dabbled in more than one heterodox creed."[110] Contemporaries contextualized Purrinton's familicidal behavior amidst the treacherous spiritual drift toward religious dissent. Edes contended, "Much of the violence of passion is often mixed with fanaticism, which makes it more tremendous in its nature and more fatal in its effects. And a tincture of both these frequently displays itself in deeds of horror, which are the result of systematic calculation upon erroneous principles."[111] The writer continues, "The natural heart is a soil in which errors flourish. Mankind being alienated from the life of GOD, thro' the ignorance that is in them, because of the blindness of their hearts, are open to delusion."[112]

Seemingly respectable patriarchs like James Purrinton and William Beadle serve as examples of early civil reputable hearts. However, from the early days of the Republic we witness a couple of cases of less than respectable men—angry drunkards, to be precise—committing familicide. Among these less reputable offenders we witness the importance of sexual jealousy, humiliation at one's failures as a man, and the unbridled anger and rage that accompanied these phenomena.

It is possible we witness sexual jealousy in the 1784 familicide perpetrated by Matthew Womble. Matthew caught a male neighbor visiting his wife. He confronted the man with an axe, threatening his life. It appears from the newspaper account that Womble was trying out some new brandy and was drunk at the time of the altercation.[113] The male visitor fled. Womble's wife appears to have reprimanded him for his behavior toward the neighbor. Matthew apparently responded by cutting off her head. He then proceeded to kill two of his four children, the other two escaping.[114] We have little information concerning Womble. Furious sexual jealousy may have fueled his familicidal behavior. However, the historical explanation remains at the level of his drunkenness and his hearing of voices from "Satan in disguise,"[115] telling him to kill his family. The prominent role attributed to Satan in the historical record reflects the fact the principal contemporary written commentary of the Womble case was a poem by John Leland, a Baptist clergyman from Massachusetts. Leland was visiting Virginia at the time of the killings. No confession graces the historical record. Neither do we learn about Matthew Womble's childhood.

On November 10, 1835, John W. Cowan, 30, murdered his wife, Mary, 25, and their two children, Thomas, three, and Sarah, one, using an axe and a knife. He fled the scene. Police apprehended him later without a struggle. On a number of occasions during the two months prior to the familicide, he had threatened their lives.[116] At John's trial, witness Harriet Boss reported that Mary asked to stay in Harriet's room overnight because she feared John. We learn that around midnight, John came to the room and forcibly removed Mary. The next morning, Harriet reported seeing Mary "much bruised."[117] Rebecca Oliver told the court Mary once sought refuge at her house. On that occasion, John came for her with a club. She accompanied him home, Rebecca testified, "on his promise not to abuse her."[118] The next day John placed arsenic in a water barrel in order to poison his family. The plan was foiled when the arsenic was discovered.

John readily confessed to the familicide, telling authorities he had no regrets about killing his wife, although he regretted killing their two children. He tells readers he killed Thomas and Sarah to prevent them living with the stigma of having a murderer for a father and also to spare them from growing up without parents.

In spite of witness claims he had been consuming alcohol for two days and was perhaps mildly intoxicated, John told Constable Madison he killed "coolly" and with "calm deliberation."[119] He also shared that he wanted to die and was contented for authorities to give him up to the mob.

On the morning of the killings, Rebecca Oliver reported hearing cries from the Cowan residence. She told the court that at that time she exclaimed, "There is Cowan whipping his wife again."[120] A Mrs. Ackerman testified seeing John and Mary walking up and down in their back yard, talking earnestly. Mrs. Ackerman told the court she heard Mary say, "Give it to me, John," presumably referring to the axe. A little later she reported hearing Mary say, "Strike me with that if you dare." Was Mary challenging John or merely expressing her resignation and emotional exhaustion? Whatever sense we make of her statement, John commenced striking her with the axe. Mrs. Ackerman reported exclaiming, "He is chopping up his family."[121]

In his summation, the judge spoke of John Cowan's "deep malignity of heart, and the revengeful spirit, engendered perhaps by jealousy, without a cause, so far as appeared in evidence."[122] He also commented on John's intemperance and his "embarrassment of circumstances and loss of character."[123]

We might expect these types of insights to emerge in the trial of a batterer for killing his wife. In many ways, John Cowan commits classic intimate partner homicide. We see a prior history of violence and tyranny, threats to kill himself and his family, attempts to kill, obsessive possessiveness, a couple that endured half a dozen troubling separations in as many years, intemperance, stalking, frantic attempts to control Mary, and so on. All these disturbing aspects of the Cowan's stormy marriage surfaced at trial. When case characteristics such as these appear today, many see them as risk markers or red flags. In this sense, the Cowan case is just one more in a long line.

John Cowan was born on June 10, 1806. His parents separated early in his life, something he reports regretting bitterly. John lived for a while with his father before eventually being sent off to school. His sister lived with their mother in Pittsburgh, where she grew into a young woman. John reported loving both parents. He was particularly distraught at his separation from his mother, someone he barely saw as he grew up. His "forlorn situation" soured his temper. John comments, "I know not what might have been the character of my *manhood* had circumstances in my early life placed me where I could have loved those around me and been loved by them in return."[124] John's father rarely visited him at school. John was overjoyed when he did visit, although he was "overwhelmed with grief" when his father left. He tells readers, "I wept until I thought my little heart would break; and the lady of the house took a switch and whipped me into silence. This taught me circumspection."[125] John learned to keep his feelings to himself, as he put it, "to indulge them by stealth."[126] He remembers living a "heartbroken" life for two years before his father once again called for him. John then traveled to Shawneetown, Ohio, to join his father.[127]

About three months into his new life, his father received a letter from his wife, John's mother. We see evidence in his father's reaction to her letter that notions of love and romance infused the lives of at least some of the working poor around 1820. John reported his father being profoundly affected: "he swooned and fell into the street."[128] For a brief period John thought his family might reunite. He was deeply disappointed when he learned otherwise. He tells readers, "I longed to see my mother and often have I wept bitterly at the thought of our separation. But I wept in silence, for I never dared to express my feelings to my father."[129] John lived with his father for a year or so after this incident. His father then dispatched him upriver to live with an uncle in Danville, Kentucky. John was 12. This separation caused further anguish, leading John to opine he "suffered more mental affliction than befalls most men at thirty."[130] He remained with his uncle until he was 15.

John's uncle apprenticed him out to a master cabinetmaker. John lasted six months. His next apprenticeship exposed John to a violent master who made him into a "drudge."[131] The abusive master beat him regularly with a cowhide whip. He lasted three years in this apprenticeship before finally quitting and moving on to a series of odd jobs. Eventually he traveled to Pittsburgh where he found his sister, living as a widow. His mother lived near his sister. When he met his mother, she did not know him. As John put it shamefully, "Even she did not know me."[132] He refused to write anything about his meeting with his mother, perhaps because the encounter was so painful. He did write, "She had been faulty, it is true, and bitterly had my life been made to pay the penalty of her errors."[133] John learned from his relatives that his father had died in New Jersey, without apparently knowing the fate of his family.

Within a short time of his arrival in Pittsburgh, John's mother died. He was 22 years old. In the year or so after his mother's death, John became aware of Mary Sinclair, a young woman who lived in a house close to his sister's. He was introduced to Mary in December 1829. At that time, Mary was engaged to be married to a man John never named, a Mr. X. According to John, Mr. X. was an apprentice saddler, due to complete his apprenticeship in the summer of 1831. John fell in love with Mary. The couple spent time together and courted. John eventually won out over Mr. X., who was apparently devastated at Mary's decision to marry John. Indeed, Mr. X. continued to visit Mary up until three days before her wedding to John. In his narrative, John wrote that, had Mr. X. been finished with his apprenticeship, Mary would have chosen him over John. Indeed, John reports weighing the decision to marry Mary very carefully. However, he wrote, "The more I reflected the more I felt that I could not live without her."[134]

John and Mary's courtship reminds us that by around 1830, patterns of upper and middle class courtship rituals had found their way into American working class life. As Peter Stearns reminds us, "Courtship periods often saw young men and women deliberately focusing on a number of possible partners rather than zeroing in, with intensity, on a single individual until the last minute. This might have occasioned some moderate jealous rivalries, but not extreme possessiveness."[135] Indeed, it seems John expressed little sense of jealousy toward Mr. X. in these early stages of his premarital relationship with Mary. John reports that a year into his marriage he learned from Mary that she had been simultaneously engaged to both men. It was around this period John's sexual jealousy manifests with some intensity.[136]

When John thought back from his jail cell, awaiting execution, he recalled just how vital Mary was to his life. In some ways this is understandable. His mother and father had both died, and he saw in Mary a brighter future, albeit one centered on her. Is it just possible that John's recollection of Mary's worth and significance constitutes one of the earliest examples of what Barbara Hart would later call *centrality*? By centrality, Hart refers to the pivotal emotional role battered woman play in their batterer's universe. Put simply, the woman is the center of his future hopes and dreams, and living without her "represents or precipitates a total loss of hope for a positive future."[137]

The rather abrupt appearance of a sense of elation in John Cowan's life upon marrying Mary Sinclair contrasts sharply with much of the despair John reports feeling as a child. John and Mary married on December 23, 1830. He was 23. She was 18. They moved in together and John reported, "for once in my life, I felt myself happy."[138] Mary quickly became pregnant. When Thomas was born on November 23, 1831, the family moved out of Pittsburgh to Ashtabula Village, Ohio. Their happiness did not last long.

Feelings of jealousy seized John early on in their marriage. He could not decide whether they had any basis in reality. John reports becoming aware of a young apprentice carpenter, Mr. Y., conversing with Mary for long periods of time, and tells readers, "I remonstrated with her on the impropriety of her conduct and she promised to avoid him in the future. She did not, however, observe her promise and I resorted to strategies in order to detect her."[139] He began to observe her talking with Mr. Y. On one occasion, after observing Mary talking for an hour with Mr. Y, John asked Mary when she had last seen Mr. Y. She replied she had not seen Mr. Y. since the last time John had confronted her about him. Her dishonesty enraged John but he apparently kept his feelings to himself. He tells us, "Though all the fires of jealousy were burning in my bosom, I chose silence rather than a quarrel. That evening I went to a billiard room and played and drank liquor till late."[140]

As John drowned his sorrows and anxieties about what he perceived might have been Mary's infidelity, his temper worsened and he became increasingly morose. Mary sensed John's emotional turmoil and withdrew from him emotionally. John comments, "I discovered a marked coldness in my wife's conduct toward me." He adds, "She soon became so ill-tempered that my anger became ungovernable and I treated her with equal, if not greater, unkindness. This only made her worse and our domestic hearth became an earthly hell."[141] According to John, Mary discontinued her household duties and failed to prepare his meals. When he challenged her about these matters he reports her saying, "If you don't like me, get someone that will suit you better."[142] If we are to believe John's narrative, Mary was no shrinking wallflower, no helpless woman without agency.

John acknowledges he became a "sot and a brute."[143] He was jailed on one occasion, apparently for beating Mary. The couple quickly reunited, Mary imploring him to get back together because she and Thomas faced dire poverty. The family moved to Cincinnati, arriving April 10, 1832. The couple later separated several times over the years, on each occasion eventually reuniting. In due course, the Cowan family moved to Pittsburgh. Mary gave birth to Sarah on October 9, 1834. Mary and John's struggles continued. At this point, John mentions the return of Mr. X. According to John, Mr. X. came in and out of Mary's life on a number of occasions, constantly arousing John's suspicions. John's extreme jealousy reached the point where he would later reflect, "I was determined to take his life, and, for that purpose, purchased a large dirk knife."[144] John tells readers he quit his job to watch for Mr. X.

Just prior to the familicide, John reports he had caught Mary with Mr. X. According to John, Mary told him her situation was none of his business. Whether her alleged retort was a form of assertiveness, bravado or a figment of John's imagination, we will never know. Clearly, without Mary's insights, we can only estimate her fear. What John does tell us is that in the immediate aftermath of their exchange, John seized the axe from the mantelpiece and struck Mary eight times, killing her. Before the last blow, John informs readers Mary uttered, "Oh, John, I am guilty."[145] There are a number of ways to interpret John's recall of Mary's final utterance. Clearly, we cannot rule out that he was delusional or simply lying. What we do know is that John then killed his two children. Later John writes, "I then started leisurely down the road, with my hands behind my back meditating on the deed I had committed and occasionally taking a pinch of snuff."[146]

Notwithstanding the possibility that in 1784 Matthew Womble killed his wife because of sexual jealousy, John Cowan's familicide unequivocally evidences the centrality of sexual jealousy. The narrative strongly implies John's sexual jealousy was delusional. John is not sure of his own perceptions. At the end of his narrative, he comments, "My early matrimonial woes may have been imaginary and might have been obviated by prudence and sobriety but the bottle made them real. My first pang of jealousy may have had its origin in my own misapprehension."[147] Certainly, at his trial, witnesses presented no evidence of any infidelity on Mary's part.[148]

Indeed, John embodies an early modern example of livid coercive masculinity. He honed his emotional style amidst the fast-changing figurations of feeling that saw mothers assuming prime responsibility for the care and emotional nurturance of children. These profound shifts in modern figurations of feeling probably contributed to John's personal insecurities, making the loss of contact with his mother all the more painful and damaging. Indeed, if we are to believe John, this loss shaped the core of his manhood.

John Cowan's opinion that his abandonment by his family affected his emotional style and his act of familicide is prescient in its anticipation of new interpretive approaches such as psychoanalysis. John's painful upbringing haunts his act of familicide at every turn, inviting readers to consider the role of his childhood abandonment and trauma. It matters little if John Cowan shared his experiences to elicit sympathy or to lessen his guilt. What we see with the Cowan confession is the introduction of new ideas about etiology, cause, and responsibility.

These new ideas invite discussion of the role of the unconscious. Avery Gordon puts it nicely, "The unconscious draws us, as social analysts, into another region or field where things are *there and yet hidden*, where things *stand gaping*, where the question of how we present a world, our own or another's, becomes a question of the limits of representation."[149] She continues that this world "is far away from that of the contemporary social scientist whose scientific covenant is precisely to ward off the mythological."[150] Bringing the unconscious into our analysis of familicidal hearts provides yet one more reminder of the importance of what appear to be the inexplicable, the imponderable, and the haunted.

We ought not lose sight of the fact there were many sources of shame and humiliation in John's life. He was an itinerant carpenter among many, struggling to make a living in a fast-changing capitalist economy. As John Cowan himself notes, he and his family lived in chronic poverty. As the familicide approached, John opines, "This was the sixth time that we had commenced house keeping, and we had been but little more than five years married. These frequent derangements in our household matters always kept me poor."[151] Put simply, John found himself in the position of many men at that time. He lived in an increasingly urban setting. Rather than work the land as an independent farmer, the lot of earlier generations of sons, he sold his labor in the rapidly expanding marketplace. His was a precarious economic existence, not unlike that of many immigrants who migrated to America in vast numbers before the Civil War. Probably his inability to provide for his family added to his sense of shame and the personal insecurity he suffered because of being abandoned by his family. Readers will recall Randolph Roth's speculation earlier in this chapter, that abusive and ultimately murderous husbands perceived themselves as failures in a fast-changing economy that increasingly emphasized honor, success and temperance.[152] John Cowan failed to live up to these cultural standards, a failure that diminished his sense of self-identity and, more specifically, his sense of his own manhood.

John Cowan's familicide is the first that we know of in the United States or Western Europe to evidence a long history of woman battering. Like the livid coercive hearts I introduce in Chapter 4, his familicidal heart was vulnerable, dependent, narcissistic, and ashamed. It was a heart frantically chasing a relatively recent historical idyll, a wife who was affectionate, loving, companionable, and a sole nurturer of the family he never experienced as a heartbroken child. As such, Cowan's heart was a product of a period that placed strong emphasis on companionate, affectionate, and loving marriage. As a young man, John found it difficult to do the things expected of new fathers. He was unable to provide successfully, unable to tap into the newly esteemed sources of honor that included being softer patriarchs, indulgent fathers, and tender, respectable husbands. In short, it was difficult for John Cowan, with his traumatic emotional biography and his inability to provide for his family, to thrive in an emerging figuration of feeling that increasingly prescribed what Lawrence Stone called *affective individualism*. It is worth revisiting Stone's notion of affective individualism, a concept I briefly introduced in Chapter 1.

Lawrence Stone's highly influential book, *The Family, Sex and Marriage in England 1500–1800*, acted both as guiding light and foil for much of the historical debate about family life in Western societies. Stone points to a plethora of economic changes during this three-century time period that fed what he calls an increasing "possessive individualism."[153] In particular, personal and familial autonomy increased, and the influence of the community declined. He comments, "Man was egotistical, vain, envious, greedy, luxurious and ambitious. His main desire was to *differentiate himself* from his neighbors in some way or another."[154]

Stone traces these changes to the mid–seventeenth century, with mercantile and professional upper-bourgeois groups taking the lead. Members of these ascendant social classes began to get married because they had fallen in love. Spouses placed greater emphasis on being affectionate and cultivating sensual aspects of their lives and personalities. Men especially cultivated the autonomous self.

Parenting became more tolerant, indulgent, and nurturing. Prospective marriage partners increasingly began to choose each other for reasons of companionship and emotional, personal, and sexual compatibility. Couples married less frequently in order to merge property, traditions, lineages, and skills. Rather, they embarked on a search for individual fulfillment through familial intimacy. Nuclear families became less permeable to community and kinship influences, interferences, and disturbances.

For Stone, these major shifts in the arena of intimacy mirrored the rise of notions of individualism in general, the proliferation of a market economy, and the appearance of strong ideas about political rights, equality, and fairness. Stone captures many of these changes in his notion of "affective individualism."[155] Randolph Trumbach concurs with what he calls Stone's trinity of changes, namely affective individualism "attacking traditional patriarchy and replacing it with romantic love, companionate marriage, and an affectionate and permissive mode of childrearing."[156] Indeed, most historians acknowledge the profound importance of the shift in the new American Republic toward selecting spouses for reasons of affection and personal compatibility.[157] They also recognize major shifts toward nurturing children, as opposed to treating them in an excessively authoritarian and perhaps brutal manner.[158] For example, Carl Degler points out, "Love as the basis for marrying was the purest form of individualism; it subordinated all familial, social, or group considerations to personal preference. The idea of love, to be sure, was not new in the nineteenth century. The Middle Ages had certainly known of it, and the troubadours had sung of courtly love. But significantly enough, not as a basis for marriage."[159] In short, there was an increasing emphasis on love, affection and romance *as the basis for marriage*. The American family became more of a private institution, a place for emotional development, nurturance, and support, a refuge from the outside world, a site for the elaboration and proliferation of new emotional opportunities. These changes lay at the heart of new figurations of feeling, haunting emotional styles, and familial atmospheres of feeling, and had dire consequences for the familicidal hearts and their families.

The gradual emergence of romantic love as the basis for marriage ought not be confused with the realization of that ideal in everyday marriages. Cultural prescriptions are one thing; their lived reality, entirely another. The historical march toward companionate, loving marriage was gradual, uneven, and contradictory. Women continued to experience exploitation and oppression within marriage. Nancy Cott opines that in selecting their mates on the basis of attraction and companionship, women chose "their own bondage."[160] In general, the nature of this bondage differed from that of the early colonial period where patriarchs enjoyed greater freedom to use physical punishment as a form of discipline.

These rising expectations for loving, companionate marriage formed an increasingly important part of the figurations of feeling John Cowan negotiated. As we have seen, at the start of his marriage John reported feeling happy for once in his life. However, after the initial period of setting up house, during which time it appears John was relatively happy, his contentment seems to have waned. Once Mary became pregnant, things worsened. Dawn Keetley suggests Mary Cowan's pregnancies precipitated John's sexual jealousy.[161] Indeed, it does appear the two principal waves of John's intense jealousy coincided with Mary's pregnancies, although John Cowan cautions readers about the accuracy of his chronology of events. To be sure, in his narrative, John acknowledges harboring thoughts of committing familicide for three years, that span of time including Mary's two gestational periods.

Keetley adopts a psychoanalytic logic to suggest John Cowan envied Mary's procreative capacities. However, any such envy was perhaps beyond conscious recall, or something John was not able or willing to articulate in his life and confession. Rather, John's acknowledgment of his sexual jealousy was perhaps as close as he could safely get to expressing any deep envy and anger toward his first love object, his mother, who abandoned him as a young child. Keetley makes much of John Cowan's desire, even as a young man, to reunite with the mother from whom "in infancy, he had been ruthlessly severed."[162] She further suggests John's "desperate desire" for his mother "seems deeply implicated" in the familicide.[163]

Keetley locates sexual jealousy and a more generalized form of men's envy of women's procreative capacities at the center of the familicide. She links this to the historical changes in modern mothering whereby mothers "came to take on a much more central and exclusive role in the emotional and psychic life of the family."[164] Put simply, as mothers became the principal or sole nurturers, their absence in the early lives of their children assumed greater significance. In general, colonial parenting was shared between more family members, including kin, servants, apprentices, and community members, than its modern equivalent. Undeniably, many colonial households had a more permeable relationship with their communities. Only later, as the sexual division of labor became increasingly polarized and mothers became the exclusive nurturers of children, have we witnessed more intense mothering, or at least a growing valorization of these maternal responsibilities.

Keetley is well aware that these changes were contingent upon geography, social class, and race. In poor and rural families, for example, she notes birth rates remained high, mobility considerable, and child mortality rates high. Many of these families also retained fairly permeable relationships with communities well into the modern era. Keetley's work raises interesting questions about familicide. For example, if, as she suggests, Cowan's attenuated relationship with his mother was a significant contributor to the act of familicide, then why do we not see much higher rates of familicide among African-Americans, themselves subject to the threatened or disrupted familial bonding endemic to slavery? Unfortunately, the archive does not permit us to answer this question with any authority or confidence.

Significantly, familicides among Caucasian families date from the birth of the Republic and the rise of more privileged men's individual rights and participation in democracy. We must wait until the Reconstruction era before we find the first recorded African-American familicide. The *New York Times*, citing the *Nashville Union*, informs us that "a negro fiend . . . . Daniel Kannon . . . . killed his wife and child with an ax."[165] According to the article, Kannon had previously killed another of his children and been jailed for his transgression. The article informs us "his wife got him released by testifying that he was innocent." After saying he was going to hang himself from a tree, Kannon disappeared from the region of Tennessee where he lived and also from the historical record.

Following Keetley's logic, it might be significant that Mrs. Kannon was pregnant at the time of her demise. The Kannon familicide occurred during Reconstruction, the first time in African-American history when black spouses and partners began to establish legally sanctioned familial networks. By 1870, Jacqueline Jones informs us that 80 percent of black families in the Cotton Belt had a male head of house and a wife, a household composition that comports with that among the neighboring white population.[166] Much to the chagrin of Southern landowners who ran the sharecropping system, many black women refused to work in the fields, leaving this task to their husband. Nevertheless, the establishment of black nuclear families was always compromised by acute poverty, endemic racism, and the terrorism of organizations such as the Ku Klux Klan. Yet more black women than ever became mothers who tended to the needs of their children above their need to earn income outside of the family. Put simply, is it mere coincidence that we witness the first African-American familicide at a juncture when figurations of feeling amongst this long oppressed group were changing rather quickly?

The timing of the Kannon familicide is significant for another reason. Just as Caucasian familicides appeared around the time of the birth of individual political rights, this first African-American familicide occurred in the same year as the Fifteenth Amendment to the U.S. Constitution was ratified, granting black men the right to vote.[167] Daniel Kannon fled quickly. Living in a remote rural area six miles south of Columbia, Tennessee, Kannon was most likely aware of the venom directed at black men by members of the Ku Klux Klan. As Howard Zinn points out, whites murdered 46 blacks in Memphis, Tennessee, in 1866, burning homes, schools and churches in the process.[168] Zinn comments, "The violence mounted through the late 1860s and early 1870s as the Ku Klux Klan organized raids, lynchings, beatings, burnings."[169] Indeed, in its description of Daniel Kannon, the *Nashville Union* newspaper captured the racial toxicity of the resistance to Reconstruction in the South, referring to him as a "black monster."

Notwithstanding the possible relevance of Keetley's arguments to the Kannon case, her suggestion of a link between Cowan's pathological jealousy of his wife, or perhaps a deeper envy of women's procreative capacities, and his act of familicide, dovetails with the rather speculative work of historians of the family. For example, Elizabeth Pleck notes, "Victorian marriage appears to have been fraught with stress and jealousy. The ideal of romantic love arose, leading to hopes of intimacy, sharing, and companionship which could not always be satisfied. Dashed expectations for marital bliss may have caused some murders."[170]

Stone identifies a shift in the nature of family homicide from the early modern to the modern period. In the former period he notes significantly more killings stemming from "casual brutality."[171] These often took the form of parents' brutally killing children. Indeed, roughly half of all family murders in Elizabethan England (1558–1603) involved parents' killing children. In modern times, Stone speculates the greater proportion of spousal killings among family killings as a whole "suggests that family homicide due to casual brutality has declined, while family homicide due to sexual passion has increased."[172]

Roth suggests a similar shift in northern New England spousal murder cases. He contends that separation or divorce "never led to murder in the post-Revolutionary era."[173] However, by the 1840s and 1850s these murders "sometimes occurred as abused spouses left troubled marriages, or even after they had left."[174]

The insights of Keetley, Pleck, Stone, and Roth speak to significant shifts in modern era emotional formations, particularly increases in people experiencing sexual jealousy and/or trying to suppress the emotion.[175] Their observations raise the question of whether modernity accelerates or somehow intensifies the kind of deep, evolutionary history of sexual proprietariness that Wilson and Daly identify as being at the heart of men's murdering their former or current mates. Was an intensification of this sexual jealousy an emerging characteristic of modern figurations of feeling that somehow contributed to the historical emergence of familicide? Clearly, with increasing geographical mobility, urbanization, the emergence of organized prostitution in American cities from the 1830s, and the increasing insularity of families from community monitoring, opportunities for sexual infidelity grew. Additionally, as romantic love slowly gained ground as the principal reason for marriage, we see more and more people attaching greater significance to contraventions of rules of sexual exclusivity. For these and other reasons we might expect to see feelings of sexual jealousy increase. However, as Peter Stearns suggests, the growing emphasis on self-control militated against the expression of such jealousy.[176] It is likely then that much overtly expressed sexual jealousy and the possible shame associated with the feeling of it was suppressed in the new American Republic.

Although 190 of the 211 familicides I examine come from the United States, it appears this new form of mass interpersonal killing may have accompanied the emergence of modernity in other parts of the Western world as well. If further research confirms my impression, the historical appearance of familicide runs counter to the decline of murder and violent behavior in public space between nonmilitary combatants in most Western societies. Any counterintuitive emergence of familicide warrants our attention.

In Britain, a nation with reliable long-term homicide data, Ted Gurr notes that homicide rates declined more than tenfold between the thirteenth and twentieth centuries, and rates of violent crime in general decreased "probably ten and possibly twenty or more times."[177] The U.S. homicide trends are more difficult to interpret. Leonard and Leonard note there are no reliable national figures for violent crime (homicide, forcible rape, robbery, or aggravated assault) in the United States before 1900.[178] The U.S. homicide data are unusual compared with many other market economies: complex, regionally nuanced, and characterized by a series of peaks and troughs. Importantly, as Eric Monkkonen reminds us, the United States has "had a murder rate dramatically higher than that of comparable nations."[179] For example, Monkkonen observes that for most of the period from 1800 to 1990, the New York City homicide rate vacillated between three and six per 100,000 people. This rate was far higher than the rates in the most violent European cities during the same period.

Gurr attributes the decline in murder in most Western societies to a combination of increasing cultural sensitivity to violence and the rise of self- and social control. As numerous historians note, medieval England was brutal and violent. Marc Bloch's seminal work on feudal society emphasizes the everyday threat of violence from war, blood feuds, and sudden outbreaks of anger in public space. Medieval men did not shy away from using violence and in many ways exhibited nonchalance in the face of bloodshed and pain. At one point Bloch comments, medieval men "had small regard for human life," and they were "very prone to make it a point of honour to display their physical strength in an almost animal way."[180]

In a recent and much more extensive analysis, Manuel Eisner builds on Gurr's insights and confirms the decline in homicide across Europe over several centuries. In relation to England, Eisner contends, "an astonishingly clear picture emerges," in part because of the richness of the English homicide data.[181] Combining data from 40 different estimates of homicide rates in thirteenth- and fourteenth-century England, Eisner notes a mean of 24 homicides per 100,000 people. This declines to 3 to 9 per 100,000 in the early modern period, falling off steadily to 1.8 by the mid-ninteenth century and 0.6 in the early 1960s.

Eisner notes similar declines in Holland, Belgium, Scandinavia, Germany, and Switzerland, with dramatic decreases occurring much later in Italy. In Western Europe the decisive turning point was the early seventeenth century. Eisner cites a number of other authors who identify this reduction in murder, occurring first among the upper classes, then slowly permeating wider society over long periods of time. Perhaps most significantly, the European declines in homicide appeared first in England and Holland, countries Eisner refers to as the "pioneers of the modernization process."[182]

The horror and allure of familicide emerged over the same period wherein we witness decreases in public violence such as branding, execution, and torturing;[183] increases in mannerly behavior and the suppression of strong emotions;[184] and growing state monopolies over the use of legitimate violence. Insofar as we might expect these pacifying tendencies in public life to wield some influence in the more private sphere of family life, the appearance and persistence of familicide is counterintuitive. On the other hand, as greater importance is attached to successful companionate marriage and men's economic success, the greater the shame associated with failures in these areas of life. It seems that for a few vulnerable souls, this overwhelming shame, seemingly unacknowledged or bypassed, drove their familicidal violence. Fortunately, the case studies that follow enable us to explore these matters further.

NOTES

1. Pleck, 1987; Appendix B, pp. 217–225. Pleck excludes infanticides and the murder of servants and apprentices.

2. Historians are suspicious of human population data, and estimates of medieval populations are subject to substantial error. Consequently, comparisons of the per capita rates of crimes such as family murder are problematic.

3. It is important to remember that, when historians make historical comparisons of homicide rates, they are not necessarily comparing similar acts of violence that caused the homicide, let alone similar types of intent to kill. Due to the effectiveness of some forms of modern medical intervention, violent behavior that caused homicide in medieval times may not have resulted in death in much later periods. Sharpe (1981) notes modern medicine saves lives that would have perished if they experienced comparable injuries in an early modern setting. He also contends modern forensic science and investigation techniques make it more likely authorities will detect and record domestic homicides. Factors such as these make it hazardous to compare levels of domestic homicide in different societies in different epochs.

4. Hanawalt, 1979: 104.

5. Hanawalt, 1979: 104.

6. For further comments on the famine and crime rates, see Hanawalt, 1979, Chapter 7, especially page 260. Other researchers have reached similar conclusions about lynching and economic conditions. For example, using a time series analysis from 1882–1930, Beck and Tolnay (1990) contend that the lynching of blacks in the Deep South of the United States was more frequent when the value of cotton was declining and inflationary pressure was increasing. They argue this violence reflected particularly the worsening plight of marginal white farmers.

7. Local historical records in England are particularly detailed compared with those of other countries.

8. See Hunnisett, 1961: 12. Authorities leveled various penalties and fines upon communities for concealing deaths or failing to notify the coroner in cases of death.

9. Hunnisett, 1961: 21.

10. Hammer (1978) cites other research illustrating the magnitude of the Oxford rate. He notes Hair's (1971) estimate of 40 per 100,000 for Bedfordshire from 1270–1276. He also cites Given's (1977) finding that rates in urban centers such as London, Norwich, and Bristol were below 20 per 100,000. The only rates that exceeded those of Oxford appeared in the Italian metropolis of Florence, although Hammer questions whether it is appropriate to compare data for the two towns.

11. Hammer, 1978: 14.

12. Hammer, 1978: 20.

13. Hunnisett, 1961: 31.

14. Given, 1977: 56. Eyre courts consisted of panels of royal justices who attended each county every few years.

15. See Pleck, 1987; Appendix B, noted above.

16. Hanawalt, 1974: 4.

17. Hanawalt, 1974: 4.

18. Hanawalt, 1979: 263.

19. Gurr, 1981: 305.

20. Given, 1977: 29.

21. Given, 1977: 30.

22. Given, 1977: 32. Italics mine. Hanawalt acknowledges that "there are no population figures for early fourteenth-century England" (1979: 18). This makes statements about changing rates of crime hazardous at best. In discussing the limitations of Given's work, she comments, "He did not take into account growth over the thirteenth century. The rates of homicide that he draws from these calculations are not sufficiently reliable to be used for analysis of the incidence of homicide; thus much of the rest of the study can only be viewed with extreme caution" (1979: 287, footnote 31). It is for these reasons Hanawalt prefers to "avoid all discussion of rates of crime until, if ever, there is more reliable demographic information for the fourteenth century" (1979: 287, footnote 31).

23. Sharpe, 1981: 34.

24. Sharpe, 1981: 34.

25. Jeffrey Adler's analysis of the relationship between changing domestic relations and the rise of domestic violence homicides in Chicago makes a similar point. He notes the domestic homicide rate ballooned from the late 1870s to the late 1890s by 378 percent (1997: 259). He traces this increase to the rise of more intensive forms of social control that lowered the violent crime rate in public space in Chicago.

26. Sharpe, 1999: 261–262.

27. The italics are mine.

28. Roth, 1999: 85.

29. Roth, 1999: 86.

30. Sharpe, 1981: 47.

31. Sharpe, 1981: 48.

32. McDonald, 1986: 58.

33. McDonald, 1986: 58.

34. West, 1967. A similar proportion of domestic murderers commit suicide in contemporary American society.

35. MacDonald and Murphy, 1993: 5.

36. MacDonald and Murphy, 1993.

37. The English remained less humanitarian than the French with regard to suicide. John MacManners (1981) identifies Enlightenment humanitarianism at the heart of the French reluctance to enforce the laws against suicide. French authorities decriminalized suicide in 1791.

38. MacDonald and Murphy, 1993: 198.

39. Halttunen, 1998: 2.

40. Halttunen, 1998: 2.

41. Growing religious dissension and increasing denominationalism reflected modern individuation and social differentiation.

42. Halttunen, 1998: 3.

43. Halttunen, 1998: 160.

44. See Halttunenen, 1998: Chapter 4.

45. Roth, 1999: 65–67.

46. Roth, 1999: 67.

47. See Cohen, 1995: footnote 102, for the sources of his claims.

48. Marietta and Rowe, 1999: 24.

49. Marietta and Rowe, 1999: 32.

50. *New York Mercury*, August 25, 1755.

51. I was unable to locate Myrack's confession.

52. John Lewis murdered his wife on June 27, 1760. She was pregnant at the time of the killing. As Keetley (2006) suggests, men's unconscious envy of their spouse's procreative capacities might have motivated them to commit murder. For information on the Lewis murder, see Marietta and Rowe (1999: 32; also footnote 9, p. 50) and McDade (1961: 180, case 605). McDade describes the killing as "the most inhuman, barbarous and bloody murder." Marietta and Rowe noted Lewis "brutally strangled his expectant wife as she neared her time" (1999: 32).

53. Marietta and Rowe, 1999.

54. Marietta and Rowe, 1999: 29, Table 3.

55. Marietta and Rowe, 1999: 35, Table 4.

56. Einstein once expressed a similar belief when he commented that he did not believe God played dice with the universe.

57. See Fitzgerald, 1971. For a more recent treatment, see Daniel E. Williams (2003). Williams's detailed analysis provides a sense of the cultural significance of these iconic mass killings.

58. Fitzgerald, 1971: 2.

59. Cohen, 1995: 728.

60. Cohen, 1995: 728.

61. Cohen, 1995: 728.

62. Cohen, 1995: 728.

63. See Fitzgerald, 1971, footnotes 2 and 3.

64. Halttunen, 1998: 51.

65. See Halttunen, 1998: 51–56.

66. Mitchell, 1805: 6.

67. Mitchell, 1805: 6.

68. Mitchell, 1805: 6.

69. Mitchell, 1805: 6.

70. Mitchell, 1805: 7.

71. Mitchell, 1805: 17.

72. Mitchell, 1805: 17.

73. Mitchell, 1805: 17.

74. Mitchell, 1805: 17.

75. Mitchell, 1805: 17–18.

76. Mitchell, 1805: 18.

77. Mitchell, 1805: 7.

78. Mitchell, 1805: 7.

79. Laudanum is a mixture of opium and alcohol.

80. Mitchell, 1805: 8–9.

81. See Chapter 5 for other examples of this orderly and respectful presentation of the dead.

82. See Cohen, 1995; Williams, 2003.

83. Williams, 2003: 646.

84. Other writers see the texts on the Yates case at the forefront of this narrative development. Halttunen (1998) adopts this position at the same time as accentuating the importance of the Beadle texts.

85. The words "gruesomely happy" are Fitzgerald's interpretation of Wieland's state of euphoria upon completion of his grisly task. See Fitzgerald (1971, p. 59). Charles Brockden Brown, a committed deist in the Philadelphia literary circles of the 1790s, eventually rejected religious dissent and returned to a more orthodox path. His own transformation probably occurred around the time he wrote *Wieland*.
86. Quoted by Fitzgerald, 1971: 55.
87. Quoted by Fitzgerald, 1971: 58.
88. My comments apply particularly to perpetrators such as Yates (1781), Beadle (1782), Womble (1784), Clemmens (1805), and Purrinton (1806).
89. Ulrich, 1990: 290.
90. Ulrich, 1990: 291.
91. Ulrich, 1990: 291.
92. Edes, 1818: 3. Edes was the editor of Augusta's *Kennebec Gazette*.
93. Edes, 1818: 3.
94. Edes, 1818: 3.
95. Edes, 1818: 4.
96. Kaufman, 1996: 71.
97. Edes, 1818: 4.
98. Edes, 1818: 4.
99. Ulrich, 1990: 291.
100. See Cohen, 1995, footnote 59, for further discussion of the drought conditions.
101. Edes, 1818: 4.
102. Edes, 1818: 8.
103. Edes, 1818: 8.
104. Edes, 1818: 8.
105. Edes, 1818: 8.
106. See Edes, note 3, pp. 10–11.
107. Ulrich, 1990: 303.
108. Cited in Cohen, 1995: 737, and footnote 61.
109. Ulrich, 1990: 296.
110. Ulrich, 1990: 297.
111. Edes, 1806: 17.
112. Edes, 1806: 17.
113. *Essex Journal*, Virginia, July 23, 1784, Issue 3, page 2.
114. See Cohen, 1995: 731.
115. Cohen, 1995: 731.
116. Trial testimony of Virginia Boss, p. v.
117. Trial testimony, p. v.
118. Trial testimony, p. vii.
119. Trial testimony, p. vi.
120. Trial testimony, p. vii.
121. Mrs. Ackerman's testimony on page vii.
122. The observations of the judge appear in Trial Testimony, p. vii.
123. The observations of the judge appear in Trial Testimony, p. vii.
124. Cowan, 1835: 9. Italics are mine.
125. Cowan, 1835: 9.
126. Cowan, 1835: 9.
127. Cowan, 1835: 9.

128. Cowan, 1835: 10.
129. Cowan, 1835: 10.
130. Cowan, 1835: 10.
131. Cowan, 1835: 11.
132. Cowan, 1835: 12.
133. Cowan, 1835: 12.
134. Cowan, 1835: 13.
135. Stearns, 1989: 17.
136. The historical study of emotions such as jealousy is fraught with difficulties. Much of the research is riddled with caveats and cautions. Most of the research derives from the content analysis of prescriptive materials such as advice manuals. Clearly, it is much more difficult to discern what readers made of these materials and how their various interpretations influenced their attitudes and behavior. What research there is regarding people experiencing and negotiating jealousy derives from studies of the more literate classes, those who left behind diaries and personal letters. These observations remind us of the rare value of John Cowan's written narrative on the role of jealousy in his life. As he was an impoverished and itinerant working class man, we cannot assume Cowan was aware of what Peter Stearns calls the "love-drenched family manuals of the 1830s onwards" (Stearns, 1989: 21). These manuals decried jealousy as a negative, selfish emotion. Such diatribes probably caused some readers to hide jealous feelings, or to feel anxious, guilty, or ashamed of those feelings. Although John Cowan later acknowledged his shame about his sexual possessiveness toward Mary, we do not get a clear sense from his narrative that he acknowledged his humiliation as he experienced it or did anything but bypass his sense of shame regarding the failure of his marriage. What is clear, though, is that John valued romantic love, engaged in what for his social class was a historically recent dance of courtship, and longed for the nuclear family idyll.
137. Hart, 1988: 242.
138. Cowan, 1835: 14.
139. Cowan, 1835: 14.
140. Cowan, 1835: 15.
141. Cowan, 1835: 15.
142. Cowan, 1835: 15.
143. Cowan, 1835: 15.
144. Cowan, 1835: 17.
145. Cowan, 1835: 18.
146. Cowan, 1835: 18.
147. Cowan, 1835: 20.
148. Current thinking about delusional behavior suggests it reflects an emotional condition as opposed to mere errors in logic. See, for example, American Psychological Association, 2007: 266.
149. Gordon, 1997: 46.
150. Gordon, 1997: 46.
151. Cowan, 1835: 17.
152. Roth, 1999: 85.
153. Stone, 1977: 172–173.
154. Stone, 1977: 173. Italics added.
155. Stone, 1977. See especially Chapter 6.
156. Trumbach, 1979: 140.
157. Critics attacked Stone on a number of fronts, far too numerous to explore

here. Alan MacFarlane points to romantic love as a potent social force well before the eighteenth century (1979: 114). He cites several examples of travelers' commenting upon the loving treatment of wives between 1558 and 1614, although such treatment does not necessarily mean spouses married for reasons of romantic love. Likewise, MacFarlane takes issue with Stone's emphasis on the novel forms of loving and liberal parenting from the eighteenth century, pointing to comparable examples dating back to the thirteenth century. Again, the existence of such examples does not necessarily negate the arguments of Stone and many others that *overall* patterns of parenting began to change with modernity.

In a nutshell, MacFarlane attacks Stone's evolutionary approach to family history; an approach he contends either ignores or misinterprets a considerable amount of evidence to the contrary. Under Stone's scheme, the modern family becomes the "hero of his book," thus espousing an essentially laudatory interpretation of the present at the expense of the past. Here MacFarlane cites E. P. Thompson's (1977) review of Stone's book. See MacFarlane, p. 109, citing Thompson (1977), p. 499. MacFarlane therefore contends many of the pivotal shifts Stone traces to seventeenth- and eighteenth-century England date back to at least 1400.

Specifically, MacFarlane argues, "England in 1400 was roughly as follows: The concept of private, absolute property was fully developed; wage-labor was already widely established, and there was a large class of full-time laborers; the drive toward accumulation and profit was already predominant; the 'irrational' barriers toward the isolation of the economic sphere were already dismantled; there were no wide kinship groups, so that the individual was not subordinated to large family structures; natural 'communities,' if they had ever existed, were gone; people were geographically and socially highly mobile" (1979: 125).

MacFarlane's critique of Stone is part of a much broader attack on the writing of English history. However, given the influence of the English in early colonial America, we would do well to bear in mind that notions of individualism and nuclear families not heavily subordinated to kinship systems might have had certain far-ranging consequences that perhaps contributed to the appearance of familicidal hearts. If this is so, then MacFarlane's caution about formerly peasant societies adopting Western methods of technology and production might be particularly prescient. He comments that these countries are "not merely incorporating a physical or economic product, but a vast set of individualistic attitudes and rights, family structure and patterns of geographical and physical mobility which are very old, very durable, and highly idiosyncratic. They therefore need to consider whether the costs in terms of the loneliness, insecurity and family tensions which are associated with the English structure outweigh the economic benefits" (1978: 202). This raises the rather obvious question, is familicide one of those costs?

158. For a sampling of this literature, see Pleck, 1987; Rothman, 1987; D'Emilio and Freeman, 1997; Degler, 1981; Demos, 1970; Fliegelman, 1982; Smith and Hindus, 1975; Woloch, 1994; Norton, 1980; Rotundo, 1987; Mintz and Kellogg, 1988; Trumbach, 1978; de Mause, 1974; Greven, 1978; Lombard, 2003; Lystra, 1989.

159. Degler, 1981: 14.

160. Cott, 1977: 78. Cott attaches considerable importance to women's legal disadvantages *vis-à-vis* their husbands.

161. Keetley, 2006.

162. Keetley, 2006: 279.

163. Keetley, 2006: 280.

164. Keetley, 2006: 273.

165. *New York Times*, August 30, 1870: 1.

166. Jones.

167. See Websdale, 2001: 22–23, for a discussion of the constitutional amendments pertaining to these matters.

168. Zinn, 2003: 203.

169. Zinn, 2003: 203.

170. Pleck, 1987: 222. Unfortunately, Pleck is unable to provide us with a list of spousal murders attributable to stress, jealousy, or dashed hopes of intimacy, sharing and companionship.

171. Stone, 1983: 27.

172. Stone, 1983: 27.

173. Roth, 1999: 88.

174. Roth, 1999: 88.

175. For the cultural variability of sexual jealousy, see Mead, 1998, and Davis, 1936.

176. See Stearns, 1989: Chapter 2. Stearns notes, "Victorian society proved reluctant to talk about jealousy" (1989: 22).

177. Gurr, 1981: 312. Gurr is talking about overall long-term patterns. He acknowledges that there are temporary reversals in the trend data. For example, he suggests a probable upsurge in violent crime in fourteenth-century England, Elizabethan England, and in locations such as early nineteenthth-century London. See page 314.

178. Leonard and Leonard, 2003: 108.

179. Monkkonen, 2000: 181. Gurr contends U.S. homicide rates began to rise significantly in the 1920s and again in the 1960s. He suggests the two major peaks in homicide during the twentieth century might reflect blacks' killing each other at disproportionately high rates compared to their presence in the population. He comments, "These waves or cycles are of such amplitude that we cannot say conclusively whether the cycles are superimposed on a longer-run decline" (Gurr, 1981: 326, and Figure 3).

180. Bloch, 1966, Vol. 2, Chapter XXX: 411. See also Huizinga, 1999, Chapter 1, for a discussion of the violent tenor of life in the Middle Ages. Huizinga remarks, "The feeling of general insecurity which was caused by the chronic forms wars were apt to take, by the constant menace of the dangerous classes, by the mistrust of justice, was further aggravated by the obsession of the coming end of the world, and by the fear of hell, of sorcerers and of devils" (p. 21).

181. Eisner, 2001: 622.

182. Eisner, 2001: 618.

183. See Garland, 1990.

184. See Elias, 1994.

4

LIVID COERCIVE HEARTS

This chapter explores the lives and intimate relationships of seven male livid coercive hearts and one female perpetrator who may have possessed a livid coercive heart. I include the case of the female perpetrator for heuristic purposes, to allow us to explore just how difficult it is to compare men and women and the livid coercion they employ. Using the Cowan case as anchor and springboard, I briefly recap the historical origins of livid coercive familicide. I then introduce eight cases of livid coercion, selected from the 77 in the familicide archive that evidence these abusive dynamics. Table 4.1 summarizes key aspects of these eight cases, providing a touchstone for readers as they engage the chapter. I will then proceed to explore the early socialization of the offenders, wherever possible using multiple sources of information about these often deeply troubled people.

My biographical and thematic approach scrutinizes perpetrators' searches for intimacy, exploring these using the themes of the lure of romance, and the role of livid coercion, sexual jealousy, and obsessive attempts to control partners. Perpetrators' attempts to force intimacy undermined any intimate connection spouses and partners might have once enjoyed, resulting in what I term Pyrrhic victories. These tensely balanced and outwardly intimate arrangements required perpetual bolstering and evidenced much impression management and bluster by eventual perpetrators of familicide. The archive contains rich information on this impression-management and bluster, and I present various excerpts as means of grasping the complex personhood of all parties to these tragedies.

The demise of their intimate relationships exacted an enormous toll from the livid coercive hearts and those they eventually murdered. I briefly note as well the pervasiveness and character of perpetrators' depression. As I argue throughout the book, the eventual victims of familicide do not emerge from the archive as paralyzed or frozen to the point that they could not function, resist, or strategize about how they and their families

Table 4.1 Summaries of the Cases Discussed in Chapter 4
(PS = Perpetrator Suicide)

Perpetrator	Victims	Summary Notes
Beckenbauer, Misook	Gerd (husband), Emily (Misook's daughter by her first marriage) and Jenny Beckenbauer. PS	South East Asian woman who perpetrated violence against her husband. In the month prior to the killings Gerd found a new lover. Misook was obsessively jealous and fearful of the breakup of the marriage and family. Gerd was a wealthy computer engineer.
Camacho, Oscar	Carmella Sifuentes (partner) and Carmella's two teenage daughters, Maria and Juanita	Interviewed in the guard's lunchroom of a maximum security prison. Grew up on the streets of a Mexican city. Oscar was sexually abused as child. He worked as a thief and a coyote. Oscar murdered his victims, hid the corpses, and fled to another state with his two young children.
Hester, Malcolm	Shirley Hester (wife), three stepchildren, two biological children. PS	Malcolm was physically abused as a child; parents divorced. Stepfathers wanted to have sex with him. Malcolm injured in U.S. Army. Suffered irreversible shriveling of muscles, limiting his ability to work and provide for the family. Sadistically terrorized Shirley.
Langdon, Bill	Marge (partner) and Peggy Clanton (stepdaughter). PS	Lived in a run-down trailer. Alcoholic with serious health problems. Sold drugs in a school zone. Langdon misled to believe Marge's mother, Katrina Spencer, was going to give him some money to set up a business. He discovered the ruse and committed familicide.
Mason, Owen	Nancy (estranged wife) and Peter Mason. PS	Owen was living with a new partner but threatened Nancy's life on numerous occasions. He was enraged by what he perceived was Nancy's allegation he raped her. Family home a mansion. Owen's financial planning business threatened with a lawsuit. He visited websites to learn how to commit murder.
Oxley, Kevin	Bonnie (wife) and two children. PS	Kevin had a serious drug problem for much of his life, stuttered as a child, dropped out of high school, and had few educational skills. His mother abandoned him at an early age. His stepmother, Connie Oxley, reported Kevin was plagued by shyness. Kevin worked sporadically on a seismic crew. He met Bonnie when she was just 14.
Ronaldo, Ben	Laurie (pregnant wife) and Kai (daughter)	Ben drove his family off a cliff after Laurie told him she wanted a divorce. In the months leading up to the killings, Ben had lost his job, only to regain it again with less pay and no benefits. He told Laurie he suspected the child she was carrying did not belong to him. Ben had a serious drug addiction and exhibited road rage. He survived the crash.
Sims, Marcus	Gloria (wife) and Alex (son)	Marcus fled the scene and was apprehended about six months later. Sims left the poetry he wrote with a female chat-room friend at the crime scene. He claimed his childhood physical and sexual abuse and abandonment by his father contributed to his act of his killing.

might survive. Victim maneuverability, resistance, and agency emerge as consistent themes and convey a strong sense of the contingent nature of domination and the problems associated with commonly used notions of "control" in violent interpersonal relationships. The eventual victims of familicide also displayed considerable perceptual acuity, something noted by others who write about interpersonal violence and tyranny. However, it remains unclear how well victims perceived the degree of shame the livid coercive hearts experienced. I explore this shame under the subheading of *ignominy*, a near-total loss of dignity and self-respect, itself an intensely uncomfortable and relatively short-lived experience in many of the cases. Perpetrators engaged in varying degrees of planning and preparation in the midst of humiliated fury, reminding us of the dangers of trying to treat rational calculation as if it is somehow incompatible with the experiencing and expression of strong emotion. Indeed, we get the impression from some cases that strongly felt negative emotions guided the rational planning and preparation for the familicide. My discussion of the final act, the familicide itself, is necessarily speculative with regard to human emotion. However, I introduce the possibility that familicide might fleetingly dissipate or dissolve unbearable feelings of humiliated fury, recovering, albeit momentarily, a lonely patina of pride, often perhaps the last gasp in the Pyrrhic victory that in 45 cases out of 74 (61 percent) for which we had data on these matters ended in the suicide or attempted suicide of the livid coercive heart.

RECAPPING THE COWAN CASE

Between the American War of Independence and the Civil War, we witness a handful of men committing familicide after having beaten, intimidated, and otherwise abused their spouses. As we saw in the case of John Cowan, men such as these possessed what I have referred to as livid coercive hearts. The emotional style of men like John Cowan was rather different from that of the civil reputable perpetrators of familicide like William Beadle. Cowan and Beadle also came from different social classes,[1] although, like the majority of perpetrators, both were Caucasian men of European ancestry.[2] Cowan, like the vast majority of the livid coercive hearts in the archive, was working class. Beadle, like most of the civil reputable hearts, was middle class. Nevertheless, both men perceived an overwhelming threat to their pride, their social status, their manhood, and their sense of connectedness and belonging in a fast-changing world.

John Cowan craved a close relationship with the mother he perceived had abandoned him. In his adulthood he was profoundly traumatized by what he saw as the sexual dalliances of his wife. In his confession, John Cowan told readers he lamented failing to create a harmonious marriage, something his parents before him had also failed to do. His lament regarding his failed marriage came at a time when companionate marriage and the liberal parenting of children were emerging at the heart of a new and powerful figuration of feeling. John's sadness about his childhood abandonment coupled with his pathological sexual jealousy tore him apart, rendering him hopelessly dependent upon his wife at the same time that he was profoundly suspicious and resentful of her. We find echoes of John Cowan's dependent emotional style in the recent research of David Adams. In his analysis of men who killed their intimate partners, Adams notes that, "Jealous men were significantly more likely than their non-jealous counterparts to say that they felt 'highly dependent' upon their partners. They were more than five times more likely to characterize themselves as 'needy or clingy.' Nearly one-third of these men characterized themselves as 'helpless much of the time.'"[3]

John's shame or dishonor at his violent treatment of his wife and his failure to support his family was at once social and personal. It was social insofar as others witnessed his violence and his failure to provide. It was personal in the sense that John perceived his wife had abandoned him in a manner akin to the way his mother had. The intensity of John's sense of abandonment was, of course, historically situated. John lived at a time when mothering became more intense, when gendered cultural prescriptions increasingly depicted mothers as the sole emotional nurturers of children, and successful fathers and husbands as the principal or sole providers for those increasingly isolated nuclear family units. He also lived at a time when wives were increasingly expected to provide intense emotional and sexual support for husbands. Put simply, with the increased expectations that mothers and wives would provide such intense emotional support, the loss of such closeness was perhaps all the more heartfelt.[4]

EIGHT CASES OF LIVID COERCION

I selected the eight cases that constitute the principal focus of this chapter from the 77 familicide cases evidencing varying degrees of livid coercion from rare or sporadic outbursts of partner assault to more continuously threatening, intimidating, and emotionally abusive relationships. As noted in Chapter 1, I selected these cases because of my ability to learn about the emotional styles of the parties. Forty of these 77 cases revealed an official history of intimate partner violence. Another 19 cases contained clear evidence of intimate-partner assault without any involvement of authorities. All of the remaining 18 cases revealed some combination of ongoing emotional abuse, threatening behavior, attempts to control the intimate partner, a partner who reported fearing for their life, intimidating behavior, and/or various forms of degrading an intimate partner.[5]

One survey question asked, "Was there a history of emotional abuse?" By "emotional abuse," I mean attacks on the partner's self-esteem, putting down the partner, humiliating the partner, and otherwise undermining their successful engagement in the social order. By asking this question I sought to identify the cases evidencing an ongoing or chronic pattern of emotional abuse, as distinct from incidents or rather fleeting episodes of such abuse. Forty of the 77 files contained insufficient information to allow me to answer this question. Of the 37 cases with sufficient information to make a determination about a history of emotional abuse, 36 of 37 (97 percent) revealed abuse. Forty-three cases contained enough information to answer the question, "Was there a history of threatening behavior?" Of these 43, 40 (93 percent) contained such evidence. Forty-eight cases provided an answer to the question, "Was the perpetrator striving to control the victim?" In all of these 48 cases (100 percent) I found evidence of such attempts to control. The records in 41 cases permitted me to determine whether the victim of livid coercion feared for her or his life at some point in the relationship. Among these 41 victims, 28 reported fearing for their lives (68 percent).

On the whole, where sufficient information existed, the livid coercive cases evidenced chronic, ongoing abuse similar to what Evan Stark refers to as *coercive control* (defined in Chapter 1) or what Michael Johnson calls *intimate terrorism*, "violence embedded in a general pattern of coercive control."[6] However, given the varying degrees of missing data, it is possible that some of the 77 cases involved situational couple violence as opposed to intimate terrorism. For this reason it is inappropriate to refer to all 77 perpetrators as livid coercive hearts. It is probably safe to say at least half of the 77 cases displayed violence in combination with various attempts to control victims, threaten them, and emotionally abuse them on an ongoing basis. These we can safely call livid coercive hearts. The remaining cases evidence livid coercive behavior on at least a sporadic basis but do not display such behavior as a dominant feature of the perpetrator's presentation of self to family members, or there is simply not enough information to confidently speak of more than sporadic incidents.

The principal point is that toward the livid coercive (left-hand) end of the emotional continuum, perpetrators express strong emotions such as rage fairly regularly, especially to their intimate partners. We do not see these strong emotions displayed at the civil reputable (right-hand) end of the continuum. In what follows, I write about seven cases, all involving fairly high levels of livid coercion. These seven male-perpetrated familicides are among the most extreme involving prior violence, abuse, threats, intimidation, coercion, and attempts to control their intimate partners.[7] In all seven cases, the eventual female victims stated they feared their men might kill them. Only one female perpetrator of familicide used violence against her husband prior to killing him, her two children, and herself. In this case the victim, Gerd Beckenbauer, did not appear to suffer recurring fears for his life. Neither, as far as we know, did the perpetrator, Misook Beckenbauer, threaten Gerd's life until the moment she committed familicide. Misook Beckenbauer is the closest we get in the archive to a female livid coercive heart. As we will see, Misook was livid and obsessively possessive. According to witnesses, she used violence seemingly mostly out of frustration rather than in attempt to control her husband. However, she did attempt to control her husband, but the archival files lack evidence of her successfully coercing him, try as she did. If the seven male livid coercive hearts appear toward the far left-hand end of the continuum, then it seems more appropriate to locate Misook to the right of them rather than in their midst. However, this is no easy placement. I will endeavor to explain why.

EARLY SOCIALIZATION

Unlike other newborn mammals, the human newborn remains dependent upon its parents or guardians for very long periods of time. Human newborns are immediately social, forming important attachments with mothers and others. For the livid coercive hearts I explore in this chapter, those early years of finding one's place in the social order were unpredictable, painful and emotionally injurious. For these men and even for the female livid heart, Misook Beckenbauer, forming reliable social attachments proved difficult, if not impossible.

The eight perpetrators who are the principal focus of this chapter all experienced serious attachment difficulties. Among the sad and abusive experiences that helped shape their character, we find examples of child physical and sexual abuse, hearing or witnessing domestic violence between their parents or guardians, and the severing of parental bonds through the loss, abandonment by, or death of a parent.[8] The archive as a whole contains only very limited data on early socialization. However, where I had exhaustive information on early socialization, I usually found these debilitating emotional wounds. It is entirely possible that in some cases the reason there was no exhaustive information on early trauma is because there was none. These socially situated psychic injuries created a clear sense of abandonment from an early age, contributing to the development of a tenuous sense of identity and often-profound feelings of vulnerability and dependence. For these budding familicidal hearts, moving forward to establish wholesome ties in the social order and the arena of romance and sexual intimacy proved inordinately difficult, and ultimately impossible. The cases themselves offer the clearest insights into these matters. It is in their direction that I now move, commencing with my trip to a maximum-security prison.

I drove past hay bales to my left and charred fields to my right. The sky was smoky. In the distance, hemmed in by metal guardrails, thousands of cows stood in their own waste. Cramped, herded together, the cattle provided a harbinger of what was in store as I approached the maximum-security prison. I exited my rental car. The air stank of cow dung and smoke. White cattle egrets with inquisitive beaks pecked at the fields. It took an hour to clear security. I eventually met Oscar Camacho in a lunchroom.

Oscar was serving life without the possibility of parole for killing his live-in girlfriend, Carmella Sifuentes, and Carmella's two teenage daughters, Maria and Juanita. The couple had two younger children of their own, Xabi and Lucinda. A prison therapist acted as a translator since Oscar's first language was Spanish. The therapist told us he was there to oversee the interview and also for "security reasons." The counselor introduced me to Oscar. Oscar eyed me carefully and we shook hands. Our conversation lasted several hours and took the form of a life-history interview. I made it clear to Oscar that I was not interested in the details of the familicide. As we became more comfortable with each other, Oscar began to address me in English rather than going through the interpreter. It soon became obvious as the interview unfolded that Oscar's English was good. Indeed, Oscar is a highly intelligent and articulate man. The counselor exited about halfway through the interview. Oscar and I sat chatting behind locked doors. Every twenty minutes or so a guard checked on us. Time flew.

Briefly, the details of the Camacho familicide are these. Oscar was a career criminal. He operated as a "coyote," organizing the transportation of what he referred to as "illegal Mexicans" across the southern border of the United States. Oscar was also a professional thief. His activities as a career criminal brought him considerable social standing. Many people saw him as a man capable of frightening violence. The archive identifies Oscar as an obsessively possessive man who sought to control Carmella very closely. Oscar and Carmella never married although they sometimes presented themselves as husband and wife. In the ten years prior to the familicide, Oscar had an on-again, off-again relationship with Carmella. For large portions of this time they lived as intimate partners in one household, although for most of the three years prior to the familicide they lived separately.

At the time of the familicide, Oscar and Carmella also had two preschool children, Xabi and Lucinda. Oscar was their biological father and Carmella was their biological mother. In the weeks prior to the familicide, Oscar and Carmella talked of living together. According to Oscar, Carmella was pressuring him to live as a family unit with all four children under one roof. Police reports note Maria, 18, and Juanita, 17, both opposed Carmella's reuniting with Oscar. According to her friends, Carmella appeared in favor of a reunification, although she had a number of reservations.

Oscar helped Carmella and the children move into a new apartment. The reunited family remained in that apartment only a night or two before Oscar committed familicide. He spared his own biological children and fled to another state with them. There he raised them on his own until police finally caught up with him some eight years later.

At the time of the familicide, friends of Carmella filed a missing persons report on her, Maria, and Juanita. Police had few leads, and it was not clear whether Carmella had taken her two girls back to Mexico. Her few friends told police she did not want to return to Mexico. Oscar, too, had disappeared, and police suspected he had killed them. It turns out that Oscar killed Carmella and her daughters with a knife, wrapped them in blankets, and transported their bodies immediately to the state where he started a new life with Xabi and Lucinda. Police unearthed the corpses two years later, although they remained unidentified until police charged Oscar. At that juncture he told them of the killings and where to find the corpses in return for the state's not seeking the death penalty against him.

As we sat in the lunchroom, Oscar told me he had found God in prison. He and his cellmate, a much younger man, studied the Bible together. As he narrated the story of his life, we moved quickly to his childhood. Oscar grew up in what he described as a "very cold family environment with very little love or affection. It was a dysfunctional family." He continued, "I had many sexual experiences as a child. That is not uncommon for men in here" (the maximum security prison). It seems that someone in his extended family sexually abused him. He also told me he had numerous sexual experiences on the streets in the Mexican city where he grew up. Oscar also told me his childhood was lacking in what he referred to as "stimulation." According to him, he came from "an ignorant home with no books or art."

Eric Fromm's classic work on the social production of sadism helps us make sense of Oscar's early life and livid coercive heart. As we will see later, Oscar sought to impose rigid controls on Carmella. As Fromm points out, at the heart of sadism is the "passion to have absolute and unrestricted control over a living being, whether an animal, a child, a man or a woman."[9] We see varying degrees of sadism among the men with livid coercive hearts. According to Fromm, the appeal of sadism is that it creates a sense of omnipotence in the face of seeming powerlessness over human existence. He comments, "It is the transformation of impotence into the experience of omnipotence; it is the religion of psychological cripples."[10] Those whose lives are devoid of productivity and joy may find sadism particularly appealing. Sadists behave sadistically because they feel "impotent, unalive, and powerless."[11] Fromm observes, "Individual factors enhancing sadism are all those conditions that tend to make the child or the grownup feel empty and impotent. Among such conditions are those that produce fright, such as terroristic punishment."[12]

Fromm also identifies what he calls "psychic scarcity" as another generator of "vital powerlessness."[13] He continues, "If there is no stimulation, nothing that awakens the faculties of a child, if there is an atmosphere of dullness and joylessness, the child freezes up; there is nothing upon which he can make a dent, nobody who responds or even listens, the child is left with a sense of powerlessness and impotence."[14] One can only imagine the disenchantment and frustration of the clever young Oscar Camacho in a home bereft of stimuli.

Psychic scarcity alone does not necessarily lead to sadistic behavior. However, the combination of psychic scarcity and sexual abuse probably rendered it much less likely that Oscar would form strong social attachments and establish a sense of belonging in the social order. Neither did Oscar appear to have experienced positive social attachments, bonds that might have rendered him more resilient to the forces around him. Rather, his life on the street seems to have compounded his difficulties at home.

We find similar themes in the early socialization of other livid coercive hearts. Marcus Sims refused my request for an interview. He currently resides on death row. At age 40, he killed his second wife, Gloria, 27, and son, Alex, eight, and fled in his wife's vehicle to another state. He was apprehended several months later, charged with double homicide and auto theft, and found guilty. The wealth of archival data in the Sims case reflects the fact that authorities at the municipal, state, and federal level vigorously pursued him. They explored every possible aspect of his life in an attempt to apprehend, prosecute, and convict him. Our knowledge of his early socialization is both clear and comprehensive.

Further on, I will examine Marcus's sadistic parenting practices. For now it is enough to note that some of the information about Marcus's own childhood emerged from interviews with him conducted by child protection service workers and police. These professionals sought to remove his three children from the home Marcus occupied with his first wife, Janine. When confronted about his maltreatment of his three children, Marcus told them that his "mother used to hit him anywhere and everywhere and that she would come at him with plastic race tracks." I learned something of Marcus's early childhood traumas from a videotape of an interview between him and a homicide detective. Marcus reported how his brother sexually abused him. He offered this evidence as a partial explanation of the familicide.

Marcus: "My brother, man, he, uh, you all probably done heard the abuse story before, or whatever, man. But when I was growin' up, man, my brother used to blow me shotguns in my sleep as a child, and I'd wake up. I wasn't sure what was wrong with me, or what was happening, but I would always find him on the back of me with his penis in between my legs."

Investigator: "Uh-huh."

Marcus: "And, uh, I couldn't figure out what he was doin' at first and everything. And he would always tell me to be quiet and shut up and everything. Don't say nothin' to Mom and everything and you know. He'd give me money and stuff and everything. And that went on for years, man, but I finally got, you know, a little bit bigger than he did and basically whooped his ass."

Regarding his familial attachments, he told investigators, "Hell, no, there wasn't no good relationship with her [Marcus's mother]. Never has been. Not with my brother, not with anybody, man. There's no such thing as a relationship, man. Bitchin', arguin', fussin', cussin', screamin'. You know I'm better off on my own. I was always on my own." The abuse heaped on Marcus by his mother and brother meant that he could not establish social ties with those close to him. Put simply, Marcus became a social isolate and continued on that path into adulthood, establishing only tenuous interdependencies among his family members and few relationships at all through the world of work.

Marcus Sims wrestled with other demons. He never knew his father and had many regrets and much resentment about this emotional black hole in his life. Investigators later asked Marcus's half-brother, Paul, about Marcus's relationship with his father. Paul noted that Marcus "tried to

contact his father on a few occasions but his father was a chronic alcoholic
and didn't want anything to do with him." In an email communication
with his recently recontacted half-sister, Marcus told her, "if I ever met my
father I'd kick his ass for doing what he did by leaving me fatherless."

Kevin Oxley, 33, murdered his wife, Bonnie Oxley, 23, and their two
children, Joanne, seven, and Rob, six. He then attempted to set fire to
their house before shooting himself dead. The fire fizzled out for lack of
oxygen. As we will see later, Kevin had beaten and intimidated Bonnie and
their children for quite some time. Bonnie reached the point where she
told Kevin she was divorcing him and moving forward with her life.

My own interviews with Kevin's stepmother, Connie Oxley, and Bonnie's mother, Georgina Lessing, greatly enhanced my understanding of
the Oxley familicide. Like Oscar Camacho and Marcus Sims, Kevin Oxley
had a deeply troubled childhood. Kevin's parents argued frequently. Connie Oxley told me Bill and Bertha "had a very volatile marriage." According to witnesses, his biological mother, Bertha, had been the aggressor
with her husband, Bill Oxley. One source told me, "Bertha was just over
five feet tall and weighed only 110 pounds but she physically assaulted Bill
from time to time. She would yell and get in Bill's face, belittling him on
many occasions." On one occasion, "Bertha hit Bill with a piece of two
by four, knocking him down onto the driveway of their family home."
According to Connie Oxley, Bill Oxley was not intimidated by Bertha's
violence and on occasion had been known to strike back. When I quizzed
Connie about Bill's character, she told me, "Oh, Bill is not controlling.
He is very passive and only hit Bertha when he was backed into a corner.
I know. I've thrown a camera at him before, hoping for a response. Bill
just walked away."

Kevin was the oldest of three children. During his childhood, Bertha
and Bill split up several times. The first split occurred when Kevin was just
two years old. According to Bonnie Oxley, Bertha kept Kevin "for show."
She doted on him. It was very important to her that Kevin be clean and
presentable to the world. In some ways Bertha smothered Kevin. On one
occasion, Bill reported that Bertha "flipped out" because Kevin, at age
two, had gotten dirty. As the first grandchild on both sides of the family,
Kevin was the favorite. However, as his siblings arrived, Bertha used licit
and illicit drugs more and more. Indeed, it seems her family encouraged
Kevin to smoke marijuana. One report shows Kevin being caught, at age 8,
smoking marijuana in a field with a friend. We can interpret this marijuana-
smoking episode in a number of ways. It might have constituted youthful
experimentation, a way of copying the behavior of adults, or, even a way
of pleasing those adults. On the other hand, Kevin might also have been
(unconsciously) reducing the anxiety of a very stressful childhood.

It also appears that Bertha and Bill had little time for their children.
Neither parent read to the children. This lack of attention, combined with
the constant moving, meant that Kevin, a "sly and clever boy," nevertheless lacked basic education skills. He could not read well and had to attend

speech therapy classes to deal with his stuttering. Connie described Kevin as "painfully shy." Kevin was also "very self-conscious about his size."[15] In junior high school, Kevin was "painfully aware of his hair and clothing." Connie recalled one incident where she took Kevin to a store. He wanted a pair of running shoes. Since Connie and Bill lived on a shoestring, Connie proceeded to purchase a cheaper pair. Kevin "zoned out" when he could not have the running shoes he wanted. Connie remembers Kevin's eyes being downcast and his chest heaving as if he was having some kind of panic attack. To Connie, "Kevin appeared both agitated and scared."

A number of witnesses in this case described Kevin as "having a deer-in-the-headlights look, a startled demeanor." Connie told me "he would just stare at people." It was only after the familicide in 2003, that his father would acknowledge Kevin "had a flat or emotionless affect."

As noted before, Bill and Bertha Oxley moved frequently, including the years Kevin attended kindergarten through fifth grade. One of the reasons was Bertha's volatility. She frequently argued with neighbors and found it difficult to settle anywhere. Apparently, Bertha took Kevin along with her when she met other men for sex. He served as her alibi so that Bill would not suspect her infidelity. Kevin was around three to five years old at this time.

As in many of these cases, raising children with little money or parental wherewithal proved a daunting task. Bill's rather traditional patriarchal attitude added to the difficulties. He felt if he brought home a paycheck his fathering was successfully completed. Bertha apparently railed at Bill's patriarchal sense of entitlement and demanded that he help out more at home. On one occasion, Bertha screamed at Bill that she "would throw the kids up against the wall if he didn't help."

When Kevin Oxley was 11 years old, his parents finally separated for the last time. Bertha moved out to a house an hour away from Bill. The three children remained with him. Eventually, Bill met Connie and started dating. After he divorced Bertha, he and Connie married. During the years after the divorce, Kevin lived with Bill and Connie and saw his mother infrequently. According to Connie, all three of her stepchildren showed signs of distrust. As time moved on, Kevin increasingly came to criticize his biological mother. Connie heard him describe Bertha as a "big fat whale." At the same time, Connie also said that Kevin sent Bertha pictures of himself, suggesting he yearned for her and that he desperately wanted a relationship with her.

According to Connie, Kevin's love-hate relationship with his mother was the principal reason "he had no trust or respect for women." Bonnie Oxley told her mother, Georgina Lessing, "Kevin hated his mother." A number of witnesses in this case pointed out that Kevin had a huge fear of abandonment. It was this fear and vulnerability and the panic it instilled that wreaked such havoc in his abusive relationship with Bonnie.

Kevin displayed his mounting rage long before he began to date Bonnie. He was a destructive boy, engaging in property damage. He was also caught shoplifting. By 14 he was heavily using drugs and alcohol. On one occasion, Bill and Connie found him passed out drunk. Indeed, Kevin's consumption of drugs was so out of control that Connie told me that she and Bill did not expect Kevin to survive to age 25. Kevin was incarcerated for a number of months in a juvenile detention center for his drug-related offenses. Indeed, Connie speculated that if Kevin had ever been sexually abused, it was in this setting.

Kevin Oxley's passage into the social order was difficult. His mother-in-law, Georgina Lessing, told me "Kevin was extremely uncomfortable in social settings." We might best describe his social moorings as perilous and his emotional style as enraged by a deep sense of loss. I asked those close to him if he was bullied or ridiculed as a child. The answer was "no." Other children apparently liked Kevin. Kevin told them what they wanted to hear. Although he was acutely shy and physically vulnerable, Kevin was also very clever and manipulative. However, as noted, he lacked basic educational skills, was painfully aware of these shortcomings and later dropped out of high school. Put simply, Kevin Oxley negotiated a tenuous, rocky reality. More than anyone else, Kevin must have known just how far out he was. He craved a sense of belonging, something he thought he had finally found in the form of his wife, Bonnie.

Ben Ronaldo, 37, deliberately drove his car off a 150-foot cliff, killing his pregnant wife, Laurie, 34, and their daughter, Kai, age four. Ben survived the crash. He was found guilty of three counts of murder, one count being for the killing of the fetus Laurie was carrying. Ben and Laurie had been high-school sweethearts. Their stormy relationship evidenced considerable domestic violence, acute sexual jealousy, and a number of threats to kill. Indeed, in one request for a protection order, Laurie wrote, "He tells me I'm never leaving him and that he will kill me then kill himself before he lets me leave." She continues, "When we drive in the car and he gets upset, he drives recklessly, saying that if I don't shut up he will drive us both off a cliff." As with many of the other men for which we have information, Ben's earlier socialization proved painful.

Ben's mother, Andrea Pilau, told police she was married to Donny Ronaldo in 1966. They had two children, Ben and Clarice. Ben was born in 1967. Donny enlisted in the armed services and was sent to Vietnam. According to Andrea, "he returned a changed man." Donny became very violent toward Andrea. The record speaks of ten different incidents of domestic violence. The couple divorced in 1971, when Ben was just four years old. Donny went on to commit a number of armed robberies and assaults. Ben and Clarice went to live with their grandparents. Although Andrea Pilau lived in the same town as her children, she only occasionally bumped into them. Investigators noted, "She was not a mother figure in their lives." It was only later, when Ben and Laurie had Kai, that Andrea reentered their lives.

According to Clarice, her grandparents raised them in a stable home, providing them with many material benefits they would not have had if they had remained with their parents. But much damage had already been done. Notwithstanding the efforts of his grandparents, interviews with Ben's workmates revealed that Ben felt "tossed aside by his parents." Like Kevin Oxley, Ben would spend a lot of time smoking dope. According to Ben's brother-in-law, with whom Ben lived for a period of three years, Ben developed a $1,000-a-month drug habit. Indeed, in the aftermath of the familicide, Ben's blood tested positive for THC, benzodiazepines, and amphetamines. Also like Kevin Oxley, Ben dropped out of high school, something that diminished each man's social standing and options, reducing their ability to participate in social networks and interdependencies.

I do not want to belabor this discussion of men's difficulties finding a niche in the social order. We find these difficulties in the lives of other men we will meet. Bill Langdon's father beat him and his parents fought incessantly before divorcing. Just six weeks before he killed his wife, five children, and then himself, Malcolm Hester told a counselor he was physically abused as a child, that his parents divorced, his father rejected him, and his stepfathers wanted to have sex with him. In their late teens, both Bill Langdon and Malcolm Hester escaped into the military. According to Nancy Mason, her husband, Owen Mason, was reared in a cold family environment and hated his mother. Finally, all we know of our one female perpetrator, Misook Beckenbauer, is that she had a "tough childhood."

We know less of the early socialization patterns among the female victims of these livid coercive hearts. Investigators sought out these details with far less rigor, and I was left to piece together earlier parts of these lives from disparate sources. However, where we have such details, the women's passage into the social order also involved negotiating abuse, loss, and heartache, particularly with respect to their own fathers. A very significant number of women who later became the victims of familicide had unfulfilling relationships with their fathers.

Ben Ronaldo's wife, Laurie Ronaldo, had to move to different states during her childhood so that her mother could escape her violent and abusive husband, Laurie's father. When Laurie's mother was eventually able to return to her home state with her two daughters, she promptly died, leaving Laurie motherless at age 13. We know little of Laurie's early relationship with her father. The archive confirms his violence against his wife, Laurie's mother. As we will see later, though, it appears Laurie developed a relatively close relationship with her father in her later life.

Bonnie Oxley's parents divorced when she was eight years old. Indeed, Bonnie told her family the pain she experienced around her parents' divorce was the principal reason she remained so long in her abusive relationship with husband Kevin, not wanting to "raise her children in a broken family." Bonnie's mother, Georgina Lessing, told me Bonnie's father was emotionally unavailable for Bonnie. In fact, Georgina reports the children's father left the state for nearly two years after the divorce, greatly reducing contact with his three daughters. In addition, Bonnie and her two older sisters reported being sexually abused by their paternal grandfather, something all three girls only shared with their mother five or six years after it happened.

When Bonnie became pregnant with Kevin's child at age 14, her father told her "she would amount to nothing" if she had the child. He offered her the money for an abortion, which Bonnie declined. One family member described Bonnie's father as "distant and detached," a man who "liked to drink at the bar."

Bill Langdon's partner, Marge Clanton, grew up negotiating her father's sexual abuse of Marge's young daughter, Peggy. Bill, Marge, and Peggy all lived in the same trailer. Marge's father, Bob Spencer, raped Peggy and received life imprisonment for his crime. After this trauma, Marge's mother, Katrina Spencer, told investigators that Marge was "always very needy and she always felt like she needed a man." The medical examiner's report noted that Marge, not surprisingly, suffered from major depression. Her daughter Peggy also wrestled with bipolar disorder and anxiety.

We know much less about Carmella Sifuentes's upbringing. A friend of Carmella's told investigators "Carmella was from Mexico. She had no family and was abandoned as a small child." The friend added, "Carmella would not talk of her growing up because it was very painful for her."

I return to the issues regarding early socialization in Chapter 6. Suffice it to say at this point that these findings invite us to explore the relationship between different ways men and women negotiate some of their early deprivations and emotional debilitations. How is it that some men end up going down the livid coercive path and some women find themselves at the receiving end of such tyrannical and abusive behavior? How is it that most men and women who experience such childhood trauma do not end up as perpetrators or victims of familicide?

IN SEARCH OF INTIMACY

The Lure of Romance

People create their identities through social interaction, engaging, reproducing, and transforming historically enduring figurations of feeling. Livid coercive hearts often form at a relatively young age. Raised in familial atmospheres of feeling steeped in the tendency to abuse, humiliate, and punish, these hearts begin their long journeys toward adulthood. Indeed, the family trees of many livid coercive hearts reveal a consistent failure to incorporate modern ideals of nurturing parenting.

The livid coercive hearts vigorously pursued the modern ideal of intimacy with spouses or partners. A few excerpts illustrate the intensity of their aspirations regarding sexual intimacy and the potential emotional benefits of nuclear family life. These fleeting examples may rather superficially appear to reflect the vulnerabilities or dependencies of personality. If they do, it is only a small part of the truth. What we see, I contend, in their longing for intimacy, is the painful negotiation by these budding familicidal hearts of figurations of feeling that prescribe complex versions of masculinity and femininity.

As we sat in the guard's lunchroom, I saw a glint in Oscar Camacho's eyes as he described his first contacts with Carmella. She instantly enchanted him. He told me in the early days of their dating, "I saw her face transformed." Just as Oscar would later tell me his "very, very violent act of familicide" was a "spiritual experience," so, too, did he describe the transformation of Carmella's face as a "supernatural sign" that she was "for me." According to Oscar, the highly charged attraction "was mutual." When pressed to clarify these insights, Oscar told me, "I longed for a respectable life and she was the passport to that life."[16] Oscar's memories of this initial attraction remained strong in spite of the fact that he later realized "she was a prostitute who worked the cantinas."

We see instant enchantment in the Ronaldo familicide. A friend of Laurie Ronaldo's told investigators that Ben was "obsessed with Laurie from the beginning." Marcus Sims seems to have felt similarly about his wife, Gloria. From the beginning of their relationship, apparently from the time Gloria was 13 years old, she "made him whole." These sentiments persisted long after his act of familicide. Indeed, during the investigation, Marcus insisted that Gloria would always be in his heart. At the remarkably bloody crime scene, police found a poem Marcus wrote, or wrote in combination with a chat-room friend. Again, notice how Gloria renders him whole.

> I give you my heart
> Mind, Body, and Soul
> I give you my love
> *For you make me whole*
> I give you this promise
> The promise to try
> I give you each breath
> And the tears I cry
> I give you my past
> My future and now.[17]

We do not find similar expressions of bone-deep romantic love and infatuation from the female victims of these livid coercive hearts. This dearth of romantic sentiments may be an artifact of an investigative motif that concentrates on the mindset and motives of almost exclusively male perpetrators. It might also reflect a bias on the part of largely male investigators to ignore the active soul hunger of women.[18] However, this absence may also reflect a gendered difference in emotional style or expression. Where we find early emotional commitment among eventual female victims, it seems to take the form of a desire to constitute a family or to seek male approval. For example, on becoming pregnant at age 14, Bonnie Oxley would tell her mother, "We just had to be a family." Many of the livid coercive men appeared to feel that their entry point to the world of social connections, interdependencies, and pride depended on acquiring a wife or partner.

Livid Coercion, Sexual Jealousy, and Obsessive Attempts to Control

Obsessive attempts to control and regulate intimate partners and children soon appeared in the intimate relationships of the men with livid coercive hearts. Indeed, it appears obsession increased as the attempts to control their partners and children met with escalating, although not necessarily overt or explicit, emotional resistance. My reading of the archival materials is that intimate female partners resisted perpetrators' obsessive attempts to control them. When faced with livid coercion and extreme violence, women's resistance often became more muted and surreptitious. The evidence does not suggest that perpetrators controlled the wills of victims. One possibility is that at a very deep level of their psyches, victims continued to resist, regroup and further strategize. At times, victims' compliance may appear complete, but such conformity to perpetrator ultimatums signifies neither submission to nor acceptance of perpetrator demands. In only a relatively small percentage of cases did the women appear resigned to their fates.

At times, livid coercion appears to reflect a generalized state of rage emblematic of the emotional style of these unhappy, depressed, and resentful men. Indeed, chronic anger typified the lives of most of these men. In all seven cases, the expression of this anger was never far from the surface. The archive does not permit a comprehensive or sophisticated analysis of the outbreaks of this rage. Because the killings themselves constituted a form of domestic violence homicide, the archive dwells on a prior history of family violence and abuse rather than addressing what might be a much more extensive biography of rage in general.

Episodic references to perpetrator rage directed at non–family members are nevertheless useful since they provide a more general sense of what angered perpetrators. For example, numerous witnesses noted Ben Ronaldo would not only drive dangerously fast, he would display great aggression toward other drivers. Ben would invite other drivers who he perceived had disrespected him or treated him unjustly to fight. Two couples the Ronaldos went out with on separate occasions both complained of Ben's road rage. One couple refused to return home with Ben at the wheel, taking alternative transportation instead. Ben's road rage probably reflected a generalized anger toward life, his hurt pride and his rather fragile sense of personal identity and manhood. It therefore comes as no surprise that Laurie Ronaldo told police Ben would drive menacingly when he was angry with her for some perceived transgression. In all these examples we might note that Ben never appears to acknowledge being disrespected or being treated unjustly. Rather, Ben bypasses his sense of humiliation and shame, moving quickly to a livid emotional state or what elsewhere I call humiliated fury.

Perpetrators directed much of their raging venom at their intimate partners. However, other family members also experienced it from time to time. Kevin Oxley became increasingly angry as the prospect of his wife's leaving him loomed ever larger. We see evidence of Kevin's rage about losing his family in an incident at his mother-in-law's house just two months before the familicide. Bonnie Oxley suspected Kevin was having an affair. She told her mother, Georgina Lessing, "I have put up with so much from him and this is one thing I won't tolerate." Bonnie dropped her children off at Georgina's house, telling her she was going to confront Kevin with the information she had gained concerning his infidelity. Bonnie told her mother, "Whatever you do, don't let him take the kids." According to Georgina, Bonnie added, "Don't even let them play outside." Within ninety minutes, and much to Georgina's alarm, Kevin screeched to a halt outside her house. Georgina immediately locked the front and back doors to the house. Within seconds, Kevin appeared at the back door, shouting and screaming to be let in. When the door remained closed, he started to slam his body against it, cracking the door. Georgina shouted to one of her own daughters to call the police. Hearing his mother-in-law make this request did not deter Kevin. His rage at being cut off from his children was extreme. He picked up a golf club and smashed the two-foot square window in the top part of the back door. Kevin pulled himself up and through the broken window, cutting his arms in the process. His blood splashed all over the wall near the door. Georgina took her grandchildren into the living room and lay on top of them in an attempt to deny their father access to them. However, Kevin entered and threw Georgina off the children. He then seized his daughter, Joanne, and left the house with her. In the aftermath of the familicide, Georgina reported, "There was this look in his eyes, so cold, so evil. There was just this coldness about him—I don't think I'd ever felt that rage from someone before."

The seven livid coercive hearts appeared angry with their lot in life. Most of the men struggled in the worlds of work and social life. With the exception of Owen Mason, none seemed to see themselves as successful providers for their families. As we have seen, a number expressed anger at their maltreatment as children. Much of their rage was associated with their inability to form close social attachments with wives, lovers, and children. At times, it appears as if their anger masked their failures to form fulfilling intimate bonds. Much rage was directed at forcing intimacy. However, once perpetrators deployed violence, their intimate relationship began to change. Intimacy became increasingly strained, with female partners understandably becoming wary, hesitant and calculating. As we will see, some perpetrators felt unjustly treated by their partners, and their anger was one way of expressing their sense of injustice.

Marcus Sims illustrates the multiple ways that livid coercion manifests. Marcus's first wife, Janine, only escaped his clutches by moving to another state, a thousand miles away. After being married to Marcus for 11 years, Janine filed for divorce. Even after her divorce, Janine called police about him several times. Marcus continually stalked her and broke into her home. Once she woke up with Marcus standing over her bed. Things worsened when she began dating. Janine's date rode with her and her children in her truck a couple of times. Marcus called her and told her he did not want to see that again. Eventually, Janine moved to another state, taking her three children with her.

Marcus moved on to Gloria. Gloria was Janine's cousin. As a 13-year-old girl, Gloria began babysitting for Marcus and Janine's three children, Marcus Jr., Kevin, and Ember. At that time Marcus was 26 years old. Over the years Marcus eventually fell in love with Gloria, marrying her.

Just as he had done with Janine, Marcus used his livid coercion in a futile attempt to cling to Gloria. The possibility of losing Gloria was never far from his thoughts. Marcus's abuse of Gloria was ongoing, creating a chronic climate of fear. One of Gloria's close friends told police Gloria "was scared to death of Marcus." According to one of Gloria's friends, Marcus raped Gloria when Gloria was 16 years old. Gloria told this friend that Marcus's abusiveness came on quickly and remained as a constant in their relationship. Marcus refused to let Gloria obtain her driving license. He drove Gloria everywhere, including to the supermarket where she worked. One witness told police that Gloria told him Marcus had beaten her "for going somewhere that Marcus wasn't aware she was going." Another witness avoided Marcus "because Marcus always had to be in control of everything around him including his family."

Gloria left Marcus in July of the year of the familicide, finding alternative accommodation and taking Alex with her. After years of beatings and close surveillance, she had had enough. Gloria's departure from the family home in July followed fast on the heels of Marcus's assaulting her. Court documents reveal that he backhanded her a couple of times, cutting her lip and blackening her eye. The assault occurred in the family vehicle in the presence of their son, Alex. Marcus warned Gloria and Alex not to tell anyone about the assault. Chillingly, he specifically told Gloria that he had a "suitcase big enough to fit her body." Courageously, Gloria reported his assault. Police arrested Marcus, and he spent 14 days in jail. During this time, Gloria moved out with their son and went to live with relatives. She had moved out before, only to return.

Against the advice of friends, Gloria took Alex to Marcus's apartment a couple of days after Christmas. There he killed her and Alex. The crime scene displayed evidence of great rage. Blood had even splashed on the notes and poetry left there. It is not clear if Marcus planned the familicide or whether his violence was a disorganized and explosive reaction to finding out about Gloria's involvement with another man.

Marcus was particularly sensitive to Gloria's interactions with other men. Numerous witnesses described Marcus as extremely jealous. One of the men Gloria dated after leaving Marcus reported Gloria telling him that Marcus told her "if he ever saw her with another man he would kill her." Marcus's sexual jealousy continued unabated for the six-month period from July to December. During this time he was living alone. Although we will never know for sure, Marcus's jealous humiliation and rage seem to have provided the emotional energy behind the familicide.

In the six months they lived apart, Gloria dated several different men. Marcus suspected she was doing this but did not know for sure. Using call data from various cell phone accounts, police traced Gloria's final hours. Investigators interviewed Fred Scholes, a man Gloria was dating in December. Fred said that at the time he was dating Gloria he thought Marcus was still in jail. Fred called Gloria just after Christmas. He told police "she was very evasive and told him she could not talk and would call him back." According to the police report, she abruptly hung up the phone on him. Fred described her behavior as "very unusual." From the timing of the call, it is likely that Fred called Gloria during the time she had taken Alex to see his father. Investigators theorized that she took the call from Fred Scholes when she was in Marcus's presence and that Marcus surmised she was talking to another man. Investigators believed Marcus's jealousy probably triggered the familicide, which most likely occurred on December 28.

Earlier emails from his chat-room activities show he suspected she was seeing another man. One email in particular, dated December 7, refers to him having a conversation with a man who works in the same supermarket as Gloria. Marcus informed the chat-room group that it turned out Gloria "was nothing but a ho." The man himself supposedly referred to Gloria as a "slut." The email continued to opine about Gloria's lasciviousness. "Come to find out the #$#$% %*() was written up for being caught in the back with other guys. HOW FUCKING DUMB."

Here Marcus engages in what Freud once called reaction formation. He attempts to diminish Gloria's status and honor, thus making her appear less deserving of his affections. At the same time he renders his own rage understandable and explicable without revealing the wellspring of his shame as a deserted husband, as a man who failed at marriage and family a second time, and, most importantly, as a man whose own livid coercive behavior drove his wife elsewhere.

What is clear is that police found poetry and letters at the crime scene that had been crafted, if not written, some time before. As noted, Marcus declined my request for an interview. Without interviewing him, it is not possible to get any further sense of whether he intended to leave the poetry at the scene as an expression of his despair. The poetry itself provides a window into his familicidal heart and is worth quoting in detail in original form. The first poem is titled "The Love of My Life."

> Here I sit and ponder
> As to why the streets I do wander
> *Alone and empty inside my heart*
> It does ache many nights I have cried
> She was mine for seven years

On her face she showed no tears
Our son she has taken away
Only in my heart do I have him today
She took me to court stripping me of our things
Our house, our son, our wedding rings
They did not care how I treated her right
They would not listen to my plight
They took it all and still want more
They shut me out and locked the door
Alone and hungry on the streets I did roam
No wife, no life, no family, no home
How did this happen? Where did I go wrong?
My love for them both has always been strong.
Inside my heart breaks as I wonder why
Did she leave me for some other guy?[19]

In spite of Marcus's bravado regarding what he perceived as Gloria's taw-
dry sexual behavior, his sexual humiliation is palpable. Further on in the
poem Marcus talks of his need to reclaim his pride. Here the chat room
provides an anonymous vehicle for Marcus to articulate his inner aching
and his need for pride.

I need to stop this aching inside
And hold my head up with pride.

Marcus's sexual jealousy was a central feature of this familicide. Only 41 of
the 77 cases evidencing some degree of livid coercion contained sufficient
information to allow us to assess the presence of sexual jealousy. Twenty-
three of the 41 cases (56 percent) had enough information to enable us to
conclude sexual jealousy played a central role in the killings.

Recognizing that it is probably impossible to draw a line between
morbid and normal jealousy, Mowat suggests that morbid jealousy
involves "delusions of infidelity."[20] Early psychiatric research by Kraepelin
described morbid jealousy as a form of paranoia. Kraepelin illustrates this
state of emotional anguish with the example of the man who accuses his
wife of infidelity and of bearing children sired by another man. As far as I
know, only one of the seven livid hearts accused his wife of having a child
by another man. In the days before the familicide, Ben Ronaldo accused
his wife, Laurie, of having an affair. Ben contended the child Laurie was
carrying was not his. In the aftermath of the familicide, paternity testing
proved Ben was the father.

In other respects, Ben Ronaldo's jealousy resembled that displayed by
Marcus Sims and Kevin Oxley. All three men appeared threatened by their
wives' associations with men at work. Laurie Ronaldo had a good job at
a computer corporation. Laurie told her father Ben was paranoid because
she spent so much time at work. Ben thought she was "fooling around"
at work. In a related vein, Laurie said Ben was deeply threatened by her

traveling for work and meeting lots of different people. At one point, Laurie told her father that Ben had inspected her vagina and found it to be "different." At this point he was convinced she was having an affair. About 15 months before the killing, Laurie returned to her home state for a high school reunion. She told Ben she was just visiting a friend. When interviewed by police, the friend reported Ben called Laurie every ten minutes to find out where she was and with whom.

Witnesses reported that Kevin Oxley was extremely possessive of Bonnie from the very beginning of their relationship. At first, he did not want her to attend college and would follow her to class to make sure she was not meeting other men. Indeed, Kevin did not want Bonnie to go places where she would meet other men. Kevin also explicitly told Bonnie's two older sisters that if Bonnie ever tried to leave him he would kill her. Indeed, in her affidavit in request of a temporary restraining order, Bonnie wrote that Kevin had threatened to suck the venom out of a rattlesnake and inject her with it. Ironically, it was Bonnie who was sure Kevin was having an affair. She met with Kevin's lover, Ruby Johnson, and tape-recorded a conversation with her. Ruby admitted the affair but said Kevin tried to control her and she wanted nothing else to do with him. Bonnie confronted Kevin with the tape recording and recorded his reaction to it. Bonnie's sister, Regina, heard both tape recordings. Kevin's allegations regarding Bonnie's potential for infidelity serve as a good example of Freud's point that sometimes men's jealous accusations constitute little more than projections onto their partners of their own promiscuous desires.

Oscar Camacho told me that he was not jealous or possessive of Carmella. However, investigators uncovered a very different picture. One friend of Carmella's, Mary Coleman, reported, "He was very jealous and didn't like anyone visiting with Carmella or the girls." Mary told police that Carmella's daughters, Maria and Juanita, had expressed "much contempt" for Oscar and "did not want to move back in with him." In addition, Mary suspected that Oscar "had done something bad" to Carmella's daughters. As we will see, Oscar Camacho displayed sexual jealousy in relation to several love objects, not just his intimate partner.

The information in the Sims, Langdon, and Hester cases reveals livid coercion and obsessive attempts to control children. Marcus Sims sought to control his children very closely. The three children he sired with his first wife, Janine, recoiled from him emotionally as he parented them in an authoritarian and sadistic manner. Detectives quizzed Marcus's son, Marcus Jr., about the discipline in their home. He reported his father "gave them whippings." Marcus Jr. added, "It was like being in prison in my own home. We were locked in our room." Their father's surveillance was extremely detailed. Marcus insisted on the brothers' sitting "Indian style" in their locked room, with their hands near their knees on the floor. In this way the boys made hand impressions in the carpet. Marcus would enter unexpectedly and inspect the impressions to see if the boys had moved from their designated spots. When investigators asked what the consequence was for moving from the spot, Marcus Jr. said, "He took a 2 x 4 to the bottoms of our feet." When asked if their father fed them, Marcus Jr. reported that his mother would feed them when she returned from work. However, even their mother's feeding them sometimes led to their seeing their father abuse their mother for paying too much attention to the children. Marcus Jr. recalled that on one occasion his father burned his mother with a hot iron for feeding the boys.

Bill Langdon and Marge Clanton lived in a run-down manufactured home in a village a few miles from a thriving tourist town. Marge's daughter Peggy lived with them. The three had lived as a family for almost five years. Marge's mother, Katrina Spencer, lived a hundred miles away. Katrina was in the process of selling her home in order to move to the East Coast with her daughter and granddaughter. Katrina Spencer knew Bill posed a major threat to her daughter and granddaughter. In the months prior to the familicide, Bill's violent abuse of both Marge and Peggy escalated. In particular, it seems Bill obsessively sought to regulate the affairs of Peggy, using violence in the process. He was arrested twice for assaults on Peggy. Bill had a history of using violence to coerce children. The police report notes interviews with Bill's two sons from his first marriage. The reporting officer comments, "Both sons told me that their father was very mean when he was drunk and he used to beat them when they were kids."

Malcolm Hester was also an authoritarian parent. In particular, he disciplined his stepchildren very strictly, making them do a lot of housework. A neighbor told investigators that if Malcolm found "a speck of dirt, he would ground them." Another witness reported Malcolm would force his stepchildren "to eat all the food on their plate whether they wanted to or not."

His wife's mother told investigators that her daughter, Shirley Hester, and Malcolm had problems from the earliest days of their marriage. Malcolm beat Shirley's son, Guy, from time to time, leaving marks on him. Malcolm also developed a sexual interest in Shirley's daughter, 15-year-old Meredith Malloy. Indeed, Meredith told one of her mother's friends she did not like "some of the looks he had given her." In addition, Malcolm was in the habit of walking in when Meredith was changing or taking a bath.

Oscar Camacho had a sexual relationship of sorts with Carmella's two daughters from a previous partner. Oscar told investigators that pornography played a major role in his life with Carmella. He said it led to his molesting Maria and Juanita. When the family lived in Mexico, he said, he had sex with Carmella in the presence of the children. They watched pornography as a family. Oscar said that Carmella "appeared to accept his fondling of the girls, as long as he didn't have sex with them." Specifically, he told police that Carmella wanted him to "save the milk" (semen) for her. I did not speak with Oscar about these matters, and I can only speculate about what they might mean. Was his statement about Carmella's wanting him to save the semen for her a means of preventing him from raping her daughters? A mere projection on his part? A pack of lies? The possibilities are many.

Men are much more likely than women to use violence to protect their love interests or exact revenge for the loss of such interests. Men's deployment of vengeful violence to protect a love interest is much more likely to intimidate and strike fear and terror into the hearts of women than is any comparably motivated violence that women might use. The familicide perpetrated by the livid heart of Misook Beckenbauer helps illustrate this point about the gender differences in being able to strike fear in the hearts of victims of violence.

Misook Beckenbauer shot her husband and two daughters to death before killing herself. Unusual though it is in cases of intimate partner homicide for the female partner to be the only one to use violence, the Beckenbauer case appears to be such an anomaly.[21] Donna Bowness, a deputy district attorney, told me Misook "*was like a batterer.* She engaged in psychological abuse and was very controlling."[22] Others involved in the case reached the same conclusions about Misook. The Beckenbauer case is the sole female-perpetrated familicide I studied where the woman was the only partner using intimate violence.

Misook resided in an upper class neighborhood with her husband of comparable age, Gerd, their biological daughter, Jenny, age five, and Misook's daughter from her first marriage, Emily, age 12. Misook was originally from Southeast Asia, Gerd from Germany. Misook shot and killed her two daughters and her husband at what had been the family home. Police discovered the bodies several days later. Investigators inferred she shot her older daughter first. Misook then shot Jenny as she lay sleeping in Misook's bed. When Gerd arrived at the house in the early evening, she shot him six times, killing him. Detectives noted Misook had to reload her .38 caliber handgun during the shooting spree.[23] She then lay down beside Jenny and shot herself in the chest.

Police found love letters from the Beckenbauers' courting days on the chair next to the bed where Misook and Jenny's corpses lay. Donna Bowness told me these love letters indicated Misook was "very controlling" from the earliest days of the Beckenbauers' relationship. Police interviewed one of the Beckenbauers' friends, Penny Wilson. She said the couple had experienced marital difficulties for at least three years. Penny reported that Misook often complained that Gerd, a successful engineer in the field of information technology, worked too hard. Misook also told Penny that she and Gerd argued "all the time."

Gerd's heavy work schedule emerges as a key issue in the Beckenbauers' relationship. Pastor Jessie Hannon, from a local church, offered insights into Misook's predicament. In one conversation with Pastor Hannon, Misook shared that she had left her first husband to be with Gerd. When she and Gerd came to the United States in the mid-1990s, Misook "was always left alone and did not speak much English." Apparently, in those early days, Misook had no friends. Pastor Hannon told police Misook described Gerd as a workaholic who was not around very often. Hannon described Misook to police as a woman "having nothing and being very miserable with the lifestyle." It is impossible to discern the impact of her degree of social, cultural and linguistic isolation, but this probably placed her in an unusually remote psychic place. As a consequence, her emotional style often sizzled with anger, much of it apparently directed at the central relationship in her life, that with her husband.

As the investigation into the Beckenbauer familicide continued, more information emerged about Misook's obsessive behavior toward Gerd. At Gerd's apartment, detectives found 24 voicemail messages from Misook recorded in the hours before the killings. The Beckenbauers' friends Ben and Charlene Murray told investigators Misook was "obsessive and controlling of Gerd." Charlene Murray reported that when the Beckenbauers argued Misook "would hit Gerd on the chest with her fists *out of frustration*."[24] Indeed, Misook attended an anger-management class to try to get her temper under control. According to the Murrays, several months before the familicide Gerd moved out precisely because Misook was both hot-tempered and controlling.

Like other friends, Charlene told police that around the time Gerd moved out, Misook told her, "I don't want to live without him." Investigators learned Gerd told Penny Wilson that upon hearing of his intention to move out, Misook grabbed a knife and tried to cut herself. However, Penny told police, unlike many obsessively jealous male perpetrators, Misook talked about the pending separation as if she was to blame. Specifically, Misook lamented she was a "bad wife" who "demanded too much of Gerd." On more than one occasion she told Penny Wilson that if Gerd left her she would die. Nowhere in the 76 familicides committed by men with prior histories of domestic violence against their eventual victims do we find men saying they are to blame for the separation, that they are bad husbands or intimate partners, or that they demanded too much of their wives or partners. Misook's reflexivity in this regard is emblematic of women's greater awareness and expressiveness; a source, as I have argued, of potential power in their relationships with men.

Jeff Jackson was Gerd's boss. It was Jeff who became suspicious after Gerd did not show up for work for three days. Having known the Beckenbauers for six years, he went to their family home and found the bodies. Jeff knew the Beckenbauers had marital problems. He told police Gerd had shared with him that Misook had had a "tough childhood and was suffering from depression." Gerd also told Jeff that Misook would "explode with emotion." Apparently, Gerd disclosed to Jeff that Misook suffered from "low self-esteem."

Jeff informed investigators that a woman by the name of Phoebe Mindham contacted him looking for Gerd. Phoebe telephoned Gerd's workplace the day after the familicide, two days before authorities found the corpses. It turned out that Phoebe met Gerd in an Internet chat room just two months before the familicide. They eventually started talking on the phone. A month before the familicide, Gerd was on a business trip in the region where Phoebe lived, and the two met. They spent the best part of two days together. Phoebe's husband did not know of their meeting. After Gerd returned home, the two continued to communicate and their relationship intensified. Phoebe told police she knew that Gerd was separated from Misook. She added that Gerd told her Misook was "physically and emotionally violent toward him" and that Misook "hit and kicked him on many occasions."

On the Friday before the familicide, Gerd picked Phoebe up at the airport in his hometown. Phoebe spent the weekend with Gerd inside his apartment. Apparently, no one else knew that Phoebe was there. Gerd and Misook's biological child, Jenny Beckenbauer, spent that weekend with her mother and half-sister. According to Phoebe, Misook called Gerd's apartment "continuously" or "had one of the girls call." On one of these calls, Phoebe heard Gerd tell his stepdaughter, Emily, she should not have told her mother something he had told Emily in confidence. Phoebe asked Gerd about this breach of confidence. Gerd shared that he had told Emily that he had no intention of getting back together with Misook. Emily apparently told her mother, who reacted badly. It is likely that learning of the permanence of their breakup was the principal reason Misook called Gerd's apartment so much that weekend. However, we cannot discount the possibility that, at a deep emotional level, she sensed the haunting presence of another woman in Gerd's life, a change, if you will, in the emotional atmosphere between herself and her husband.

Misook did not stop at telephoning Gerd continuously. On Sunday night, she went over to Gerd's apartment. According to Phoebe, Misook rang the doorbell "numerous times." Phoebe and Gerd remained quiet inside the apartment until Misook left. The next day Phoebe returned home to her husband. Gerd took the day off from work to prepare his taxes.

At 5.00 P.M. on Monday, Gerd and Misook attended a counseling appointment. Phoebe talked with Gerd after the session. She informed the police that during counseling Gerd told Misook "that the chances for reconciliation were slim to none." Apparently enraged and screaming, Misook stormed out of the session. Phoebe and Gerd talked once more that evening, around 8.00 P.M. Gerd had just left a wireless telephone store. There he purchased two cell phones, one for himself, one for Phoebe. According to her, the new lovers wanted to "keep in constant contact." Gerd informed Phoebe that he was then going over to pick Jenny up from Misook's house. They arranged another phone conversation around 9.00 P.M. However, the two never spoke again. It appears Gerd was shot soon after arriving at Misook's house. The autopsy revealed he died of massive internal bleeding caused by four shots to the chest. By the time he arrived at Misook's house, his wife had already murdered Jenny and Emily. Having disposed of her husband, she then shot herself.

As noted, Donna Bowness, a skilled prosecutor of domestic violence cases, pointed out that Misook was "like a batterer." This comment was telling. She was not calling Misook a batterer. Neither was she saying that women could not be batterers in the same way as men. Clearly, Misook's behavior toward Gerd exhibits a number of the traits we see in men who beat their partners.

First, she used violence from time to time. As noted, her violence may have constituted misdemeanor assault. She slapped, kicked, and beat him on his chest with her fists. Had Gerd called the police, they might have arrested her under the domestic violence statutes.[25] Witnesses attested to her beating on his chest "out of frustration." It is not clear if Misook was frustrated with Gerd, herself, or both. Gerd seems to have interpreted Misook's violence as stemming from her low self-esteem. He did not like her violent outbursts, but Gerd does not appear to have cowered in the face of them.[26] Misook's violence does not appear to have seriously attacked Gerd's personhood and autonomy. As we have seen, Gerd was a well-respected, successful, and wealthy engineer of European descent. For the duration of their marriage, Misook was a homemaker. She was born and raised in Southeast Asia and not well integrated into American life. Her family life was her chief source of pride and, ultimately, her highly destructive shame. Just prior to the murders she had begun working as a waitress. In other words, their social standings differed significantly, with Gerd in the ascendant position.

Second, a number of witnesses described Misook as very controlling of Gerd. She was terrified of his abandoning her and stated to a number of people she could not live without him. In this sense, her behavior resembles that of male batterers. Such men are often vulnerable and highly dependent on the women they abuse. Her depression and self-destructive impulses upon finding out he was leaving comport with her frantic vulnerability. On a number of occasions she accused him of having affairs, although the archival files provide no evidence of Gerd's having an affair prior to his meeting Phoebe.

On the weekend before the familicide, her numerous telephone calls to Gerd, her visit to his apartment, and the 24 voicemail messages all evince a high level of obsession. Put simply, her obsessive, controlling, and at the same time highly dependent behavior resonate strongly with that of male batterers.

Misook sought control over Gerd, but Gerd's success and social standing rendered these attempts futile. Indeed, we might even say that his advantages further humiliated Misook, reminding her of her vulnerability and her limited engagement in the social world beyond her family. He came and went as he pleased. He lived separately from her. Gerd enjoyed a sizeable income and lived in his own apartment. He saw his girlfriend there. He had free access to his children during the separation. Misook was not in a position to regulate his schedule or monitor and scrutinize his daily activities. Misook was not able to isolate Gerd or entrap him to any significant degree. In fact, it was not in her material interests to do so, since Gerd was the principal breadwinner. As we have seen, Misook had to take a job waiting tables in order to begin to make money for herself. Her economic clout was inconsequential compared to his, particularly in light of the fact that the Beckenbauers lived in a very wealthy community. Livid with rage as she may have been, it seems a stretch of the evidence to equate Misook Beckenbauer's familicidal heart with those of the men discussed in this chapter. I do not say this because I do not think females are emotionally capable of reaching such a remote and destructive style. I think they are. Rather, my reticence stems from the nature of her violence and its seeming effects in the case.

My concerns on these matters remind us that violence and attempts to control others must be interpreted in terms of their context and the social meaning of such actions and behaviors. Part of such an interpretation must include the fact that, as a general rule in modern times, men's individuality and sense of otherness and autonomy is more accented than women's. I return to these important matters of context and meaning in Chapter 6 when I draw upon the influential psychoanalytic feminism of Nancy Chodorow and her critics. Suffice it to say at this juncture that when we assess attacks on personhood it is important not to essentialize the notion of personhood. Rather, we must appreciate personhood as a sociohistorical construct that varies, for example, by race/ethnicity, class, gender and sexuality.

Gerd's advantages enabled him to negotiate Misook's violence and attempts at control. Nevertheless, in the end she murdered him, regardless of his privileges as a successful engineer in an industry whose time had come or as a member of a dominant group, men of European ancestry. The archive contains minimal information on Gerd's life and upbringing, and I do not want to reduce his complex personhood to some form of undifferentiated male privilege. By all accounts Gerd was a workaholic, a driven man. He probably had his demons, and we miss his complexity if we only see him in terms of his privilege or as a victim of an occasionally violent and oftentimes controlling woman. As Avery Gordon reminds us, "even those who haunt our dominant institutions and their systems of value are haunted too by things they sometimes have names for and sometimes do not."[27]

The anti-domestic violence movement still grapples with the issue of women as perpetrators of intimate partner violence, the contexts within which this occurs, and what it might mean. I will return briefly to these discussions in Chapter 7. Suffice it to say at this point that Evan Stark's linking of coercive control to the power relations of gender does not mean he is saying women are incapable of using coercive control. Michael Johnson, using different terminology from Stark, emphasizes, "It is clear that there are women intimate terrorists in heterosexual and same-sex relationships."[28] Importantly, Johnson acknowledges, "it is not clear that all intimate terrorism, even men's, is rooted in patriarchal ideas or structures."[29] Indeed, some survey research points to hitherto unrecognized levels of men's fear in intimate relationships. It is worth considering this research in the light of the Beckenbauer familicide.

Drawing upon random population surveys rather than more specialized shelter, clinical, and agency samples, a growing number of researchers emphasize that male and female intimate partners deploy similar levels of violence in their relationships. Much of this violence is routine, sporadic, and not linked to broader campaigns of coercion, domination, and terror. Michael Johnson calls this "situational couple violence"; violence that is circumscribed and deployed to express resentment, to resolve a dispute, or to dissipate stress. These spouses and partners do not use such violence to isolate or erode their partner's sense of personhood. Neither is such violence used as part of an ongoing campaign to intimidate or strictly regulate the partner. Rather, Johnson locates the roots of such violence in "the situated escalation of conflict."[30] As Evan Stark comments, "However uncomfortable this may make feminist-oriented researchers, it is incontrovertible that large numbers of women use force in relationships, including the types of force classified as severe or abusive."[31]

Weighing the evidence from the files in the Beckenbauer case, it appears to me that Misook's violence was closer to situational couple violence than intimate terrorism. It is true that men are probably much less likely to share their fears of female-perpetrated intimate-partner violence than are women of male-perpetrated intimate-partner violence. This is one of the major reasons for my hesitancy with the Beckenbauer case. Nevertheless, I feel more confident the violence used by the seven male livid coercive hearts constituted intimate terrorism and not just situational couple violence.

Using data from the General Social Survey (GSS) on victimization and spousal violence conducted by Statistics Canada in 1999, Denis Laroche compares men's and women's experience of minor and severe violence within the contexts of Michael Johnson's notions of situational couple violence and intimate terrorism.[32] Regarding severe violence in settings of intimate terrorism involving current or previous partners, Laroche observes, "The prevalence rate (per 1,000) of victims having suffered physical or clinical consequences in intimate terrorism with severe violence was significantly higher in women compared to men. This was the case for victims who suffered injuries (19 for women vs. 5 for men), received hospital care or medical attention or follow-up from a doctor or nurse (8 vs. 1), notified the police (16 vs. 6), received help from a crisis centre or shelter (7 vs. 1), or feared for their lives (19 vs. 4)."[33]

With regard to previous partners only, Laroche observes, "The prevalence rates (per 1,000) of physical and clinical consequences among victims of a previous spouse/partner were significantly higher in women compared to men. This was the case for victims who suffered injuries (41 vs. 15), received hospital care or medical attention from a doctor or nurse (16 vs. 4), notified the police (33 vs. 18), received help from a crisis centre or shelter (14 vs. 2), or feared for their lives (39 vs. 10)."[34]

Another way of considering these rates is through the raw numbers. Laroche examines victim reports of "fearing for their lives" in the five years preceding the survey. It is not clear if respondents reporting such fears are reporting transient fear of lethal violence in association with a particular incident of domestic violence or whether they are reporting an ongoing fear. Notwithstanding these problematic issues, Laroche notes 41,000 episodes of men and 258,700 episodes of women reporting fearing for their lives as a consequence of domestic violence by a current or previous spouse or partner, and 34,000 episodes of men and 207,800 episodes of women reporting the same from previous partners only.[35] These numbers reveal at least a six-fold sex difference in reports of fear of lethal violence between women and men (6.3 more reports for women regarding current or previous spouses/partners; 6.1 for previous spouses/partners only). This particular data snapshot from the GSS comports with Laroche's much broader observation that "women who were victims of severe violence were more likely than men to report devastating psychological effects that ensue from physical abuse."[36]

If men reporting fearing for their lives are reporting a fleeting fear in connection with a violent episode(s), then this is very different from men reporting ongoing fear as part of an experience of intimidation, entrapment, and attacks on their personhood. The Beckenbauer archive does not permit us to make a clear determination of Gerd Beckenbauer's fear. We might speculate Gerd was afraid at the time Misook produced the knife, even though she said she intended to cut herself, not him. It is also possible to argue that any fear he had was transient and offset by his advantageous social position *vis-à-vis* Misook and his greater resources. Another possibility is that Gerd, like men in general, underestimated women's potential for violence. He knew she could hit and threaten to harm herself, but perhaps because she was a woman he mistakenly thought her incapable of murder. His gendered view of his wife may have prevented him from fearing for his life in the way that female victims tend to.[37] Clearly, Misook's status as a full-blown livid coercive heart does not depend upon Gerd's actually feeling coerced by her hostile overtures. It is probably safe to say that at times Misook's angry outbursts sought to change Gerd's behavior; for example, influence him to spend more time at home.

The information in the cases of the livid coercive hearts of Malcolm Hester, Bill Langdon, and Owen Mason showed no signs of sexual jealousy. Rather, the livid coercion of these men was linked to concerns about the breakup of the family unit, threats to their pride as providers or heads of household, and a range of perceived injustices or things they felt entitled to but did not receive from their intimate partners. Two of these three men, Malcolm Hester and Bill Langdon, faced debilitating medical conditions; the other, Owen Mason, wrestled with major depression and despair for which he was seeing a physician and a psychiatrist.

Shirley's Hester's twin sister, Amy Ferdinand, described Malcolm Hester as "very domineering" in his relationship with Shirley. Investigator interviews with Amy in the aftermath of the familicide revealed that Malcolm "liked to get Shirley crying and he would then laugh at her." According to Amy, Shirley developed a nervous twitch because of Malcolm's threats and intimidation. Shirley confided to her twin sister that Malcolm "liked to hurt her mentally." Another witness told investigators that Malcolm threatened to "tie Shirley and the kids up and burn down the house with them in it." Apparently, Malcolm carried a hunting knife and kept guns and knives hidden all around their house. Shirley told Amy she "was afraid to go to sleep at night." In short, Shirley lived in a state of what seems to have been something approaching perpetual fear. Family friends told police that during her last pregnancy, Shirley came over to their house to use the phone because she was spotting blood. Shirley nervously told the friends that Malcolm had pushed her up against the wall. During this episode, Shirley reported fearing physical violence because Malcolm "had a violent temper." Shirley Hester's pastor would later tell police that Shirley confided in him that Malcolm would "try to drive her crazy by displaying various weapons, mostly a knife, in front of her." In this older case dating to the early 1980s, a few people close to Shirley knew of Malcolm's sadism.

The point is not that these people as individuals proved unable to do anything to prevent the Hester killings or any of the other familicides discussed in this chapter. Rather, these cases illustrate just how insulated nuclear families had become and how the permeability between family and community had sharply declined in the two hundred or so years modernity unfolded. In some ways, this permeability seems to be changing, not because of an urgent desire to rediscover community, but rather because of the increasing breakdown and reconstitution of nuclear families and the increasing supports provided to women like Shirley Hester.

PYRRHIC VICTORIES

We have seen how the early socialization of the livid coercive hearts was riddled with emotional uncertainty, disruption, and trauma. As they entered adulthood, many of these men craved intimacy, falling hook, line, and sinker for their love objects. Establishing the harmonious familial unit they never experienced as children assumed great importance. The nuclear family provided a vehicle for legitimately incorporating themselves into various social networks; in short, the nuclear family offered a means of belonging. The developing familicidal hearts often entered these relationships with alacrity, at the same time guarding lovers nervously, like a hungry predator protects its food. A wife or partner and a family provided a source of pride, something often in short supply for these hearts growing up.

With two hundred years or more of history behind it, the modern nuclear family ideal offered a sense of home, security, love, affection, and links to the community—in short a means of entering into increasingly lengthening chains of human interdependencies. The livid coercive hearts, especially the younger ones, were particularly vulnerable to the lure of companionate relationships, childrearing, and the emotional potential and opportunities they held. In their renewed scramble for a sense of intimacy long denied, subverted, frustrated, disrupted, or simply stolen, the fragile emotional styles of these familicidal hearts ill-prepared them for the give and take of marriage and intimacy and the challenges as well as the pleasures of childrearing. In many cases, the inevitable disappointments with the family idyll feverishly dovetailed with and compounded the disappointments and injurious memories of their own childhood, opening old wounds in a way they had perhaps never been opened before.

As these men entered marriage, had children, and set up households, they faced numerous challenges. They had much to gain, and, as it might have seemed to them, little to lose. But the reality was different. Once established, their emotional fragility made it very difficult to sustain intimate relationships with partners and children. Once the honeymoon ended, some men briefly pined for the familial idyll that failed to materialize. Soon, as we have seen, they moved to force the hearts of their loved ones toward them, even if social and familial forces pulled those hearts in different directions. As they forced, their loved ones resisted. This resistance took various forms: some covert, subliminal and subtle; others overt, blatant and bold. Outward compliance with men's manipulations, threats, and tyrannies came at an enormous price to women, children, and the men themselves. In the end, the families paid the ultimate price for what I will describe as men's Pyrrhic victories. By "Pyrrhic victory," I refer to men's hollow, precarious, and fleeting sense of ascendancy created through force, intimidation, and instilling a deep fear in loved ones.[38] It is undeniable that batterers benefited from their ascendancy, receiving various services, labor, and privileges.[39] However, I contend these various material benefits are not the primary reason the livid coercive hearts exploit women and seek to control them. Rather, it is the intimacy and promise of belonging batterers crave. At every turn, men's interpersonal domination slowly and paradoxically corrodes the love, affection, and romance that the livid coercive hearts initially tasted or thought they experienced and that they longed to retain. These Pyrrhic victories ultimately proved ruinous. Any outward compliance on the women's part belied the beginnings of their moving away from their partners emotionally. Such emotional estrangement, as we will see, involved much more than mere physical separation or the specter of divorce and usually happened well before these more formal moves. With the haunting ebb and flow of tense emotions, the men sensed the women's emotional estrangement, just as the women read the men's emotional demeanor and mood.

The livid coercive hearts, like everyone else, engaged in what Erving Goffman once called *impression management* in an attempt to save face.[40] Inevitably, men began to see the failing familial idyll as, to employ Sybil Shell's mid-1950s language, "a ship going down at sea." The livid coercive hearts fought this sinking feeling. Depression often prevailed, accompanied by a growing panic about the demise of the family unit. It is during the panic of loss that we witness men's vulnerability and dependence in full-blown form. These men emerge from the archive as neither powerful over nor in control of their lives. The archive requires us to dispense with the commonly asked question, "Why does she stay?" replacing it with another query, "Why does he pine and cling to the point of death?"[41] As argued earlier, victims of intimate-partner violence don't just "stay," and their maneuverability, resistance, and agency challenge the belief that battered women are subject to men's power and control until death do them part. These observations remind us power is contested and contingent, involving a balance of forces.

It is the livid coercive familicidal hearts, as opposed to their victims, that are closer to what Dennis Wrong once described as the "over-socialized conception of man."[42] But people, men and women alike, are not the hapless recipients of historical and cultural forces, or indeed interpersonal pressures. As I will demonstrate, even up to and including the act of familicide, these men made choices, as did these women. A number of men engaged in significant planning and preparation before committing familicide. These activities proved enervating, depleting the men, draining them of emotion and any vitality that remained. It is not therefore surprising that Oscar Camacho, now serving life imprisonment without the possibility of parole, locked his fingers in the shape of a church steeple, met my eyes and then looked down and talked candidly of his enormous sense of relief at having killed. His deeply disturbing comments, reported below, comport with other findings from the research. Oscar's words, spoken behind the razor wire and guard towers of his maximum-security prison, allude to his release from a uniquely modern form of confinement, one that held forth what turned out to be for him the unrealistic promise of familial intimacy and enchantment he never knew but often craved. As we will see in Chapter 6, Oscar's implicit commentary on experiencing psychic relief through his act of familicide may reflect his release from the pressures of modern masculinities.

IMPRESSION MANAGEMENT AND BLUSTER

The archive provides a number of examples of how livid coercive hearts actively attempted to manage their public image. Often, they confined their cruel glances, slaps, shoves, punches, and viciousness to their own households.[43] Many men appeared different in public or at least tempered their venom. The livid coercive hearts navigated their hostilities as best they could, choosing certain strategies over others, wherever possible sanitizing their intimate relationships for public consumption. However, given the extent of their interpersonal desperation and rage, it was difficult and often impossible to create the impression that violence, strife, and discord did not characterize their intimate relationships. Those closer to the victims knew the truth, or at least some of it.

Marcus Sims was distraught after his first family left him and moved out of state to escape his terror and threats. When he lost his second wife, Gloria, and their son, Alex, Marcus was similarly if not more devastated. Numerous witnesses told investigators how Marcus had threatened to kill Gloria if she dated other men. His first wife reported similar behavior. Understandably, very little of Marcus's panic about losing Gloria emerges from his conversations with people somewhat removed from his everyday life. As noted, police found blood-spattered letters and poetry close to the corpses. Most of the written material remained legible. Much of it appears to express Marcus's views on the familicide and is written in his handwriting. The writing provides a curious window into Marcus's familicidal heart. However, in going through Marcus's computer and emails, investigators discovered he owned a Web TV business that included a chat room. The co-host of that chat room, Amanda, resided in a West Coast state. Amanda had corresponded with Marcus about his feelings concerning his separation from Gloria. In keeping with the clever impression management of many batterers, Marcus communicated a picture of a family drifting apart and a wife who was losing interest in her husband.

Through analyzing phone bills, investigators soon learned Marcus and Amanda talked at great length on the phone. Indeed, Marcus even knew where Amanda lived. Police informed Amanda of their suspicion that Marcus had killed his wife and son. She was shocked and expressed concern that Marcus might harm her. Amanda turned over the electronic communications and provided a brief explanation for each email. It turned out that *Amanda* had penned the poetry found at the crime scene. In regard to this poetry, Amanda told police they spent "hours on the phone" talking through Marcus's feelings. She had no idea the poems would end up beside Gloria's corpse. It was almost as if Marcus needed a woman like Amanda, a pseudo-anonymous woman at that, to act as a conduit to the inner world of feelings.

One email, posted in the chat room by Marcus, dated December 26, just two days before the familicide, is titled, "My Christmas Wish Came True." The opening line tells readers, "Yesterday was wonderful, my wife an son came 2 c me on xmas. 2 c and hold them again was the best. She told me that we're going 2 get back 2 gether but we need 2 take baby steps in doing so. This is so we can get 2 know each other all over again. I would do n e thing in the world 4 my wife an son. I need them to breathe. They make me whole."

Gloria and Alex did not visit Marcus on Christmas day. Neither did Gloria tell Marcus the family would reunite. Perhaps what we see in the December 26 email is chat-room impression-management, an attempt to salvage some pride in the midst of an audience of anonymous others. If this was the case, Marcus's strategy was indicative of his humiliation at the loss of his family. Another possibility is that the email reflects Marcus's fantasies about possible reunification. Whatever he was thinking, it is possible Marcus had convinced himself he would reunite with his wife and son.

Bill Langdon had served time for domestic violence offences, drunken driving, and selling drugs in a school zone. He worked sporadically and lived in a run-down trailer park with his partner, Marge Clanton, and her deeply troubled, semiliterate, bipolar daughter, Peggy. Bill's body was deteriorating. He had high blood pressure, excessive cholesterol, and was an angry alcoholic. Yet Bill still engaged in brief bouts of bluster. Prior to committing familicide, Bill gave his sons from a previous marriage and a neighbor the impression he was about to enjoy a getaway vacation in Hawaii. Apparently Bill told these witnesses that Marge's mother, Katrina Spencer, was going to provide the funds for his trip. Bill also led his sons to believe that he had not been consuming alcohol "for some time." The sons told investigators that although they had not seen their father in the months prior to the familicide, he assured them he was doing well.

It turns out that Bill might have believed he was going to come into some money from Katrina Spencer. Other witnesses said Bill had told them he was about to set up his own business and that Katrina was putting up the money. The reality, as we will see, was very different. In regards to his drinking behavior, Bill was either engaging in impression management or he was simply delusional. We might speculate that Bill Langdon wanted to appear favorably to his sons. Sadly, Bill's consumption of alcohol seems to have increased significantly in the weeks prior to the familicide. At the time of his arrest for assaulting Peggy, just two weeks before the killings, the investigating officer noted, "During my conversation with Bill, I detected a strong odor of alcohol and him to have an unstable demeanor." Bill's instability consisted of "red, bloodshot eyes, slurred speech, and rambling and repetitive statements."

Impression management in familicide cases preceded by domestic violence is not limited to male perpetrators. Misook Beckenbauer was deeply ashamed of the failure of her marriage to Gerd. It was her second marriage. She told witnesses she had driven Gerd away by making too many demands on him. Shame about divorce and the failure to live up to one's wifely role seems particularly acute in Asian immigrant families.[44] These cultural pressures probably commingled with Misook's limited income as a waitress. The Beckenbauers lived well and enjoyed the status trappings that came with their station. They presented themselves to the world as a happy family. Their Christmas card, issued four months before the familicide, showed the family smiling in front of the Christmas tree. They attended block parties and participated in the neighborhood watch. On Easter Sunday, just four days before the familicide, Misook and Jenny dropped off flowers and a drawing to elderly neighbors. The principal at Emily Beckenbauer's school was shocked by the killings. He was quoted in the press as saying, "This is very bizarre." The principal was quick to point out, "Emily was a delightful child. There was no sign that she came from a *troubled* home."[45]

To those who knew him, Malcolm Hester had a habit of trying to create the impression that he was a loving parent toward his stepchildren,

Shirley Hester's three children from a previous marriage. As noted above, Malcolm was anything but loving, picking on them in an authoritarian manner. Shirley's sister-in-law, Brenda Thomas, told investigators that Malcolm would "hug and kiss the children in front of the family but the children would state when they were at home he was a totally different person, not showing them any love at all."

Owen Mason's brother-in-law, Norman Keane, told me, "I never liked Owen. He had an edge to him." Owen dragged himself up out of British council (public) housing. He mocked Nancy and Norman's cohesive Irish-Catholic family. Norman told me, "For years, Owen gave me every indication that he was superior." Again, as we will see, Owen's bluster belied a profound sense of alienation and disconnectedness.

DEPRESSION

In the cases where I obtained detailed-enough emotional, psychological, or psychiatric data (24), most of the livid coercive hearts (22; 92 percent) had histories of serious depression. Their depression was either formally diagnosed or otherwise identified by those close to them. These observations about serious depression ought to come as no surprise. Mostly happy, relatively well-adjusted people, with firm familial and social bonds and a sense of pride about their place in the world, do not appear to commit familicide. A couple of examples of depression help illustrate the debilitating effects of these feelings.

Kevin Oxley's stepmother talked of Kevin's history of depression. It was something, she said, that ran in his father's family. By the ninth grade, Kevin was taking antidepressants. Like a number of other budding familicidal hearts, Kevin also used street drugs heavily, including marijuana and amphetamines. As noted previously, it was only after the familicide that Kevin's father would recognize that, as a child, adolescent, and young man, Kevin had a "flat or emotionless affect." As his relationship with his wife, Bonnie, deteriorated, Kevin would threaten to commit suicide as well as murder Bonnie.

Ben Ronaldo threatened to take his own life if his wife, Laurie, left him. These feelings permeated the married lives of the Ronaldos for many years. Fully seven years before the familicide and in the aftermath of Ben's assaulting her, Laurie wrote in an affidavit in request of an order of protection that Ben "grabbed a knife that was in my hand and held it to his heart and told me to kill him. He kept yelling for at least 30 minutes."[46] In another incident just six months before the familicide, police took Ben to a psychiatric facility for 72 hours because he had threatened suicide after Laurie had walked out. Like Kevin Oxley, Ben Ronaldo self-medicated with illicit drugs, consuming enormous amounts of marijuana, benzodiazepines, and amphetamines. Indeed, the day after the familicide, Ben's blood tested positive for all these substances. As noted, Ben's brother-in-law estimated Ben spent $1,000 a month on marijuana alone.

The Ronaldos had the financial resources to use mental health services. However, from information available in the archive, Ben Ronaldo does not seem to have availed himself of those services. In a similar vein, the Beckenbauers and Masons had sufficient resources to benefit from medical and psychiatric interventions. I have already noted Misook Beckenbauer's self-destructive behavior, including her attempts to cut herself. As noted, Misook told her friend Penny that if Gerd left her she would die. Readers will recall Pastor Hannon's comments that Misook had a "miserable lifestyle," and Gerd's boss, Jeff Jackson, saying Gerd had told him Misook was suffering from depression. Owen Mason was seeing both a physician and a psychiatrist, and was taking antidepressants for some time. It is not clear if he was taking these medications at the time of the familicide. That these offenders suffered depression is beyond doubt. However, theirs was not a depression born out of the burying of all their anger and rage, but a depression that accompanied the expression of anger and hostility.

VICTIM MANEUVERABILITY, RESISTANCE, AND AGENCY

As we saw in the Beckenbauer familicide, Gerd Beckenbauer's considerable maneuverability and resources were not able to inoculate him against his wife's murderous behavior. Setting the Beckenbauer case aside, the rest of the intimate partners who lost their lives to their livid coercive partners were women. In general, these female victims seemed to enjoy less maneuverability and resources than Gerd Beckenbauer. However, they do not emerge from the archive as paralyzed or frozen to the point they could not function, resist, or strategize about their own survival and that of their children. Rather, they appear perceptive and aware of what their male partners were capable of doing. A number of these women reported to witnesses that they felt they exercised some control over their men. Through case excerpts, I illustrate women's maneuverability, resistance, and agency. My reluctance to use the word *control* in the sense that men realize control over women is not intended to romanticize women's resistance or deny their fear or terror. Rather, my choice to emphasize victim maneuverability, resistance, and agency reflects the emotional complexity of the cases and the complex personhood of those involved. Explaining the livid coercive cases only in terms of men's power over and control of women is imprecise and a denial of the complex personhood of perpetrators and victims alike.

When Georgina Lessing asked her daughter, Bonnie Oxley, "Why don't you leave Kevin?" Bonnie replied that she did not want to raise her children in a broken home. Georgina told me she felt guilty because she and Bonnie's father had separated when Bonnie was eight. Like Connie Oxley, Kevin's stepmother, Georgina was aware that her son-in-law was dangerously possessive of Bonnie and capable of extreme violence. Yet Georgina was also aware of her daughter's pride and strength. In one conversation she told me that Bonnie vacillated between thinking that

Kevin could kill her and feeling that "she could control him." Georgina told me that Bonnie did not trust the criminal justice system to protect her. Indeed, the prosecutor's office inadvertently dropped charges against Kevin in this case. Bonnie recanted her testimony and sought the dropping of the protective order in her case because "she did not want to look over her shoulder." Georgina said, "Bonnie wanted to have Kevin close by because she would know what he was doing. She thought she had control over him, especially when their children were present. Kevin was a good father for the most part and Bonnie never thought he would hurt his children." Kevin's stepmother told me the same thing.

Numerous witnesses attested to the fact that Bonnie was a good mother, continually reading to her children and coloring with them. Although she became pregnant at 14, she finished high school and enrolled in university classes. She had completed her university general education requirements on a part-time basis, waiting until her children attended elementary school before attending university full-time. Had Kevin not murdered her in November, she would have started nursing classes the following January.

According to her mother, Bonnie's pride made it difficult for her "to ask people to help her." When Kevin broke into his mother-in-law's house to take his daughter, he was arrested and charged with criminal mischief. During the time Kevin sat in jail, Bonnie filed charges against him for partner assault and petitioned for a temporary order of protection. The night she filed, her sisters took her out to a bar. Kevin had warned Bonnie about the dangers of going to bars. She went anyway. However, her sisters reported she left early to go home to her children. Kevin's stepmother visited Bonnie at home when Kevin was in jail and the children were in school. Connie Oxley told me, "Bonnie was not rational. She chain-smoked and said she planned to buy a gun and was going to leave Kevin." According to Connie, one of Bonnie's plans was to get money from her father for breast implants. She could then earn good money dancing at a local strip joint. Eventually Bonnie dropped the charges against Kevin and sought to have the temporary no-contact order quashed. We ought not see this as Bonnie acting solely out of fear of Kevin, for, as David Ford writes, battered women obtain and sometimes drop orders of protection because the process gives them a modicum of control.[47] Also, significant numbers of battered women love their batterers and hope the relationship will somehow work out.

A domestic violence advocate present in court described Bonnie as hysterical, like a "teapot on a stove." It was as if Bonnie had absorbed some of Kevin's acute anxiety. In becoming like a "teapot on a stove," Bonnie's emotional demeanor mirrored Kevin's venom at his mother-in-law's house when he broke in by smashing a window with a golf club. Bonnie may have behaved "hysterically," although we might arrive at a less politically loaded adjective to describe her plight. However, we cannot leave her experience with the courts on this note. Bonnie was strategizing at the same time as she was going through some kind of emotional meltdown. These dual and seemingly incompatible realities evidence her complex personhood, not her resignation or lack of agency.

Notwithstanding Bonnie's fear, she was making plans to leave Kevin and live independently. As she aged, her family members noted she found increasing emotional energy to challenge Kevin's abusiveness. In the months preceding the familicide, Bonnie had inherited money from her grandfather and made plans to purchase the house she and Kevin rented from her father. Kevin was to leave and Bonnie was to assume ownership. Bonnie refused to go to a shelter. Three days before the familicide, Bonnie and her children moved into her father's house. Two days before the killings, Kevin approached his father-in-law and asked if he could take the children out to see *Harry Potter*. The father-in-law relented. Kevin did not return the children. Instead he took them to a motel, where they spent the night. Bonnie's sister spent time with her the night before the killings. She would later tell the media, "Bonnie was leaving him, she was so confident."

Kevin's stepmother told me she tried to warn Bonnie of the threat her stepson posed. Connie Oxley told me Bonnie said, "My dad bought me Mace, I'm just going to take care of myself." Bonnie added that she "knew how to work with Kevin and calm him down."

We find considerable victim maneuverability and complex resistive forces in the Ronaldo case. As noted, at age 13, Laurie Ronaldo lost her mother. It was soon after this loss that she took up with Ben. Unlike most female victims of livid coercive hearts, Laurie seems to have enjoyed a close relationship with her father in spite of the fact her father used violence against his wife, Laurie's mother, in earlier life. The two talked twice a day on the phone up until the day of the familicide. Indeed, her father told police after the familicide that he had liked Ben and got along well with him. Laurie's seemingly close and positive relationship with her father appears to have enhanced her confidence and provided her a certain edge in dealing with Ben's violence, jealousy, and attempts to control her. Eight months before the familicide, police arrested Ben for assaulting Laurie. The couple had been on vacation in their home state. Laurie told her father and stepmother that she did not want them to bail Ben out of jail. As she told them, "Ben needed to stay in jail so he would realize what he had done."

Pregnant with her second child, Laurie told her father that after the birth she would leave Ben, return to her home state, and live in her father's household. A number of witnesses told investigators that Laurie felt confident that Ben would not bother her at her father's house because he respected her father.

Laurie's active planning to leave her violent, jealous husband was consistent with her successful, seemingly confident performance at work and at home. In some ways the Ronaldos had a fairly traditional sexual division of labor in the home. Laurie performed the housework and the bulk of the child care. Ben was apparently a distant father. None of the family photographs showed Ben involved with their daughter, Kai. Ben did most of the cooking, although he seemed to do it with an air of resentment, commenting to his workmates that "Laurie couldn't cook worth a shit." In other ways their relationship was not traditional. It was Laurie, by virtue of her professional job, who earned the lion's share of the family income. It was also Laurie who made the important financial decisions, including those entailing the purchase of vehicles and houses.

A number of witnesses attested not only to Ben's violence, threats, and intimidation but also his surveillance of Laurie, his need to know where she was and with whom. If we examine these insights closely, to the exclusion of viewpoints regarding Laurie's behavior toward Ben, it is easy to see how one might end up concluding that it was only Ben who sought control over Laurie. Indeed, notwithstanding Laurie's many talents and strengths, we can see how attempts to control or the actuality of control can appear unidirectional.

However, when investigators talked with one of Ben's workmates, he described Laurie as the "controlling one." Andy Monkton told investigators that Laurie "controlled all the money that came into the house." It was Laurie who gave Ben "an allowance." Ben's paycheck was deposited directly into the bank. Andy acknowledged that Ben's regular expenses included paying for his drug habit, although he would not go so far as saying that this was the reason Laurie sought to control Ben. Andy did recall a number of occasions when "Laurie would call Ben at work and scream at him on his cell phone." Indeed, Andy contended that Laurie paid for Ben's cell phone so that she could keep tabs on him, adding that Laurie did not trust Ben and wanted to know where he was. With evidence like this it is possible to see how some researchers have argued that attempts to control and/or the realization of control cut both ways or are *bidirectional*. For example, Donald Dutton argues the "Use of controlling behaviors and verbal abuse appears to be bidirectional in intimate relationships."[48]

I will return to these challenging issues. Suffice it to say at this point that the familicide archive offers such a complex picture of these attempts to control, let alone the realization of control, that the logic of directionality itself seems questionable. Emotion does not move in straight lines. The desire to conceive of emotion in such ways reflects the will-to-truth of feminist perspectives and psychological approaches alike, and this is perhaps one reason they butt heads so much.

Gloria Sims displayed considerable savvy and courage in negotiating her separation from her husband, Marcus. Having moved out of their shared household with her son Alex in July, Gloria began to pick up the pieces of her life. She changed aspects of her life, started dating other men, and by all accounts was growing in stature by the day. One of her friends later told police that Gloria was happier, that she had "gotten a tattoo of a butterfly on her ankle and had her belly button pierced." We might see the butterfly tattoo as a symbol of her metamorphosis. She spent most of the six months between July and the fateful night of the familicide

(December 28) with Manny Singlet, a cousin, and Manny's girlfriend, Brigit Burns. Manny told investigators that Gloria was "happy to be away from Marcus." However, "she worried about what he would do when he got out of jail." Investigators asked what precisely she worried about. Manny told them "she was scared he would kill her." Marcus's terrorizing threats provided an ever-present touchstone of fear that deeply affected and duly limited Gloria's maneuverability. However, it did not, I contend, remove her agency. Her strategizing continued. Investigators found a letter Gloria wrote to Marcus, dated December 23rd, just five days before the familicide. She opens the letter with, "Hey sweetie, what's up?" Gloria continues, "I hope you are having lots of fun down there because I am not having fun up here. But I am glad you have called me every day because you make me happier when I talk with you. Wish you were here with me to go through the next few days." Finally, Gloria concludes, "Well, I miss you and will be waiting for your call everyday. Hugs and kisses. Lots more where that came from. Yours always. Gloria (Baby)."

When we put this letter alongside the plethora of witness statements talking about Gloria moving steadily away from Marcus, one interpretation is that Gloria was letting Marcus down as lightly as possible. Another possibility is that Gloria had mixed feelings about Marcus. She loved him but wanted the violence and threats to kill to cease. Either way, Marcus's death threats weighed heavily on her strategizing. In another letter, she tells him she loves him but is not in love with him. I do not wish to imply that Gloria's negotiation of Marcus did not come at a high price to her emotional well-being. In the wake of the familicide, Gloria's mother shared another letter Gloria had written describing her plight. Gloria talked of being controlled to the point she could not "even talk or think for herself." In this same letter, Gloria says that she "hates herself." However, at another point in a letter that comes close to depicting herself being without agency, exhausted, and thoroughly resigned to a state of submission, she tells of her need to survive to be there for her young son, Alex.

We have already seen how Nancy Mason was terrified of her estranged husband, Owen. Even though Owen eventually took a new lover, moving in with her, Nancy was still deathly afraid of him. At the same time, her attitude seems to have been that her professional life was in the town where she and Owen raised their children, and that she was not going to let Owen intimidate her to the point that she had to relocate. As her brother, Norman Keane, told me, "As time went by and Owen moved on to another relationship, Nancy's strength increased." Norman described Nancy's courage during the 14 tense months after she told Owen she was divorcing him, as "huge."

PERCEPTUAL ACUITY

Nancy Mason's haunting feeling that her husband, Owen, would "come for her" was not unusual. She had these feelings in the weeks before her demise, even though Owen left the family home some 14 months previous. Nancy's ominous sense persisted even although Owen had taken another lover. A significant number of women had this perceptual acuity about their partner's potential for lethal violence, and we would do well to see it as an aspect of their emotional awareness and emotional capital, as well as their intelligence. These women somehow discerned the emotional tension and the danger, and we ought not dismiss or downplay the importance of such feelings merely because many batterers kill women who have not reported similar perceptions. One way of conceiving of this perceptual acuity is to see it as a way that women sense changes in the emotional field. Needless to say, these changes can manifest physically. Kathleen Ferraro reports women knowing "that look" on the faces of their abusive partners that spells trouble. Women's special knowledge also extends to reading men's body language and their tone of voice. She notes, "Many women referred to the strange look that came over their partners' faces or into their eyes that made them look 'evil' or 'like somebody else.'"[49] Ferraro also provides interview data suggesting that women know, for example, that taking out an order of protection is not only futile but also constitutes a means of disrespecting or shaming their partner, a very dangerous thing to do.[50]

My emphasis on battered women's resistance, agency, and perceptiveness in the face of fear and intimidation does not mean that I agree with the conclusions of commercially successful entrepreneurs of risk like Gavin De Becker. In *The Gift of Fear*, De Becker writes, "Though leaving is not an option that seems available to many battered women, I believe that the *first time a woman is hit, she is a victim and the second time, she is a volunteer.*"[51] De Becker continues, "*Staying is a choice.*"[52] De Becker's simplistic formulation is perhaps popular with the "pull yourself up by your own bootstraps" crowd. However, it fails to recognize that batterers kill women *after* those women have exercised their so-called choice to leave. As the familicide archive clearly shows, the spatial separation of the parties in domestic violence cases is no panacea or guarantee of safety. As noted, 44 percent of female victims of livid coercive familicide already lived apart from the men that killed them. Livid coercive hearts commit their atrocities within the same household or from a distance. What is important, I suggest, is the tipping point beyond which emotional estrangement convinces eventual perpetrators of the inevitability of being abandoned and their intimate familial arrangements being torn asunder. It is this inevitability and the threat that it poses that simultaneously shames and inflames many of the highly vulnerable and dependent livid coercive hearts, thus contributing to the act of familicide.

We find various spatial relationships between livid coercive perpetrators and their victims. More than a quarter century ago, Shirley Hester remained with her livid coercive husband, Malcolm, until he murdered the family. A number of people close to the case asked why Shirley did not leave. Indeed, Jimmy Benson rather uncharitably described his sister,

Shirley, as a "helpless, dependent nervous woman who lived in a dream world." Shirley told Jimmy that she was too fearful to leave Malcolm. Six weeks before Malcolm killed Shirley, their five children, and then committed suicide, Shirley walked from her house to a local gas station with a paper sack. Ronnie Novak, the manager of the gas station, told investigators the sack contained "a hunting knife, a piece of rope, a small hatchet, and a tire iron or jack handle." Shirley told Ronnie that her husband had threatened to tie her up with the rope and kill her. She had come to the gas station because Malcolm was out of town. Shirley broke down and cried, telling Ronnie she was afraid.

The Langdon and Oxley familicides occurred while the female victims of livid coercion were in the process of physically separating from their abusive partners. Both women sensed imminent danger. Marge Clanton was planning with her mother, Katrina Spencer, to flee to New York. In the days before the familicide, Marge told an old friend that Bill had threatened to shoot her. After slapping and punching her at the residence they shared just weeks before the familicide, Bill told an arresting officer, "I'm going to kill that bitch and you can take that to the bank." Sensing the danger, Katrina Spencer urged her daughter not to return home to remove her personal belongings.

Bonnie Oxley had reached an agreement with Kevin Oxley that he would move out of their family home. In the weeks before the killings she told Kevin's stepmother, "He will come and kill me." But as Connie Oxley and Bonnie's biological mother, Georgina Lessing, both told me, Bonnie vacillated between thinking Kevin was capable of killing her and feeling that he would never do such a thing. No one in the Oxley case thought it possible that Kevin would destroy the whole nuclear family.

For most of these women, their perceptual acuity was not a uniform, unchanging, or certain feeling that the livid coercive hearts they loved or once loved, had children with, and built homes with would annihilate all that had gone before. Rather, the perceptual acuity was socially situated and subject to change. At times, perhaps under a certain confluence of circumstances and emotions, their perceptual acuity is heightened. In other periods, women's ominous sense of foreboding took more of a back seat, was more tempered or even denied, dismissed or ignored. It seems to me that unless we are willing to rob battered women of their agency and survival instincts, their perceptual acuity is a state of feeling and cognition that is negotiated, navigated, subject to reinterpretation, and at times utterly terrifying. Battered women sometimes behave inconsistently in response to their abusive partner's unpredictable and inconsistent behavior. At another level, we might note the role of their own conflicting feelings about their partners in producing inconsistent or paradoxical behavior.

Separated from Marcus Sims for six months and having recently filed for divorce, Gloria Sims, butterfly tattoo and all, was growing in confidence. We have seen how her letters to Marcus helped her to negotiate her exit from the marriage. As noted, Gloria told Manny she feared

Marcus would kill her. Manny went on to say that he asked Gloria if she really thought Marcus would kill her. Gloria replied "yes." Brigit Burns was with Gloria when Gloria received the news that Marcus was released from jail. Brigit told detectives she remembered "Gloria falling to the floor and freaking out." Brigit tried to calm Gloria down telling her there was an emergency protection order in place, preventing Marcus from coming near her. Brigit reported Gloria's retort, "You don't understand, he said he was going to kill me and Alex."

IGNOMINY

Battered women's determination to extricate themselves from the livid coercion in their lives is often accompanied by a more sinister transformation in their abusers. The archive suggests that in the period immediately before the familicide, and, in some cases, for a much longer period, men enter what I describe as a *state of ignominy*. By "ignominy," I refer to something akin to mortification or disgrace, where they experienced a nearly total loss of dignity and self-respect. This ignominy represented an intensification and transcendence of the chronic and sometimes acute and toxic shame that permeated perpetrators' lives. The appearance of ignominy marked another stage in the death of the self, the numbing of the emotions, and the mortification of the spirit. We might ask: Does the appearance of ignominy coincide with or indeed encourage planning and preparation for the kill? If there is a relationship between ignominy and the act of killing, might this not be a focus for those who purport to identify and even quantify risk?

I now turn briefly to the emergence of ignominy in the lives of the perpetrators. We may commence by noting its multiple origins and its continuities with lifelong feelings of social disconnection, anomie, and sporadic or even enduring feelings of shame from early childhood maltreatment. Indeed, to the extent perpetrators' panicked feelings of loss resonated with childhood abandonment, we might speak of the compounding of shame over the life course. However, what men saw as abandonment by their partners and families was the principal precipitant of homicidal ignominy. Try as some men did to soften this blow, save face, or hide their humiliation at the breakup of their families, it was this breakup and how perpetrators somehow sensed it reflected on them that was a potent source of shame. Nevertheless, men's paths to ignominy, although usually related to the shame of family breakup, had other sources. The cases help explore these paths.

Bill Langdon, for example, was tired of life and full of rage. He faced a plethora of medical problems, including high blood pressure, high cholesterol, severe back pain, and alcoholism. He was also facing a number of domestic violence charges. Of all the perpetrators, he is apparently the one least concerned about the pending loss of his partner, Marge Clanton, and her troubled daughter, Peggy. Bill knew they had plans to leave the home.

Before shooting himself and after killing Marge and Peggy, Bill would tell the SWAT team, "My life is over. I am done." He had a turbulent, abusive relationship with Peggy, 17, and did not appear to lament her leaving. Just ten days before the familicide, he would announce to Peggy in the presence of sheriff's deputies, "Get the fuck out of my house."

The principal source of Bill's homicidal ignominy seems to have been that he felt duped by Marge and Peggy. A neighbor said that Bill was happy the morning of the familicide. The neighbor told investigators that Bill told him, "Marge's mother was going to be giving him some money and that he was going to start his own business." Apparently, Marge had led Bill to believe he would somehow benefit financially from the sale of her mother's house. This prospect seems to have reignited Bill's pride. Marge may have used the prospect of the payout to negotiate her way out of the violent relationship. Readers might also remember Bill telling his sons that he was going to Hawaii with money he would receive from Katrina Spencer.

Whether Bill was to receive money to go to Hawaii or to set up his own business, it is clear that in Bill's mind and in his presentation of himself to his sons and neighbors respectively that he had something to be proud of, to look forward to. In the aftermath of the murders, Katrina Spencer dismissed the idea of giving Bill money as absurd. The investigator noted the following: "When I asked Katrina Spencer about some money she was supposedly going to give to Langdon to start his own business, she laughed, and stated she had heard from her daughter, Marge, that he was believing he was going to get some money from her, but that in actuality she was taking all the proceeds from her house, buying the motor home and getting her daughter and granddaughter away from him. She saw no reason to give him money and stated he was the one beating on her daughter and granddaughter and would not give him a dime." Katrina went on to tell investigators that Langdon's learning that he was not going to see any money from her may have lain at the root of the fight they had the night of the familicide.

Owen Mason had built a magnificent family home. With his divorce he would lose this source of pride and joy, and his soon to be ex-wife and two children would be spread far afield. He was also losing his share in a financial planning business, and facing bankruptcy. One ex-employee was suing the company for many millions of pounds. While the other partners wanted to settle out of court, Owen wanted to fight the suit. In terms of the emergence of ignominy, the economic losses paled in comparison to the breakup of Owen's nuclear family unit and the humiliation Owen incurred because of the manner of the breakup. As noted, Owen was mortified by what he saw as Nancy's claim in the court affidavit in request of an order of protection that he had raped his wife. Not only did he vehemently reject her allegation, he seems to have seen it as Nancy's way of publicly demeaning him and rendering publicly visible the fact that she no longer wanted him sexually.

Of all the livid coercive hearts, Owen Mason was the man who seems to have brooded over killing his family the longest, some 14 months. According to Nancy's brother, Norman Keane, Owen decided to commit familicide the day Nancy told him she was divorcing him. For a man who had escaped from poverty and built a luxury home and a successful business, the threatened dissolution of what he saw as his home and family was ignominious. For Norman Keane, Owen's wife and children constituted little than more trophies, symbols of his success and worthiness. The loss was too much to withstand. At the same time, Owen's understanding of his masculinity revolved around his belief he ought to control Nancy and that he was entitled to her body and her respect without engaging in emotional give-and-take.

For Ben Ronaldo, like Owen Mason, the prospect of divorce and the dissolution of the family constituted a principal source of ignominy. Ben experienced delusional jealousy even to the point of saying his wife Laurie's unborn child did not belong to him. Yet other indignities plagued Ben, probably feeding his feelings of disgrace. As Laurie worked her way forward in her job with a major computing corporation, Ben's performance in the workplace deteriorated to the point where his supervisor was getting ready to fire him. Apparently, six months before the familicide, Ben quit his job. He was later rehired with greatly diminished pay and benefits, much to his chagrin.

Among researchers and practitioners in the field of domestic violence, it is understood that homicidal batterers rarely "just snap." Rather, it is recognized that the emotions driving domestic violence-related killings tend to build over time, culminating in a lethal outcome after a series of lesser transgressions. Clearly, Ben Ronaldo moved up the ladder of transgressions. However, we would miss something about Ben Ronaldo if we did not contrast his ignominy with that of Owen Mason. Owen festered in his growing ignominy for 14 months, biding his time, picking a moment to strike. Ben Ronaldo had an entirely different emotional style, having a more explosive temper. Ben waited only a matter of hours after Laurie shared with him she would seek a divorce, before he drove his family, unborn fetus and all, into the ocean.

Malcolm Hester had back problems stemming from missing vertebrae and a curvature of the spine. He also suffered from an irreversible and untreatable condition that involved the shriveling and shrinking of his muscles, diagnosed just two months before the familicide. These problems stemmed from his service in the U.S. Army. According to Malcolm, his numerous health problems relegated him to sporadic, marginal, poorly paid labor that did not enable him to provide for his family. The deterioration of his body and his inability to provide adequately for his family very likely hurt his pride. With three stepchildren and two young children of his own, Malcolm could not pay his bills. In his suicide note to the father who Malcolm claimed abused and rejected him in earlier life, his feelings of ignominy loom large.

Dear Dad:
I'm sorry things had to end this way. I could never be anything but
worthless since I hurt my back in the army. I could never find work
and take care of Shirley and the kids the way I should have. I'm sorry
I wasn't much of a son and this is a terrible way to pay you back for
all you've done.

Like Bill Langdon, Malcolm Hester does not seem to have killed out
a sense of his family's breaking up or some delusional perception of his
wife's infidelity. Rather, Malcolm's ignominy stems from his inability to
provide. However, Malcolm was filled with rage, venting frequently at his
wife and children in what were often sadistic attempts to control them.
Although Shirley Hester had broached with her family the possibility of
leaving or divorcing Malcolm, it is not clear from the archive whether or
not Malcolm was aware of her intentions.

PLANNING AND PREPARATION IN THE MIDST
OF HUMILIATED FURY

At some point before they committed familicide, many perpetrators crossed
a threshold into a state that seemed to move rather close to emotional and
spiritual death. They may have ached with shame and sizzled with rage but
amidst all their humiliated fury they became increasingly numb.[53] James
Gilligan has argued that men such as these kill to try to feel alive.[54]

As with female victims, perpetrators do not lack agency or the ability to choose in the face of irresistible social, historical, and biographical
forces. Their humiliated fury does not deprive them of their reason or ability to think, calculate, scheme, and eventually kill. What we see is a range
of planning and preparation, from meticulous and long-term to short-
term and seemingly improvised.

According to a number of witnesses, Owen Mason planned to kill his
wife Nancy from the moment she told him she was divorcing him. Over
this period of 14 months, Owen moved in with another woman, worked
at his failing business, and became increasingly detached from the daily
life of Nancy Mason. In the first three months after Owen left the family
home, Nancy's diary revealed he made numerous telephone threats on
her life. After eight or nine months, his direct threats diminished. In the
four- or five-month period prior to the familicide, Owen visited websites
that described how to commit murder. On the day of the killings, he called
Nancy to obtain her permission to drive onto her driveway to drop a guitar
off for their 16-year-old son, Peter, a promising musician. Normally such
proximity would have been a breach of the court-mandated understanding between the parties. Nancy consented to his request. Owen pulled up
on the driveway and parked. A neighbor saw Owen retrieve something
from the trunk of his car. It was perhaps the shotgun he used to murder
his family. Peter met his father on the driveway, only to be murdered there

as Owen shot him a number of times. Owen entered the house. Nancy hid in a storeroom, from where she called police. The police dispatch log recorded the last minutes of Nancy's life. The log tells us that Owen, in a fit of rage, called Nancy a "fuckin' whore" before murdering her and committing suicide.

In the aftermath of the familicide, police found several bottles of gasoline in his trunk, suggesting Owen had also planned to burn down the house. Investigators even found written materials saying that if Owen failed in his plan to commit the killings, he had paid a large sum in cash for someone else to finish the task. All of these facts indicate considerable planning and preparation.

Owen Mason's approach contrasts with that of Marcus Sims. The principal trigger for Marcus appears to have been the ignominy he experienced when Gloria received a phone call from her current lover, Fred Scholes. Even in the heat of his fury, the crime scene evidence and later investigative interviews suggest some element of thought in the execution of familicide. As we have seen, Marcus killed Gloria with his barbell, a symbol of masculinity. Yet we also learn that he did this while eight-year-old Alex was playing with his trucks in a neighboring room. He then killed Alex. As spontaneous as the Sims familicide seems, it was not devoid of calculation because Marcus clearly mapped out an escape route, taking Gloria's car and surviving on the road for some time.

THE FINAL ACT

Given the data available through the archive, it is not possible to gauge the emotional feeling of perpetrators after they killed. Kevin Oxley, Owen Mason, Malcolm Hester, Bill Langdon, and Misook Beckenbauer all committed suicide. Marcus Sims refused my request for an interview. I was able to talk with only one perpetrator in the group, Oscar Camacho. As noted, Oscar's version of the facts was so at odds with the version suggested by numerous alternative sources that its veracity was questionable. Nonetheless, we can consider Oscar's own description of his feelings in the wake of the familicide.

Oscar described himself to now be "a spiritual man." He does not like institutionalized religion but he now lives the "spiritual life." His cellmate reads the Bible a lot. In other words, in his early fifties, with a younger cellmate, Oscar's new prison identity is as a spiritual man. This may explain why Oscar reads spiritual meaning into his act of familicide. Oscar would not talk in detail of the act of familicide. He said only that it was "very, very violent." He told me that, "A massive force overcame me, taking total control of my personality and my being," and the killings constituted a "spiritual act," an act of transcendence. Oscar also talked of feeling an enormous sense of "emotional relief" in the wake of the familicide.

The psychiatric literature references experiences similar to those of Oscar. I have already noted Nesca and Kincel's coverage of the familicide committed by Mr. X., noting in particular Mr. X.'s post-offense interview statement that he agreed with a psychological test item "I have never felt better in my life than I do now."[55] In his discussion of the "catathymic crisis," Wertham reports the "rutlike fixation"[56] among those patients who acquired the idea they "must carry out a violent act against others."[57] Wertham notes "a tremendous urge to carry it out."[58] Once the patient commits the violent act, "It is followed immediately by an almost complete removal of the preceding emotional tension."[59] Interestingly, Wertham talks of a period of profound inner adjustment in the aftermath of the killing. This leads to a "complete shift in the person's attitude and results in the gain of insight and the reestablishment of an equilibrium which is lasting."[60] Finally, when Wertham contextualizes the violence against the development of the perpetrator's personality, he sees the violent act as a "benign feature."[61] As he puts it, "It is an expression of the fight on the part of the patient for the safeguarding of his personality. One gains the impression that the violent act in these cases prevents developments that would be far more serious for the patient's mental health."[62] In short, violence such as familicide might stave off "chronic neurotic developments" or "even a progressive estrangement from reality."[63] In his book *Violent Attachments*, J. Reid Meloy notes that catathymic homicide requires "a borderline or psychotic personality organization."[64] He continues, "The perpetrator attributes increasingly malevolent and controlling characteristics to the symbiotic partner."[65] Meloy suggests the relief realized after the killing "marks the end of a disruptive symbiotic attachment, which probably had its roots in early attachment pathology."[66] Meloy's description comes close to describing the way Oscar recalled his own life and final relief at committing familicide.

The psychiatric and psychological research offers us a set of insights regarding the emotional condition of perpetrators. Broader sociological and historical insights extend these oftentimes individualistic ways of seeing the world, moving them toward a complex analysis of familicide and a rather critical interpretation of modernity. Interdisciplinary approaches are helpful here because they do not feed into the false dichotomies between psychopathology and social pathology that plague many of the analyses of interpersonal violence. Rather than remain locked into the language of psychology and psychiatry, I prefer to see the men we have met being tyrannized by the demands of modern masculinities.

At the level of individuals like Marcus Sims, Oscar Camacho, or Kevin Oxley, it is difficult to argue that their male privilege offers the key to unlocking the mysteries of their familicidal hearts. Rather, it is the thwarting of their aspirations to realize male privilege and honor that undid them and humiliated them to the point of fury. Even in the case of Owen Mason, a far more successful man in economic terms, we have only to appreciate his humiliated fury at the breakup of his nuclear family idyll to realize his edgy emotional location in the social order. As the livid coercive hearts go, it is also a stretch to see them as powerful or in control in terms of their social standing. Marcus Sims could not hold down a regular job because of a back injury. Malcolm Hester's muscle disease prevented him from working. Bill Langdon worked sporadically and seems to have sold drugs on the side. Kevin Oxley worked on a seismic crew for only part of the year. Ben Ronaldo lost his job, only to return at lower pay and without benefits. Oscar Camacho worked for a period of time but was also a coyote and a professional thief. A lawsuit from a former employee even threatened Owen Mason's economic security.

These men's lack of control, whether personal, emotional, interpersonal, economic, social, or political, is striking. Male supremacy in various arenas is not a thing of the past. However, we need a more nuanced theory of power and control. It should consider a range of perspectives, including those of the socially disconnected, hapless, livid, often self-medicating, depressed, and interpersonally violent and cruel men present in the familicide archive.

NOTES

1. See Appendix I: The Occupational Backgrounds of the Livid Coercive and Civil Reputable Hearts.

2. See Appendix II: The Racial/Ethnic Backgrounds of the Livid Coercive and Civil Reputable Hearts.

3. Adams, 2007: 47.

4. I address the gendering of familicide in Chapter 6. Readers might well wonder why more women did not suffer the emotional debilitations of the men to the point that they, too, resorted to familicide. The interim answer to this question is that women were not subject to the same pressures to individuate as men, were not socialized into the use of violence as a means of supposedly solving problems, and on the whole remained more socially engaged and had an emotional intelligence that enabled them to problem-solve in alternative ways.

5. For practical purposes, I defined livid coercion as including partner assault (officially recognized or otherwise identified)

6. Johnson, M. 2008: 2–3.

7. Due to the fact that some case studies contained less information on these matters, we cannot assume that the seven cases selected are the most extreme examples of livid coercive hearts. Neither is it easy to assess what the abuse meant to each of the victims.

8. Violent offenders and murderers report disproportionately high rates of childhood physical and sexual abuse. For a general discussion, see Gilligan, 1996. Smithey (1997) notes the importance of early childhood physical and emotional abuse by the parents of mothers who end up killing their children.

9. Fromm, 1973: 322.

10. Fromm, 1973: 323.

11. Fromm, 1973: 326.

12. Fromm, 1973: 332.

13. Fromm, 1973: 332.

14. Fromm, 1973: 332.

15. The autopsy report showed Kevin weighed 125 pounds and stood five feet four inches tall.

16. Given Oscar's work as a coyote, I found his use of the word "passport" interesting.

17. Italics mine.

18. I am indebted to Kathleen Ferraro for her observations regarding the soul hunger in this case.

19. Italics mine.

20. Mowat, 1966: 21. Assessing whether jealousy is delusional is extremely difficult. As Daly and Wilson caution, "It cannot be assumed that the jealous suspicions of abusive husbands are necessarily delusional" (1988: 208).

21. In my analysis of 24 women who killed male intimates, I concluded, "Male victims of intimate partner homicide almost always precipitate the killing through proximal violence, distal violence, or both" (Websdale, 1999: 164). More specifically, I found that five female victims had offensively assaulted their male intimate in the past (see Websdale, 1999: Table 5.3, page 122). This compares with 20 men who had offensively assaulted the women who eventually killed them (see Websdale, 1999: Table 5.4, page 123). When we sharpen the focus, we find that 16 of the 24 case files reveal the eventual male decedent was the only party to have used offensive intimate violence during the relationship. This compares with only one case where the female killer was the only party to have used offensive violence in the course of the relationship.

22. My emphasis.

23. Misook purchased the gun at a local sporting goods store. The owner of the store, Bob Cowley, recognized Misook's photograph from the television coverage of the familicide. Bob told police he tried to sell Misook a shotgun. She opted for the handgun. Misook told Bob she wanted it for home protection. Bob told police he thought Misook knew nothing about guns and "was a bit apprehensive to handle the gun." When quizzed about Misook's demeanor, Bob told police it was "normal, as she seemed happy and was laughing at times." According to police records, Bob did not observe the mandatory 10-day waiting period in selling the gun to Misook.

24. My emphasis.

25. Family court records revealed no protection orders in the Beckenbauer case. Neither did law enforcement records indicate police had attended either residence on domestic violence calls.

26. Upon autopsy, Gerd stood six feet tall and weighed 170 pounds. Misook stood five feet six inches and weighed 124 pounds.

27. Gordon, 1997: 5.

28. Johnson, 2006, footnote 2, page 1015.

29. Johnson, 2006, footnote 2, page 1015.

30. Johnson, 2006, footnote 2, page 1015.

31. Stark, 2007: 92.

32. Laroche, 2005. The GSS relied upon 25,876 respondents from all 10 of Canada's provinces. The respondents comprised 11,607 men and 14,269 women. See Figure 1, page 5, for the criteria used to distinguish between minor and severe violence. See Figure 2, page 10, for the statements used to identify controlling behaviors in relationships. Combining elements of violence and controlling behaviors, Laroche separates respondents into those experiencing situational couple violence and those experiencing intimate terrorism. He finds the majority of cases of intimate terrorism among those reporting on previous rather than current partners.

33. Laroche, 2005: 14.

34. Laroche, 2005: 14.

35. See Laroche, 2005, tables 6 and 8, pages 13 and 16.

36. Laroche, 2005: 9.

37. I am indebted to one of the reviewers for helping me make at least some sense of Gerd's relationship to fear.

38. In defeating the Romans at Heraclea in 280 BC and Asculum in 279 BC, King Pyrrhus's army suffered enormous losses that could not be replaced. Pyrrhus's hollow victory contained the seeds of long-term failure.

39. Evan Stark emphasizes, "coercive control is unintelligible apart from the immediate material, sexual and other benefits perpetrators garner from exploiting victims" (2007: 207).

40. Goffman, 1959.

41. I am indebted to Chic Dabby for her insights on these questions.

42. Wrong, 1961.

43. These observations comport with those of David Adams, a psychotherapist who studied men who killed or tried to kill female partners. Adams notes, "Eighteen of the twenty victims of attempted homicide in our study rated abusers as 'charming to others'" (2007: 26).

44. See, for example, Wang, 1996; Masaki and Wong, 1997; Gap Min, 2006.

45. My emphasis.

46. Note the similarities between Ben Ronaldo and Misook Beckenbauer with regard to asking their partners to kill them.

47. Ford, 1991.

48. Dutton, 2006: 127.

49. Ferraro, 2006: 161.

50. See the case of Danielle and Tony, reported by Ferraro, 2006: 51.

51. 1997: 216; italics in the original.

52. 1997: 216; italics in the original.

53. Lewis, 1971: 494.

54. Gilligan, 1996: 41.

55. Nesca and Kincel, 2000: 48.

56. Wertham, 1937: 976.

57. Wertham, 1937: 976.

58. Wertham, 1937: 976.

59. Wertham, 1937: 976.

60. Wertham, 1937: 977.

61. Wertham, 1937: 977.

62. Wertham, 1937: 977.

63. Wertham, 1937: 977.

64. Meloy, 1997: 65.

65. Meloy, 1997: 65.

66. Meloy, 1997: 65.

5

CIVIL REPUTABLE
HEARTS

In the last chapter, we saw how the humiliated fury of the livid coercive hearts drove their acts of mass interpersonal killing and how these perpetrators spent much of their energy anxiously striving to control the activities of their partners and children. In this chapter, we move toward the right-hand end of the emotional continuum. Civil reputable hearts have more guarded emotional repertoires. In many familicide killings, especially those that men commit, perpetrators appear conformist, proper, respectable, almost emotionally constipated or tightly constrained. By virtue of their social locations, upbringings, physiologies, and temperaments, civil reputable hearts subdue extreme emotions such as rage or perhaps experience them much less than the livid coercive hearts. Unlike livid coercive hearts, they tend to maintain their intimate relationships, find common ground with spouses and partners, and make various accommodations, including playing their specific part in a gendered division of labor. Yet, civil reputable hearts may be neither satisfied nor fulfilled by their family life. In fact, the evidence suggests many of these men and women lived lives full of tension and apprehension about the future, often quietly worrying away their days.

If livid coercion appears to continue that line of cruel and punitive marriages sometimes evident in premodern times, then the civil reputable relationships might appear to epitomize the ideal of modern companionate marriage. When livid coercive hearts commit familicide, the force and violence they finally deploy marks the culmination of their ongoing threats toward and intimidation of their spouses or intimate partners. Their acts of interpersonal killing, although rare and highly unpredictable in any statistical or risk-assessment sense, are, for their victims, nevertheless consistent with their prior behavior. However, when civil reputable hearts commit familicide, the surprise is much greater for victims and the communities in which they reside. These familicides therefore tend to be more shocking and disturbing. When men and women of honor and respectability commit familicide it raises the possibility that other like-situated persons have the same potential, and it makes us doubt the genuineness of manifestations of honor, civility, caring, and nurturing.

Civil reputable hearts inhabit a different sector of society than their livid coercive peers. For the most part, civil reputable hearts live in well-to-do or at least upwardly mobile or economically aspiring families. They are well thought of in their communities, sometimes pillars of them. Simply put, they have much farther to fall than their livid coercive peers. Indeed, the prospect of losing face, of falling from grace, looms large in the lives of civil reputable hearts. These worries appear to reflect nervousness about their social status.

Men make up the majority of civil reputable hearts in the sample. Women constitute only seven of the 47 civil reputable hearts.[1] Women's presence among these offenders contrasts with their absence among the ranks of livid coercive offenders. This may reflect social prescriptions for women to be civil and reputable and not angry or coercive.

My analysis of the lives and murderous behavior of the civil reputable hearts takes us to the very limits of the modern social enterprise. While killings by civil reputable hearts are rare, the emotional hurt that characterizes them is not. The acute anxieties, humiliations, and heartaches evident among the lives of the civil reputable hearts are commonplace in modern and late-modern life. What drives civil reputable hearts to familicide while other people with similar feelings do not commit this offense is the focus here. In particular, I focus on *fitting into the social order*, *latent discontent*, and the various *pathways to familicide*. I introduce the cases I discuss in the chapter in Table 5.1. As in earlier chapters, the table provides case summaries and a frame of reference for readers.

FITTING INTO THE SOCIAL ORDER

I commence by considering the rather limited information we have about the early socialization of perpetrators. Given that 39 of the 47 (83 percent) civil reputable hearts committed suicide as part of their act of familicide, authorities had little need to dig deeply for information that might support a prosecution. Consequently, it is usually only in cases where perpetrators survived that significant information about their childhood experiences and early upbringing was gathered. A common and persistent theme is that perpetrators and their families were responsible and respectable citizens. Those who knew the offenders saw them as loving their children and as either loving or liking their intimate partners, or being willing to raise children with them despite their differences, animosities, or disappointments.

Perpetrators did not seek to especially control the activities of their partners or children, although some appeared to be strict disciplinarians with their children. Rather, they lived out the social roles they thought

Table 5.1   Summaries of the Cases Discussed in Chapter 5

Perpetrator	Victims	Summary Notes
Ali, Ibrahim	Indira (wife) and three children. PS	Suffocated his three children as they slept and shot dead his pregnant wife before committing suicide. Principal cause seems to have been his large gambling debts that pushed him toward bankruptcy.
Allen, Patricia	Benjamin (husband) and three young children, six-year-old Gillian, five-year-old Paul, and two-year-old Sadie. PS	Patricia lost her mother at age two. Maltreated and humiliated by her stepmother. Coroner concluded she was temporarily insane. Oral history contacts revealed Patricia was a battered, terrified woman. 1950s case.
Baines, Priscilla	Bobby (husband), Steven (son), and Carrie (daughter). PS	Long oral history with chief investigator. No rhyme or reason to the killings. Beautiful home and successful dairy farm business. Well established local family of considerable repute. Principal investigator suspected hidden mental health problems.
Brandley, Lillian	William (husband) and Lucas (son). PS	According to authorities this was the "act of one suddenly gone mad." No apparent reason for the killings, no known domestic violence, no financial difficulties.
Bronski, Kenny	Sara (wife) and Eddie (son). PS	Esteemed police officer in financial difficulties caught stealing money from the possessions of an arrested drunk driver. Bronski's theft was recorded on video. He at first denied the theft and was then confronted with the video recording. He returned home to shoot his family members, set fire to his house, called the fire department, and shot himself.
Curtis, Mary	George (husband) and Marjorie (daughter). PS	Health problems for family members in the wake of an automobile accident. She killed them "to leave them in peace." Medical examiner describes Mary as "mentally unbalanced due to worry." NYT describes Mary as a "crazed wife."
Holcombe, Heather	Billy (husband) and two children. PS	Billy was stiflingly controlling. Heather practiced with the gun before the familicide. Shot the victims as they slept. She'd been receiving treatment for anxiety and depression and might have been "shopping for a disease." Munchausen case?
List, John	Helen (wife), three children, mother	John List killed his wife and three daughters, fled, and lived under the pseudonym of Robert Clark for 18 years before police finally apprehended him. During this period he cleverly assumed a new identity, remarried, made new friends and developed a new career. Westfield, N.J., 1971.

(continued)

Table 5.1 *(Continued)*

Perpetrator	Victims	Summary Notes
Miller, Mandy	Andrew (husband) and two of their three children. PS	The Millers lived in the wealthy suburbs of a mid-western city. Her husband, Andrew Miller, owned his own design company. Andrew had taken a new lover and decided to leave Mandy.
Mochrie, Robert	Catherine (wife) and four children. PS	Hammered to death his wife and four children as they slept, stayed with the bodies for up to 24 hours before hanging himself. Police found the bodies eleven days later in an advanced state of decay. Mochrie was an ex–British civil servant before becoming a successful independent businessman. Business failures led to a pending bankruptcy and notices of foreclosure on the mortgage. Barry, Wales, 2000.
Motson, Paul	Wife and two children. PS	Motson donned a Halloween mask as he killed his family. Successful financier facing charges of embezzlement. Deeply depressed and anxious.
Wagner	Wife, four children, plus a number of villagers	German schoolteacher who wanted to be a well-known dramatist. Obsessed with being found out as someone who had engaged in sodomy in his earlier life.
White, Nancy	Paul (husband), Ruth (eldest daughter). PS	Nancy, a 26-year-old homemaker, slit the throat of her eldest daughter, Ruth Eckles-White, three, killing her; stabbed her middle child, Claire Eckles-White, 23 months, in the throat, injuring her; killed her husband, Paul Eckles, 47, by stabbing him in the chest; and then committed suicide by slicing open her own neck. Nancy and Paul's youngest child, Jill Eckles-White, seven months, was left unharmed. No clues as to motive in spite of extensive fatality review.
Wu, Kevin	Mary (wife), Craig and Wayne (sons). PS	Respectable Chinese family. Kevin was depressed and anxious, worried about business-related lawsuits. Killed his family while they slept. Kevin Wu placed gold bullet-shaped objects under the bodies of his wife and two sons.

they signed up for. Usually these roles involved a traditional gendered division of labor with men as sole or principal economic providers and women as homemakers, nurturers, and caretakers.

Early Socialization

Few civil reputable hearts reported experiencing physical violence or sexual abuse as children. Of those whose childhoods we know about, many experienced attenuated or disrupted bonding with their parents; some experienced varying degrees of parental neglect. Case excerpts illustrate these observations.

On September 3, 1913, a German schoolteacher by the name of Wagner murdered his wife and four children. He then set fire to the village of Muelhausen, Germany, and shot dead ten villagers and injured many more. We learn through Wagner's psychiatrist of many years that Wagner's father was an alcoholic who died when Wagner was two years old. Apparently, Wagner's mother had the reputation of being promiscuous.

Paul Motson shot to death his wife and two daughters as they slept. His modus operandi comports with that of many of the civil reputable hearts, who murdered their victims when they were unconscious. As a child, Paul experienced parental neglect. In a letter to his mother, a film star, Paul commented, "You were never around much when I needed you." Paul's biological father told him that he was an unwanted child, sired in a vain attempt to rekindle his romance with Paul's mother. Paul wrote his mother, "And when the marriage fails, as it did, and the child is now five years old, the sense of personal guilt for the failure is likewise substantial." His stepfather fought frequently with his mother, who it seems became an alcoholic. Paul's life included seeing his mother intoxicated, passed out, surrounded by bottles and pills. Likewise, Paul complained his mother never noticed his many achievements because she was too busy indulging her own desires. Paul told investigators he loved his own wife and daughters but he got himself into major financial difficulties, the only way out of which was to commit familicide.

Male civil reputable hearts commonly experienced rigid and authoritarian parenting in childhood, especially by their fathers. The case of John Emil List exemplifies this point. John List killed his wife and three daughters, fled, and lived under the pseudonym of Robert Clark for 18 years before police finally apprehended him. During this period he assumed a new identity, remarried, made new friends, and developed a new career.

His mother, Alma List, gave birth to John Emil List on September 17, 1925, in Bay City, Michigan.[2] She was 39 years old. Her husband, John Frederick List, was 60 years old. He met Alma when she worked as a nurse, attending to his ailing first wife before she died. According to Joe Sharkey's record of the List case, Alma was a protective mother and John Frederick a distant, authoritarian father. Sharkey opines, "John grew up in a cocoon protected by his mother, whose warmth was in sharp contrast to her husband's coldness."[3]

In contrast, John List recalled his father as a hard worker and someone with whom he enjoyed many good times. He fondly remembered going with his father to the docks to buy fish, selling items such as candy, magazines, and tobacco out of the small store his father operated, and learning of his ancestors in conversations with his dad on the porch.[4] Specifically, John noted, "As far as I can remember, most of the time I spent with Dad was quality time. He only had to spank me once, when I earned it by being unruly in church."[5] Similarly, John gave an overall positive impression of both sides of his family. He commented, "All in all, my dad was a kindly man, the same as the rest of my relatives on both sides."[6] John also reported his parents demonstrating their love for each other. He wrote,

"My parents often showed that they loved each other. They would do this by hugging and kissing at various times. Often they pulled me close to them so that I was a part of the hugging."[7]

The "true crime" accounts of List's life and his own observations agree on the fact that the young John List was a loner, socially disengaged except for his relationships with immediate family and church members, and reserved. John did not play with boys in his neighborhood; in fact, boys in the neighborhood teased and taunted him. List himself acknowledged "my social life all the way through high school was pretty much limited to a tightly drawn circle of close relatives and church members. I never went to school dances."[8] John noted, "I had no regular play-mates in my neighborhood and rarely stayed after school to play sports on the playground with kids of my age."[9] John was also acutely aware of his ungainly physical nature. He commented, "There always seemed to be a problem in communication between my active brain and my un-coordinated extremities."[10] John's awkwardness resulted in his being constantly subject to humiliating experiences. He noted, "In choose-up-side games, I was always the last kid to be picked, and often I wasn't chosen by either team captain, so I joined the last team to choose by default."[11]

John shot his wife and children. He rationalized his killing as a means of rescuing his outwardly well-to-do family from the horrors of bankruptcy and from drifting into a non-Christian lifestyle. Although he killed them in face-to-face encounters with a handgun, he arranged their bodies with apparent care, covering them with blankets, and tuned the radio to the classical music station, leaving the music playing until authorities found the bodies almost a month later.

Patricia Allen killed her husband of seven years, Benjamin, and their three young children, and then committed suicide. She shot six-year-old Gillian, five-year-old Paul, and two-year-old Sadie in their heads as they lay in their beds. She shot Benjamin in the forehead in their living room. Police found the handgun used in the killings next to her corpse. No police records survived from this case in the early 1960s in Hayden Wick, a small village in the Midwest. At the coroner's inquest the six-member all-male jury concluded that Patricia Allen had experienced temporary insanity. Her murderous acts appeared so incomprehensible and out of character that the temporary insanity verdict explained away an otherwise unblemished life as a hardworking wife and mother and respected member of the community. Oral history interviews later revealed that Benjamin Allen had abused his wife, suggesting that Patricia Allen's act of familicide laid to rest more demons than the public knew about.

Patricia Allen lived with deep emotional wounds. In this respect, her personal insecurities also mirrored those of the livid coercive men described in Chapter 4. When Patricia was two years old, her mother died. Her father eventually remarried. The stepmother dominated the household and was abusive. Her father and stepmother argued long into the night. Patricia's sister, Angela Kearley, told me, "She would not let him rest."

According to Angela, their father was "not a strong character." Her step-mother was highly religious. Angela remembered the stepmother assaulting Patricia for shouting at the stepmother's dog. In general Angela resisted the abusiveness of her new mother. Patricia did not have the emotional reserves to do so, and paid a high price for this. The stepmother bullied Patricia incessantly, picking on her both physically and emotionally. Significantly, Angela remembers the stepmother's forcing Patricia to wear old clothes that humiliated her. In addition, the stepmother constantly put Patricia down, attacking her self-esteem on an ongoing basis.

Local journalist Kevin Moore wrote an article about the Allen familicide. In response he received an anonymous letter from a reader who remembered Patricia Allen. The anonymous writer described Patricia as a "delicate person" and "not evil." Patricia "was a very needy person" and "a sweet little girl." From the writer's perspective, Patricia "was very young when her mother died, and she seemed lost. Her father did his best, but he couldn't do it all." The writer, clearly female, befriended Patricia. She noted, "Patricia was only two years my junior but she latched onto me as if I were a much older sister. In grade school she was waiting for me every morning with hairbrush in hand for me to fix her hair. She needed her homework checked, advice on clothes, etc."

Patricia's early childhood traumas and losses resemble those of the livid coercive hearts. However, unlike those perpetrators, Patricia became the victim of intimate-partner violence before becoming a perpetrator of familicide. These differences raise important issues about the way males and females cope with trauma in later life.

Responsible and Respectable Citizens

Among civil reputable hearts, we witness the signatures of responsible, respectable behavior. Most of the men held well-paid jobs, often working as successful managers or businessmen. A minority held more modest but nevertheless well-thought-of occupations. The majority of female perpetrators were married to men with impressive jobs, their families enjoying high social standing in their communities.

Robert Mochrie, who would later hammer to death his wife and four children as they slept, was an ex-British civil servant before becoming a successful independent businessman. His wife was secretary of the local parent-teacher association and a student at Cardiff University in Wales. Catherine Mochrie's best friend, Debbie Zeraschi, described Robert as a "good friend, a good man, a loving father and a good husband."[12] The evening before the familicide, Robert drove Catherine and Debbie into Cardiff, 45 minutes away, so they could attend a graduation party. He would later pick the women up at the train station. According to Zeraschi, Robert was laughing and joking. She told a reporter, "I remember my last words to him were: 'Rob, you're an angel.'"[13]

Like Robert Mochrie, John List had been a successful businessman. In many ways List was a pillar of his community. He came to New Jersey to assume the vice presidency of a bank. His family lived in a mansion in Westfield, New Jersey. John and his children were active members of the Lutheran Church. He was a seemingly devout family man with a beautiful wife. List evinced a strong commitment to hard work, Christianity, and familial solidarity. In some ways he was almost absurdly respectable. For example, neighbors reported seeing John working in his yard wearing a collar and tie. John sought to control his children closely, choosing their schedules, whom they associated with, and the lessons they took at school and church.

Paul Motson was a vice president, head futures trader, and economist at an investment bank. After he had shot his wife and two daughters and committed suicide, friends and family wrote letters to the editor of the local newspaper. One friend, for example, described the Motson family as "the sweetest, most generous, and definitely the most caring family I have ever known."

Wagner was a German schoolteacher of good reputation.[14] In the aftermath of his acts of familicide and mass killing, numerous witnesses interviewed in the wake of his mass killing described him as "an admirable citizen, dignified, somewhat quiet, more soft-minded than rough."[15] Wagner, like List, at times found it difficult to gauge precisely how to behave. Although Wagner lived in a part of Germany where educated and uneducated people alike spoke with a heavy dialect, Wagner "insisted on using High German, even in his private life."[16] Like John Emil List's habit of gardening in a collar and tie, Wagner's excessive, perhaps absurd insistence on using High German reflects an uncertainty of status, a nervousness, a sense that these men felt as if they really did not belong.

According to a family friend, police officer Kenny Bronski, 39, "worshipped his wife, Sara, 40, and adored his son, Eddie, nine." The friend was stunned at Bronski's familicide, an act that entailed his shooting Sara, Eddie, and the family dog, and then committing suicide, setting their home ablaze in the process. A neighbor told reporters that Bronski "did everything with Eddie. Just last week he was teaching Eddie to play golf." According to the maid of honor from her wedding, Sara Bronski "was a devoted wife and mother." We learn from witnesses that Eddie would emulate his father by wearing a tool belt, helping out on household jobs. The principal at Eddie's school described the young Bronski boy as "an excellent student" who was "very well liked." The family lived in an average house in a "quiet, well-kept subdivision." Neighbors noted the family "seemed happy." Another neighbor described Kenny Bronski as "a great family man." Neighbors knew the Bronski family by name. The Bronskis would walk their dog in the neighborhood.

The neighbors also knew Kenny Bronski as a police officer of some notoriety. About a year before the familicide, Kenny had solved a highly publicized Jane Doe case, reuniting a missing woman with her family.

Indeed, neighbors knew Kenny Bronski as "Officer Kenny." Another neighbor described how Kenny was "quick to crack jokes." Kenny's coworkers described him as "hard-working."

Female perpetrators drew much of their social esteem from their husband's standing in the community and from their own roles as successful wives and mothers. As with the men, case illustrations tell the story. The *New York Times* informs us Mary Curtis, 45, shot and killed her husband, George H. Curtis, her daughter, Marjorie, seven, and herself on August 13, 1925. She also shot and wounded her 20-year-old son George H. Curtis, Jr. Mary belonged to the wealthy Curtis family.[17] Her father-in-law, Fayette S. Curtis, was president of the Old Colony Railroad Company. Her husband, George H. Curtis, was assistant superintendent of foremen in the building department of the Boston Terminal Company.

On March 11, 1915, in Newark, New Jersey, Lillian Brandley shot and killed her husband, William Brandley, and their son, 12-year-old Lucas Brandley, before killing herself.[18] According to the press, investigators remained convinced "that it was the act of one suddenly gone mad."[19] The newspaper reported the family lived "happily."[20] According to William's brother, George Brandley, there was "no reason"[21] for the shootings. However, he did tell police that his sister-in-law "had been irritable and nervous of late, but that she and her husband seemed to be happy."[22] George also ruled out any "domestic or financial difficulties"[23] in the family. We cannot do the same. Again, an air of mystery and the inexplicable haunts this case. Rather like the Emma Cooper tragedy, authorities knew the funeral would attract a throng of people. They therefore deliberately kept the time of the funeral a secret to reduce the attendance of the curious. What we are left with is detailed media coverage of the forensic aspects of the deaths of these responsible and respectable citizens, an analysis that elsewhere Alex Alvarez and I have referred to as "forensic journalism."[24] The inexplicable does not appear to be newsworthy at this particular historical juncture. Rather, we learn of the logical process of elimination whereby investigators identified Mrs. Brandley as the only one who could have fired the lethal shot into her own brain. We read that "the muzzle of the revolver must have been inserted in her mouth as her teeth were uninjured by the bullet. There were no powder burns on her face and the interior of her mouth was blackened."[25] All this evidence reassured police that "it was impossible that her wound could have been other than self-inflicted."[26] At some level, these observations might have reassured readers, eliminating one form of the impossible, such as an unknown or unexpected perpetrator, someone lurking dangerously at the edge of police inquiries. However, it seems to me that in cases such as these, a range of other "impossibilities" warrants consideration, possibilities that do not necessarily lend themselves to the logic of abstract empiricism, and that may not be admissible in court.

My conversation with Danny Barak, a retired detective who investigated the familicide committed by Priscilla Baines in the late 1970s, revealed Priscilla was the wife of a well-to-do independent dairy farmer. Priscilla shot dead her husband, Bobby, and her son, Steven, as they slept. She then called her pastor, Greg Rooney (now deceased), and apologized for the killings, saying, "She'd messed up real bad this time." Priscilla then told Pastor Rooney that she was going to kill her daughter, Carrie, and then take her own life. Detective Barak knew the Baines' extended family, remembering them as follows: "Priscilla was a beautiful young woman. The Baines family was super-nice. They lived in a beautiful new home." Nevertheless, there is more than a hint of the inexplicable in the Baines familicide. The Baines extended family cooperated fully during Danny's investigation and knew of no reason for Priscilla's behavior. Barak also told me that he and Pastor Rooney had discussed the case over the years, and neither man knew of any reason for the familicide. As we talked, he cautioned me that there was no hint of economic problems or marital infidelity and no police calls to the residence for "family problems" or any knowledge of such problems. However, he did say, "You never know what goes on behind closed doors." I quizzed him closely on this comment, asking him if it was his way of telling me about family problems or domestic violence that the community did not want uncovered. He said "no."

There were two possibilities left in Barak's mind. The first was some kind of hidden mental illness, a common knee-jerk response for many who investigate these cases and who are essentially flummoxed by the outcome. The second struck me as equally interesting. Barak said, and I quote verbatim, "there was no rhyme or reason to those killings." We are back to the uncanny, the inexplicable, and the haunting presence of Priscilla's emotional style and its relationship to prevailing figurations of feeling.

Mandy Miller killed her husband and two of their three children in the 1970s. The Millers lived in the wealthy suburbs of a Midwestern city. Her husband, Andrew Miller, owned his own design company.

Heather Holcombe, who shot to death her husband, Billy, and their two children before committing suicide, lived in an affluent suburban neighborhood of a Southern city. Her husband ran his own small business. A neighbor said the Holcombes "seemed like the ideal couple, the ideal mom and dad." Heather volunteered for the local Parent Teacher Association, engaged in community recreational activities, and was held in high regard. The press even tells us their expensive house was situated in a "tightly knit neighborhood" with "neatly cut lawns and well-kept shrubbery." In short, the Holcombes lived in the midst of order and plenitude.

Similarly, Nancy White, who stabbed her husband and daughter to death before committing suicide, lived in a wealthy residential community. Her husband, Brian Eckles, ran his own successful computing business out of their home.

Finally, we must reemphasize the warm regard community members expressed for Patricia Allen, a fact that might have contributed to the conclusion of the coroner's inquest that she suffered from temporary insanity. In the wake of the familicide, neighbors of the Allen family expressed their shock and disbelief. They told the press they could not explain the deaths. None had ever heard of any "family trouble" at the Allen residence. A number of neighbors described the children as "especially nice." The newspaper boy said the Allen family was "very friendly" and "never caused any trouble." A female neighbor described Patricia Allen as a "wonderful person," a commonly expressed sentiment in this case.

Impression Management

A difference between the livid coercive and civil reputable hearts is that the former sought to control their partners, whereas the latter seem to have negotiated their differences or learned to live with them, sometimes with what seems to have been enormous disappointment. However, civil reputable hearts did seek to control the impressions people had of them and their families. To some extent, most families regulate what personal information about family members is made public, wanting to present the family as favorably as possible. Given that the civil reputable hearts perceived their family life to be disintegrating or under grave threat, it appears that many expended tremendous emotional energy to prevent the disclosure of such information. For the most part, we might conclude they were successful. In a number of cases, perpetrators even concealed their concerns from other family members. Male perpetrators in particular, appeared to view protecting family members from such negative information as part of their responsibilities as head of the household.

The secretiveness of some of the civil reputable hearts lessened what researchers might learn about family life in these cases. For example, did Robert Mochrie know of his wife's two previous affairs before he killed her and the children? According to the newspaper account and the coroner's inquest, it appears not. However, I cannot help but think that at some level he sensed she had moved on. Did his wife know that every Tuesday and Thursday night after he dropped her off at university, he would use her car to pick up a prostitute? In fact, did Catherine Mochrie know that the family was facing bankruptcy? The archive does not allow us to answer these important questions. However, we do know that Robert Mochrie had received treatment over the years for depression and some delusional behavior, treatment that his wife apparently knew nothing about.

When John Emil List was fired from his job as bank vice president, he never told his wife. Rather, he left home every morning, supposedly to attend work. John later admitted, "My professional career had reached a dead end, but I was too proud—or ashamed—to admit it to my family *or even to myself.*"[27] He continued, "I tried to cover my firing by pretending to go to work every morning, wearing a suit and a tie and driving off in the only car we had left after I sold our second car. Sometimes I went to New York City to contact employment agencies and killed time at the city library between appointments. Some days I just stayed in the car at the railroad station."[28] After six months of misleading his wife, he began to sell insurance out of his home, at a drastically reduced salary.

John List later acknowledged that his taking out of a second mortgage on his house "was needed to pay for the goods and services to maintain the image of prosperity that both Helen and I craved. It was an example of *conspicuous consumption* in the extreme."[29] At the same time, John refused to apply for unemployment insurance after his various layoffs because "I had been too proud."[30]

Ibrahim Ali returned home from a gambling trip to suffocate his three children as they slept and to shoot dead his pregnant wife, Indira, before committing suicide. Ibrahim managed to keep his gambling addiction a secret from his neighbors and business associates alike. He never gambled in his home state, instead traveling long distances to Las Vegas and Atlantic City. A successful businessman for a time, Ibrahim was facing bankruptcy. One neighbor described Ibrahim as "all about family." It is difficult to know how the neighbors reached this conclusion, given that Ibrahim traveled so frequently and seems to have had little contact with them. However, Ibrahim had enough contact to tell his neighbor he had won $5,000 on a slot machine in Las Vegas. The impression he conveyed was that of a lucky man. Just before the familicide, Ibrahim told his brother-in-law, Tugrul, that he was considering filing for bankruptcy. Tugrul told investigators that Ibrahim did not "appear to be despondent." Marcy Barker, a close friend and neighbor of Ibrahim's wife, Indira, told investigators Indira never mentioned any problems other than Ibrahim's health difficulties. Apparently, Ibrahim had been gaining weight and smoking excessively.

Successful Chinese businessman Kevin Wu, 55, shot to death his wife, Mary, 49, and their two sons, Craig, 21, and Wayne, 17, in their large house in a beautiful, leafy suburban community. He then killed himself. Friends described him as a "brilliant and financially successful businessman, a devoted family man." Neighbors watched the sons sit for hours in their bedroom windows, poring over their schoolbooks. But according to neighbors, the family was also very private. It is still not clear from the archive whether friends and family knew about Kevin's battle with depression. After the familicide, their family doctor told reporters that Kevin's cultural background made it very difficult for him to admit he suffered from depression. Kevin was also suffering from acute anxiety for which he was taking medication. Such an admission would have been seen among some people as a sign of weakness. Neither was it clear to neighbors or those who knew the Wu family the extent that two pending lawsuits plagued Kevin.

Men like Robert Mochrie and Kevin Wu felt shame about what they perceived to be the end of family life as they knew it. Officer Kenny Bronski did not expose his wife and son to his disgrace. Caught on video stealing money from the stored possessions of a drunk driver, Bronski was immediately suspended from duty, his gun and badge removed. Within hours, he had committed familicide and set his house ablaze.

Paul Motson donned a grotesque Halloween mask before killing his wife and two daughters, all of who were sleeping at the time of the murder.

188 FAMILICIDAL HEARTS

The disguise might have been an attempt by Motson to transform him-self into something sufficiently monstrous that could commit familicide. Paul was managing his own impression of himself. Episodes such as these remind us of the centrality of impression management to the workings of the social order, an order where individuals try to convince not only others of who they are, but themselves, too.

The female civil reputable hearts also managed their presentation of self. The older cases contain relatively little information in this regard. For example, the coroner's inquest into Patricia Allen's familicide did not reveal evidence of her husband's intimidation and tyranny. Indeed, oral history evidence suggests few people knew of the extent of Benjamin Allen's abusiveness. Official records revealed no prior history of domestic violence. The coroner's inquest mentioned none. No police records sur-vive. According to the police chief's testimony at the coroner's inquest, police never went to the Allen residence because of a family disturbance. Mr. Allen emerged from the coroner's inquest as a rather flamboyant, easygoing sort of man who knew many of the residents of Hayden Wick.

Reverend Hicks bumped into Benjamin Allen at the Hayden Wick post office the day before Patricia sought him out for spiritual guidance, two days before the familicide. Benjamin seemed in "very good humor." Although he was not a member of Reverend Hicks's church, the two men discussed the possibility of Benjamin's taking some photographs at an upcoming Sunday school rally, as Benjamin Allen was an amateur photographer.

Police Chief Goddard told the inquiry that everyone he talked with described Mr. Allen as a quiet sort of man who loved his children and his wife. He had apparently heard that Mrs. Allen was a person who seemed to be in a daze in the weeks preceding the killings. He specifically noted that she "would seem to go out of her mind at times."

Other witnesses attested to Benjamin Allen's good-natured demeanor. Just two hours before the killings, Mr. Allen ventured into the grocery store run by Mr. and Mrs. Don Phillips. Mrs. Phillips told the inquiry, "Benjamin came to the store around 8:30 p.m. and we talked about being related. He laughed and talked with Don and me. Finally, he said he had better take his groceries home. He never mentioned any troubles at home. He seemed in real good spirits."

Mr. Sangster, the local pharmacist, provided other insights. Late Wednesday afternoon, Benjamin was in the store to pick up medicine for his wife. Mr. Sangster described Benjamin as "normal in all ways." Therefore Benjamin Allen, according to the official historical record, was a relatively easygoing, albeit quiet, man who loved his wife and children.

The range of examples showing the way families and perpetrators pre-sented themselves to each other and community members reveals just how difficult it is learn the truth about these killings. The secretiveness of the civil reputable hearts is hardly surprising, given that all people manage the way they present themselves to others. However, the civil reputable hearts anxiously guarded the degree to which they felt their lives were spinning painfully and shamefully out of control. Their taciturn emotional styles meant they could not reach out to others or share with others just how desperate they had become. We find evidence of this in the next section.

LATENT DISCONTENT

Despite the impression of happiness, stability, and well-being presented by the civil reputable hearts, there is evidence of latent discontent in their lives. Such discontent seems to have many origins. Many experienced acute emotional isolation, even amidst the hubbub of family life. They kept a lot to themselves, appearing socially marginal, even secretive. Unlike the livid coercive hearts, most civil reputable perpetrators displayed little anger and rage, either apparently choosing to exercise considerable emotional restraint in their affairs, or not actually feeling the bite of these emotions.

As their latent discontent grew, often in response to forces beyond their control, the civil reputable hearts endured various forms of emotional suffering. In some cases, their difficulties and troubles emerged relatively quickly, apparently in response to a perceived threat that others often saw as innocuous, inconsequential, or simply groundless. Nevertheless, the emotional style of the civil reputable hearts did not permit them to cope well with these perceived threats. Facing threats like bankruptcy, illness, or a controlling spouse, the perpetrators appeared to be overwhelmed to the point they felt that killing was their only way out.

Acute Emotional Isolation

People are social beings. They form acquaintances, friendships, romantic ties, and other intimate networks in specific social settings at particular junctures in their lives. They also disengage or withdraw in these various settings; some people becoming more guarded, even emotionally detached. It may sound trite, but at some level we are all guarded, even secretive about certain aspects of our lives, feelings, and behavior. I mention these matters not to point out the guarded and anxiously reflexive ways we build our identities in modern societies, but rather as a way of introducing and qualifying what appears as a principal theme, especially among some of the male civil reputable hearts: their acute emotional isolation. The emotional demeanor of civil reputable hearts comports with Fox and Levin's observation that mass murderers are "intensely isolated, physically or psychologically, from sources of emotional support."[31]

The civil reputable hearts felt isolated despite living with family members. Often they appear distant, disengaged, and detached. We saw this in the cases of William Beadle (1784) and James Purrinton (1806), men who held their cards close to their chest, even in the presence of their wives and children. There is evidence of emotional alienation, not only immediately prior to and during the familicide, but also long before the killings.

This acute emotional isolation emerges in the context of the specific social arrangements of family life and the networks of interdependencies of which they formed a part. In the case of John List, he was increasingly distant from his wife, Helen, and their children. Years before, John had fallen in love with the beautiful and flamboyant Helen Taylor. Helen had just lost her husband, Marvin, in the Korean War. According to Helen's daughter, Brenda, Marvin's death devastated Helen. After burying Marvin, she was seeing a lot of different men. Brenda would later tell the New York *Daily News*, "I guess she just settled on John."[32] In fact, John stood in stark contrast to Marvin. Unlike Marvin, John was timid, quiet, and taciturn. Marvin had been aggressive and was, to most observers, observers a much better fit with Helen's personality. A number of people reported Marvin could keep Helen's spending habits in check. In later years, Helen would compare John unfavorably with Marvin.

Whatever their level of compatibility, John married Helen on December 1, 1951. The fact that Helen told John she thought she was pregnant appears to have played an important part in John's decision to marry her. He told a friend at that time, "Helen is pregnant, we've been intimate several times. What in the world can I do? We have to get married."[33] Benford and Johnson report that John would later explain to the trial psychiatrist the way he "obsessively 'debated in my mind' over and over whether or not to marry Helen."[34] Ultimately, John married Helen, though it later turned out that Helen was not pregnant.

Both partners brought their problems into the marriage. Helen's mother had physically abused her as a child, and John's shyness and rigidity remained. John's compulsiveness and righteousness about religion bothered Helen. The couple had three children, Freddy, Johnny, and Patty. John successfully climbed the career ladder as an accountant, though he developed a reputation for being meticulous, obsessive, and socially disengaged.

Those who knew John List prior to and during his marriage to Helen described him as quiet, shy, snobbish, prim, and uptight. However, after he committed familicide, fled, and developed a new life in Denver as Bob Clark, we witness a change of personality and emotional style. Elements of his personality endured: his meticulous nature, his precision, his pensiveness, his quietness, and his religious devotion. However, one of his first bosses in his new life, Gary Morrison, was angry to read newspaper stories describing the man he knew as Bob Clark as "arrogant and dogmatic."[35] Gary experienced Bob as flexible in matters regarding religion. He also described Bob as "great with people" and not at all shy.[36]

As "Bob Clark," List married Delores Miller in 1985, some fourteen years after committing familicide. as John List. Joe Sharkey describes Delores as a "shy, religious person."[37] It was almost as if Bob had calculated precisely what he needed in his second wife. After Bob's arrest in 1989, Delores wrote a statement for the media. "This is not the man I know. The man I know is kind, loving. A devoted husband and dear friend. He is a quiet yet friendly man who loves his work and the people he works with. We both enjoy going to church. Bob is a man of devotion and faith."[38] The pastor at Bob's Lutheran church also refused to acknowledge that Bob was anyone other than a devout religious man of principle.

John List transformed into the kinder, gentler, more sociable, less emotionally reserved Bob Clark. We might suggest possible reasons for this longer-term transformation. A psychiatric interpretation might posit that John cut off into a split personality as a way of coping with the trauma of the familicide. Perhaps "Bob Clark" was not subject to the high-stakes pressure that John List faced in his business and family life. It seems he was much better matched with his second wife than his first. Neither can we rule out the possibility that somehow the commission of familicide dissipated some of John List's reservoir of anxiety and despair. John List explains his more relaxed demeanor as he fled to Colorado in the following terms. "I had absolutely expected to be caught by law enforcement officers within a day or two, a week at the outside."[39] He tells readers this expectation "must have produced in me a sort of fatalistic peace of mind."[40] According to John this put him "on a sort of mentally relaxed cruise control as I moved into my new life."[41] Ought we see John List's new life as Bob Clark as an example of the emotional opportunities available in modern era figurations of feeling, a new opening with a different set of social networks and interdependencies?

Acute emotional isolation is present in a number of other cases. In the following two cases, surviving family members, friends, neighbors, workplace peers, and other witnesses identified the ways the perpetrators' emotional isolation manifested itself. Those who knew Robert Mochrie said he did not disclose much about himself. His wife Catherine's best friend, Debbie Zeraschi, put it as follows, "Rob was one of the least aggressive men I have ever known. He was quiet—not the most sociable of people. Telephone conversations were impossible—long silences, that sort of thing. That was Rob."[42] Piecing the evidence together, journalist Kevin Toolis explained, "Beyond his family circle, Robert had few, if any, real male friends. His social entertainment amounted to little more than having a few pints down the pub, watching the occasional rugby match. He was shy, but not a social misfit."[43] It seemed Mochrie did open up to Cardiff street prostitute, Charmaine Jacobs. Toolis told readers Jacobs told him that the Mochrie's marriage was in trouble. Robert shared with Charmaine that he and Catherine were not having sex any more. Charmaine knew details of Robert's family life, that he had a handicapped daughter and that the family used to play musical instruments. She also knew Robert had owned hotels. As well as providing hand-relief (genital stimulation) to Robert on a weekly basis, Charmaine Jacobs also listened to and consoled Robert. According to Charmaine, she met with Robert just hours before the familicide. She recalls, "It was pissing down with rain, and at first he flashed past me. I flagged him down by stepping into the road and then we went to the usual location. He was quiet that night."[44]

One case that contrasts with the others is the case of Nancy White. There was little evidence of emotional isolation, and investigators described the case as an utterly inexplicable familicide. In other words, there was relatively little in the life of Nancy White that suggested she would commit familicide.

The facts of the case are these. Nancy, a 26-year-old homemaker, slit the throat of her eldest daughter, Ruth Eckles-White, three, killing her; stabbed her middle child, Claire Eckles-White, 23 months, in the throat, injuring her; killed her husband, Paul Eckles, 47, by stabbing him in the chest; and then committed suicide by slicing open her own neck. Nancy and Paul's youngest child, Jill Eckles-White, seven months, was left unharmed. Nancy arose in the morning of the familicide and wrote to her husband Paul a suicide note in which she revealed intent to kill their eldest daughter, Ruth, and then commit suicide. In another note to Paul, she told him the locations of the children's medications, so that he could care for them after her death.

Despite her apparent plans to kill only her daughter, Nancy ultimately murdered other family members. Paul was stabbed in the torso. As he lay in bed bleeding, he called the police and told the dispatcher his wife had stabbed him. On the tape of the call, one of the surviving children is heard screaming in the background. Paul died while on the phone.

The evidence suggests that Nancy was a socially engaged mother of three young children. By all accounts, Nancy and Paul had a good relationship, getting along well. Police ruled out the possibility that either party was having an affair or that there was a history of domestic violence. Nancy was twenty-one years younger than Paul. It seems as if the couple entered the marriage and the childrearing arrangements with eyes wide open, as far as this is ever possible. They are the only family in the archive to have retained both partners' surnames, suggesting an egalitarian relationship despite the traditional gendered division of labor in their household.

Paul ran his own business from the basement of their home in a well-to-do neighborhood. Two employees worked for him. Investigators interviewed these employees, both of whom knew of the working arrangements at the White household. Paul was a successful, hard-working businessman. Unlike in the Mochrie case, there was no pending bankruptcy or any lesser form of financial threat. Paul would come up from the basement at lunchtime to take meals with his family. Detective Bohm described their family life as "fairly normal." He added, the "household was well maintained."

Amid all the evidence in this case, there are only two clues as to why Nancy might commit suicide. One friend described Nancy's sense of being emotionally alone. In addition, Nancy had anxiety about her eldest daughter's medical problems. I address the first clue at this juncture and address the second clue in the discussion of ignominy.

In spite of the fact that Nancy appeared to have a good relationship with her husband and also had relationships with her siblings, a close friend described her as a young mother with three very young children, living in a neighborhood populated mostly by families with middle-aged parents. According to the friend, in this setting Nancy was alone. She met other mothers on her daily excursions to the park with her young children, but somehow she was cut off.

The source of Nancy's sense of isolation may have been linked to her lifestyle as a young mother in a setting well outside her range of experiences. Was it the case that her mothering experience was not what she thought it might be? In spite of concerns to develop an egalitarian marriage, was it perhaps the case she felt trapped by their gendered division of labor? However, the archive contains no evidence to suggest that Nancy White experienced physical or sexual abuse or any disruption of parental or other familial bonds.

In the aftermath of the killings, police would not release any medical information to the press. The press reported the observations of experts on issues such as postpartum depression or postpartum psychosis, two potentially pertinent psychiatric conditions that might help explain Nancy White's bizarre and inexplicable act of killing.[45] Readers learned many women feel depressed after childbirth. However, only one in one thousand of these women become psychotic. Postpartum psychosis usually develops in the first two to three weeks after delivery. In these rare instances, women sometimes become delusional or paranoid and might perceive their child or husband as a threat. Some might suffer suicidal or homicidal thoughts, insomnia, and extreme feelings of anxiety or agitation. For most experts who offered an opinion on the White familicide, the fact that Nancy's youngest child was seven months old ruled out postpartum psychosis. Detective Bohm told me Nancy suffered none of the symptoms normally associated with postpartum psychosis. Nancy had displayed no signs of anxiety, depression or suicidal thoughts. She had received no counseling. To the best of Detective Bohm's knowledge, the only call Nancy made was to request assistance with shopping for groceries. The haunting presence of the inexplicable looms larger in the White case than in any other case in the entire archive.

The acute emotional isolation of the two female perpetrators (Patricia Allen, Heather Holcombe) who had been subject to the intimidating, controlling, and abusive behavior of their husbands warrants closer attention. Patricia Allen and her children visited Reverend Roy Hicks on the Wednesday afternoon before the familicide. The Reverend Hicks and his wife, Janice, had formed their own church in Hayden Wick. He told the coroner's inquiry that Patricia sought "spiritual guidance." Reverend Hicks described Patricia as "quite despondent." He was unable to say what caused Patricia's despondency. The reverend's testimony at the Coroner's Inquest proceeded as follows:

Coroner (C): Was she perturbed or preoccupied?
Reverend (R): Yes, quite a bit.
C: She didn't say what the trouble was?
R: No.

C: Did she have any fears?

R: Yes, there seemed to be a little fear.

C: Fear of what?

R: It left an indication that there might have been *a little family diffi-culty.* If we surmised that there was any deep trouble we would prob-ably have done something more than we did. [*All italics mine.*]

C: Had she ever been under a doctor's care for *nervousness?*

R: It seems as though I heard that she had been.

C: She was an emotionally stable person generally?

R: I would say so.

C: Was there any difference at that time?

R: Only that she was not very talkative.

Patricia left the Reverend's house and went to see her brother, Barry Barille. Barry also felt something was bothering Patricia, although he said he did not know what it was. After leaving her brother's house, Patricia returned home with her children. She then telephoned Reverend Hicks. Patricia asked the Reverend for something to read "for comfort." He directed her to the fourteenth chapter of St. John: "Let not your heart be troubled. Ye believe in God; believe also in Me." Later, Patricia called Reverend Hicks's wife, Janice, who was also Patricia's stepsister. Janice Hicks visited Patricia Allen and prayed with her.

The coroner questioned Benjamin's father, Ralph Allen, about Patricia's mental condition.

C: Had she ever been under a doctor's care within the last year or so?

RA: I couldn't say.

C: You don't know if she was in the habit of taking sedatives?

RA: No.

C: Had Benjamin been under a doctor's care?

RA: Only for a cold or something like that.

C: Not for tension?

RA: No.

C: They got along nicely in their home life?

RA: As far as I know when we were up there they seemed to.

C: They seemed compatible that Sunday?

RA: Outside of not being as talkative as usual.

C: No financial trouble, as far as you know?

RA: No.

Patricia's circumstances seemed quite desperate to her sister Angela, who reported that her sister experienced loneliness in the midst of a busy life as a mother. She had "no money." Her husband, Benjamin, was a factory worker who earned little. The Allens had three young children. Patricia was acutely aware of their financial difficulties and had taken an afternoon/early evening job to make money. As a mother of three young children she was under enormous stress, though she was also "a docile person and very nice."

Angela described Benjamin Allen as a man who showed no interest in the children and did little around the home to assist Patricia. He expected "dinner to be ready at a certain time." Unlike the impression of Benjamin Allen that emerged from the coroner's inquest, quiet yet sociable, Angela said he was a "social isolate" and "antisocial." When Angela and Barry would go over to see Patricia and the children, Benjamin would shut himself in a bedroom. She added that Benjamin came from a different community and that his mother "was very strange."

Patricia's emotional isolation within her marriage continued a long-established pattern dating back to the loss of her mother. She herself had developed into a mother of three and a part time wageworker. But she was engulfed by her husband's abusiveness, her commitments as a loving dutiful mother, and her economic plight.

The emotional styles of the civil reputable hearts are similar to those of mass killers in general, including serial killers. All are emotionally isolated to some degree. However, as we have seen, the emotional isolation of the civil reputable hearts occurs within familial atmospheres of feeling. But it might be precisely because such estrangement emerges in the midst of a seeming abundance of emotional connections that the alienation or even disenchantment and loneliness are all the more debilitating. The intrafamilial emotional entanglements emerged because romantic love forms the basis of marriage in the modern era. By definition, modern families, much more so than their premodern predecessors, concern themselves with partners' needs for companionship, sexual compatibility, and romantic love. In a sense, the ethos of intimacy, some might argue the ideology of intimacy, plants the seeds of its own destruction, perhaps by setting up unrealistic expectations for people like John List, Robert Mochrie, Nancy White, and Patricia Allen. In premodern times, family members had lower expectations of intimacy from spouses. Likewise, given the more permeable relationship between families and communities, emotional bonds tended to be more spread out, more diffuse, perhaps less vulnerable to the kinds of disappointment we see in cases like List and Mochrie. The emotional isolation among some of the civil reputable hearts reflects the workings of both social and historical pressures.

This socially and historically situated value placed on intimacy has the potential to breed emotional disappointment and suffering at the same time as it provides opportunities for emotional growth and the refinement of personal identity. In their lives, the civil reputable hearts display an overabundance of this suffering, albeit often in subterranean, covert, unarticulated, or disguised forms. It is to examine their anger that I now turn.

Anger and Rage

Living as they did at the more subdued (right-hand) end of the continuum of emotional drives, the civil reputable hearts expressed relatively little anger and rage compared with their livid coercive counterparts. In the following discussion, I review two exceptions, cases in which a civil reputable heart overtly expressed anger. Both examples come from the List case.

Over the years, List's wife, Helen, developed addictions to alcohol and Doriden.[46] She had a difficult time mothering their children. With growing resentment, John found himself returning from long days at work, only to prepare meals for his children. At times, according to Sharkey, Helen would taunt John, attacking his rule-bound, repressed nature. At Helen's suggestion, the couple took to viewing pornography to enhance their sex life. On occasions when Helen socialized, she sometimes flirted with other men. John assaulted one man he caught kissing Helen at a party. John's frustrations grew. On one occasion after Helen tormented him about getting a buzz cut, he overturned a table and smashed some plates. Yet these outbursts were isolated. Although considerable tension, frustration, and disillusionment permeated the List marriage, John was deferential to her in many ways, buying her things to placate her. Joe Sharkey opines, "At home, he was terrified of Helen."[47]

For the most part, the civil reputable hearts, men and women alike, internalized modern prohibitions against the expression of powerful emotions such as anger and rage. This made them conformists at two interrelated levels. Socially, they blended into their communities, adhering to the norms and values that came with the prestige they earned. Psychologically, offenders exercised considerable self-control, either subduing any strong negative emotions or reining them in, or not realizing in any conscious way they even had such feelings. However, this assessment is incomplete because we cannot in any way be sure that this was the case. In short, the civil reputable hearts kept much of their suffering to themselves. It is in that direction that I now turn.

Emotional Suffering

Most of the civil reputable hearts experienced anxiety and depression, much of it severe. The two abused women Heather Holcombe and Patricia Allen also suffered very specific fears. At times, as we will see, these women reached a state of despair, especially prior to the familicide, although this was not necessarily obvious to those around them. Fewer civil reputable hearts engaged in obsessive behavior, and only rarely do they appear to have experienced delusions. The evidence for this suffering derives from a variety of sources, including the more formal assessments of physicians, mental health professionals, relatives, friends, and others, and the presence of metabolites of antidepressants, anti-anxiety, and sleep medications in autopsy reports.

Patricia's sister, Angela Kearley, indicated that Patricia suffered from depression but definitely not from delusions, schizophrenia, or other mental health conditions. She reported that Patricia's doctor "did not realize the extent of the problems she was facing." Regarding the relationship between Patricia and Benjamin, she said that Benjamin was "verbally abusive" and "was constantly putting Patricia down. He called her ugly, fat. He would get mad at her. In fact, my brother and I never heard him say one nice thing about Patricia." Patricia shared with Angela that her husband frequented taverns in the evenings. He would return to his home smelling of perfume.

As to why Patricia had gone to see Reverend Hicks the day before the killings, Angela reported Patricia had sought support from Reverend Hicks on the day before the familicide because "Benjamin had threatened to kill Patricia and the children." We do not know if Patricia communicated this threat to Reverend Hicks. I asked Angela if Benjamin had threatened Patricia in other ways. She told me, "Benjamin would sometimes put a stocking over his head to scare Patricia." Angela recalled a number of other incidents where Benjamin terrorized her sister. Civil and reputable as she was, Patricia Allen lived in a state of acute fear that most people seem to have interpreted in terms of a rather generic nervousness. Such interpretations have been common assessments of women's concerns, with the old stereotypes of women being hysterical remaining strong. Angela's references to Benjamin's terrorizing of Patricia probably described the "little family difficulty" that Reverend Hicks referred to at the coroner's hearing. The Reverend's understatement bespeaks the hesitation of authorities in addressing family violence and tyranny in mid–twentieth century America.

The interdependencies in the Allen family between Benjamin and Patricia evidenced a balance of power that heavily favored Benjamin. But these interdependencies were breaking down. Patricia was taking a paid job in spite of her speeded-up mothering. Her husband showed little interest in family life, returning at night from the bar smelling of other women. Benjamin's tyranny and intimidation continued. These failing interdependencies echo the case of Emma Cooper. Indeed, Patricia and Emma remind us that speeded-up mothers who can no longer rely on the interdependencies they think they signed up for have their breaking points.

More than half a century on from the Allen case, Heather Holcombe murdered her husband and their two children, and then committed suicide. The newspaper reports tell us the police had gone to the residence for a domestic disturbance some six months prior to the killings. No one was arrested, and no assaults took place, as the couple was simply arguing loudly. Detective John Stinchcombe, one of the senior investigating officers in the Holcombe familicide, told me that interviews with neighbors revealed the husband, Billy Holcombe, was extremely jealous of other men and their contact with his wife, Heather. At block parties the couple attended, Bill forbade Heather to have any contact with men.

Heather Holcombe was receiving medical treatment for depression and anxiety. Detective Stinchcombe opined that in the months prior to the killings, Heather was "shopping for an illness." When I pressed him on this, he said Heather had approached doctors thinking she had a number of different serious illnesses in addition to her depression. The last fear she expressed just prior to the familicide was that she had contracted AIDS from an affair she had had some ten years earlier. Her gynecologist said there was no indication of this but agreed to run tests. Heather was also convinced she had passed AIDS on to her husband and children. The test result for HIV was due back to her doctor the day after the familicide. The HIV test, like the one she had had for other illnesses, proved negative. Stinchcombe's suggestion that Heather was paranoid is one possible interpretation of her plight. Another possibility is that Heather's behavior was an adaptation to the abuse she suffered at the hands of her husband. In other words, her behavior reflected something similar to the symptoms of post-traumatic stress disorder.

Detective Stinchcombe contended that Heather feared learning her HIV test was negative and therefore committed familicide to avoid dealing with that revelation. A negative result would have meant that her sense of her own illness was "in her head," to use Stinchcombe's words. For Stinchcombe, her gynecologist had implied as much by prescribing Xanax for her anxiety on top of her antidepressant medication. According to Stinchcombe's interpretation, Heather Holcombe needed attention and sympathy, rather like someone suffering from what psychiatrists might call "factitious disorder."[48]

However, Stinchcombe's interpretation is open to considerable criticism. Heather's concerns about HIV might have reflected her husband's concerns about the matter. It is possible he had verbally abused her by claiming she was infected, perhaps through an extramarital affair. Indeed, he may have used such suspicions to justify his own close surveillance of her, keeping her from talking with other men. In addition, we must note that Heather's anxiety was real. Had her doctor suspected her anxiety was "in her head," it would have been unethical for him or her to prescribe Xanax. Finally, it is common for abused women to suffer from anxiety and depression at the same time and to receive medication for both. Indeed, Billy's intense striving to control Heather lay at the root of her depression, anxiety, and possible paranoia. It is therefore perfectly appropriate to see her act of familicide as a reaction to such a suffocating form of intimacy.

In 1990, when he was still a civil servant, Robert Mochrie saw a psychiatrist, Dr. Brian Harris, for treatment for depression. He complained of sleeplessness, weight loss, fatigue, and low mood. He admitted to the psychiatrist that he felt suicidal. At one point he confided that work-related problems made him feel "as if someone had blown his head open with a shotgun."[49] In spite of these symptoms, Mochrie declined admission to an inpatient psychiatric facility. Like other civil reputable perpetrators, he kept much of his emotional suffering to himself. He would not even allow his wife to be informed about his treatment. According to the psychiatrist, antidepressants helped Mochrie through this emotional crisis. However, he returned to the psychiatrist again in November 1993, reporting depression and some hallucinations. Dr. Harris told the coroner's inquest, "He said that he felt there was someone on his shoulders, sometimes seeing a light."[50] Harris continued, "He was obviously disturbed by that and was thinking of going to see a priest. He had a feeling of futility and doubts about whether it was worthwhile carrying on."[51]

Journalist Kevin Toolis contended that Mochrie's emotional suffering, particularly his depression and delusional beliefs, "appear to be directly connected to moments of crisis in his professional life—on the first occasion, problems at work in the civil service; on the second, his new life as an independent businessman."[52] Robert Mochrie did not seek further treatment for his suffering in the months and weeks prior to committing familicide. He felt heavily burdened. His reputability added to rather than lightened his sense of carrying a weight on his shoulders. At the coroner's inquest, Dr. Brian Harris opined that Robert was delusional at the time of the familicide, thinking familicide was his only or best option.

We cannot leave our interpretation of Robert Mochrie's behavior at the level of his own psychiatric history, his hallucinations, his delusions, his suicidal ideations, and his depression. I suggest Mochrie was experiencing the haunting presence of changes in the emotional field, itself an aspect of the social interdependencies in which he actively participated. Prominent amongst these interdependent relationships were his familial and business responsibilities, aspects of his life that were fast unraveling. We cannot separate the material and the emotional as if they were mutually exclusive realms of activity. Robert Mochrie was feeling the weight of the modern era figurations of feeling, persistent and intense prescriptions about the performance of respectable middle class fatherhood and appropriate husbandly behavior. Seen in this light, his feelings of pressure might be construed as the somatic manifestation of what he perceived as his failure to meet these demands, reflected through his lack of sexual intimacy with his wife, his resort to the services of a prostitute, his possible sense that his wife had been unfaithful, and his sense that two of his four children, in spite of his love for them, needed special support and care. These were Robert's anxieties. We find similar fears in other cases.

Fired for fraudulently diverting company funds into his mother's bank account, Paul Motson's blood profile revealed his body was saturated with medication designed to treat emotional suffering. The medical examiner's report lists the presence of Elavil (antidepressant), Valium (anti-anxiety), marijuana, alcohol (trace) and Fastin (appetite suppressant). His wife's body revealed the presence of Elavil, Valium and marijuana. It seems Paul had been anxious and depressed for a long time. He also had longstanding heart and circulatory problems. However, three days before he committed familicide, he was fired for his swindling activities. Like Robert Mochrie's news of impending bankruptcy, we must suspect Paul's firing was the final straw.

The cultures of some of the civil reputable hearts appear to have made negotiating their emotional suffering even more difficult. Evidence of such difficulties surfaced in the case of Chinese businessman, Kevin Wu. Few of Kevin's friends or acquaintances knew he was taking anti-anxiety and antidepressant medications. Those who noticed a change in Kevin's behavior remarked he had become quiet and withdrawn and at times had shown uncharacteristically slow thought processes. In meetings with his personal banker, Wu would ask questions and then repeat them again without realizing he had already asked them. His family doctor, a Chinese physician, told reporters that Wu might have felt he would appear weak to his Chinese friends and associates if they perceived he had a mental problem.

It is likely too that Kenny Bronski's handling of his initial surge of shame at being caught stealing $500 from a drunk driver was made much more difficult because he worked in the subculture of law enforcement. As we have seen, Bronski committed familicide within hours of having his gun and badge removed by police administrators. For Kenny, the shame probably proved utterly overwhelming. There is no evidence that Kenny Bronski suffered from long-term emotional distress, although the archive in this case is limited. It remains an open question as to whether he was unusual among the civil reputable hearts, nearly all of whom experienced chronic emotional distress.

I have already mentioned John List's obsessive-compulsive behavior. List himself suggested it contributed to his meticulous planning and execution of the familicide. In his autobiography, List informs readers of other emotional suffering that he suggests contributed to the demise of his marriage and eventually to the familicide. According to List, he suffered from post-traumatic stress as a result of World War II action he experienced as a soldier in Europe. In spite of the fact that his fellow soldiers recollected heinous experiences of being shelled and captured, John List recalled nothing. He contends his amnesia is a symptom of post-traumatic stress; a way the mind dissociates and therefore copes with extreme stress. John suggests his post-traumatic stress adversely affected his ability to engage in intimate relationships and to form close social bonds. Citing the research into PTSD, List also argues his emotional trauma limited his ability to solve problems, including the difficulties associated with dealing with his pending bankruptcy in the run-up to killing his family. If List is correct, then his PTSD might be one more way that past trauma contributed to his familicide. However, there is room for doubt here, because if his alleged PTSD lay at the root of his inability to solve problems and engage in intimate relationships, then we might ask how he managed to do a better job of these things the second time around in Denver. None of this should be taken to mean that the effects of the post-traumatic stress do not have the potential to undermine a person's sense of belonging, perhaps destabilizing social attachments and interdependencies or inhibiting their development.

We ought not leave the analysis at the level of John List's possible PTSD. It is also possible to see his behavior, PTSD included, as a byproduct of the kind of masculinity prescribed in times of war and honed in military conflicts. Another way of seeing the PTSD is as a form of emotional distress, repression, and social disconnection resulting from or associated with activities designed to kill enemy combatants, other human beings. These forms of masculinity also valued suffering in silence, not displaying terror and grief, an exaggerated form of the individualistic masculinity of capitalism that emerged in nineteenth-century America and that I return to in Chapter 6.

Using the interpretations of mental health professionals and those close to the civil reputable hearts, I reached the conclusion nearly all of these people were plagued by various forms of anxiety, depression, and shame. Roughly half of the civil reputable hearts had received some kind of mental health treatment in the years preceding the killings, although fewer than a quarter were receiving treatment at the time of the familicide. As was their way, these men and most of the women kept the full extent of their chronic suffering secret from those closest to them. Nevertheless, they also had sufficient emotional strength to carry on in society, albeit in many cases as rather isolated people. It was this strength or toehold in the social world that separated these civil reputable hearts from that small number who lost touch with reality and drifted into delusional, schizophrenic, or other states where the self breaks down.

PATHWAYS TO FAMILICIDE

Just as in the case of livid coercive hearts, many civil reputable hearts experience *ignominy* or something approximating mortification. Again, my assessment relies on a subjective reading of the archive. It is not as if perpetrators reported their feelings of disgrace or somehow articulated a total loss of dignity or self respect. Rather, I read these emotional states from the trace evidence of their lives, variously captured in the archive. I prefer "ignominy" to words such as "humiliation" or "embarrassment," because the latter words do not seem to capture the depth and magnitude of wounding, exposure, and vulnerability. Case illustrations help flesh out the social character of ignominy among the civil reputable hearts. As in the case of the livid coercive hearts, we also find evidence of planning and preparation. Finally, unlike their livid coercive peers, the civil reputable hearts engage in what I call "killing with care."

Ignominy

In many cases, we see some kind of terminal disgrace or mortifying humiliation. Their days of enjoying some semblance of honor or repute, the esteem of those around them, were about to vanish. In the light of fast-disappearing material resources, it was this final episode of shame that that threatened to expose the civil reputable hearts and their families to gossip, possible scorn, and the reality that they would no longer occupy their cherished place in the social order. For Paul Motson, it was the letter terminating his employment as the vice president, head futures trader, and economist at an investment bank. For Ibrahim Ali, it was his bank's refusing to honor his checks that he wanted to use to pay off massive gambling debts. Kevin Wu committed familicide the day before he was due to give testimony in a wrongful-death lawsuit filed against his company. The Wu family physician said "the lawsuits were really bothering him." Kevin's wife was named as a defendant in one of the suits, suggesting her own family fortune was under threat. Witnesses suggested Kevin would have felt enormous shame at jeopardizing his wife's family fortune in this manner, striking at generational networks of interdependencies on his wife's side of the family that traced their roots back to Hong Kong. In Robert Mochrie's case, the source of ignominy was probably the receipt of final notices of foreclosure on their mortgage and the need to file for bankruptcy. With female perpetrators, the ignominious trigger or precipitant, as we will see, involved them seeing themselves as failures as mothers or wives. This included cases where female perpetrators like Heather Holcombe and Patricia Allen experienced abuse at the hands of their spouses.

An increasingly uptight John List was mortified about a number of things in his life. He was ashamed of the fact that his wife, Helen, would not accompany the rest of the family to the Lutheran church on a regular basis. Rather, Helen would attend only when it suited her, and she openly rejected the church elders. As his children entered their teenage years, John perceived they became unruly. As his daughter, Patty, grew up she performed in school plays. According to Sharkey, these sometimes embarrassed John. Without Helen's support in providing the children with a solid religious upbringing, John perceived them drifting from Christianity. John saw his children's drift from faith as part of the much broader cultural climate of the 1960s, a permissive milieu that John saw as both self-indulgent and dangerous.[53]

John carried his sense of shame through his life. When Helen mentioned she thought their marriage might not last, John talked of experiencing shame about the possibility of getting divorced. He comments, "the prospect of divorce filled me with a sense of shame, since mine would be the first ever in the List family."[54] Similarly, when John's employers terminated him, he was "too ashamed to tell Helen that I was being fired."[55] John tells us he was "too proud to apply for unemployment compensation, which would have cushioned my loss of income. Instead I had to take out a second mortgage on the house."[56] In addition, he acknowledges "most of the money was needed to pay for the goods and services to maintain the image of prosperity that both Helen and I craved. It was an example of conspicuous consumption *in the extreme*."[57]

John List took his responsibilities as a provider very seriously. His seriousness in this regard is consistent with his emotional demeanor as a taciturn, shy, and rule-bound man. In his internal deliberations about whether to commit familicide, John contends his thoughts "focused mainly on my failure to provide for my family coupled with my desire to ease their suffering from our collapsed financial situation."[58] John was flooded with shame because he perceived he had failed his family. His sense of failure must be seen against the prescriptions of the modern era gender regime and ideas about what it takes to be a real man. I return to these matters in the next chapter.

On the eve of the familicide, John List, like Robert Mochrie, Paul Motson, and a number of other civil reputable hearts, was facing bankruptcy. For a man who had made a career out of managing money, this was the final ignominy. In many ways John List's money, like that of many of the other male civil reputable hearts, was a proxy for his masculine potency. Indeed, according to Benford and Johnson, John List had learned from his father that "to go on welfare was to admit that you were not a man."[59] We learn that John mulled over in his mind the possibility of declaring bankruptcy and receiving welfare. However, the prospect of living among the poor and subjecting his family to the challenges of such a life mortified him and was tantamount to a public acknowledgement of his own impotence.

We must see the emergent ignominy of men like John List in relative rather than absolute terms. It is not the case that John List's failure was greater than that of like-situated men. Rather, the intense shame of men like John List only makes sense when seen balanced against their tenuous, anxious place in a social order they never really fit into or felt a part of. Carving out their reputations as men who climbed social ladders and enjoyed considerable success, prestige, and honor also defined them as men who had a long way to fall. Given that many of these men shepherded their families along with them, their powerful sense of patriarchal responsibility amplified their shame and fear.

Readers will remember Wagner, the German schoolteacher who killed his family and members of the village of Muelhausen, where he once taught for ten years. At age 26, Wagner apparently engaged in an act of sodomy during a drunken escapade. The secondary reports on the Wagner case do not reveal whether he was the victim or perpetrator of the sodomy, or whether the acts were consensual or forced. He felt that the villagers of Muelhausen somehow knew of his criminal act. According to the psychiatrist Hilda Bruch, from his act of sodomy onward, Wagner "felt himself continuously observed, mocked, and ridiculed, and lived in constant dread of arrest. He was determined not to suffer this public shame and humiliation, and therefore he always carried a loaded pistol."[60]

Wagner rose from his peasant roots to occupy a teaching position that placed him on the fringes of the respectable middle class. However, he never seemed happy about his achievements. He always felt he should become a well-known dramatist and was bitterly disappointed when he failed to realize his dreams in this regard. Wagner felt superior to those around him. In particular, he felt superior to his wife, a woman he impregnated and felt compelled to marry. He also saw himself above those of lower social standing who he thought gossiped about him because of his act of sodomy. His use of High German, as opposed to the local dialect, represented a constant effort on his part to elevate himself in the eyes of others.

For anthropologist Elliott Leyton, Wagner's social mobility contributed to his act of mass killing. Leyton notes:

> Yet few things are so corrosive to the individual as rapid social mobility: He is no longer in the world that he knows; he does not know quite how to behave, nor how much leeway the public will allow him in the performance of his role. All he knows is that the penalty for failure is disgrace and an unceremonious return to the ugly status from which he has escaped; hence the common quality of a defensive status hysteria—which manifests itself as a kind of extreme personal insecurity—that is found so often among those who have risen or fallen dramatically in the social hierarchy.[61]

Leyton's words resonate loudly with the Bronski case. Kenny Bronski, as we have seen, was something of a local hero. Community members knew him as a police officer who had served his community and department with honor. When Kenny stole $500 from a drunken driver he had arrested and booked into custody, he became in his own eyes something worse than that driver. In short, Kenny failed the character test and got caught. He felt he could never return to the Thin Blue Line of which he was a part: this line, in his mind, was what separated good from bad, right from wrong, moral from immoral. Kenny became the very thing he worked against, a criminal. When senior officers confronted Kenny about his transgression, he denied their accusations. Eventually they presented him with the videotaped evidence of his thievery from the storage locker, and he confessed. Kenny then agreed to go home, find the money, and return it. Fellow officers accompanied the disgraced Kenny Bronski to his residence, taking his gun and badge. He was officially suspended on suspicion of theft. Kenny's disgrace was total, immediate, and something he could not envisage surviving. He left a suicide note in the van parked in his driveway, telling those who remained he could not live with his disgrace.

Men like Paul Motson, Kenny Bronski, and Ibrahim Ali all committed financial crimes of some sort to try to make ends meet and to fulfill an ideal they strived for.[62] Their fraud, theft, and financial impropriety reflected desperation, greed, narcissism, and dishonesty. In contrast, Kevin Wu, Robert Mochrie, and Wagner did not engage in such financial impropriety, although Mochrie did engage in illegal acts of prostitution. Put simply, male perpetrators differed significantly in their lawbreaking behavior.

None of the female perpetrators resorted to criminality prior to the familicide. This may reflect a lack of opportunity on their part; less contact with the world of paid work where opportunities for example to commit fraud presented themselves. As we will see, women's ignominy was rooted in their sense they somehow failed their families, their husbands, and their children.

Readers have already met Nancy White, a homemaker with three young children and a husband, independent businessman Paul Eckles. The White familicide is unusual because there was no obvious motive. Although Nancy was subject to the rigors of speeded-up motherhood, with all its potential difficulties and challenges, she lived in a wealthy community and was not confronted with economic problems, the threat of bankruptcy, or destitution. According to family and friends, she did not experience childhood abuse and had no history of mental illness, including postpartum depression.

To the best of Detective Bohm's knowledge, the only call for help Nancy made was to request assistance with shopping for groceries. The only thing about the White familicide that Detective Bohn identified as significant was Nancy's exaggerated concern about the health of her three-year-old, Ruth, who suffered from stomach problems and urinary tract infections. Investigators ruled out any possibility that Ruth had been sexually abused. Apparently, Nancy felt bad about Ruth's lingering health problems, and according to detective Bohm, may have felt some shame about her mothering abilities. Under the pressures of speeded-up motherhood, would such a feeling of shame have become so overwhelming to the point it might drive an act of familicide? As noted, the case for Nancy's shame in regard to her daughter is weak, and the White familicide is best seen as an exemplary example of the need to recognize the role of the inexplicable in cases of familicide.

We are on surer ground with Mandy Miller. Her act of familicide appears to principally stem from her husband's passing her over for another woman. Mandy's ignominy resembles that that of the livid Misook Beckenbauer, although Mandy's ignominy was seemingly muted, secretive, and not accompanied by any violence or obsessive attempts to control her husband.

Motives and Beliefs

Many of the civil reputable hearts appear to commit familicide for what they define as altruistic reasons. As we will see later, perpetrators also occasionally exhibit care for their victims. Perpetrators express concerns about the misery their families endure due to things like financial destitution, social disgrace, and illness.

Elements of narcissism or selfishness may accompany perpetrators' sense of altruism. Some perpetrators simply did not want to face the ignominy or disgrace associated with their gambling, theft, embezzlement, or financial mismanagement, to name just a few. The civil reputable hearts appeared to view their family members as extensions of themselves as opposed to autonomous individuals.

The civil reputable hearts almost always made the decision to commit familicide on their own. Only in rare cases do we see them even broaching the topic with loved ones or others. Their solitude in this regard probably provided them with some semblance of control, although the archive does not really allow access to perpetrators' sense of control. It is also clear that many perpetrators saw committing familicide as part of their responsibilities as a parent, spouse/partner, or both. Perpetrators appeared to have a sense of entitlement to kill. Some perpetrators clearly betrayed proprietary beliefs, akin to premodern notions that the head of the household is the final authority on matters of crucial importance. We must be careful with reading a sense of entitlement solely from the act of killing, however. We have no way of knowing whether the killers actually felt a sense of entitlement or whether they felt that what they were about to do was immoral but they would proceed regardless. Clearly, it is possible some perpetrators felt a sense of entitlement to kill and at the same time thought what they were doing was immoral or wrong. It is difficult to know how to assess the presence or weigh the relative importance of themes such as altruism, attempts to exercise control, narcissism, a sense of entitlement, and proprietary beliefs. As usual, returning to the cases helps us flesh out some of these important issues.

Many civil reputable hearts expressed concerns about the future well-being of their families, or we might reasonably deduce the presence of such anxieties from their behavior. Men like Robert Mochrie, Kevin Wu, and Paul Motson exhibited grave concerns about their families' facing financial destitution. Their own ignominy and desire to avoid further public humiliation spurred their decisions to kill. Robert Mochrie was perhaps concerned about his two youngest children, Luke and Bethan. At age eight, Luke contracted a life-threatening brain tumor that resulted in his having minor learning difficulties. Bethan was autistic and received special education. How would these youngsters have fared had their father only committed suicide? Mochrie may have believed that killing his children as well as himself was preferable to killing himself only, because the latter option would not ensure that his children's special needs would be addressed in the absence of a father. Mochrie's motives for committing familicide reflect an exaggerated belief in his own importance as a father. It seems he thought his wife or extended family could not look after the children in his absence. Neither did Mochrie appear to think the state could somehow look after his children in the event he committed suicide.

Perhaps Kevin Wu also refused to explore the option of his wife's carrying on in his absence. It is difficult to know what options Kevin weighed prior to committing familicide. Rather than frame Wu's familicidal behavior in terms of his sense of entitlement, narcissism, or self-importance, his family doctor, who had known Wu since high school in Hong Kong, explained Kevin's decision to commit familicide instead of suicide as "his way of loving his family."

In some ways the elements of narcissism in the Motson case appear stronger than in those of Mochrie and Wu. Such differences are those of degree, not kind, and I am not suggesting the existence of subtype of civil reputable hearts that we might call "overly narcissistic." Paul Motson actively contemplated suicide, eventually deciding to kill his family as well because he could not stand the thought of them dealing with his suicide as well as the potential destitution. Even stronger evidence of narcissism emerges in the Bronski, Wagner, and List cases.

Bronski's suicide note was clear; he could not live with the disgrace of being caught stealing from a drunk driver. According to what he told his psychiatrist, the German schoolteacher, Wagner, engaged in what he saw as an act of mercy in killing his wife and four children. In killing them all, he removed any possibility of their being humiliated by revelations about their father's act of sodomy. In Wagner, in addition to any possible altruism, we see both narcissism and condescension. Wagner was petrified of being publicly humiliated through the circulation of information regarding his prior homosexual experiences. However, the element of condescension is also strong, especially given the way Wagner looked on his wife as his social inferior. Yet again we note the powerful influence of ideas about the appropriate way of being masculine in the modern era. It is here in the making of masculinities that we see the insidious workings of a very productive form of power in the modern era. Wagner was acutely fearful of people's identifying him as a homosexual, widely viewed as a deviant form of sexuality, utterly inconsistent with being a successful man.

We find similar themes in John List's familicide. He had come to resent his wife, who at the time of her death was in the advanced stages of syphilis. She supposedly contracted this disease from her first husband, although she somehow kept this information from John for 18 years. Yet John's resentment toward his wife was only a part of the motive. He feared his family was drifting away from what he saw as important Christian values. Killing his wife and children meant for certain they would go to heaven. John said he knew his God would forgive his act of killing, even although it was contrary to one of His commandments.[63] As John would later comment, "I convinced myself that this was the only way out, and I had to carry through with it. . . I did not consider how this would affect others. It was almost like I was looking in the wrong end of a set of binoculars."[64] He may have killed partially out of a sense of altruism. However, there was a strong element of narcissism in this case, with John planning the killing in such a way that he could escape.

There is only one case of a female civil reputable heart where her motives and beliefs appear to involve some sense of altruism. Mary Curtis, mentioned earlier in this chapter, sent several letters to friends telling them that she committed familicide "to leave them all in peace."[65] Mary had been worrying for some time about her son, who had just been released from hospital and was experiencing intestinal problems. The entire Curtis family had been injured in an automobile accident a year before the familicide. As a result, Mary suffered partial paralysis and was crippled. Mary shot her family members as they slept. Authorities attributed Mary's motives to her worrying about her family as a result of their automobile accident. The *New York Times* captured the popular sentiment that Mary was temporarily insane at the moment of the killings. Medical examiner Leary concluded Mary was "mentally unbalanced due to worry."[66]

If we train our gaze on Mary's mindset, psychological problems, or supposed break with reason, we miss some rather important aspects of the case. Mary was partially paralyzed as a result of the automobile accident, crippled to the point that she could not climb the stairs of her house to kill her daughter. As we have seen, Mary was the daughter-in-law of the president of a railroad company. We do not know the extent of her husband's injuries in the automobile accident, but we do know that her son, George Jr.'s, injuries forced him to give up his job as a ticket seller. We learn George Jr. had been an "invalid" for some time, and that he'd been recently discharged from hospital because of intestinal problems. These injuries undermined the ability of family members to depend upon each other and to work together, creating a bleak future and great anxieties for Mary Curtis. Mary's personal mental condition was clearly important in terms of making sense of the familicide; however, I contend her shifting emotional style reflected a profound transformation of the interdependencies within the Curtis family.

Planning and Preparation

Many of the livid coercive hearts appeared to kill in haste, with sometimes explosive, vengeful violence, often in response to what they perceived as intolerable acts of provocation, abandonment, or betrayal. Readers will remember Marcus Sims's believing that his ex-wife had received a phone call from a boyfriend; Kevin Oxley's learning that his wife, Bonnie, was going to purchase a home independently of him; or, Ben Ronaldo's learning that his wife, Laurie, wanted a divorce.

The civil reputable hearts generally displayed considerable planning and preparation in the lead up to committing familicide. They planned and prepared physically, emotionally, and spiritually. In the extent of their planning and preparation, offenders like Robert Mochrie, Kevin Wu, John List, Paul Motson, and Lonnie Shell epitomize the performances of the civil reputable hearts. Where ignominy appears almost instantaneously and with overwhelming intensity, we find less time for planning. The widespread availability of firearms facilitated quick kills of this nature. The hitherto celebrated police officer, Kenny Bronski, killed within hours of being exposed as a thief and a liar, although some degree of rather hasty planning still accompanied his act of familicide. After killing his wife and son, he telephoned emergency services.

Some civil reputable hearts appear to have killed sparingly, thoughtfully, and clinically. The Mochrie case is one in point.

"It was not mayhem or a bloodbath," said Detective Inspector Paul Bethell, the leading investigator in the case. "It's methodical. It's controlled, managed. He's used some degree of pre-planning. Picture the scene. The house is in darkness, the house is silent and he is walking round. He goes from room to room. He strikes each of them with a blow or blows to the head."[67]

As we have seen, Robert and Catherine Mochrie had both engaged in marital infidelity in the last year or two of their long marriage. It is not clear if either spouse knew of the other's unfaithfulness or whether such transgressions would have mattered. It remains an open question whether any such knowledge of infidelity, at least on Robert's part, informed the familicide. Journalist Kevin Toolis opined, "Forensic reports show that her head wounds were no more or less severe than those inflicted on her children, which would suggest that, despite their respective infidelities, sexual anger was not a factor in the killings."[68]

Clearly, another interpretation is that Robert did know or sense Catherine was moving in a different direction, and that he suppressed and contained his sexual anger until he could do so no more. In this interpretation, the fact he used similar force on each of his five victims does not mean he did not do so in humiliated fury. It is just possible that he saw his children as extensions of their mother and therefore killed them with a similar level of venom. Unlike the livid coercive hearts, Robert was able to manage his rage, perfecting a stoic and quiescent emotional style that sustained him until the collapse of his business and the unbearable feelings of failure and shame this generated.

Yet another possibility is that Robert knew about his wife's infidelity but had reached a point where he did not really care about it. His family had become a continuous burden to him and providing for them was more than he could manage. In this hypothesis, Robert Mochrie emerges as the male equivalent of the speeded-up mother, someone emotionally exhausted and disaffected by the performance of his patriarchal role. If we find clues anywhere, it is in a longer-term appreciation of Robert's life and decline.

Robert Mochrie's life had been spinning out of control for a number of years. We might speculate that the option of at least taking his own life and perhaps even killing his family had surfaced from time to time, perhaps for some years. Fully seven years before the familicide, he told his psychiatrist that he wondered if it was worthwhile living.

Mochrie's planning in the wake of the murders was easier to discern. On the morning of Wednesday, July 12, 2000, after killing five people, Robert Mochrie put a note out for the milkman that read "no milk until Friday." At 5:30 a.m., he left a telephone message for the school bus driver saying that his daughter, Bethan, 10, would not attend school for the rest of that week. He used his then-dead wife's mobile phone to send a text message to her best friend, Debbie, canceling their arrangement to attend a parent-teacher association meeting that evening. The message, timed around noon on Wednesday, simply offered the excuse, "My mother's ill; we'll speak tomorrow." Robert then let the family dog and cat out of the house before hanging himself.

We will never know why Robert chose this particular juncture to commit familicide. Perhaps he wanted his wife to enjoy a graduation party before he killed her? Perhaps her graduation marked a watershed in their lives, bringing into sharp focus her desires to move in a different direction? Whatever his reasons for planning to kill when and how he did, it is clear he did not want the world to intrude until the familicide was complete. The precautions he took to keep people at bay for a couple of days raise the possibility that perhaps he wanted to mull over his decision to take his own life, or consider carefully how he might do this. It seems reasonable to suggest that he needed time to keep the world at bay, perhaps just for a few hours. Perhaps he needed a space for the hubbub to die down? As it turned out, no one found the bodies for 11 days. When authorities entered the home, the stench was unbearable. One cannot help but wonder if in all his meticulousness and fastidiousness, Robert Mochrie knew the foul scene the authorities would encounter. It was almost as if he was trying to tell us something about the charade his respectable family or at least its head of household was living.

Paul Motson apparently began planning his familicide at least three weeks in advance, if not longer. It is around this time we find what appear to be at least the beginnings of the emotional preparation. Indeed, twenty days before the familicide, Paul praised his wife and children in his diary and took full responsibility for their calamitous financial situation. In this particular diary entry, Paul somewhat cryptically noted, "There is really only one choice now." Eight days before the familicide, Paul wrote in his diary that he had had a prayer meeting with a friend. Entries that day included the comment that God was his only parent; a likely broadside to the parents who he perceived essentially deserted him. The next day we learn from Paul's diary that "Now a plan is in place should God give me the sign."

John List's act of familicide was remarkable, not just because of his meticulous planning, but also because he seems to have either explicitly or implicitly communicated his murderous intent to others. As noted, the job that brought John to New Jersey was a vice presidential position at a bank. Ultimately, he was fired and spent six months pretending to his wife and family he was going to work. He eventually found work selling insurance out of his home office at a drastically reduced salary. On the eve of the killings, he was facing bankruptcy.

According to Joe Sharkey's account, at some point in those final weeks, John sat his children down and told them to prepare to die. He asked them whether they preferred burial or cremation. From this point on, all three children perhaps understood he was going to try to kill them. Each child in his or her own way tried to communicate their plight to adults around them. None of them succeeded in doing so, although some of their teachers expressed major concerns about life in the List household. Patty, at age 16, told her drama teacher that her father intended to kill her.

John had assessed his options carefully. He could not commit suicide. Suicide offended his religious beliefs and was a sure path to hell. It also left his family to fend for itself, something a responsible patriarch did not do, especially not when the only other adult was ailing and, in John's mind, ineffectual as a parent and provider.[69]

On November 9, 1971, he murdered them all. John told people he was taking his family to North Carolina to visit a seriously ill relative. They would be gone for some time. The corpses remained in the house for a month before police finally entered the residence. By that time, John was long gone. Like Robert Mochrie, John List cancelled the milk and all appointments and commitments family members had made. Unlike Mochrie, List did not commit suicide. Instead, he successfully eluded authorities.

Police arrived at the Miller residence in time to see Mandy Miller raise a handgun to her temple and shoot herself to death. Mandy killed her husband as he attempted to flee out the front door of their house. She had already killed the youngest two of her three children. As police moved through the residence, they found a stash of ammunition in Mandy's sewing box. Investigators later discovered that Mandy had purchased the gun two months prior to the killing. They also found a letter from Mandy to her husband, Andrew Miller, dated ten days before the purchase of the handgun. Her eldest daughter, Alison, was out of the home at the time of the shooting. Alison later told investigators her mother "had been acting normal and did not appear upset recently." However, she also advised police that "her mother knew that Mr. Miller had been seeing another woman."

In this letter, Mandy says "I have been pushing love at you so strongly. It finally occurred to me that that is not what you are looking for. You are tired. You are disgusted with life in general." After acknowledging Andrew's seeming state of disenchantment, she continues, "I have found my something—it is you, in every sense of the word. It hasn't always been this way. I have prayed to God that it isn't too late. I pray you will find your something in me. If I could have a second chance. There are so many things I want to tell you but I realize I must try to be patient and wait for you, give you your much-needed chance and not think only of myself. I am ready to try living our lives your way, although many times I thought we were."

I will return to this letter in Chapter 6. The letter registers Mandy's attempt to reconnect with her husband and salvage their family life. We can probably assume Andrew Miller had already moved on. The purchase of the gun ten days after the dating of the letter suggests that during that intervening period Mandy reached the conclusion that her husband was not returning to her and that her family life as she knew it was over. The purchase of the gun marks a significant change in Mandy's problem-solving. It suggests she became alive to the possibility of killing herself and/or other family members. The killings were confrontational, raising the possibility that Mandy did not necessarily plan to kill precisely when she did. At one point, her son ran into the street, yelling to a neighbor that his mother was killing everybody. He ran back into the house before being killed. We might surmise that she became embroiled in an altercation with her husband and reached for the gun.

The fact that she hid her gun and ammunition in her sewing basket is a bleak reminder of the rigidity of the separate spheres of physical labor in this family, a division that also mirrored what had become major emotional fault lines between the spouses. All we can do here is map the chronological parameters of her planning. It took her six weeks or so from the purchase of the gun to commit familicide. Without knowing more about Mandy Miller's comfort level with guns, we can only surmise that somehow she developed a relationship with that weapon as it sat in secrecy in her sewing closet, working its way seamlessly into her heart as a means of righting her despair and humiliation as a failed wife.

We learn a little more about the relationship between a female civil reputable heart and her weapon of choice from the case of Heather Holcombe. Like Mandy Miller and all the other female civil reputable hearts, Heather was a stay-at-home mother and homemaker and her husband the principal provider. Unlike Mandy Miller's husband, Andrew, as far as we know Heather Holcombe's husband, Billy, was not seeing another woman. Rather, Billy was stiflingly controlling, forbidding Heather to even talk with other men in the neighborhood. In the lead-up to the killings, Heather began practicing with the eventual murder weapon. Police found shell casings in several areas of the residence, suggesting Heather practiced firing the gun before using it to commit familicide.

Described by neighbors as a "very sweet" wife and mother, Heather Holcombe shot her husband and children as they slept. Test-firing the weapon probably provided her with important information about how she might successfully commit the familicide. Her nervousness with the gun reflected her overall state of acute anxiety. With all her anxieties and depression, Heather managed to carefully plan these killings. Her emotional style was embedded in the atmosphere of feeling within her family, and particularly her husband's attempt to restrict her contact with other men in the neighborhood. Heather's concern to kill family members as they slept may have mirrored her fear of her domineering husband, her love for her children, and her unbearable anxieties.

Killing with Care

By *caring*, I refer to the care used at the crime scene; for example, killing victims as they slept, or cleaning up the corpses, and so on. I distinguish this from the term *altruism*, which I employ to refer to an overall sense on the part of perpetrators that they were saving their family members from negative consequences such as destitution or illness.

Among the male civil reputable hearts we occasionally find evidence of what might be construed as caring for the bodies. The decision of perpetrators like Heather Holcombe, Robert Mochrie, Kenny Bronski, Paul Motson, and Kevin Wu to kill family members as they slept may reflect attempts to spare victims the conscious experience of a violent death.

However, it is also possible perpetrators killed slumbering or otherwise unconscious victims because it was an easier and surer way of getting the job done, engendering little if any resistance. Mandy Miller's act of familicide was most likely angrier, probably reflecting her humiliated fury at her husband for moving on to another woman.

Given the crime scene evidence, we are often on safer ground talking of the possible presence of caring in the aftermath of the killings. For example, Kevin Wu placed gold bullet-shaped objects under the bodies of his wife and two sons. These seem to have been some kind of talisman, functioning symbolically to bring wealth in the world to come. Robert Mochrie mopped up blood that had splashed on the wall behind his 16-year-old daughter Sian's bed, where he had hammered her to death. Mochrie pulled duvet covers up over the heads of his two sons and his wife, Catherine. Readers will remember how William Beadle took the corpses of his three dead daughters, laid them out on the floor, and covered them with a blanket. In her original suicide note to her husband saying she was going to kill their three-year-old daughter, Ruth, and then commit suicide, Nancy White told Paul where to find the medications that he would need to take care of the two children she intended to leave behind.

The fact that some of the civil reputable hearts displayed altruism and caring as they killed makes their familicidal acts all the more shocking and disturbing. Whereas these perpetrators might have seen their killings as forms of euthanasia, the majority of the population, in accord with the prescriptions of the criminal code, defines such acts as murders.

The juxtaposition of their respectability and their latent discontent raises important questions about modern notions of intimacy and companionate family life. If indeed the life of the heart is continuous with the social construction of reality, then it is important that we further train our gaze on the emotions that feed the tendency toward familicide.

NOTES

1. The cases are Curtis, Brandley, White (pseudonym), Allen (pseudonym), Holcombe (pseudonym), Miller (pseudonym), and Baines (pseudonym).

2. For a longer discussion of the John List familicide, see Sharkey, 1990; and Benford and Johnson, 2000. John List (2006) provides his own account of his life and the influences shaping his decision to commit familicide.

3. Sharkey, 1990: 16.

4. List, 2006: 3–4.

5. List, 2006: 4.

6. List, 2006: 5.

7. List, 2006: 5. It is possible that John List is romanticizing and idealizing his early childhood experiences in order to cast himself in a more favorable light. Those who have written about John List tend to describe a much colder childhood, a tendency in their writing possibly born out of a need to paint a picture of a somewhat negative upbringing for a man who committed such a heinous familicide.

8. List, 2006: 5.

9. List, 2006: 6.

10. List, 2006: 7.

11. List, 2006: 7.

12. Kevin Toolis, *The Guardian*, July 13, 2002.

13. Kevin Toolis, *The Guardian*, July 13, 2002.

14. Leyton, 2005: 340–345.

15. Bruch, 1967: 694.

16. Bruch, 1967: 694.

17. *New York Times*, August 14, 1925: p. 1. "Crazed Wife Kills Two and Herself."

18. *New York Times*, March 12, 1915: p. 8. "Insane Wife Kills Family and Herself."

19. *New York Times*, March 12, 1915: p. 8. "Insane Wife Kills Family and Herself."

20. *New York Times*, March 12, 1915:. p. 8. "Insane Wife Kills Family and Herself."

21. *New York Times*, March 12, 1915: p. 8. "Insane Wife Kills Family and Herself."

22. *New York Times*, March 12, 1915: p. 8. "Insane Wife Kills Family and Herself."

23. *New York Times*, March 12, 1915: p. 8. "Insane Wife Kills Family and Herself."

24. Websdale and Alvarez, 1998.

25. *New York Times*, March 12, 1915: p. 8. "Insane Wife Kills Family and Herself."

26. *New York Times*, March 12, 1915: p. 8. "Insane Wife Kills Family and Herself."

27. List, 2006: 59. Italics mine. They emphasize John List's unacknowledged shame in the period immediately preceding the familicide.

28. List, 2006: 59.

29. List, 2006: 59. Italics in the original.

30. List, 2006: 59.

31. Fox and Levin, 2005: 178.

32. Sharkey, 1990: 27.

33. Sharkey, 1990: 29.

34. Benford and Johnson, 2000: 123.

35. Sharkey, 1990: 189.

36. Sharkey, 1990: 194.

37. Sharkey, 1990: 204.

38. Sharkey, 1990: 274.

39. List, 2006: 79.

40. List, 2006: 79.

41. List, 2006: 79.

42. Kevin Toolis, *The Guardian*, July 13, 2002.

43. Kevin Toolis, *The Guardian*, July 13, 2002.

44. Kevin Toolis, *The Guardian*, July 13, 2002.

45. The term *psychosis* describes a psychiatric disorder where one loses touch with reality. This may involve schizophrenia or mania. Symptoms of these conditions include delusions, hallucinations, incoherence, and distorted perceptions of

reality. For a good discussion of postpartum psychosis, see Ewing, 1997: Chapter 5; McLellan, 2006.

46. Doriden was used at this time to treat insomnia.

47. Sharkey, 1990: 75.

48. According to the DSM-IV-TR, *factitious disorder* refers to any group of disorders where the patient "intentionally produces or feigns physical or psychological symptoms solely so that he or she may assume the sick role" (APA, 207: 363). The extreme manifestation of this disorder is referred to as Munchausen syndrome. It involves both physical and psychological signs and symptoms. For more information on Munchausen syndrome by proxy, see Cleary, 2005; Raitt and Zeedyk, 2004; Gross, 2008.

49. Kevin Toolis, *The Guardian*, July 13, 2002.

50. Kevin Toolis, *The Guardian*, July 13, 2002.

51. Kevin Toolis, *The Guardian*, July 13, 2002.

52. Kevin Toolis, *The Guardian*, July 13, 2002.

53. See Sharkey, 1990, for a discussion of these matters.

54. List, 2006: 45.

55. List, 2006: 47.

56. List, 2006: 59.

57. List, 2006: 59. Italics in the original.

58. List, 2006: 69.

59. Benford and Johnson, 2000: 68.

60. Bruch, 695.

61. Leyton, 2005: 344.

62. One of Ibrahim Ali's debtors filed suit after the familicide, alleging that Ali had defrauded him of $280,000.

63. My observations are drawn from John List's letter to his pastor, Reverend Rehwinkel, published in its entirety in Benford and Johnson, 2000: 267–269.

64. Benford and Johnson, 2000: 287.

65. *New York Times*, August 14, 1925, p. 1. Crazed Wife Kills Two and Self."

66. *New York Times*, August 14, 1925, p. 1. Crazed Wife Kills Two and Self."

67. Toolis, 2002.

68. Toolis, 2002.

69. Indeed, Helen List's syphilis eventually caused blindness in one eye and brain damage. At John List's trial, Dr. Miller testified that in the later stages of the disease Helen became a paranoid recluse. See Sullivan, J., 1990.

6

FAMILICIDE AS A CONSEQUENCE OF MODERN EMOTIONAL FORMATIONS

We are now in a position to recap briefly. First, the historical evidence tells us familicide is a modern transgression. In premodern settings we find no trace of the mass killing of a spouse or partner and one or more of their children, with or without the suicide of the perpetrator. In short, familicide is a consequence of modern emotional formations. Second, many of the familicidal hearts experienced acute feelings of social disconnection. Offenders also endured intense feelings of anxiety, fear, shame, jealousy, rage, depression, and revenge. These two related aspects of their emotional styles, their social disconnection and their negative feelings, lay at the root of the familicide. Third, familicide appears to be socially patterned. Men commit the vast majority of familicides, although women commit enough to caution against any crass essentialism. Indeed, the gendering of familicide looms large in the findings.

In Chapter 6, I explore modern era figurations of feeling, familial atmospheres of feeling, and the emotional styles of perpetrators as means of making sense of familicide. These various emotional formations intermingle, and it is not my suggestion we can neatly separate them from each other. Indeed, because emotion ebbs and flows with social life, essentially constituting the lifeblood of social interdependencies, it is best to see these emotional formations as mutually constitutive rather than mutually exclusive. From birth onwards, human emotion is contagious, moving in complex ways that defy facile linear interpretations.

One of the hallmarks of modern life is the increasing value attached to controlling one's emotions and one's interactions with others. Such self-control was particularly emphasized among the ranks of bourgeois men. The chapter commences with a discussion of these cultural imperatives for self-control and emotional restraint. In what follows, I underscore the prominent place of anxiety, shame and anger among familicidal hearts. I commence by examining the place of anxiety in the lives of a handful of the perpetrators we have already met. My purpose here is not to reexamine exhaustively the prominent place of this primary emotion, but rather to affirm its central importance and its relationship to the emotional frailties of these offenders. I then go on to discuss shame and anger in the lives of the familicidal hearts. These analyses lead me into a broader ranging discussion of modernity, emotional styles and familicide.

CONTROLLING EMOTION IN THE MODERN ERA

Sociologists have long talked of the way modernity has altered patterns of human interaction. Ferdinand Tonnies wrote of the shift from community life (*Gemeinschaft*) evidenced by close human contacts and enduring relationships between kin, friends, and neighbors of fixed and known status, to a more urban way of life (*Gesellschaft*) involving less stable associations of people that were more instrumental, that pursued specific ends, and did not involve the whole person but rather were related to the increasing number of roles people played. George Simmel talked of the way urban life altered personality, rendering it more calculating, more individuated, and detached. For Simmel, webs of human interaction changed in urban centers, increasingly involving those not related by blood or marriage. He contended that the pace of life quickened, focusing increasingly on contractual relationships and the exchange of money. Erving Goffman's notion of "civil inattention" or "civil indifference" addressed the way strangers on the street acknowledge each other's presence with a brief glance or fleeting eye contact, thus reaffirming generalized trust among strangers and increasing social integration.[1] These interaction rituals are specific adaptations to modern life and are not found in the same form in premodern settings. Such interactions are emotional adjustments to the impersonal nature of modern societies, and yet another way in which people present themselves to others in everyday life. Giddens put it nicely: "In many traditional contexts where the boundaries between those who are 'familiars' and those who are 'strangers' is sharp, people do not possess rituals of civil indifference. They may either avoid the gaze of the other altogether, or stare in a way that would seem rude or threatening in a modern social environment."[2]

These measured public interactions in modern life contrast sharply with the tenor of life in the Middle Ages, an epoch of much greater violence and extremes of emotional expression. Johan Huizinga observed:

> So violent and motley was life, that it bore the mixed smell of blood
> and of roses. The men of that time always oscillate between the fear of

hell and the most naïve joy, between cruelty and tenderness, between harsh asceticism and insane attachments to the delights of this world, between hatred and goodness, always running to extremes.[3]

The early American Republic witnessed an increasing emphasis on the control of emotion. C. Dallett Hemphill noted, "the period's strongest advice to mask one's feelings was directed to *men alone*. More than women, men were implored to keep their faces as calm and unmoved as possible."[4] The fast-changing and increasingly companionate nuclear family became the principal target of these messages. Writings such as Lord Chesterfield's *Letters to His Son* influenced many parents, particularly those of the middle class.[5] This American bestseller, published posthumously in 1775, was reprinted dozens of times and cited and excerpted from frequently by authors of parental advice manuals. Chesterfield's principal message to his son was that he ought present himself to the world with poise and grace, regardless of how he felt. Parents cultivated these qualities in their children.

The upwardly mobile members of the middle class proved especially receptive to these messages, often incorporating them into their parenting practices. This cultivation of an outwardly personable and genteel demeanor emphasized hiding or disguising one's emotions. In a classic statement pre-scribing emotional restraint and careful calculation about human interaction, Lord Chesterfield advised, "The general rule is to have a real reserve with almost everyone, and a seeming reserve with almost no one."[6] Hemphill commented, "This disguised reserve was a new feature of genteel behav-ior, and thereby hints further at the manipulation (of both self and others) implied in the new self-presentation."[7] Chesterfield advised men to cultivate gracefulness to the point that such demeanor did not appear contrived. He begged his own son to become the master of his own countenance and to keep his face "as unmoved and unembarrassed as possible, whatever you may feel inwardly," for "a tell-tale countenance. . . is a great unhappiness."[8]

The control of one's emotions proved especially valuable to the rising middle class in instilling a sense of trust and confidence. Emotionally stable, even-keeled men made for good, reliable business partners. Unlike the landed aristocrats who relied upon extensive personal connections and the esteem they derived from their ascendant social position, the achievements of the rising middle class depended much more on their own efforts. The self-discipline of the middle class male provider slowly came to speak volumes about his character and reliability. His self-disci-pline increasingly became the aspect of his personality and presentation of self that others trusted. Instilling a feeling of confidence in others signaled that the man functioned well in the more and more competitive capi-talist market place, one increasingly populated by unknown others who responded, not to the cues associated with aristocratic notions of defer-ence, but instead to emotional styles evincing controlled comportment and rationality.

Men's achievements as sole providers were sources of pride. However, their failures led to shame and disillusionment. Sometimes this shame and disillusionment, as we saw with men like John Cowan, aggravated childhood feelings of abandonment, creating a swirl of insecurities. In other words, the links between men's paid work and their emotional style were clear and acute, acting, in a rare number of cases, to inform, unconsciously or consciously, their decisions to commit familicide.

Anthony Rotundo describes the desirable form of manhood in colonial New England as *communal.*[9] In this setting, men served not only their families but also their communities. A man's honor derived in significant part from his contributions to the community: his public usefulness. Much of this philosophy harked back to the landed aristocracy of Western Europe and its paternalism and concern for those below them in the social hierarchy. This dominant form of colonial manhood was fed by religious and other ideas that saw men as superior to women, as possessors of greater reasoning powers.

However, as Rotundo points out, during the first few decades of the nineteenth century, rising notions of self-made manhood gradually eclipsed those of communal manhood. It was between 1810 and 1820, for example, that the term "breadwinner" was coined to denote the responsible family man.[10] As Republican government emerged, the market economy expanded, the middle class became more prominent, and individualism flourished, increasingly "a man took his identity and his social status from his own achievements, not from the accident of his birth. Thus a man's work role, not his place at the head of the household, formed the essence of his identity."[11] The image of the self-made man of the rising bourgeois class gradually superseded the ideal of the genteel patriarch, a version of manhood tainted with aristocratic pretensions, privileges, and the exploitative colonialism of the British. The self-made man was also considered superior to the rough-and-ready worker, the emasculated slave, or the infantilized and dependent Asian or Indian. Michael Kimmel writes, "Avoiding the taint of aristocracy and subduing the working classes, the Self-Made Man was now, at mid-century, the dominant American conception of manhood."[12]

Rotundo identifies the emergence, toward the end of the nineteenth century, of a ratcheted-up version of self-made manhood he calls *passionate* manhood.[13] He notes that people increasingly came to revere male traits such as ambition, competitiveness, combativeness, toughness, and aggressiveness. Rotundo contends that as passionate manhood stretched self-made manhood to unprecedented levels, and that important qualities of communal manhood such as tenderness became "a cause for scorn."[14]

Summarizing attempts at controlling emotion from the closely supervised emotional life in the early colonies to the present, Stephanie Shields contends, "The goal seems to be one of achieving an idealized state of focused and controlled experience and expression appropriate to the evoking circumstances."[15] As noted in Chapter 1, in modern times the nuclear family increasingly became the location for this emotional social-ization. Although industrial capitalism deprived the family of much of its productive function and public schooling removed some of its formal educational work, the nuclear family became a site of nurturance, a cru-cible of intimacy, all engineered as romantic love increasingly formed the basis for the marital union. Firm social bonds became more intensively concentrated within the nuclear family.

Norbert Elias's historical argument about the increasing regulation of strong emotion sees emotions acting in concert, rather than as distinct phe-nomena such as anxiety, shame, and rage that can be neatly separated. At some level it is inappropriate to talk of individual emotions as if they existed separately from each other. Nevertheless, in what follows, I discuss anxiety, shame, and anger bearing in mind their fundamental connectedness.

Social performances and impression-management by the gender groups is one of the principal means of defining and authenticating the self, the individual. As we have seen, both the livid coercive and civil repu-table hearts failed here, albeit for seemingly different reasons. The former mostly lost out as intimate partners, also allowing their emotions, par-ticularly their anger, to get the better of them. The latter failed as provid-ers and also internalized their emotions to a dangerous degree, appearing profoundly inexpressive.

ANXIETIES

Anomie and alienation are two of the primary feeling states in modern-era figurations of feeling. In general, modern era figurations of feeling and familial atmospheres of feeling render modern emotional styles anxious in ways that their premodern counterparts did not. It is not that modernity is an epoch that is inherently more anxiety-provoking. People have always become anxious in the face of what they sense as a persistent and general threat to their well-being. Under modern social arrangements, much anxi-ety arises from who individuals perceive themselves to be and how they sense others view them. Therefore, under modern social arrangements the cultivation of the self becomes an increasingly reflexive and energetic enterprise. It is this reflexive tension, lacking the signposts and sureties of tradition, that generates much anxiety.

Giddens describes anxiety as an "unconsciously organized state of fear."[16] As he points out, anxiety differs from fear insofar as the former is not a response to a specific threat or danger. With anxiety the threat is diffuse and generalized, coming to haunt a person's emotional style and body. Most familicidal hearts experienced anxiety about the future. At the heart of this anxiety was the fact that perpetrators felt they did not really fit into the social order. Rather, they felt disconnected from it, feeling only a nominal sense of belonging.

At the livid coercive end of our continuum, perpetrators cowered, recoiled, and raged as they anticipated and experienced the loss of their intimate partners and/or their nuclear families. For men like Kevin Oxley and Marcus Sims, this heartfelt loss represented, not just the loss of their principal love object, but also an undoing of their already tenuous ties to the social order. The threatened or actual departure of their mate was a seismic threat to their already weak sense of belonging as social beings. For these particular men, this threat echoed and resonated with their early existential insecurities, their childhood traumas, their disrupted bonding, and their abandonment by their parents.[17]

How people proceed in the face of loss and grief depends in part upon their confidence, their trust in the world, and their personal sense of power. The livid coercive hearts had little confidence, trust, or emotional security, often feeling out of place or inadequate. Their emotional styles evidenced much less confidence in who they were, the nature and meaning of their existence, and particularly their identities as men. Indeed, their power was often limited to an immediate and highly circumscribed command over their partners and children.

It is no accident that so many of the lives of the livid coercive hearts were awash with mood-altering substances, especially alcohol, Readers will recall Ben Ronaldo's $1,000-a-month drug habit, Bill Langdon's angry alcoholism, the judge who passed sentence on John Cowan referring to the offender's "intemperance," and Kevin Oxley's longstanding and eclectic drug use dating back at least as far as smoking marijuana in a field at age eight. I suggest the addictive use of alcohol and drugs by the livid coercive hearts was a conscious or subconscious attempt on their part to ease anxiety, anger, and depression that sometimes had roots deep in their troubled childhoods.[18] As we saw, Kevin Oxley's anxieties were powerfully connected to his mother's abandoning him, the frequent relocations of his family during Kevin's early years, his accompanying his mother on her frequent marital infidelities, his small physical stature, his stuttering, his poor educational skills, and eventually his failure to graduate from high school. All of these difficulties made Kevin apprehensive, shy, and angry.

Kevin Oxley was struggling to define who he was. Modernity breeds these anxious personal travails over self-identity. Drawing on the work of Winnicott, Erikson, and Sullivan, Anthony Giddens argues that an infant's early sense of security derives from the nurturance of caretakers, principally mothers. Giddens comments, "Anxiety is felt through a—real or imagined—sensing of a caretaker's disapproval long before the development of consciously formed responses to the disapprobation of the other. Anxiety is a 'cosmic' experience related to the reactions of others and to emerging self-esteem. It attacks the core of the self once a basic security system is set up. . . . Rising anxiety tends to threaten awareness of self-identity."[19] Kevin Oxley felt that those closest to him, particularly his mother, disapproved of him, used him, and pushed him away. These feelings contributed greatly to his personal insecurity, something he would carry into his relationship with his young wife, Bonnie.

Most of the civil reputable hearts lived with enormous anxiety. The psychic energy of men like Robert Mochrie and Lonnie Shell was blocked or jammed, and their frustrations sufficiently high that (paradoxically) they were willing to depart from their commitment to law-abiding behavior and seek illegal sexual satisfaction through resort to a prostitute (Mochrie) or Peeping Tom activities (Shell). Their helplessness and emotional near-paralysis in the face of various threats greatly contributed to their decisions to commit familicide. Simply put, they perceived no options other than to kill.

As noted, many civil reputable hearts added to their anxiety by walling off various parts of their emotional lives, shielding them from onlookers, even those supposedly closest to them. Perhaps the most extreme walling-off occurred in the lead-up to the familicide. Perpetrators probably worried about being exposed as frauds or hypocrites. Indeed, the secretive behavior of these men continued until the very end: as we have learned, few people if any had an inkling of their familicidal intensions.

It strikes me that this compartmentalization involved something significantly deeper than surface acting. Arlie Hochschild helpfully distinguishes between surface and deep acting. *Surface acting* involves changing "feeling from the 'outside in.'"[20] *Deep acting* involves changing "feeling from the 'inside out.'"[21] Clearly, deep acting uses an array of strategies that go far beyond changing one's expression to actually effecting a feeling change. From her research, Hochschild offers a number of examples of how social actors alter their state of feeling: by changing their bodily state, such as engaging in deep breathing; by focusing sharply on a specific mental image; by "deliberately visualizing a substantial portion of reality in a different way."[22] Deep acting requires recognizing the existence of a viable and profoundly important inner self. Hochschild remarks, "To develop the idea of deep acting, we need an a priori notion of a self with a developed inner life."[23] She goes on to note that such a notion of an inner self is generally absent from Goffman's analysis. Hochschild observes, "From no other author do we get such an appreciation of the imperialism of rules and such a hazy glimpse of an internally developed self."[24]

The cultivation of the self in the face of uncertainty and rapid social change becomes a major endeavor for modern people, especially men. In this endeavor, the civil reputable hearts experienced enormous tension. Their homes were models of a traditional sexual division of labor, with wives being primarily nurturers and homemakers and husbands being the principal economic providers. In a sense the false modern dichotomy between rationality and emotion was reproduced by the gendered roles of men and women respectively. Nearly all of the male civil reputable hearts for which we have data mostly left the emotional work to their wives and female partners, often appearing quiet and taciturn, lonely and isolated. This emotional work included nurturing children, nurturing husbands, and providing for them emotionally. These men served as sole or principal providers by working in the capitalist marketplace. It was through their successes in the marketplace the men principally cultivated their self-identities. Their performances at home and in the workplace still involved much emotional work, including considerable emotional restraint. However, the emotional energy used to restrain oneself is not the same as emotional energy used to nurture and care for others. The former is more passive and restrictive, the latter more involved with the active negotiation of social interdependencies, and expansive.

In their occupational lives, the emotional styles of our men may appear to have served them well. Their concern with order and detail, their self-restraint, their discipline, and their commitment to routine meant they had an edge in their authoritative jobs as financiers, bankers, schoolteachers, businessmen, accountants, police officers, independent farmers, engineers, and doctors. However, for many, their inflexibility, compulsiveness, inability to fit in, seeming lack of creativity, and despondency undermined and diminished them as human beings.

It is possible the demands of their workplaces exacerbated these problems. The impersonal and bureaucratic nature of their jobs, the capitalist hierarchies most operated within, and the controlled communicative exchanges expected of them contributed to what Eva Illouz calls "cold intimacies." For Illouz, the capitalist workplace and particularly the managerial roles within it lead to a split between "an intense subjective life on one hand and an increasing objectivization of the means to express and exchange emotions on the other."[25] The deliberate "therapeutic" form of communication that developed as capitalism modernized "instilled a procedural quality to emotional life which makes emotions lose their indexicality, their capacity to orient us quickly and unself-reflectively in the web of our everyday relationships."[26] Illouz contends, "The precondition to 'communication' is, paradoxically, the suspension of one's emotional entanglements in a social relationship. To communicate means to disengage from my position in a concrete and particular relationship to take the position of an abstract speaker, affirming my autonomy or understanding."[27] It might have been that the cold intimacies many of the civil reputable hearts engaged in at work rendered them less able to participate spontaneously and wholeheartedly in interdependencies within their families. In particular, such effects of these inflexibilities may have adversely affected their ability to solve problems in their family lives.

We see various manifestations of their emotional inflexibility. Readers will recall how William Beadle, in the early days of the American Republic and in the face of his failing business, adopted a rigid plan for the family economy even while he maintained the façade of wealth. He displayed a similarly meticulous approach to the control of his victims' blood after axing and knifing them, laying bodies over the sides of beds or on the floor side by side to prevent the bedding "from being besmeared with blood."[28] Inspector Paul Bethell, who investigated the Mochrie familicide, commented, "Downstairs, we found a mop and bucket that had been used to wipe the blood off the wall in one of the rooms. The mopping was a fascinating act. It wasn't the action of someone trying to clean up a crime scene. It was like tidying up."[29] After Mochrie had murdered his wife and four children, he placed a note for the milkman stopping the milk deliveries, he cancelled his wife's appointment with a friend, and he left a message for a school bus driver saying his child would not need a ride to school.

In the period preceding the familicide, these civil reputable hearts brooded endlessly. They agonized about a range of looming threats, including a bad harvest (Purrinton), pending bankruptcy (Mochrie, List, Ali), financial ruin and criminal prosecution (Motson), or other forms of ignominy (Wagner, Bronski, Wu). Over time, these worries proliferated to the point of these men contemplating and planning familicide. The worrying of these men was cyclical, self-reinforcing, and self-referential. It was also a product of their roles as providers in modern nuclear family arrangements. Their inhibited emotional styles, including their narcissism and need to be in control, made it difficult for them to reach out to others and at the same time further distanced them from moral reasoning. In the end, of course, the murder of their families was immoral. As outwardly respectable as their concern with order and discipline might have implied they were, the civil reputable hearts lived rather compulsive routines as little islands increasingly isolated from the social whole and the collective conscience.

The civil reputable hearts suffered profound social disconnection of long standing. This made it difficult for them to enjoy creative social engagement with others and to participate actively in the chains of social interdependencies increasingly characteristic of modern life. Their ontological insecurity and nominal sense of belonging, even in the midst of the hubbub of family life, made it difficult for them to recognize the autonomy and individuality of others. This is one of the principal reasons they were able to murder the ones they professed to love and care for. Their concerns with orderliness, discipline, and structure reflect a nearly compulsive enactment of routines rather than a more rhythmic engagement with family members and life, with all the joy and sorrow this might have entailed. Their long-standing emotional constipation rendered it much more difficult for them to handle any looming catastrophe, whether that calamity appeared in the form of a foreclosure notice on a mortgage or a more general threat of exposure as a failure.

Robert Mochrie consumed slug pellets and weed killer before hanging himself. Essentially, he was consuming chemicals designed to eradicate animals and plants that grow in the wrong place, animals that are seen as lethargic, slimy, and disgusting, and plants that are ugly and choke out beautiful flowers.[30] Is it just possible that Mochrie's unconscious mind was speaking to us, telling us he was an unappealing life form in the wrong place at the wrong time? If this is the case, then his own unconscious sense of his nominal belonging, his disconnection, help us understand how Mochrie, and indeed a handful of other civil reputable hearts, were able to spend many hours in the presence of the corpses before killing themselves.[31] It is possible that for Mochrie, like the livid coercive heart Oscar Camacho and others, the familicide temporarily dissipated their enormous anxiety, serving on a much grander scale as something akin to the sense of release Lonnie Shell fleetingly felt as a Peeping Tom or Ibrahim Ali experienced as a compulsive gambler.

Men's civil reputability derives from their achievements as fathers, husbands, and esteemed employees. As we have seen, most of these men were soft patriarchs and employees who worked in high-status jobs. Female civil reputability stems almost entirely from women's roles as mothers and homemakers and, indirectly, as the wives and sexual partners of successful, honorable men. In the small number of cases where well-thought-of women killed their families, people saw those women first and foremost as mothers and wives. It appears the anxieties of the female perpetrators largely stemmed from their roles as overburdened mothers, nurturers, and caretakers. In two cases, those of Patricia Allen and Heather Holcombe, women's anxieties stemmed in large part from the terrorizing, intimidating, and controlling behavior of their husbands. There are no male equivalents of these women among the familicidal hearts, reminding us that committing familicide as a reaction to tyranny is profoundly gendered. Significantly, in the Allen and Holcombe cases, men's livid coercive behavior did not find its way into the police report, medical examiner report, or coroner's inquest, or the newspaper coverage of the killings. For all the general public knew, these female-perpetrated familicides remained something of a mystery.[32]

The roughly fifty-year-old case of Patricia Allen illustrates just how careful we have to be when assessing the socially situated meaning of coroner's verdicts that explain women's familicide in terms of temporary insanity.[33] As we saw in the last chapter, I was able to trace relatives who still remembered the Allen killings and were willing to share what they knew. Patricia's personal insecurities and dread had their roots in childhood abuse. Her mother died when Patricia was two years old. Her rather ineffectual father remarried, and Patricia's domineering stepmother tyrannized and humiliated the young girl. Patricia's abusive husband, Benjamin Allen, would only reopen these old wounds, creating new anxieties and compounding existing ones. As in a number of these cases, at some juncture, perhaps a few days before the killings, Patricia passed a point of no return. It is likely Benjamin's abuse resurrected Patricia's deep childhood injuries. The fear he instilled probably tapped an enormous reservoir of emotional pain. In the days before the killings, Patricia assumed a silent air. Whether this reflected abject fear of Benjamin or her decision to commit familicide is something we will never know.

One lesson from the Allen case is clear: Had it not been for the oral history evidence's surfacing, we would never have learned of Benjamin Allen's intimidation and livid coercion. The extant record, enshrined in the limited work of the all-male coroner's jury, was that she committed familicide while "despondent and temporarily insane." Our findings of a hidden history of livid coercion in the Allen case raise doubts about earlier familicides such as Brandley (1915) and Curtis (1925), both hastily attributed to temporary insanity.[34]

Other researchers make similar points about the way criminological theorizing and popular interpretations tend to overemphasize the mental state of female offenders.[35] In relation to women who kill their young children, Ania Wilczynski makes the point, "it is fallacious to equate the undeniable emotional and physical upheaval of the birth with mental illness, or even temporary insanity. Further, there is usually no evidence of psychosis or mental illness either before or after the birth."[36]

It is easy to see why authorities, coroners and police spokespersons alike, used notions of temporary insanity or something similar to explain female-perpetrated familicide. As noted in the Cooper and Allen cases, the label "temporary insanity" functions at one level to rescue women who somehow strayed from the path of reason. Of course, the price of such rescue is paradoxically to purge the familicidal act of any semblance of rationality. To reach the conclusion that these killings somehow made sense would have been enormously subversive. That married women who had fulfilled their alleged biological calling to reproduce could destroy the modern familial idyll from within with one implosive act of familicide, warranted swift resort to an explanation that put such behavior beyond the bounds of reason. We do not see the explanatory language of *temporary* insanity in any case involving a male perpetrator of familicide, a fact that indicates the gendered nature of the rather makeshift "temporary insanity" or "mentally unbalanced" verdict.

SHAME

Many of the familicidal hearts experienced deep shame and humiliation. By *shame*, I refer to a powerful negative evaluation of the self, deriving from a person's sense of how others might see them. We can feel shame in the absence of other people. Humiliation is a negative evaluation of self based upon a sense of how others might judge our behavior or action. Shame therefore cuts deeper than humiliation because the former involves a negative assessment of the self in its totality, whereas the latter results from negative evaluations based on a particular incident or particular behavior. The damage to the self from humiliation is less than that with shame, but humiliation can clearly contribute to shame. Embarrassment is more fleeting than either shame or humiliation and usually results from a passing feeling that one has not acquitted oneself appropriately in a particular endeavor, incident, or interaction.

Like everyone else, our familicidal hearts experienced embarrassment from time to time as they went about their lives. However, I suggest the familicidal hearts experienced crushing levels of shame that debilitated, depressed, and often enraged them. Among the 77 cases evidencing livid coercion, in 35 there was sufficient information to determine the presence or absence of shame and humiliation. In 30 of these 35 cases (86 percent) I inferred the presence of perpetrator shame as a powerful precipitant of familicide. Similarly, among the 41 civil reputable offenders, 25 cases provided enough material to identify the presence or absence of shame. Of these 25, I deduced that 23 (92 percent) revealed perpetrator shame and humiliation as a primary reason for the mass interpersonal killing. Many perpetrators killed to relieve their unbearable feelings of shame and humiliation. Many of our perpetrators failed to acknowledge their sense of shame, bypassing, repressing, or sublimating it, thereby often allowing it to intensify.

Perpetrator experiences of shame and humiliation are as prevalent as their nominal sense of belonging. The co-occurrence of shame and a nominal sense of belonging ought not surprise us, because shame is the emotion of social disengagement. We are shamed by actions or behavior that others find objectionable, leaving us vulnerable, exposed, and feeling inferior. Shame therefore profoundly threatens social bonds and the attachment of the individual to the social order. The resolution of shame and humiliation in people's lives can mend social bonds and enhance social solidarity. However, in the lives of our perpetrators, pride and shame worked divisively to further distance offenders from their families and communities.

One of the principal sources of shame and humiliation among the livid coercive hearts was the failure of their marriages and intimate relationships. In 52 of the 61 cases (85.2 percent) for which we have data, the intimate partner of the perpetrator was exiting the relationship or distancing herself, and to a much lesser extent himself, either physically or emotionally. Most perpetrators saw this as abandonment and in some cases betrayal. Perpetrators' sense that their partners had abandoned or betrayed them publicly identified them as unlovable and unworthy.

We find feelings of shame and humiliation in the case of Mandy Miller, whose husband had left her for another woman (see previous chapter). We find convergences between her behavior and that of Misook Beckenbauer, although unlike Misook, Mandy did not engage in a campaign of violence and obsessive attempts to control her husband. Rather, Mandy's approach appears on the surface more controlled, rational, and calculating, evincing a civil reputability that belied her deep distress and obvious homicidal strategizing. In her final letter to her husband, Andrew, she revealed her feelings about their marriage: "I have secretly wanted a man that would sit me down and say, 'my dear wife, this is our plan and this is the way we should do this' not 'I am going to do this and you can do that.'" It seems Mandy wanted more parity, more sharing in the making of decisions. She continued, addressing a common theme in the lives of female perpetrators of familicide, the traditional sexual division of labor in their families: "I have pushed myself through the years with child rearing, housework, thinking these were the right things to do. On the other hand I have wanted you to be proud of me for engaging in volunteer work, however small it seems." Mandy then addressed what she saw as the connectedness they experienced through their sex life, something we sense her husband had long since disavowed because he had moved on to take another lover. She continued, "And then there is our sex life. It too has always been a great symbol of love. It does relieve tension but it also reunites us each time. It fuses us together and it is somewhat like taking a renewal of our oath, giving to each other, sharing with each other."

Mandy Miller's relational orientation to Andrew, her desire for fusion, oneness, and re-unification reveal her disappointment and her longing. In this sense she resembles Misook Beckenbauer, who at various points talked about not being able to survive without her husband, Gerd. Mandy also wrote a preface to the letter in which she told Andrew, "I am alone—you are with me though. I wait for your phone calls and the encouragement they bring me." Her aching vulnerability is touching, and her awareness and expressiveness emblematic of her emotional capital. As I noted in the preceding chapter, it seems Andrew continued to exit the relationship, and Mandy's humiliation, like that of Misook Beckenbauer, eventually pushed her in the direction of committing familicide.

Unlike the case involving Misook Beckenbauer, where we had a smidgeon of knowledge that she had a tough upbringing, the Miller case archive tells us nothing of Mandy's upbringing or possible early childhood traumas. In this sense the Miller case reflects one of the greatest weaknesses of the archives, the dearth of information on the early socialization of perpetrators. It is therefore impossible to know how many perpetrators already felt unlovable and unworthy because of their early childhood experiences. Notwithstanding the spotty archival data regarding the early childhood socialization of offenders, the livid coercive hearts seemed to experience considerably more physical and sexual maltreatment than their civil reputable peers. Even with the limited information available, it seems reasonable to suggest that many livid coercive hearts grew up with rather strong feelings of inferiority or unworthiness. Displays of anger and rage punctuate many of the biographies of the men. Their inability to do well in school, to become successful employees, and to establish lasting, successful nuclear family units compounded these preexisting feelings, often with alarming intensity.

Many of the livid coercive hearts did not directly acknowledge or recognize their state of shame, leaving me to draw inferences regarding its presence and potency. Sometimes men referenced their shame indirectly. Readers might remember Marcus Sims's poem left at the crime scene where he used a barbell to bash to death his wife, Gloria, and knifed his son, Alex, in the heart. He told of his need to reclaim his pride:

> I need to stop this aching inside
> And hold my head up with pride.

The over-controlled civil reputable hearts probably experienced unbearable levels of fear and anxiety as they anticipated their public exposure as failed parents and spouses. It was their anticipation of their fall from grace, the loss of family dignity and pride that strongly influenced their decision to commit familicide. By definition, the civil reputable hearts were often taciturn, reserved, restrained, and conformist. Many of these perpetrators, at least superficially, appeared as bastions of respectability. Typically the civil reputable perpetrators sensed the inevitability of material failure, the looming presence of poverty or destitution and all that that implied about them. We cannot easily separate the material threat from the anticipation of shame because these are in many ways opposite sides of the same modern cultural coin.

In some cases the threat of material failure loomed very large. Readers will remember Robert Mochrie's mounting debts. With the other civil reputable hearts, the threat of material failure was more distant, indirect, and subdued, and the role of immediate disgrace or ignominy more prominent. As we saw in Chapter 5, local hero and police officer Kenny Bronski's unbearable shame and humiliation stemmed almost entirely from his unmasking as a thief and a liar. One might make the argument that such an unmasking had severe material consequences such as the loss of his job, diminished future income, and so on. However, it was the social implications of Kenny's transgression, the anticipated alienation or loss of social prestige that drove his familicidal act.

In both the Mochrie and Bronski cases, the eventual perpetrators had much to lose. Mochrie had been a successful civil servant and businessman; Bronski, an esteemed police officer and community member. In this sense the civil reputable hearts tended to face the prospect of losing more in terms of their public image than did the livid coercive hearts, who tended to be less well established as fathers, providers, and esteemed community members.

A number of other researchers identify shame and humiliation as the root of aggression, violence, and murderous behavior. Scheff and Retzinger argue that shame, if not acknowledged and if not respectfully communicated, can generate aggression and violence.[37] For these authors, a person's pride reflects the degree of their social integration and acceptance by others. Those accepted and appreciated experience pride. As they put it, "solidarity causes and is caused by shared pride."[38] For Scheff and Retzinger, humans have a basic need for attachment to their fellows, for a sense of belonging. They comment, "The nearer people are to a state of bondlessness, the more likely it is that violent emotions and behavior will arise. To the extent that people literally have no one to turn to, they are likely to become violent or mentally ill or both."[39]

Unfortunately, much of the feminist research literature on intimate partner violence and homicide has not seized the opportunities embedded in the extant psychiatric and psychological research. To some extent this is understandable, as this literature tends to explain murderous behavior in terms of the characteristics of individuals and their psychological biographies. However, the psychiatric and psychological research has much to tell us about the workings of shame and humiliation in cases of murder, even although these studies largely fail to position the emotional states of perpetrators on a social and historical canvas. It is indeed rare for these bodies of research to ask why it is that killings such as familicide are restricted to modern times or that the perpetrators are largely men. Nevertheless, in documenting the persistent presence of shame and humiliation in interpersonal killings, we ignore this literature at our peril.

In one of the classic psychiatric analyses of murder, professor of psychiatry John MacDonald reports the case of a 55-year-old dentist who murdered his wife and son with a claw hammer. MacDonald tells us the dentist had not been feeling well for several months. The man appeared to have been depressed, experiencing forgetfulness, lack of sleep and an inability to concentrate. His professional work suffered as a result, and his income declined. Understandably, the dentist became increasingly worried about his declining income. In addition, he was concerned over his wife's ill health. Socially, he felt his friends were avoiding him, a sign of his shame at his worsening social position.

As his plight deteriorated, the dentist began to hear the voice of the Devil telling him to kill his wife and son. His depression deepened. The dentist gave away his guns because he felt like committing suicide. He eventually sought hospital treatment. Just prior to the familicide, the dentist reported "I was worthless,"[40] another thinly veiled reference to his increasing shame. At one point he picked up a hunting knife. He later said, "I thought I would gash myself with it across the jugular vein."[41] The dentist brooded over the kinds of things many of our civil reputable hearts seem to have ruminated over, telling us, "I kept thinking about the bills coming, the house taxes. Piling up, piling up in my mind. . . . I thought everything was going to fall around my head. I knew it could be a catastrophe in a short time. My son wouldn't be able to stand the stigma, my wife wouldn't have the things she was used to."[42]

The dentist's words were those of the modern, civil reputable provider in a relatively closed nuclear family system. His sense of self was under threat, facing fragmentation. He was hearing voices and was unable to get out from under the pressure of the financial burden. Like a number of the civil reputable hearts we have met, our dentist said he cared about his wife and son and did not want to the leave them behind by committing suicide. Yet his sense of shame was central and palpable, although not explored by MacDonald, or others who have also resurrected this case in their own studies of familicide.[43]

Psychiatrist Manfred Guttmacher reported the case of Willie W., a houseman for one of the Johns Hopkins University professors.[44] Willie W. was so reliable that he had access to the liquor closet and transported his employers' children to school. Two days after Christmas, this trusted houseman killed his wife and only child. Guttmacher reported interviewing Willie in jail. Willie had been manacled for his own protection. The psychiatrist soon learned that at the police station Willie had held his mouth under a spigot and allowed "great quantities of water to gush

into it."[45] He repeated this behavior in jail, leading authorities to conclude he was trying to kill himself. Guttmacher reported Willie "felt he
was being spied upon from all sides."[46] Willie worried about a number
of things, some of which seemed to cause him acute shame. Willie's son,
Theodore, had been identified as a serious delinquent from an early age.
Theodore had just been expelled from the public schools, and they could
not find an alternative placement for him in a private setting, apparently
because of his bedwetting. When asked why he committed the killings,
Willie replied it was an easy way out. He told authorities, "Every time
we planned anything there was an obstacle. The boy was part of it. We
planned to buy a home and that fell through. . . . Something was pulling
us down all the time."[47] When interviewed under light sodium-pentothal
narcosis about the incident with the spigot at the police station and in jail,
Willie commented, "I had a black heart. I was dirty. I was trying to wash
my mouth out. One of the police told me I had a black heart. Everybody
was against me."[48]

Rather cryptically, as is sometimes the style of communication of those
experiencing delusions, Willie wrote his mother just before the familicide,
"I have eaten something here at home and the vultures are waiting to
get fat."[49] Prior to receiving sodium pentothal, Willie could not even
remember writing this note. Under the influence of this drug, designed to
elicit subconscious thoughts or information consciously withheld, Willie
said, "I thought the buzzards would eat me when I was dead and would
pick my bones."[50] One interpretation of Willie's note and his reflections
on it is that he was suffering acute shame about his son's plight and his
family's reputation. Perhaps shame was the "something" he had eaten at
home rather than acknowledged, something he knew deep down would
eventually allow the vultures to get fat.

Reinterpreting these comments some fifty years later, I suggest Willie
was articulating a sense of disgust with himself as a provider and father. As
a black man in a Caucasian world at Johns Hopkins in the 1950s, Willie
had won the trust of those he worked for. However, the labeling of his son
as a delinquent from an early age and Willie's own sense he could not get
out of a rut economically led to an acute sense of shame. Under sodium
pentothal he said he felt *dirty*. He felt vulnerable. Willie told authorities
he felt spied upon or exposed. All these are classic symptoms of shame and
humiliation. In the police station and jail he tried to cleanse his mouth
with gushing water. My interpretation is that he mostly swallowed his
disgust, repugnance, and shame. But as Scheff and Retzinger have argued,
shame not acknowledged or dealt with festers, sometimes leading to violence. Intuitively, at some deep emotional level, Willie knew or felt this,
hence his comments in the note to his mother just prior to the familicide
that the vultures were waiting to get fat. It may be significant, too, that
Willie had broken through some racial barriers and won the trust of his
employers. Is it possible that Willie became more susceptible to shame
because he had moved up in the world? Did Willie's social mobility create

strains that were as disorienting as they were potentially giddying? In such a setting was Willie now more likely to take the blame for his own failures to move forward?

Other pioneering research into homicide-suicide unwittingly identified the presence of acute shame. D. J. West's detailed documentary analysis of 78 cases from England and Wales included an interesting one, Case Number 72. West informs us the offender was a middle-aged man, describing him as "quiet, hesitant and decent living."[51] The man "had a marked stammer and was suffering from some nervous trouble for he was under treatment by his doctor."[52] His emotional difficulties caused the man to miss work. He fell into financial difficulties. Eventually, like many of the civil reputable hearts we have already met, the man was threatened with the loss of his home. He gassed his wife and child before committing suicide. The man's suicide note informed authorities he had killed his family to avoid the scandal of losing his home.

Talk about avoiding scandal concerns saving face or not being ashamed. This man's shame was unbearable, and I suggest it contributed greatly to his murderous behavior. It seems likely his shame built on and was linked to earlier sources of humiliation such as that associated with his marked stammer, which West reports being linked to nervous trouble. Neither West nor the researchers who have subsequently made nodding reference to Case Number 72 explored or developed these issues of shame.[53]

We find similar cursory nods to shame in the work of other researchers. Malmquist, who, in discussing a case of what he terms "altruistic familicide," reports the worsening depression of a man who felt "worthless and no good to anyone."[54] Wilson, Daly, and Danielle's important pioneering study of familicide reports a 52-year-old English librarian who killed his wife, daughter, and mother before taking his own life. The librarian was obviously despondent. The researchers quote from his suicide note, "For some years now I have wished to die. However, this would have meant leaving the three persons dearest in the world to me without my protection. I can't leave them to the threat of death from radiation sickness after the coming atomic war. . . . I have been dead professionally for 12 years, of which the last 10 have been a nightmare. . . . I am a man who thought himself a poet and wished to be nothing more, yet I have not succeeded in having published as much as a single line."[55] His sense of personal failure recalls the lament of the German schoolteacher, Wagner, whom we met in Chapter 5. Like the unfortunate librarian, clearly a civil reputable heart, Wagner, too, had grandiose ambitions to rise above his station, in his case to become a well-known dramatist. It is not so much the despondency of these men that drove them toward familicide; it was their shame and their hyper-individualism. The ambitions of the librarian and Wagner reflect modern drives for public acclaim and recognition over an inward sense of accomplishment in the community. For these perpetrators and for many others we have met, modernity seems to create inexorably painful public standards that the self sometimes finds impossible to meet.

The importance of shame in these detailed psychiatric case studies of familicide is implicit rather than explicit. It ought to come as no surprise that those working with, observing, or studying perpetrators of acts such as familicide, as well as those who commit these acts, often bypass or shy away from acknowledging or exploring the shame and humiliation present.

In her pioneering studies of shame, Helen Block Lewis suggested, "At least in our culture, shame is probably a universal reaction to unrequited or thwarted love. By its nature, it is a state with which it is easy to identify, and at the same time it is painful, so that both the patient and the therapist turn away from it."[56] It is not easy for perpetrators of familicide to recognize their shame, in large part because it is such a painful emotion, and also because in modern life failure also increasingly becomes the fault of the individual; the liberal, autonomous, and responsible self. Lewis adds, "Shame reactions, taken lightly, dissipate of their own accord. The self recedes into its more automatic background position and resumes its more taken-for-granted functioning."[57] Here shame regulates people, encouraging conformity with social norms, values, and behavior. She also contends, however, that many people deny their shame, suggesting "some intrinsic connection between shame and the mechanism of denial."[58]

People's avoidance of shame epitomizes the way this master emotion courses covertly and subliminally through modern social life. In premodern times, shame was much more out in the open.[59] For Norbert Elias, the suppression of feelings of shame and the ever-closer management of this emotion are among the essential hallmarks of modernity. The historical tendency to drive shame underground, to mask it, to not acknowledge it, and to deny it is one of the principal features of modern figurations of feeling, contributing a necessary although not sufficient emotional prerequisite for familicide. I now turn to Elias's work as a means of providing important historical context for my identification of shame at the heart of the modern generation of familicide.

In the development of modern Western societies over the last half-millennium or so, people have come to feel increasingly ashamed, humiliated, and embarrassed by an ever-proliferating array of behaviors and experiences. We have become much more susceptible to shame, even to the point of feeling ashamed of experiencing shame, humiliation, and embarrassment. At the same time, modern people often hide their shame, making it difficult for others to know how they feel. Sometimes the telltale signs are obvious: casting the eyes down, blushing. On other occasions the shamed person might experience symptoms such as tightness in the throat, nausea, and stomach pain, all of which are difficult for onlookers to see.

Elias identifies increasing feelings of shame, humiliation, and embarrassment at the center of the way modern societies are regulated. For Elias, these emotions promote social cohesion, albeit at the cost of injecting increasing amounts of anxiety into everyday affairs. In modernity, we are much more self-conscious about behaviors such as cleaning the body, expressing aggression, using violence, the proper relationships between adults and children, the conduct between the sexes, and our interactions with those above and below us in social hierarchies.

Elias sees the civilizing process as involving the transformation of human behavior. His detailed historical analysis of etiquette manuals, teaching materials, works of fiction, paintings, and other documentary sources identifies gradually increasing tendencies to check one's own behavior. The modern development of self-monitoring and emotional restraint commenced in courtly circles, gradually spread to the bourgeoisie, and only much later influenced the sensibilities of the working class.[60] A few examples illustrate the core of Elias's argument.

Elias quotes from Tannhauser's thirteenth-century poem of courtly good manners:

> "A number of people gnaw at a bone and then put it back in the dish—this is a serious offense."[61]
> "Do not slurp with your mouth when eating from a spoon. This is a bestial habit."[62]

Quoting from a song by the Marquis de Coulanges, dating to between 1640 and 1680, Elias excerpts:

> "In times past, people ate from the common dish and dipped their bread and fingers in the sauce.
> "Today everyone eats with spoon and fork from his own plate, and a valet washes the cutlery from time to time at the buffet."[63]

As modernity unfolded, social attitudes toward bodily functions also underwent a marked tightening. As early as 1530 Erasmus warned readers, "It is impolite to greet someone who is urinating or defecating."[64] We find growing concerns about blowing the nose. Erasmus' readers learned, "To blow your nose on your hat or clothing is rustic, and to do so with the arm or elbow befits a tradesman; nor is it much more polite to use the hand, if you immediately smear the snot on your garment. It is proper to wipe the nostrils with a handkerchief, and to do this while turning away, *if more honorable people are present*."[65] Behaviors like spitting increasingly became the targets of regulation. For example, in *The Habits of Good Society* (1859), readers learned that "spitting is at all times a disgusting habit. I need say nothing more than—never indulge in it."[66]

In the Middle Ages, people often slept in the same rooms and the same beds. As modern life unfolded, sleeping became increasingly private, something that happened between intimates, behind the scenes of social life. Elias informs us that the nightdress came into use at "roughly the same time as the fork and the handkerchief."[67] These items of etiquette and social dressage—the knife, the fork, and the nightdress—are what Elias refers to as the "implements of civilization."[68] These implements increasingly took into account the feelings of others, conveying a sense of decorum, a concern to avoid offending others. Elias contends,

"Sensitivity toward everything that came into contact with the body increased. Shame became attached to behavior that had previously been free of such feelings."[69]

Elias sees the steady march of feelings of shame, humiliation, embarrassment, and repugnance that affected behavior such as cleaning the body, expressing aggression, using violence, the relationship between adults and children, conduct between the sexes, and the proper ways of interacting with those above and below one in the social hierarchy as at the heart of modern social order. The parents of the increasingly private modern nuclear family became the principal means of inculcating these inhibitions and sensibilities. These modern shifts in human sensibilities and the growing differentiation of modes of proper conduct accompanied the rise of the individual and the constitutive political subject. For Elias, this shift operated at both a conscious and subconscious level. However, it was the subconscious adoption of these sensibilities that was the hallmark of their widespread adoption in modern Western societies. He observes, "people have begun to construct an affective wall between their bodies and those of others. The fork has been one of the means of drawing distances between other people's bodies and one's own. . . . For many centuries, this wall did not exist."[70]

The gradual and uneven internalization of these constraints and prohibitions contained elements of liberation and repression. It was liberating insofar as it rendered modern societies generally more peaceful, less riddled with overt aggression and public rage. In short, compared with their medieval ancestors, modern Western citizens live in relative safety and security, at least *vis-à-vis* the immediate public depredations of others. As noted in Chapter 3, one manifestation of this peace and security is the dramatic decline in homicide rates, measured recently by criminologists such as Manuel Eisner. Eisner examined local historical records of homicide rates from the thirteenth to the twentieth centuries in Western Europe and found very significant decreases over the long term.[71]

At another level, the modern individual is less at the mercy of his extreme emotions, better able to rein in strong feelings and to think before he acts. However, the internalization and gradual intensification of emotional inhibitions and various forms of social dressage raised levels of anxiety. As we have seen, modern anxiety is also intensified by the loss of traditional moorings, urban anonymity, and the alienation and anomie associated with less communal and more competitive ways of life.

The aristocracy and, later, the bourgeoisie did not simply impose these constraints and prohibitions upon the masses. Rather, Elias sees court society as one of the experimental locations that crafted these refinements in conduct and personality. He comments, "I don't think that a single class could be the author of changes while the rest follow passively."[72]

The gradual growth of distant markets and trade built trust, confidence, and sensitivity to others. These interdependencies were linked to the increasing rationalization in Western societies and the state monopolization of the use of violence, themes Elias and Weber both explore. Indeed, Elias observes, "No less characteristic of a civilizing process than 'rationalization' is the peculiar moulding of the drive economy that we call 'shame' and 'repugnance' or 'embarrassment.'"[73]

Modern Western societies operate through legal contracts and credit. In a sense, modern economic competition and free enterprise replaced the internecine strife of feudalism. As Christopher Lasch puts it, for Elias, free enterprise represents a "highly sublimated form of warfare."[74] For Elias, such developments are preferable to the violent feudal social arrangements based on the hierarchical subcontracting-out of military services between monarchs, aristocrats, and knights in order to realize political control and the right to tax subject populations.[75] However, in focusing on the internalization of psychic constraints and the overall advance of socially negotiated thresholds of shame and repugnance, Elias's approach tends to downplay the divisive aspects of capitalist markets and class strife. Clearly, the development of distant markets required an increased sensitivity to the needs of trading partners far away. However, modern capitalism has also exploited distant markets and workers, causing great dissension and disaffection in the process. Lasch puts it as follows, "Elias takes for granted what many of us have come to doubt, that history records the triumph of order over anarchy."[76]

It lies beyond the scope of my current project to explore the numerous debates concerning Elias's work. Unlike Marx, Elias does not see an economic base as largely determining or shaping social life, ideas, ideologies, the law, and so on. As Jonathon Fletcher points out:

> The marketplace was only able to flourish in conditions where there was a monopoly of the means of physical force in a particular area; that is, within pacified social spaces. Thus in contrast to Marx, Elias stresses that monopolization is not confined to the economic sphere and points out that a relatively successful monopoly of the means of production is only one type of monopolization.[77]

The covert circulation of inhibiting emotions such as shame and embarrassment contributed to the pacification of modern social life, especially when compared to the much greater levels of public violence in feudal societies. Modern Western societies are safer and more secure than their premodern predecessors in the sense that public interaction is more orderly, polite, and peaceful. Nevertheless, modern capitalist economies with their competitive divisions between haves and have-nots are also potent generators of shame and embarrassment. Indeed, many familicidal hearts perceived themselves failures as spouses, partners, parents, providers, and workers.

The livid coercive hearts often externalized their shame by using humiliated fury against those closest to them. The civil reputable hearts behaved with much more restraint and control. They, too, denied their shame or failed to address it, keeping their plight and what they perceived as the gloomy prospects for their family largely to themselves. The accumulated shame of the civil reputable hearts often steeped for long periods of time, manifesting as deep depression and, more rarely, as fragmentation of the self, including a drift toward a schizoid-type delusional behavior. However, the common emotional experience among the livid coercive and civil reputable hearts was their nominal or token sense belonging. Indeed, their shame was both emblematic and constitutive of their isolation at the same time as being the principal force behind their acts of familicide.

ANGER AND RAGE

Familicidal hearts run the gamut from those who venomously attack, coerce, and angrily seethe at loved ones, to those who appear to mostly acquiesce amidst the numerous frustrations and difficulties of raising a family. By "anger," I refer to those feelings of tension, potential aggression, and hostility that arise in the face of threats or perceived danger. Fear and anger are important human emotions that can, if used wisely, enhance people's chances of survival. These emotions are deeply rooted in human instinct and are accompanied by powerful bodily sensations that prepare the body for fight or flight. In the face of danger, the body shunts blood to the large muscle groups such as those found in the legs, to prepare itself for possible flight. In this state of fear, the face whitens— hence the expression, as Daniel Goleman points out, that one's blood runs cold.[78] Goleman continues, "the body freezes, if only for a moment, perhaps allowing time to gauge whether hiding might be a better reaction."[79] When one is enraged, blood moves to the hands, "making it easier to grasp a weapon or strike at a foe; heart rate increases, and a rush of hormones such as adrenaline generates a pulse of energy strong enough for vigorous action."[80]

Modern people face different threats than those of their premodern and indeed pre-historic ancestors. We may no longer face the threat of death from a wild animal or a marauding horde, yet we still use anger to deal with fear and threats, calculating our options of whether to flee or fight. Solving interpersonal problems through the use of murder and violence may have diminished over the last half-millennium but this does not mean that anger has no role to play in resolving conflict. As one popular author on emotion puts it, "Our disputes are carried on by others means today, but they still require grit and determination, and anger provides just such internal motivation. People who never get angry never get ahead."[81]

The historical tendency to control anger is a part of that much more sweeping development that Elias has called "the civilizing process," entailing the slow but sure reining in of strong emotions. Although Elias focused primarily on Western European civilizations, his observations regarding anger comport with the work of historians of the United States. According to Carol and Peter Stearns, modern Americans have been taught to subdue their anger in all its forms. Over the last three centuries the movement to subdue anger gathered considerable momentum. The seventeenth-century moralists focused mostly on excessive anger, rather than anger per se. The growing disapproval of anger, especially among the rising middle class, intensifies with the birth of the Republic, when the Stearnses note important changes in child-rearing practices that discouraged and stigmatized certain forms of angry expression. In premodern times, many parents used corporal punishment to break the wills of their children, inculcating obedience. Such harsh, coercive practices, often meted out with livid parental demeanor, did not teach children that anger per se was wrong. Rather, they militated against directing anger toward one's parents. The Stearnses observe, "The simple fact was that traditional Western society lacked the mechanisms and even the vocabulary to socialize children against anger in any general way."[82] As these authors document, premodern life was often angry, evidencing considerable hostilities.[83]

We find some of the earliest American attempts to regulate intrafamilial anger among the Puritans of Massachusetts Bay. Elizabeth Pleck observes that the Massachusetts "Body of Liberties" of 1641 prescribed that "Everie marryed woeman shall be free from bodilie correction or stripes by her husband unlesse it be in his owne defence upon her assault."[84] This prescriptive document was the first known written attempt in the American colonies to reform the practice of using violence within families. Significantly, it was the investors in the Massachusetts Bay colony who called for a written criminal and civil code to regulate conduct. Ironically, the Massachusetts "Body of Liberties" linked self-restraint to individual liberty as a means of furthering economic development and colonization. We see parallels here with Elias's arguments concerning the development of economic interdependencies and the need to become more aware of the sensibilities of others in distant markets.

By the eighteenth century, the campaign to regulate anger had gathered considerable momentum. Diary evidence increasingly revealed concerns about taming angry outbursts among the more educated and the well-to-do. The proliferation of advice regarding the control of anger was also socially situated. The advice manuals addressed men much more than women. The Stearnses note the appearance of words such as *tantrum* that have a negative edge that stigmatizes and even ridicules certain angry expressions. They date the first appearance of the word *tantrum* to mid-eighteenth century English plays and the early decades of the nineteenth century in the United States.

The civil reputable hearts were drawn almost exclusively from the ranks of self-made men. Although many were ambitious, they were mostly not aggressive or combative. However anxious and depressed these men became, they did not display anger and rage at their predicament. Onlookers described these perpetrators as mild-mannered, quiet, peaceful, and reserved. Even their acts of killing displayed little evidence of rage. We cannot read into the crime scene evidence that these men did anything other than use sufficient violence to take life. There is little evidence of mutilation or brutalization, a terminal emotional meltdown, a grand dissipation that somehow seemed to function as a final release. In short, the emotional style of the civil reputable hearts evinced an exaggerated capacity to suppress or impound their anger. We might speculate that their suppression of this instinctive and powerful human emotion contributed to their deep depression and ultimately to the familicide. Indeed, psychiatrists and psychologists have long reflected on the complex relationship between the suppression of anger and the development of depression.[85] Throughout human evolution, anger paved the way for fight or flight. Was it the case that familicide constituted the only flight option these isolated, hapless men thought was left to them?

There is more than a little irony in the lives and murders of the civil reputable hearts. Outwardly, these men almost bristled with compliance and conformity. In short, they embody the essence of the pacified individual in the public sphere. In a historical sense they appeared to have deeply internalized that long line of advice, dating back at least to Lord Chesterfield, to rein in the expression of strong emotion and re-present it to the world as grace or at least more than a patina of contentment. If it were not for their acts of familicide, once-successful businessmen like William Beadle, James Purrinton, Robert Mochrie, Paul Motson, Kevin Wu, John List, and Ibrahim Ali might have continued to serve as examples of those who kept a lid on their anger, foot soldiers of the modern psychic formation that held strong emotion in place for the good of all. In a sense these men embodied modern-era drives to "make oneself" while also harking back to earlier forms of communal manhood, of service to others, or at least devotion to their immediate nuclear family. Men such as these represent the historical embodiment of what the Stearnses have argued "has remained the most persistent motif in the emotional reconstruction of the American personality"; that is, the "need to keep the lid on anger."[86]

As noted, the restraint of public anger and rage has made life more peaceful, improved public security, probably contributed greatly to the significant decline in the murder rate since medieval times and to the disappearance of unsightly forms of public punishment such as branding and hanging.[87] It is my argument that the historic repression of anger and rage, seemingly so successful among our placid civil reputable offenders, contributed significantly to the rise of familicidal violence. Hence my earlier comment that modern notions of intimacy can contain the seeds of their own destruction. Seen in another way, the murderous acts of the civil reputable hearts remind us that the pacification processes of modernity work differently in public space and within families. Indeed, it is a problem of Elias's work that he fails to explore in detail the way the family facilitates the seeming pacification of social life through more permissive parenting and inculcating certain modes of communication between spouses, thus preparing children for a world increasingly imbued with a sense of affective individualism. The civil reputable hearts remind us of the precariousness of the pacification process and its complex interweaving with the politics of gender and particularly men's notions of entitlement, responsibility, and control.

With the civil reputable hearts, the absence of anger and rage from everyday family life renders familicide all the more shocking. These seemingly placid men led lives as reliable providers in the midst of fairly traditional sexual divisions of labor. With the benefit of hindsight, we now know many of these men must have experienced quiet desperation, unable to articulate it through their constrained emotional styles. On the other hand, the civil reputable hearts in their placid quietude present us with various combinations of acute anxiety, ignominy, suppressed anger and rage and depression emblematic of our modern lifestyles. Indeed, men like Robert Mochrie, Paul Motson, Kevin Wu, William Beadle, and James Purrinton require us to look more critically at the nature of civil human interaction, the so-called intimate/companionate family, the often-hidden workings of pride and shame, and the secret life of the heart.

MODERNITY, EMOTIONAL STYLES AND FAMILICIDE

The phenomenon of "honor killings" in traditional societies provides us with a vantage point from which to view modern familicide and to conclude this chapter. Gideon Kressel situates honor killings among the Bedouin as part of the struggle for status and social mobility among patrilineal kin groups. At the heart of "group honor" is the appropriate behavior, particularly sexual behavior, of females. Kressel notes, "Prior to Western interference, 'purging' the family honour was a public act."[88] He reports male elders recalling a time during Ottoman rule "when the murderer would sprinkle his victim's blood on his clothes and parade through the streets displaying the bloody murder weapon to increase his honour."[89] According to Kressel, there was widespread public approval for these rare acts, and the perpetrator was "a 'purger,' one who restored honour, not a murderer."[90] In these traditional settings, most victims of honor killings are females and most perpetrators are their brothers or less commonly, their fathers. At times, female relatives such as mothers, grandmothers, sisters, and aunts assist with the honor killing by arranging the setting or enticing the victim to the scene. Victims' perceived transgressions included initiating inappropriate associations with men, loss of their virginity, adultery, pregnancy, and causing problems over an arranged marriage. Kressel traces the plight of these young women to their relative weakness in a man's world.

Importantly, these honor killings coexist with community norms and civil legal codes. As Kressel and others show, an honor killing is more likely if the alleged transgression is widely known and if the social group to which the victim belongs is ascending the social hierarchy. Kressel is clear: "Realization of the threat actualizes its solemnity, helps deter the disobedient, and thereby reinforces male dominance."[91] In essence, honor killings bolster traditional male authority and reproduce hierarchical social arrangements.

Unlike familicide, honor killings in traditional societies often involve several perpetrators and one victim, nearly always female. The perpetrators and their conspirators are principal enforcers of the sexual rules of the kin group and the wider community. Their acts of killing restore honor to the shamed kin group. The public disgrace leads to a public resolution. The shame of the kin group is there for all to see, so too is the restoration of esteem through honor killing.

More recent scholarship identifies the existence of "fake honor killings" of women who have not "dishonored" their families through engaging in some kind of transgression such as adultery. In their research into *Karo-Kari*, a form of honor killing in Pakistan, Patel and Gadit uncovered examples of women becoming the targets of *Karo-Kari* attacks merely for seeking divorces from their husbands.[92] Men who perpetrate *Karo-Kari* attacks for these "bogus" reasons are able to "obtain the customary endorsement for their actions and avoid retribution."[93] In poorer communities in Sindh, fake honor killings also sometimes occur "when a woman is felt to have become a financial burden on the household."[94]

Other scholars have suggested that honor killings of women in the forms noted above ought properly be defined as a form of violence against women and "that the terms 'honor based violence' and '*honor killings*' should be dropped."[95] Aisha Gill argues, "There is no honor involved in these murders, and that calling them honor killings belittles the victims and plays down the severity of these crimes."[96] Gill continues, "Honor is actually less important as a concept than the desire on the part of male leaders within these patriarchal social groups to retain their political and cultural authority by reinforcing established gender roles and expectations."[97] Gill admits her argument to remove the language of honor killings and replace it with the language of violence against women is "unashamedly polemical."[98] Gill's polemic to align honor killings with the vast array of other forms of violence against women is understandable. However, she provides no evidence that male leaders' desire to retain their political and cultural authority somehow trumps their commitment to an honor code. More important, she implies that the code of honor of these male leaders is somehow distinct from the societal subordination of women, when, in fact, the two are interwoven into the same cultural cloth.

My reason for mentioning honor killings is that they do reflect the vestiges of premodern patriarchal arrangements in which shame operates explicitly and overtly. As I have argued, modern era figurations of feeling result in shame becoming increasingly hidden, masked, and subterranean. Under these modern-era emotional formations, we witness the rise of emotional styles and familial atmospheres of feeling conducive to the emergence of familicidal hearts. In addition, the shame of the modern familicidal heart is borne individually, not collectively. As we have seen, many of the familicidal hearts bypassed or failed to acknowledge their enormously painful feelings of shame and humiliation. Familicidal hearts are therefore products of their time, archetypes of modernity. Unlike honor killings, familicides do not comport with community or even patriarchal mores. Neither do they restore "honor." Rather, modern communities stand incredulous in the face of these massacres, wondering how perpetrators could have engaged in such depravity. The incredulity alone reminds us just how much modernity transforms gender regimes in the direction of equality, regardless of the stubborn persistence of livid coercion and gender inequalities.

The historical workings of shame connect honor killings in traditional societies and the killing of intimate partners in the modern era. Nancy Baker, Peter Gregware, and Margery Cassidy identify breaches of honor as a factor in the modern era killings of female intimates.[99] Like Kressel and others, they contend that female "misbehavior" in traditional societies can dishonor the men of the family, kinship group, clan or community. Female behavior and specifically their sexuality therefore become the target of close surveillance and control, in part because female reproductive capacities are so highly valued and coveted. Indeed, the failure to control becomes a source of dishonor in these traditional settings. In modern Western societies they point out that batterers have killed women who challenged their control, thus restoring their pride in a manner akin to honor killings in premodern settings. They comment, "The difference is that the male *who kills to assert his control* is the intimate partner and not the brother or father of the victim."[100]

Another way of interpreting the killing of females in traditional and modern societies is not as an assertion of male control but rather as a means of relieving or discharging shame and humiliation and restoring a sense of pride and honor. In my analysis of familicide, it is the latter interpretation I prefer, although I have no doubt from the archive that the livid coercive hearts *sought* control over their wives and intimate partners. Readers might remember Marcus Sims telling those who found the body of his wife and child that he needed to hold his "head up with pride." In the panic of loss, Sims used extreme and homicidal violence to discharge his unbearable feelings of shame. His acts recall Eric Fromm's reminder that "one of the most effective ways of getting rid of anxiety is to become aggressive. When a person can get out of the passive state of fright and begin to attack, the painful nature of fright disappears."[101]

Marcus's brutal murder of his wife and son using barbells and a knife temporarily relieved his humiliated fury at hearing his estranged wife receive a phone call from another man. Since time immemorial, one way men have relieved their fear, anger, and shame is through the use of violence. Indeed, one of the many important points James Gilligan makes is that violence distances the self from the shame it feels, short-circuiting the pain, if you will. Gilligan's astute insights apply to many of the episodes of violence in the Sims case and those of the other livid coercive hearts, outbursts of rage that appear totally disproportionate to what appear to be the merest of slights. Readers might remember the report from Marcus's son, Marcus Jr., that Marcus burned his first wife, Janine, with a hot iron for feeding the boys when she returned from work. We can only speculate that Marcus felt ignored and therefore disrespected by Janine's attention to the boys. Such a "slight" may appear trivial to readers, but as Gilligan points out, it cuts to the heart of the feelings of shame violent men possess. From his work with prisoners, Gilligan observes that violent men hide their vulnerability to shame as if their lives depended on guarding this secret. He comments, "This is a secret that many of them would rather die than reveal."[102] He continues, violent men "feel ashamed— deeply ashamed, chronically ashamed, acutely ashamed, over matters that are so trivial that their very triviality makes it even more shameful to feel ashamed about them, so that they are ashamed even to reveal what shames them. . . . Often violent men will hide this secret behind a defensive mask of bravado, arrogance, 'machismo,' self-satisfaction, insouciance, or studied indifference."[103]

Saving face is at the root of much of the intimate violence of the livid coercive hearts. The stakes are much more significant when it comes to their acts of killing. At these junctures the livid coercive hearts are responding to a threat to their very identity as men in a world policed by the imperatives of modern masculinities. Again, Gilligan puts it well when he observes that violent men kill when they feel they are faced with a "total loss of honor, prestige, respect, and status—the disintegration of identity, especially their adult, masculine, heterosexual identity; their selfhood, personhood, rationality, and sanity."[104] Significantly, among the livid coercive hearts, men were bereft of other sources of pride that might have bolstered the self, shored it up, so to speak. As we have seen, the livid coercive hearts enjoyed little if any esteem through the ways they provided for their families, callings that many of them sensed they failed at. Following Gilligan's logic, the livid coercive hearts lacked nonviolent options for reducing their intense feelings of shame.

The intensity of shame among the livid coercive hearts and their meager social standing nurtured their familicidal hearts. However, Gilligan notes a third aspect of the emotional styles of the prisoners he worked with that fed their violent tendencies: that is the absence, at least at the time of their murderous behavior, of emotions that typically inhibit violence.[105] These emotions are love, guilt, and fear, particularly fear for the self. All of the livid coercive hearts exhibited a dearth of these inhibiting emotions in the lead-up to the kill and also on occasions where they had used great violence against their partners.

Another characteristic of the livid coercive hearts was their vulnerability and their dependence on their spouses and partners. Indeed, as I pointed out in Chapter 4, the livid coercive hearts often clung to and pined for the partners they assaulted and attempted to control. Their inner sense of this vulnerability was at odds with the imperatives of dominant notions of masculinity, that successful men are strong, independent, providers upon whom others depend. We might then rightly ask ourselves what the livid coercive hearts were attempting to gain control over as they murdered their loved ones. In a logic that parallels Gilligan's, I suggest that they gained fleeting control over their alarming and sometimes inchoate sense of vulnerability and dependency by vanquishing the immediate love objects they pined for and clung to. It is also possible these perpetrators killed to feel alive, in part because they had become deadened through the routines of emotional dressage that in modern families more than any other historical versions of the family, are supposed to provide nurturance, sustenance, and love.

Whether one is feminist or anti-feminist, the debate about men's control or ebbing control is a bit of red herring. As Susan Faludi points out, these conflicting perspectives "are rooted in a peculiarly modern American perception that to be a man means to be at the controls and at all times to feel yourself in control."[106] However, this perception confuses the prescriptive ideologies of influential writers like Lord Chesterfield with the lived experiences of men themselves. Again, as Faludi indicates, the problem with the feminist and anti-feminist views of male control is that neither "corresponds to how most men feel or to their actual positions in the world."[107] Faludi's observations derive in part from her time spent talking with men in a batterer's intervention program. After many years of working with men in such settings, psychologist Donald Dutton makes a similar point: "in intimate conflict men appear to feel generally powerless, threatened, and out of control."[108]

We can debate until we are blue in the face whether one "controls" something by destroying it. One interpretation of such destruction is that it leaves nothing to control or even attempt to control. Another interpretation of the destructiveness of familicide is that it provides an ultimate form of control at that particular moment in time; only later do perpetrators reflect on the futility of their acts, assuming they do not take their own lives in the process.[109] In the final analysis the livid coercive hearts clearly failed to control their own rage. In this sense, the livid coercive hearts are far removed from those successful self-made men of modern capitalism who reined in their anger, creating an emotional style that spelled success in the competitive marketplace. Rather, the livid coercive hearts were marginal to capitalist production, relatively unsuccessful providers, and often at a loss in the arena of intimacy. Probably this marginality constituted another source of shame, as they struggled to provide for their families and create the much-vaunted nuclear family idyll they themselves probably did not have as children. Their failings were their own, as was their shame. However, their destructive emotional styles must be framed against the repressive emotional climate of modern society, a society where ontological insecurities reign; where to be successful, strong emotions must be suppressed; and where one's shame is not shared but absorbed or inhaled, not by extended kin or the community but into one's viscera and heart. Indeed, it is no accident that many premodern cultures have ceremonies for the ritual discharge of shame, processes that reintegrate people into the social order. As John Braithwaite, among others, points out, in many Western industrialized societies, punishment involves degradation ceremonies that stigmatize and further alienate offenders rather than bring people back into the fold.[110]

The emotional styles of the civil reputable hearts were exaggerated versions of those of the successful self-made middle class men of modern capitalism. We might see the civil reputable hearts as over-internalizing the historic strictures of men like Lord Chesterfield, taking them to an extreme, taking them too much to heart. They lived overly anxious yet highly secretive lives. Readers will remember the sexual obsessions and compulsions of johns like Robert Mochrie and Peeping Toms like Lonnie Shell, both well-established businessmen of superficial repute in their communities. These hearts brooded and wrestled with the inevitable shame that their unmasking through bankruptcy or some ignominy would bring. With over-controlled emotional styles, these men and a handful of middle class housewives faced the demise of that which they prided in most, their well-established, respectable nuclear family units and their own (tenuous) adherence to the prevailing imperatives of masculinity and femininity. As soft patriarchs living in the midst of traditional sexual divisions of labor, the men assumed responsibility for the family's fall from grace. But as patriarchs they presumed to make life or death decisions for their family members, effectively sacrificing them, in a manner that curiously resembles the sacrificial behavior of the honor killers in traditional societies. Among the civil reputable hearts we appear to witness narcissism in an acute or particularly grandiose form, an enormous extension, some might say, of the modern cult of the individual, or, on the other hand, a failure to realize a fully blown sense of an inner self.[111] Unable to access their rage, or at least express it, many of the civil reputable hearts turned inward, often becoming depressed to the point of emotional near-paralysis. Others carried on sinisterly, seeming happy and contented, quiet and peaceful just days before the killings. Again, one cannot help be struck by the exaggerated internalization of the disingenuous emotional posturing of these perpetrators under these circumstances. How lonely they must have felt as with careful calibration and perhaps a strong yet inchoate sense of duty to the honor code of the gender order they hacked, hammered, incinerated and shot the ones they purported to love.

Among many, many other things, modernity produces the anxiety, shame, rage, and nominal or minimal sense of social belonging that are the hallmarks of the emotional styles of the familicidal hearts. The perpetrators we have met trace their lineages to different classes and the emotional formations associated with them. We may even speculate that racial and ethnic minorities commit much less familicide than criminologists might predict based on their disproportionate commission of homicide and intimate partner homicide precisely because their families have not assumed the acutely insulated forms evinced by their more privileged and supposedly successful Caucasian counterparts. Notwithstanding the interesting questions that arise regarding the relationship between class, race, and ethnicity and familicide, my principal focus remains firmly on gender relations and familicide as a profoundly gendered modern phenomenon.

It is not my intention to engage in an attack on modernity. Clearly, modernity provides enormous opportunities for emotional development and fulfillment that take individuals away from some of the ties and pressures of their kinship lines and broader communities. Selecting mates based on personal attraction, companionship, and compatibility represents a marked change from arranged marriages that blend property, traditions, skills, and so on. However, in setting up modern idylls, whether it is the respectable nuclear family or the modern romantic life partner, there are casualties. Familicidal hearts and their victims are among these casualties, one of the downsides of modern hopes, dreams, and emotional possibilities. This observation invites us to explore some of the possible reasons for men's marked over-representation among the ranks of the familicidal hearts. It is not enough to say that men, because of their position as principal providers in modern nuclear families, are those most likely to suffer the acute shame, rage, and anxiety so emblematic of perpetrators. Rather, we must also explore the individuation of boys and girls in modernity, for it is here that we see the beginnings of some men's nominal and tenuous sense of belonging.

In *The Reproduction of Mothering*, Nancy Chodorow argues it is primarily modern mothers who nurture young children, developing close social bonds with them.[112] Fathers tend to be more distant, often working for wages outside the family. This emotional asymmetry in the provision of maternal and paternal nurturance has profound implications as boys and girls separate and form their own self-identities. According to Chodorow, because girls are female they are experienced as being like their mothers, both anatomically in terms of the possession of the same genitalia but also symbolically in terms of what those genitalia signify. Girls gradually break away, all the while maintaining a relationship with the mother. For boys the process is more abrupt. Being experienced as unlike their mothers, boys tend to repress their feminine side and reject much of the warmth and closeness they experienced with their mothers early on in their relationship. Chodorow contends boys' more abrupt and repressive separation from their mothers comes at a heavy emotional price.[113] This gendered individuation happens at both conscious and unconscious levels and contributes significantly to boys' growing into men who value independence, autonomy, and competition with others. As a consequence of these gendered developmental processes, men have a harder time than women establishing intimate social bonds and expressing themselves emotionally. Nevertheless, in crude terms, this gendered individuation fed male workers into a system of capitalist production where they were primed for emotional isolation, competition, and alienated labor. This was the contribution of modern mothering to the incarnation of self-made manhood, a manhood that for many is steeped in loneliness and disconnected from communal responsibility.

In contrast, girls grow into women who value relationships and emotional connections with others and experience some difficulty maintaining personal boundaries that emphasize their distinctiveness as independent people. Chodorow puts it as follows, "Women experience a sense of self-in-relation that is in contrast to men's creation of a self that wishes to deny relation and connection."[114]

Chodorow's use of feminist psychoanalytic tools adds flesh to the bones of Elias's historical observations about the way the modern family serves as a principal molding mechanism, a location for the mediation of much broader-ranging figurations of feeling. Elias's work awaits significant development through the various lenses of feminism. At this juncture, we must note how Chodorow's observations about the gendered nature of individuation extend Elias's important points about the role of the family in socializing children. Elias pays insufficient attention to the differential socialization of boys and girls, stopping short of a gendered analysis. For example, Elias notes the class origins of the historic perfusion of the control of drives, and the way the family eventually mediates many of these processes. Understandably, with Elias, we do not have a strong sense of the gender power relations within modern nuclear families. Nevertheless, when seen in combination with Chodorow's insights, Elias's stress on the importance of the family for instilling emotional dressage assumes renewed relevance and zest. He comments:

> Stricter control of impulses and emotions is first imposed by those of high social rank on their social inferiors, or at most, their social equals. It is only comparatively late, when bourgeois classes comprising a large number of social equals have become the upper, ruling class, that the family becomes the only—or more exactly, the primary and dominant—institution with the function of installing drive control. Only then does the social dependence of the child on its parents become particularly important as leverage for the socially required regulation and molding of impulses and emotions.[115]

Noticeably, it is during the period in American history when the bourgeoisie became more prominent and bourgeois families became more affective units that we witness the emergence of familicide. The historic correspondence between the appearance of familicidal hearts and broader social, economic, and political changes, particularly changes in familial atmospheres of feeling, remind us of the importance of the nuclear family as a generator of social change. Elias pays insufficient attention to the power of the family in this regard.

However, as Chodorow points out, the social dependence of children on parents differs significantly between boys and girls. When boys "deny relation and connection," their molding, to use Elias's language, differs in general from that of girls. Elias is imprecise with respect to gender when he points out that each individual is "constrained from an early age on to take account of the effects of his own or other people's action."[116] Here, he is really only referring to boys, not girls, a serious omission.

Chodorow's point that boys develop a much greater sense of separateness than girls is enormously important. However, as Elizabeth Spelman points out, this does not mean that men inhabit public worlds devoid of connection with others. Spelman comments, "What Chodorow describes as the public world (or sphere) of work is teeming with affect—whether it be boredom, pride, anger, jealousy, hope, contempt, or fear."[117] The issue is not whether men's world of work is an affective arena—it is. The question is whether men's emotional styles recognize and acknowledge the ebb and flow of feeling among people and the overall figurations of feeling they inhabit. She continues, "It is thus not the absence of affect that characterizes the public world, but perhaps it is an absence of affective ties. *Men have feelings, but not the kind that reflect relations with other people—* if they fear, it is for themselves; if they feel pride, it is in themselves."[118] Spelman is making an important point that resonates with my arguments about familicidal hearts. Most of these familicidal hearts are men. But the more important point is that the familicidal hearts are socially disconnected, isolated, and have difficulty, whether because of their angry emotional styles or seriously emotionally inhibited styles, in feeling a part of intimate human interdependencies. Under the conditions of modern life men are more likely to possess such emotional styles, but, as we have seen, women also reach these remote emotional locations.

Spelman also contends Chodorow pays insufficient attention to the way mothering differs among different racial and ethnic groups. Acknowledging that Chodorow makes the point that "mothering is not an unchanging transcultural universal,"[119] Spelman nevertheless argues that Chodorow's work, like that of others that focuses primarily on gender oppression, "keep[s] race and class, racism and classism, at the periphery of feminist thought."[120]

Briefly, Spelman suggests that boys and girls of different racial and ethnic groups learn their gender identity in tandem with learning about other aspects of their identities, and that this process of learning is complex to the point that notions of gender cannot be teased apart from those of race, ethnicity, class, and sexuality. If, as Chodorow suggests, boys distance themselves from their mothers and identify with their more powerful fathers, Spelman asks us to consider how race and ethnicity might mediate such differentiation. Spelman rather pointedly remarks, "The ideology of masculinity in the United States hardly includes the idea that Black men are superior to White women."[121] Chodorow's observation about the differential individuation of boys and girls does not apply equally to all races and ethnic groups. For Spelman, the mothering of African-American sons does not entail the same kind of preparation for male superiority as the mothering of Caucasian boys. Spelman comments, "Insofar as a Black mother's mothering is informed by and takes place in a social context in which there is racism, it cannot be said that she is preparing her male child to assume his appointed superior place among the 'men' as Chodorow argues."[122]

Chodorow's work helps us understand why modernity spawns the kinds of emotional styles that lend themselves to familicide. As we have seen, in modernity, mothering becomes more intense, although racial, ethnic, and class locations clearly mediate this intensity. Many mothers, more than at any other time in history, increasingly have become the primary or even sole nurturers of children at the same time as their direct and socially valued economic contributions to the family have diminished. The changing role of mothers accompanied the rise of capitalism, the growing separation of home from workplace, the decline in the fertility and infant mortality rate, and the increasing disconnection between family and the community. As increasingly isolated mothers assumed more and more responsibility for emotional nurturance, the process of individuation became more intense and painful, especially for boys.

In her later work, Chodorow uses her ideas about mothering and the differential individuation of boys and girls as a window into understanding why men commit so much more violence and murder than women. She suggests, "Humiliation may also in some way adhere more to men than to women."[123] Gilligan reports violent prisoners saying that "they felt dead inside: empty, numb."[124] He continues, "they found the feeling of deadness and numbness more intolerable than anything, even pain."[125] Is it not possible that it was these feelings of numbness and emptiness that enabled men like Marcus Sims to mutilate himself, to slash his Achilles tendon and his throat, after killing his wife and son, and men like Robert Mochrie to murder five people and then ingest slug-pellets and weed-killer and hang himself?

Both these men experienced certain entitlements within the sexual and emotional divisions of labor that they negotiated. Is it not possible that notwithstanding their relative authority within their little gender regimes at home, these men felt ashamed of the nature of their relative ascendancy and the foundation of sand that it rested on? Perhaps this was more likely the case with Marcus Sims, who had to more overtly attempt to force compliance through violence, something that immediately pointed to the precariousness of his supposed domination. We might make a related point about Robert Mochrie, a man who no longer enjoyed an intimate sexual relationship with the woman whom he allegedly oversaw in his capacity as a soft patriarch. According to the prescriptions of the gender regime, soft patriarchs should not have to use the sexual services of a prostitute.

I have highlighted the centrality of emotions such as anxiety, shame, fear, and rage at the heart of the lives of perpetrators. Working class men committed the vast majority of livid coercive familicide, often battering and attempting to control their spouses or partners before the killings. Only one woman, Misook Beckenbauer, committed familicide after using livid coercive behavior against her husband. In all cases of livid coercion, the perpetrators' disgrace was not simply a reflection of their economic predicament, although as we have seen many struggled to eke out a living and many were saddled with deep feelings of inferiority. Rather, their ignominy derived much more from the demise of their intimate lives or the downfall of their nuclear family arrangements and the implications these had for their social standing as men.

By definition the civil reputable hearts were much more emotion-ally constrained than their working-class peers. On the whole, these civil perpetrators were members of social classes that enjoyed a much higher standard of living, more resources, and significant social esteem. It is essential that we see the plight of the civil reputable hearts in historical terms. Their social standing and significantly greater resources signified their membership in the rising successful class of capitalism. Perpetrators evinced many of the behavioral and psychological qualities that accompa-nied such social locations: they were usually stoic, polite, meek, kind, and so on. In their lifetimes they had enjoyed considerable success and their familial atmospheres of feeling exhibited aspirations and expectations for success that were consonant with their class position.

The civil reputable hearts included a larger proportion of female per-petrators than their livid coercive peers. The social standing of the female civil reputable hearts derived from the achievements of their husbands, although their personal esteem was in each case related to their perfor-mance of their roles as wives and mothers. These women killed in the face of the pending failure of their nuclear familial arrangements and their sense they had failed as wives, mothers, or both. They killed because of their perceived failure of their own emotional labors. In sharp contrast, but in concert with Chodorow's observations, the male civil reputable hearts killed out of a surfeit of responsibility, entitlement, shame, and nar-cissism concerning their perceived failure to provide. These men secretly occupied extraordinarily lonely places, seemingly feeling little connection even amidst the hubbub of family life. Unlike their working class peers, the middle class civil reputable hearts had a greater distance to fall and had to handle their predicaments without resort to the humiliated fury of the livid coercive hearts. In other words, the civil reputable hearts internalized rather than externalized their emotional plight, exhibiting classic symp-toms of depression. The shame of the civil reputable hearts was rendered all the more intense by the expectations and aspirations of the social class to which they ever more tenuously clung.

My effort to map some of the continuities between the gender, class, and emotional styles; familial atmospheres of feeling; and historic figu-rations of feeling, may appear unduly esoteric. However, tracing these continuities is not just another way of talking about the inexplicability of familicide. Rather, it is a means of pointing to its complexity and the complex personhood of those party to it. In summation, it appears there are certain modern conditions necessary for the commission of familicide. I have identified the important role of shame among the livid coercive and civil reputable hearts. Shame circulates in a much more subterranean man-ner in the modern era and this fact helps explain the historical emergence of familicide.

It also seems that the spirit of familicide is associated with a failure to measure up to or a breakdown in the adherence to the prescriptions, standards, and imperatives of what Robert Connell calls hegemonic masculinity.[126] By *hegemonic masculinity*, Connell means the versions of masculinities that dominate in a particular society at a particular time; for example, in modern times, Caucasian heterosexual norms are seen as more appropriate, worthy, and desirable than other forms, such as homosexuality. We see these failures or breakdowns in the misguided efforts of the livid coercive hearts to force intimacy and in the senses of entitlement and responsibility among the male civil reputable hearts.

With the livid coercive hearts I documented their rather grave abuses, disrupted bonding, abandonment, and other traumas of early childhood. I suggest these may contribute to the development of the familicidal heart. The problem is that the archive remains weak on these matters, and we can only speculate about the role of such disturbing events and episodes of early childhood. It is not my suggestion that early childhood traumas rise to the level of a *necessary* condition for the later maturation of the familicidal heart, although this remains a distinct possibility. At the same time we must point out that women experience much more sexual abuse in their early lives than men, and yet they commit much less familicide. This fact reminds us that it is the affective individualism of modern life, and men's peculiar assumption of its most lonely dimensions, that are central to the development of the familicidal heart.

Identifying what appear to be the *necessary* emotional and sociohistorical conditions for the rise of familicidal hearts is not to say what the *sufficient* conditions might be. My choice of words here is deliberate because I maintain that, whatever the pretensions of sociology, criminology, history, and psychology, and whatever interdisciplinary interweavings we might deem appropriate among these disciplines, in the final analysis the commission of the uncanny act of familicide is about haunting, something subliminal and diffuse that defies categorical or empirical analysis. Confronting the inexplicability of familicide serves as a reminder to freshen up some of our approaches to the study of intimate violence. It is in the direction of the implications of some of these observations about familicidal hearts for the study of intimate violence and murder that the last chapter turns.

NOTES

1. Goffman, 1963.
2. Giddens, 1991: 47.
3. Huizinga, 1999: 18.
4. Hemphill, 1998: 44. My italics.
5. See Hemphill, 1998: 36–40.
6. Hemphill, 1998: 37.
7. Hemphill, 1998: 37.
8. Hemphill, 1998: 39.
9. Rotundo, 1993: 2.
10. See Kimmel, 2006: 15.
11. Rotundo, 1993: 3.
12. Kimmel, 2006: 29.

13. Rotundo, 1993: 5–6.

14. Rotundo, 1993: 6.

15. Shields, 2002: 145.

16. Giddens, 1991: 44.

17. As psychiatrist Willard Gaylin once contended, "Abandonment by a source of love is central to our earliest definition of death" (Gaylin, 1989: 33).

18. See Goleman, 1995, citing the research of Tschann, 1994. Goleman suggests the small proportion of children and young adults who experiment with drugs and alcohol and eventually become addicted are those "who reported higher levels of emotional distress." He suggests those who become addicted use alcohol and/or drugs "to soothe feelings of anxiety, anger, or depression" (1995: 253).

19. Giddens, 1991: 45.

20. Hochschild, 1983: 121.

21. Hochschild, 1983: 121.

22. Hochschild, 1983: 121.

23. Hochschild, 1983: 226.

24. Hochschild, 1983: 227.

25. Illouz, 2007: 38.

26. Illouz, 2007: 38.

27. Illouz, 2007: 38.

28. Mitchell, 1805: 8.

29. Cited in Toolis, 2002.

30. I am indebted to Kathleen Ferraro for her input on the Mochrie case.

31. A handful of civil reputable hearts remained with the corpses for some considerable time before committing suicide or informing authorities.

32. It appears that one other woman, Bertha Eckinger, committed familicide because of her husband's livid coercive behavior. We cannot describe Bertha as a civil reputable heart. Rather, I include her among the perpetrators occupying contradictory/intermediate locations on the emotional continuum. Briefly, the details of the case are as follows: Late in the evening of August, 8, 1899, in Canton, Ohio, Bertha Eckinger shot dead her 25-year-old farm-laborer husband, Edward, and their three-year-old daughter, Ruby, before killing herself. The couple had married in July 1896. Neighbors reported the Eckingers' marriage had "not been pleasant" and that they had "parted company a year ago." Witnesses stated that the couple quarreled chronically. They apparently reunited in the spring of 1899, but the altercations continued. Neighbors and others reported that Edward consumed considerable quantities of liquor. It was on these occasions in particular that he quarreled with Bertha. The *Canton Repository* described Edward's relationship with liquor as follows: "Most said they knew he used liquor and they had known him to be intoxicated and to quarrel with his family." In her suicide note, Bertha tells us, "He choked me once, and he will never do it again." At another point she comments, "I am nearly crazy." My excerpts are drawn from the following newspaper accounts: *New York Times*, August 10, 1899: Page 1: "Entire Ohio Family Dead." *Evening Repository*, (Canton, Ohio), August 10, 1899, Page 1: "Her Last Wish Ignored: Bodies of Edward Eckinger, Wife and Babe Will Not Rest Side by Side in One Tomb." *Evening Repository*, (Canton, Ohio), August 10, 1899, Page 1: "Father, Mother, Child: Three Dead Bodies in a Home Below Waco Bear Silent Testimony of an Awful Tragedy." *Evening Repository*, (Canton, Ohio), August 10, 1899, Page 1: "Coroner's Testimony."

33. "Patricia Allen" is a pseudonym.

34. The Brandley, Curtis, and Allen cases continue a legal tradition dating back to the Civil War period. Ann Jones enlightens us regarding the use of the temporary insanity defense by women tried for first-degree murder as a result of killing men who had mistreated them. In these cases the male murder victim perhaps made prior and inappropriate sexual advances, made false promises of marriage, or abandoned the female perpetrator. Often these hapless female defendants fit the stereotype of the "typical seduced-and-abandoned maiden." As Jones points out, women such as Mary Moriarty (1855), Mary Harris (1865), Fanny Hyde (1872) and Kate Stoddart (1873) were "young, poor, friendless and innocent" (Jones, 1980: 153).

Jones notes Fanny Windley was one such young woman (Jones, 1980: 154). Fanny's mother died when the girl was four. At age ten Fanny found work at a factory owned by George Watson, a 45-year-old married father of five. He seduced her, impregnated her, and forced her to take medication to effect an abortion. Fanny's health suffered greatly. She eventually married a man named Hyde, becoming Fanny Hyde. However, George Watson, after promising to let her be, continued to harass her. Eventually she killed George, shooting him dead in cold blood. At her trial, Fanny's attorney, Samuel Morris, argued she was temporarily insane at the time of the murder. He traced the commencement of her insanity to her first seduction by George Watson when Fanny was 15 years old. Morris recited to the jury the words of noted authority Dr. William Hammond: "There is a form of insanity, which, in its culminating act is extremely temporary in its character, and which, in all its manifestations, from beginning to end, is of that duration.... By authors it has been variously designated as transitoria mania, ephemeral mania, temporary insanity and morbid impulse" (Jones, 1980: 164). One of the causes of this condition was menstruation.

As Jones notes, most observers at the time saw through the insanity defense for "deserving" young women such as Fanny Hyde as "trumped up" (Jones, 1980: 166). Prosecutors saw such defenses as vehicles for placing otherwise inadmissible evidence (e.g., prior seduction) in front of juries. However, as Jones astutely observes, some of the women benefiting from such defenses never recovered their mental faculties and spent the duration of their lives in mental institutions. Jones cites the case of Mary Harris, who "failed to recuperate and had to be returned to Washington to the asylum where she spent the rest of her life" (1980: 166). For some women their emotional disturbance was deep, enduring and significantly above and beyond its utility as a means of legal defense.

35. Alder and Polk, 2001: 5.

36. Wilcczynski, 1991: 7; quoted in Alder and Polk, 2001: 5.

37. Scheff and Retzinger, 2001: x.

38. Scheff and Retzinger, 2001: 22.

39. Scheff and Retzinger, 2001: 26.

40. MacDonald, 1986: 187.

41. MacDonald, 1986: 187.

42. MacDonald, 1986: 187.

43. Wilson, Daly, and Danielle, 1995: 288, discuss this case as an example of a despondent perpetrator of familicide. However, they do not make the inference that he was suffering from acute shame, in spite of the dentist's talking of feeling worthless, referencing the stigma his son would face, or the fact that his wife would not have access to the things he usually gave her.

44. Guttmacher, 1960: 103–106.

45. Guttmacher, 1960: 103.

46. Guttmacher, 1960: 104.

47. Guttmacher, 1960: 105.

48. Guttmacher, 1960: 105.

49. Guttmacher, 1960: 106.

50. Guttmacher, 1960: 106. For legal and ethical reasons, clinicians no longer use drugs such as sodium pentothal or amobarbital to conduct interviews. See also APA, 2007: 46, entry concerning amobarbital.

51. West, 1967: 53.

52. West, 1967: 53.

53. Wilson, Daly, and Danielle cite West's work as they explore the makeup of the despondent perpetrator (1995: 288).

54. Malmquist, 1980: 301.

55. Wilson, Daly, and Danielle cite *The Times*, April 28, 1984: p. 3, as the source of the suicide note. See Wilson, Daly, and Danielle, 1995: 288.

56. Lewis, 1971: 16–17. Comparing shame to guilt, Lewis observes, "Shame is intrinsically more difficult to discharge than guilt, particularly because hostility evoked in connection with shame is trapped by the position of the self" (1971: 503).

57. Lewis, 1971: 27.

58. Lewis, 1971: 196.

59. For example, Hanawalt notes that in some cases of rape, it appears the motive of the rapist was to directly shame an enemy. She observes, "Raping the wife or widow of an enemy was a way of bringing shame on him. It showed that he was too impotent to protect his own property against defilement" (1979: 273).

60. The civilizing process does not simply consist of the linear progressive development of social constraints. Rather, as Elias points out, the process of development is uneven and complex.

61. Elias, 1994: 68.

62. Elias, 1994: 69.

63. Elias, 1994: 75.

64. Elias, 1994: 106.

65. Elias, 1994: 118. Italics in the original.

66. Elias, 1994: 128.

67. Elias, 1994: 135.

68. Elias, 1994: 135.

69. Elias, 1994: 135.

70. Fontaine interviewing Elias, 1978: 245.

71. Eisner, 2001.

72. Fontaine interviewing Elias, 1978: 251.

73. Elias, 1994: 282.

74. Lasch, 1985: 709.

75. Elias notes, "War, rapine, armed attack and plunder constituted a regular form of income for the warriors in the barter economy" (1994: 317).

76. Lasch, 1985: 708.

77. Fletcher, 1997: 36.

78. Goleman, 1995: 6.

79. Goleman, 1995: 6.

80. Goleman, 1995: 6.

81. Evans, 2001: 40.
82. Stearns and Stearns, 1986: 23.
83. Stearns and Stearns, 1986: 24–28.
84. Pleck, 1987: 21–22. Pleck goes on to note the Pilgrims enacted a law against spouse abuse in 1672.
85. A discussion of the relationship between suppressed or impounded anger and clinical depression lies beyond the scope of this chapter. However, the absence of rage responses in clinically depressed patients is well documented. As psycho-analyst William Gaylin once put it, "the fixed relationship between the impound-ing of anger and the feeling of depression is an empiric fact that will not go away" (Gaylin, 1989: 121). Civil reputable perpetrators like Robert Mochrie, Kevin Wu, and Paul Motson had received formal diagnoses of depression, as had their female peers, Nancy White and Heather Holcombe. These perpetrators seemed largely helpless and hopeless and suffered low self-esteem. These debilitating experiences very likely affected their coping ability and contributed to their seemingly incom-prehensible decisions to commit familicide.
86. Stearns and Stearns, 1986: 214.
87. The new nuclear family was the principal, but not the only, social loca-tion where people learned to subdue their anger. We see similar developments in the workplace, long before the advent of trendy safe working and learning envi-ronments in places like universities. American capital-labor history is among the bloodiest in the world, with the period between the great railroad strikes of 1877 and the unionization drives in the automobile industry during the 1930s witness-ing enormous levels of violence and public conflict. Capital–labor strife subsequent to the Great Depression has been tame in comparison. Likewise, in the field of leisure, rules and referees have done much to dampen down the overt display of anger and hostility.
88. Kressel, 1981: 143.
89. Kressel, 1981: 143. Note Joseph Ginat's comments on Kressel's point that honor killings increase one's honor. Ginat contends, "By killing a woman an individual does not *gain* honor but restores it" (Ginat, 1981: 153; italics in the original).
90. Kressel, 1981: 143.
91. Kressel, 1981: 152.
92. As Patel and Gadit define it, *Karo-Kari* is a form of premeditated honor killing that originated in rural and tribal areas of Sindh, Pakistan. These killings mostly target women who are perceived to have brought dishonor to the family by virtue of their illicit premarital or extramarital relations. The authors note, "a female is labeled a Kari because of the perceived dishonour that she had brought to her family through her illicit relationship with a man (other than her husband) who is subsequently labeled a karo. Once labeled a kari, male family members have the self-authorized justification to kill her and the co-accused karo in order to restore family honour" (2008: 684).
93. Patel and Gadit, 2008: 686.
94. Patel and Gadit, 2008: 686.
95. Gill, 2009: 3.
96. Gill, 2009: 3.
97. Gill, 2009: 3.
98. Gill, 2009: 3.

99. Baker, Gregware, and Cassidy, 1999.

100. Baker, Gregware, and Cassidy, 1999: 174. The italics are mine. These authors also cite Kenneth Polk's analysis of 58 case studies of intimate partner homicide involving sexual jealousy and possessiveness and 15 cases involving suicidal masculine depression. They quote Polk on the relationship between violence and control, "The power of the male to control is demonstrated by the very act of destruction of his 'possession'" (1999: 175; citing Polk, 1994: 44).

101. Fromm, 1973: 224.

102. Gilligan, 1996: 111.

103. Gilligan, 1996: 111.

104. Gilligan, 1996: 112.

105. Gilligan, 1996: 113–114.

106. Faludi, 1999: 9.

107. Faludi, 1999: 10.

108. Dutton, 2006: 162.

109. I am grateful to one of the five anonymous reviewers of the manuscript for help in clarifying these points.

110. Braithwaite, 1989: Chapter 10.

111. For an interesting discussion of the relationship between shame and narcissism, see Morrison, 1989.

112. The pros and cons of Chodorow's work on mothering lie well beyond the scope of my current project. She has been criticized for universalizing the notion of mothering and not paying enough attention to the different experiences of mothers from different racial and ethnic groups. As we have seen, African-American slave mothers had a different experience of mothering than mothers of European ancestry whose households they serviced. Migrant women who work as nannies experience another form of motherhood still. If it is the case that certain racial and ethnic groups, because of various disadvantages, have been less able to provide the kind of exclusive, intensive mothering found among some Caucasian households, then we must ask if this inability somehow, ironically, reduced their offspring's susceptibility to reaching the kinds of emotional remoteness associated with the familicidal hearts.

Drawing from an array of empirical studies, Miriam Johnson (1988) challenges Chodorow's argument that mothers treat boys and girls differently. Johnson concludes mothers provide comparable nurturance to boys and girls. Johnson's point does not negate Chodorow's claim that boys move in the direction of much greater independence than girls as a means of distinguishing themselves from their mothers and as a means of developing their self-identities.

113. Citing the work of French analyst Janine Chasseguet-Smirgel, Jessica Benjamin points out that the little child's unconscious image of its mother is anything but the castrated and powerless person depicted by Freud. Benjamin comments, "While the little boy may consciously represent the mother as castrated, clinical evidence reveals that unconsciously the boy sees this mother as extremely powerful" (1988: 94).

114. Chodorow, 1999: viii.

115. Elias, 1994: 112.

116. Cited in Van Krieken, 1989: 198.

117. Spelman, 1988: 108.

118. Spelman, 1988: 109. My italics.

119. Spelman, 1988: 87, citing Chodorow, 1978: 32. Spelman's insightful critique contains many pearls of wisdom, far too numerous to examine here. Significantly, Spelman questions Chodorow's use of some of the troubling parts of Freudian theory, Chodorow's seemingly uncritical use of the public–private sphere dichotomy, her assumption of women's heterosexuality, and her implication that sexism is the basis for racism and classism.

120. Spelman, 1988: 16.

121. Spelman, 1988: 89.

122. Spelman, 1988: 98–99.

123. Chodorow is well aware that women use violence. Indeed, she comments that among her patients, "the women most prone to feeling humiliated are also those most liable to outbursts of rage" (1998: 35).

124. Gilligan, 2003: 1152.

125. Gilligan, 2003: 1152.

126. Connell, 1987. See also Connell and Messerschmidt, 2005.

7

SOME IMPLICATIONS: A FEW CLOSING THOUGHTS

We must first put behind us (or at least agree to return to it later through a much more substantial body of research) the fact that familicide appears to have increased over the last four or five decades, while intimate partner killings as a whole declined.[1] These paradoxical counter-trends may be more than mere coincidence. The decline of the intimate-partner homicide rate, especially among racial minorities, particularly African-American male victims and to a lesser extent African-American female victims, probably reflects improved medical responses to violence and injury, the mass incarceration of younger African-Americans, and the post-1970s extension of various support services to domestic violence victims in the inner city. The reasons for the apparent increase in familicide, particularly over the last two decades, remain unclear.

Whatever the precise relationship between changing rates of intimate partner homicide and familicide, it is clear that, of the total number of intimate-partner homicides, relatively few are accompanied by the commission of familicide. Likewise, a relatively low proportion of all filicides and suicides occur during familicides. Nevertheless, when these different forms of killing manifest in what some researchers refer to as *family annihilation*, we must ask what this might mean. Familicide is a consequence of modern era emotional formations, one of the signatures of modern times, an outcome of the imperatives of the gender regime. Is it possible that the emotional styles associated with familicide, blocked shame, acute anxiety, heavy and suicidal depression, humiliated fury, and acute social disconnection, are becoming more prevalent as late modernity unfolds?

258

My somewhat speculative findings suggest familicide is much more than a form of mass killing and much more than the sum of its parts, an intimate partner homicide here, one or more filicides there, and perhaps a suicide. Rather, familicide involves the implosive undoing of a *uniquely modern set of lineages and interdependencies*, mediated through the expectations of romantic love and increasingly liberal parenting. Such an implosive undoing, I contend, even though relatively rare, raises important questions about the very fabric of modern social life and the ways we seek to make sense of it.

However, perpetrators of intimate-partner homicide as opposed to familicide also experience considerable shame, fear, anxiety and rage. Why is it, therefore, that the rate of intimate-partner homicide has gone down as familicide has increased? We might try to answer this question by suggesting that the intensity of the emotions of the familicidal hearts is much greater than that among perpetrators of intimate-partner homicide. Such intensity therefore has more drastic effects, resulting in the deaths of more people. Since we cannot socially map the patterns of intensity of these emotions, this particular explanation will provide little solace to those who want empirical evidence regarding differential motives or causes. We might also suggest that it is less likely medical services will be able to respond to familicidal killings in a rapid and effective manner because there will be few if any survivors remaining to summon the necessary emergency intervention.

Whatever the possible explanations for these paradoxical counter-tendencies among the offense types, familicide differs significantly from intimate-partner homicide. The former may include the latter, but familicide includes much more. Killing a partner is one thing. Murdering the children as well and then perhaps taking one's own life represents a quantum leap that reaches back into the past and forward into the future, destroying a lineage and eliminating new blood. It is not only the number of victims the familicidal hearts claim that marks the gravity of the transgression. Rather, its seriousness stems from the undoing of romantic attachments and sets of interdependencies emblematic of modern freedom of choice in intimate life. It is perhaps for this reason that we saw thousands of mourners and gazers file past the coffins of the dead Coopers in 1908 in Cadillac, Michigan. Familicides haunt communities because of the intensity of their illogic and because they interrupt the ebb and flow of emotion and interdependencies we all feel. At some deep level, they are uncanny acts.

My approach draws significantly from the work of Elias and his emphasis on the importance of lengthening chains of interdependencies in modern life and the role of psychological restraint. I have included the insights of feminist psychoanalytical theorists to emphasize the significance of particularly intense intrafamilial interdependencies and expectations about the identities and degrees of individuation of men and women. My admittedly unusual analysis of familicide relies in large part upon a curious blending of the language of history, sociology, and psychoanalysis. My findings are worth restating.

At the livid coercive (left-hand) end of the continuum, we witness significant failure to control emotions, particularly anger and rage. These men simmered and bristled with anger for much of the time. As we saw, the livid coercive hearts exhibited many of the traits we see among male batterers, including the use of violence and intimidation, threats, attempts to control partners and children, and frequent tendencies to self-soothe using alcohol or drugs. We also see high levels of personal vulnerability, dependency, and fear of abandonment amidst all the posturing and bluster of their emotional styles.

When we glance at the civil reputable (right-hand) end of the emotional continuum, the emotional styles differ considerably from those of the livid coercive hearts. Male and female civil reputable hearts lived out their assigned gender roles in traditional sexual divisions of labor, suffering for failing to live up to them. They exhibited good control of strong emotions, particularly anger, but suffered from shame, depression, and anxiety about the breakdown of their nuclear family arrangements.

Readers might well object that comparing livid coercive and civil reputable hearts is like comparing apples and oranges. Insofar as one evidences a history of domestic violence and tyranny and the other seemingly enjoy tranquil, traditional nuclear familial arrangements, the objection may appear apropos. However, at the level of emotional style, we see the similar workings of submerged shame and humiliation across the continuum. In a related vein, shame being the emotion of social disconnection, livid coercive and civil reputable perpetrators evidence a painfully nominal sense of self and often-acute isolation, even in the midst of the practical swirl of family life. Indeed, we might argue that this practical swirl, with all its expectations of intimacy and a warm place for the heart to settle and soothe itself, not only confuses and complicates matters but also paradoxically compounds the perpetrator's isolation.

I begin my recap of these interrelated observations and their possible implications by acknowledging, once again, the complexities of the gender regime, modern patriarchy, and the seeming ebb and flow of advantage and domination. My recognition of these complexities enables me to question the appropriateness and usefulness of situating concepts such as power and control at the center of our analysis of domestic violence. The evidence from the familicide archive points to the central importance of relationships between emotional styles, familial atmospheres of feeling, and modern figurations of feeling as ways of comprehending these offenses. In other words, as an alternative to the language of power and control, my analysis suggests the importance of appreciating the role of emotion in these killings. It is crucial that the role of emotion be historical, sociological, and psychological in a way that clouds or dissolves the boundaries between these subject disciplines. It is in the cracks at the boundaries of these disciplines where the light gets in, enabling us to view things a little differently.

If, as I have argued, familicide constitutes one of the consequences of modernity, then two emotions emerge as centrally important: shame and anger. Using the findings from the familicide archive, I suggest a greater appreciation of the workings of these emotions in making sense of intimate violence, the dangers various parties confront, and the complex person-hood evident throughout the archive. I insist upon recognizing, not only the complexities of the people involved in these tragedies, but also the per-ils involved in predicting outcomes such as familicide or intimate-partner homicide. I therefore couch my discussion of risk alongside another per-vasive theme permeating the archive, that of haunting.

Finally, I visit the thorny issue of social change and what we might do to alter the way we approach intimate-partner violence, abuse, and murder. Just from my personal involvement it strikes me the anti–domestic violence/violence against women movement and the fields of psychology and psychiatry have reached something of an impasse, with proponents on either side obstinately insisting on the virtues of their own positions. In their extreme forms, these factions cling imperialistically to their theo-ries like batterers cling to their victims. Perhaps it is time to pay closer attention to the ancient warning, one that reverberates through the fami-licide archive, that "pride goeth before a fall." As Helen Lynd once put it, "But since every way of seeing is also a way of not seeing, it is pos-sible that the very multiplication of categories and the very precision of techniques may sometimes act as barriers instead of as means of access to understanding."[2]

MODERN GENDER REGIMES

I devoted considerable space to discussing the ways in which the power relations of gender change with time and how they intersect with struc-tures of race and ethnic and class relations. There are still significant dif-ferences between the social, economic, and political positions of men and women. For example, most men can still expect to earn significantly more than like-situated women during the peak earning years of their lives, although the reasons for this are complex and contested.[3] Men still occupy many more positions of power than women in the arenas of government and business. Women's ongoing disproportionate responsibilities in the arena of child care and housework still impede their progress in the work-place.[4] However, as modernity marches on, the gender gap in terms of pay, power, the distribution of executive positions, and family labor seems to be diminishing. Women are breaking new ground, and growing num-bers of men are spending more time with their children and sharing in household responsibilities. At the same time, increasingly large numbers of people are electing to live alone rather than live out unfair or onerous sexual divisions of labor.[5]

Modern gender relations exact a toll from both genders. Men do not wield unlimited or monolithic power over women, even in that small proportion of intimate relationships where men maintain a tyrannical physical presence in women's lives.[6] As the archive suggests, both men and women exercise power within intimate relationships and families, sometimes in different ways and in different social locations and situations, other times not. Numerous writers attest to men's burdens as well as women's. A number of these authors remain sensitive to the goals of feminism but also seek to point out the ways men are often oppressed by their roles as breadwinners in modernity.

Barbara Ehrenreich documents what she calls a "male revolt" away from their roles as breadwinners, sole providers, and tamed employees in a capitalist economy increasingly deficient in decent jobs that pay a wage that can support a family. Herb Goldberg points out that in the nineteenth-century, men lived on average longer than women.[7] However, as women's death in childbirth diminished and diseases more prominent among men came to replace more traditional killers such as pneumonia and tuberculosis, women's life expectancy surpassed that of men's. He also points out that, compared with women, men suffer disproportionately from alcoholism, drug addiction, disease, suicide, imprisonment, and accidents. For Goldberg, these phenomena are all part of the modern hazards men face, perils that cause him to question whether it is really appropriate to talk of male privilege *vis-à-vis* women.

In similar fashion, Warren Farrell points out that white females live seven years longer than white males (79 years compared to 72) and black females live nine years longer than black males (74 years compared to 65).[8] He attributes this discrepancy to the greater stressors men face in modern social, political, and economic life. Farrell comments, "If power means having control over one's life, then perhaps there is no better ranking of the impact of sex roles and racism on power over our lives than life expectancy."[9]

Goldberg and Farrell treat complex issues a little too cursorily for my liking. Both men and women suffer from the gender regime. Women live longer than men but they also experience higher rates of disability, so we might ask, "Are they better off?" These are very complex matters, and many things influence life expectancy. Insofar as their work points to the existence of alternative interpretations regarding gender and privilege, it is helpful. However, it is difficult to deal with the complex intersection of race, ethnicity, class, and gender in the rather rhetorical manner they adopt.

Farrell also contends that men suffer because of the social expectation that they will protect women. He reports a male friend of his asking, "What would you pay someone who agreed that, if he was ever with you when you were attacked, he would intervene and try to get himself killed slowly enough to give you time to escape? You know that is your job as a man—every time you are with a woman . . . any woman, not just your wife."[10] We might also note that men are much more likely than women to face death or serious injury because of their disproportionate performance of dangerous jobs, from serving in a combat capacity in the military, to fighting fires, to mining.

On the whole, men enjoy more political, economic, and cultural capital than women, although as I have noted, modernity narrows these gaps. However, women have greater emotional capital, and I argue we must factor this into our understanding of the power relations of gender. As Leslie Brody puts it, "Women are more facially expressive of most emotions than are men, with the possible exception of anger. . . . Women also use words to express feelings more than men do. They express a wider variety and more intense positive and negative feelings than men do."[11] In their intimate relationships, women's emotional capital empowers them *vis-à-vis* men. It is wholly inadequate to theorize away women's more eclectic emotional skills and talents, honed at least in part out of their intense modern involvement in child care and nurturing, as merely a symptom or byproduct of their patriarchal oppression. It may be the case that, for many women, their emotional skills and talents develop out of resisting various traumatic emotional experiences connected with their relationships with men. Even so, this does not diminish the importance of women's emotional capacity as they contest and negotiate the power relationships with their spouses or partners and in their families. Indeed, as Giddens contends, "Women have prepared the way for an expansion of the domain of intimacy in their role as the emotional revolutionaries of modernity."[12]

We saw in Chapter 6 the stifling emotional prescriptions laid at the feet of the new self-made man. Self-made manhood required the adoption of a stiff emotional demeanor or style reminiscent of the physical constraining of women by devices such as the corset. As Heather Formani remarks, "whatever masculinity is, it is very damaging to men."[13] (I will return to masculinities and the awareness and expression of feeling a little later.)

Modern gender regimes and the familicidal violence they accommodate are complex, multifaceted, and not accurately depicted by dichotomous oppressor/oppressed models. Rather, I have explored the ebb and flow of emotion as a means of challenging these simplistic binary formulations. Acknowledging the ebb and flow of emotion between spouses and partners, within families and among modern figurations of feeling allows us to question the notions of power and control. It is crucially important that notions of power and control be seen as social and historical phenomena as opposed to psychological characteristics of individuals.

POWER

As I have argued throughout the empirical exploration of the lives of the familicidal hearts and those they murdered, seeing one group as powerful oppressors and the other as hapless, powerless victims is inaccurate and a denial of the complexity of the cases. Men and women exercise power in different ways. Within most of the relationships, the preponderance of power resides with men, even in relationships where women committed familicide. A key question, then, seems to be, "To what extent does that power differential contribute to or drive the act of familicide?"

What is striking about the archive is that men and a few of the female perpetrators were failures within their own gendered family lives. Many of the men, dominant in their spousal or intimate relationships, were relatively unsuccessful in meeting the exacting standards of successful masculinities. These men exerted power over the women they abused. However, their female partners were not powerless. Rather, an important source of women's power was their emotional awareness, expressiveness, and acumen *vis-à-vis* the men that abused them.

I have argued that perpetrators sought power because they perceived their power was ebbing. The livid coercive hearts often felt their spouses or partners slipping away from them, deserting them, betraying them. Their panicked sense of loss was rooted in dependency, vulnerability, and shame, revealing the precariousness of what some in the anti–domestic violence movement tend to see as men's relatively unfettered ascendancy. My point is that any power perpetrators enjoyed was contingent, relational, and contested. The civil reputable hearts had enjoyed considerable esteem in their communities. It was the anticipated undoing of their social standing and that of their families, and the shame and humiliation this engendered, that lay at the root of the killings. Therefore, as in the case of the livid coercive hearts, it was the diminution or evaporation of a feeling of power that seems central to understanding the familicide.

Interpreting domestic violence as an expression of an intimate's power *vis-à-vis* the partner has a long history. In 1874 in the English Parliament, Frances Power Cobbe explained the root causes of wife beating:

> The general depreciation of women *as a sex* is bad enough, but in the matter we are considering, the special depreciation of *wives* is more directly responsible for the outrages they endure. . . . It is even sometimes pleaded on behalf of poor men, that they possess *nothing else* but their wives, and that consequently, it seems doubly hard to meddle with the exercise of power in this narrow sphere![14]

Over a century later, feminist activists Ellen Pence and Melanie Shepard informed readers that the Domestic Abuse Intervention Project (DAIP), based in Duluth, Minnesota, rejected theories of battering that focused on batterer abnormalities, the abusive relationship, or the victim, "because these promote treatment strategies which do not alter *the power system which creates the foundation of battering behavior.*"[15] My findings from the familicide archive suggest that although the "power system" among families is alive and well, this system is not the immediate generator of familicide. If it were the immediate generator, we would see much more violence. Rather, the power relations of gender provide a crucially important context for understanding familicide, yet it is the shame perpetrators felt at not being able to meet the exacting standards of dominant notions of masculinity and femininity that drove these tragic killings. These punishing demands, emblematic of the modern era, exposed perpetrators as failures, as losers in a world ideally comprising of winners or at least aspirants.

Rebecca Emerson Dobash and Russell Dobash reported important findings from their interviews with 122 men and 134 women involved with criminal justice–based intervention programs for violent men. They contextualized men's intimate-partner violence against male authority and dominance within their intimate relationships and families. They commented, "Violence is often used to silence debate, to reassert male authority, and to deny women a voice in the affairs of daily life."[16] Their excerpts from interviews provide important insights into men's behavior and motives for violence and are clearly consistent with an interpretation that men seek to establish or affirm their interpersonal ascendancy over women.

I include a sample from their work of men's responses to the question "Why did you hit her?"

"I was wanting to show her who was the boss."[17]

"Because she knows how to wind me up."[18]

"She does my head in."[19]

In response to the question, "Is there something she could have done to stop you being violent toward her?" men commented, "Yes, shut her mouth."[20]

In response to the question "Do you think that this violence can be stopped?" one man replied, "If she just shuts up and accepts what I say and do."[21]

Clearly, one interpretation of these excerpts is to see them as an expression of male authority and dominance or as an effort to reassert that authority and domination. Indeed, the Dobashes conclude, "Violence is used as a means of obtaining an end, as a product of men's power over women, and is deeply rooted in men's sense of masculinities."[22]

Many men enjoy social, political, and economic authority over women, although their ascendancy in this regard is slowly but significantly eroding. To the extent that the livid coercive hearts realized such authority in their intimate relationships, it is understandable that we would want to draw an arrow from this authority to their violence, an arrow that signifies that their authority causes their violence. It is not men's authority over their spouse or partner that drives the violence. Rather, it is their lack of authority, recognition, and success *vis-à-vis* the imperatives of modern masculinity. Men do have overall power at the group level over women. However, men can be relatively powerless at the individual level; for example, when they fail to get their way or when their female partners leave them.

It is instructive to ask questions of the responses of men reported by Dobash and Dobash. For example, How does he get "wound up" by her actions? Why does he want to be the boss? Why does he feel "done in" by her? Why does he want to silence her? If we ask these questions, I suggest that an alternative possibility is that men who appear socially, economically, and politically superior to their spouses or partners are simultaneously fearful, vulnerable, and dependent upon them. Is it not possible that she "winds him up" because she is more linguistically accomplished and better able to articulate a sense of the prevailing atmosphere of feeling? The context and relational dimensions of my observation remain key. I am not suggesting, for example, that female victims of domestic violence exhibit exceptional emotional intelligence or cognitive abilities. From my experience, the reverse can be the case. What I am suggesting is that in relation to the men that abuse them, female victims often have more emotional acumen, even if that acumen pales in comparison to that of women in general. I propose that her emotional capital is a source of authority (albeit subtle and either unacknowledged or under-appreciated,) that she enjoys within her relationship with him. Indeed, we might go further and suggest that her emotional awareness and expressiveness sometimes shames him at a level that he perhaps bypasses or does not acknowledge.[23] Women's emotional power and acumen are important sources of power. Both parties can also be authorities in different social arenas, perhaps simultaneously.

None of this ought be read to mean that I do not see the overall balance of power in nearly all of the familicide cases as residing with men. However, when we use words like *balance*, we must also be aware of the contingent nature of the domination it reflects. The word *balance* reminds us that power is a complex contest, subject to negotiation and change. Dobash and Dobash provide other important insights that comport with the interpretation I am offering. Specifically, they opine, "It also seems likely that although a man may reaffirm his masculine identity through the *outcome* of a violent encounter with a woman (i.e., getting her to shut up, keeping her at home, punishing her for some wrongdoing, and the like), it is not reaffirmed through the process of using violence itself."[24] If the baseline prescriptions of modern masculinities call for men to be in charge of their wives and intimate partners, and violence expresses or indeed consolidates men's ascendancy, ought we not expect men, even during their acts of violence, to feel an inner glow, a surge? Why must we await the outcome and the seeming arrival of her consent to the tyrannical arrangement before realizing an affirmation of his masculinity?

I suggest that the reason men do not sense a reaffirmation of their masculinity while actually committing violence is that the violence functions, not to reaffirm masculinity, but rather to temporarily discharge humiliated fury. It is likely that this visceral discharge dissipates anxiety and fear, just as violence in general temporarily solves the primal fight-or-flight dilemma. However, we ought not expect to see violence, abuse, and tyranny linked to a reaffirmation of masculine prowess, because such malevolence originates in feelings of vulnerability and inferiority and is not merely a lapse or hiatus in his dominance. Rather, his malevolence is a symptom of the precariousness of his unraveling romantic allure, his potency. Only later, when he sees her behavior and demeanor change, seemingly in accordance with his actions or stated wishes, does his bluster return. "Bluster" is the significant word here. The violence alienates the person to whom it is directed. The malevolence destroys intimacy as surely as it simultaneously and desperately seeks to bolster the crumbling edifice of romantic love.[25]

The violence and tyrannical tendencies of the livid coercive hearts simultaneously express men's desires for authority and their relative vulnerability and dependency. These observations remind us that modern notions of masculinity are social constructions, hauntings, ideal types, and in the final analysis, abstractions. Rather than seeing modern men's behavior as a mere reflection of the triumph of these masculine prescriptions, I suggest that we explore the divergences between these prescriptions in the world of men and the lived realities of those men. This requires a much more nuanced theory of power than one that merely argues that masculine dominance provides the generative juice that reproduces men's ascendancy.

It is not my suggestion that we ignore the power relations of gender or their specific articulation within the families whose lives we have journeyed through. Rather, I contend we ought to critically appreciate the complex workings of power imbalances when we discuss the origins of familicide. We might expect the women subjected to the depredations of the livid coercive hearts to consistently engage in responses that range from appeasement, to dissimulation, to cowering and weeping. As James Scott points out in his discussion of what he calls the "weapons of the weak," "Dissimulation is the characteristic and necessary pose of subordinate classes everywhere most of the time—a fact that makes those rare and threatening moments when the pose is abandoned all the more remarkable."[26] What I have tried to emphasize in the lives of the battered women that appear in the familicide archive is the everyday middle ground they travel, somewhere between outright refusal and obeisance; the ceaseless negotiation that is at once equivocal and ambiguous.

CONTROL

Much of what I have said about the notion of power is relevant to discussions about the concept of control. In the anti–domestic violence movement, *control* is frequently portrayed as the goal of male violence and tyranny.[27] In their discussion of the counseling sessions at the DAIP, Pence and Shepard note, "The concepts of control and dominance are introduced as the purpose and function of battering. The education groups emphasize this further by focusing on the use of abuse as a means of controlling the thoughts, feelings, and actions of the victim, and challenges the assailant's belief system."[28] Similarly, Evan Stark's treatment of the notion of coercive control refers to the subordination of a woman's will through depriving her of, amongst other things, her social connectedness.[29]

Are we really to believe that batterers control the thoughts and feelings of their victims? Are Pence and Shepard referring to just some of victims' thoughts and feelings, or all of them? Presumably the reference cannot refer to all thoughts and feelings, because this would presume an enormous knowledge of the lives of battered women that those women themselves are unlikely to be able to accurately recall. Strong emotions (terror, rage, fear) can reshape memory, alter it, and obscure it, rendering it very difficult to interpret at a later date. We might take a similar tack with Stark's logic that women are subordinated in part through being deprived of their social connectedness. Again, this goes too far for a number of reasons, not least of which that it flies in the face of women's generally greater and deeper ontological sense of social connection, or, to use the language of psychoanalytic feminism, their relational orientation. When we examine the way the livid coercive hearts appear to have changed women's overt behavior and physical movements, we may be tempted to jump to the conclusion that men have pulled off some grand act of disconnection. However, if we explore the women's emotional styles, their sensitive and perceptive awareness, and their negotiation of familial atmospheres of feeling, the picture becomes much more complex.

The familicide archive suggests to me that those subjected to the abusive and tyrannical behavior of the livid coercive hearts exhibited an array of responses that included acquiescence, resignation, seeming consent to their plight, compliance, resistance, rebellion, and cynicism. Even in the cases of the high levels of livid coercion evidenced in Chapter 4, we would do well to at least consider James Scott's cautious observation derived from the field of social psychology that "coercion, it would seem, can produce compliance but it virtually inoculates the complier against willing compliance."[30] Scott continues, "Put another way, the greater the extrinsic reasons compelling our action—here large threats and large rewards are comparable—the less we have to provide satisfactory reasons to ourselves for our conduct."[31] In his discussion of the lives of the English peasantry, Scott contends they clearly imagined living arrangements contrary to those that kept them in bondage. He comments, "The obstacles to resistance, which are many, are simply not attributable to the inability of subordinate groups to *imagine* a counterfactual social order."[32]

Scott's historical analysis of the resistive stances of slaves, serfs, untouchables, and peasants tends, as Steven Lukes argues, to see the victims of domination as "tactical and strategic actors, who dissemble in order to survive."[33] We do not need to go as far as Scott in this regard and propose that those subject to domination consistently or even continuously strategize. Indeed, the personal nature of resistance to intimate terrorism and tyranny makes comparisons with more publicly articulated resistance expressed by slaves, serfs, and others risky. In the arena of intimate domination, Scott's phrase "virtually inoculates" ought not be taken as a guarantor of resistance to the same extent as we might see among those linked in public, less personal hierarchies. There is ample evidence that abused women psychologically bond to their abusers. But does such merging necessarily deprive victims of their agency? Is it not possible to see such merging as a form of acutely disingenuous yet willful strategizing? Indeed, one such form of merging, popularly referred to as "the Stockholm syndrome," has recently come under attack precisely because it looks much more like an urban legend than a specific nosological entity.[34]

Notwithstanding these observations, there is ample empirical evidence in the familicide archive to conceive of those subject to livid coercion as doing more than imagining a different way of life. Indeed, as I pointed out in Chapter 1, in familicides evidencing a prior history of domestic violence, fully 44 percent of victims had already exited the family home by the time of the killings. To me the exodus of these women does not signify that the men controlled either their thoughts or their feelings. Rather, such brave endeavors reveal much more than imagining a different way of living and feeling. Nevertheless, as Steven Lukes points out in his critique of Scott's argument, in the face of coercion we also witness genuine resignation and consent that coexist with more thoughtful and nuanced responses that only appear to take the form of acquiescence. Indeed, as Lukes suggests, consent and resignation can be seen "as both expressing and resulting from relations of power."[35]

I have chosen to avoid using the word *control* in any sense other than to denote that people *attempt* to control others. It is for this reason that I developed the notion of *livid coercion* as opposed to using terms such as *coercive control* because the former, unlike the latter, does not imply that perpetrators actually realize control of the complex personhood of another. As Kathleen Ferraro has impressively argued, the language of perpetrators and victims does not serve us well in some of our attempts to understand intimate-partner violence and terrorism.[36] We might say that those subjected to the violence and tyranny of the livid coercive hearts are at once more than and less than victims. Whatever a battered woman's apparent degree of compliance with a so-called perpetrator's imperatives, whatever her physical movements might appear to signify, my reading of the archival files involving livid coercion points to the complexity of her response, a complexity I argue that is better seen as a form of relative autonomy that either consciously or unconsciously guides her actions and behavior. If we are critical of vague concepts such as "battered woman syndrome" and "learned helplessness" because they appear to depict victims as pathological and because there is no universal or catch-all stereotype of women's responses to battering, then we ought be equally suspicious of modern notions of control that posit a socially situated emotional style that in the final analysis is essentially devoid of human agency.[37]

Finally, striving for control of one's life, to define oneself in ways that make one appear desirable to others, forms part of the cultural lifeblood of the modern Western societies, particularly the United States. I showed how self control became a key character trait of the successful self-made man from the early nineteenth century. Indeed, one of the great problems of the modern era, an epoch shorn of many of the sureties of tradition, ritual, ceremony, and community mores, is a lust to know what life has in store for us. Let us not confuse these modern cultural calls for self control, control over nature, control over our health, and so on, with the actual realization of control, whether it is with regard to global warming and melting icecaps or men's desire to control the women they eventually murder in acts of familicide.

THE ROLE OF EMOTION

Familicide is one of the consequences of modern emotional formations. It remains a mystery why many men, and in all likelihood a (much smaller) number of women, experience this insurgent array of emotions and yet do not commit familicide. The insurgent array of negative emotions in the familicidal hearts seems profoundly linked to the ways men and women live out various ideas about masculinities and femininities. It is almost as if these gender prescriptions offered an all-too-important lifeline for reinforcing their vulnerable senses of self and senses of belonging in the social order. This observation raises the question of whether some offenders "perform gender" as they commit familicide. It is possible to argue that when Marcus Sims killed his estranged wife, Gloria, with his barbells, he was *doing* his version of manhood, his particular form of masculinity. Sensing that Gloria had abandoned him for another man, Marcus temporarily discharged his unbearable sense of shame with humiliated fury. Similarly, Mandy Miller, replaced in her husband's life by another woman, stashed her bullets in her sewing basket, a place where her husband Andrew would not go. She bided her time for several weeks, then wrote Andrew a letter reminding him of her contributions over the years, her child-rearing, her housework, and their lovemaking. Unlike Marcus Sims, Mandy did not use violence or fly into a rage at her departing husband. Her approach was more considered, her emotional style more subdued and civil, even reputable. Mandy told him she wanted him to be proud of her modest achievements in the field of volunteer work. Andrew moved on anyway. As she committed familicide, did Mandy perform the gender work of the humiliated housewife and mother, rejected for another woman?

The insurgent array of emotions that plagues the lives of perpetrators of familicide reflects the way these offenders were unable to live up to the gendered cultural prescriptions of their day as breadwinners, lovers, fathers, mothers, wives, and nurturers. It is probably no accident we see these killings (where data exist) in homes evidencing a traditional or conventional sexual division of labor, with women being principally responsible for child care and housework and men for primary breadwinning. Perhaps it is among these nuclear family forms that we see the greatest potential for profound shame and painful disappointment about the seemingly inadequate performance of gender scripts. It is the failure to fulfill one's perceived responsibilities within intimate interdependencies that strikes me as particularly important.

The failure of offenders like Marcus Sims and Mandy Miller to maintain intimacy with their departing spouses robbed them of a mechanism that the modern self avails itself of for bolstering its own authenticity. The appropriate living out of gender prescriptions identifies the self as lovable, deserving, and socially acceptable. For Marcus and Mandy to lose this avenue of affirmation and social integration eroded their standing in their own and others' eyes. The familicidal hearts had to deal with the exacting demands of modern hyper-individuality and the ever more elaborate calls to cultivate self-identity. When contextualized against the rigors of these modern prescriptions for individuation, the attack on the precarious self-identity of the familicidal hearts proved catastrophic.

The power relations of the modern gender regime are a necessary although not sufficient condition for the perpetration of familicide. Embedded in this wider exercise of power, modern nuclear family life provides a contextual frame for familicide, one flush with innovative notions such as the self-made man, the breadwinner, the isolated and intensely nurturing mother, the increasingly dependent and precious child. It is against this backdrop that I now consider the part played by the pivotally important emotions of anger and shame.

THE CENTRALITY OF ANGER

Since both angry and relatively placid men and women both commit familicide it might be tempting to jump to the conclusion that the management of anger is of little importance. It seems to me that the reverse is true and that the handling of anger is of central importance to understanding the actions of the livid coercive and civil reputable hearts. Modern societies actively discourage the overt display of anger and rage in everyday public and private life, with the exception of socially approved outlets; for example, sports. Indeed, some historians have argued that the suppression of anger is the hallmark of modern emotional life.[38] It strikes me as highly significant that, compared to the general population, the livid coercive perpetrators under-internalized this historical tendency to rein in anger, and the civil reputable hearts over-internalized these cultural prescriptions. We might say both groups had a skewed relationship to societal norms regarding the management of anger.

Many feminist interpretations of battering pay less attention to batterers' anger, arguing instead for the centrality of abusers' need for and realization of power and control. In this model, anger is not the cause of violence. However, researchers clearly acknowledge the presence of anger in domestic violence situations. For example, in their interview work with interpersonally violent men, Dobash and Dobash note, "Men do, however, describe a number of intense emotions and specific orientations that *accompany* their decision to use violence. They often describe themselves as intensely angry and usually blame the woman for their anger and their subsequent violence."[39] The word "accompany" portrays the anger as epiphenomenal rather than central. The familicide archive points to the centrality of anger and its management in the process of violence and mass interpersonal murder. Psychologists also identify anger as an important component of batterer behavior and personality profiles.[40] For example, in discussing his clinical observations of men who batter women, Donald Dutton remarks, "Fury is the magic elixir that restores an inner sense of power. In an instant, the powerlessness and jealousy evaporate; the accumulating tension dissipates."[41]

The handling and expression of anger differ among the familicidal hearts. As psychiatrist William Gaylin reminds us, in the face of threat, danger, and assault in prehistoric times, "The two great devices of survival for the adult were flight and fight. The physiology of fear subserved the first, and the physiology of anger was a reasonable preparation for the assault."[42] In a very real sense, the anger of the livid coercive hearts serves as a temporary visceral or somatic solution to the immediate threat or hazard presented. The violent response allows the batterer to assume a superior posture. One way of interpreting this is that anger is not an expression of his domination, but rather a manifestation of his fear and vulnerability in the face of an interpersonal threat or challenge. Another possibility is that in some men, anger may have been the only emotion they learned to express. Perhaps they learned anger was an acceptable alternative to fear, an emotion they learned was unacceptable for them to experience, or at least to express. For these men, their anger is not a manifestation or displacement of other emotions, but rather an alternative to them or a replacement of them.[43]

It is not my point we ought recognize anger and rage merely as intrapsychic phenomena. Rather, I argue that social and historical manifestations of anger are highly relevant to our grasp of mass interpersonal killing. Under what specific social and historical conditions do people feel threatened and angered to the point they will kill their spouses and children and perhaps commit suicide? This question links the handling of anger in the familicide cases to modern figurations of feeling and changes in the political, economic, and cultural landscape.

In talking about the literature on what she calls "different masculine possibilities," Barbara Ehrenreich notes a "physically expressive, macho and overtly aggressive" form and a version of manhood whereby men are "uptight, emotionally inhibited and fastidiously devoid of affect."[44] These masculine possibilities roughly correspond with the livid coercive and civil reputable hearts, respectively. Ehrenreich also notes that these masculine possibilities also "corresponded to stages in the middle-class male life cycle. Little boys were forced to prove themselves athletically; they learned to fight or at least to swagger. Once grown into a professional or managerial occupation, the male acquired the verbal means of command and the emotional distance necessary to function in a bureaucratic setting."[45] In other words, there are class and biographical dimensions to the manifestation of anger, with working class men tending to wield their expressions of anger much later into life, sometimes using it as a bargaining chip against employers.

The humiliated fury of the livid coercive hearts is a vitally important piece of the familicide puzzle. It might be tempting to deny the centrality of anger because of the need to promote power/control explanations and to explain men's intimate violence in terms of their patriarchal or sexist beliefs. Psychologists or psychiatrists might want to eschew the social, historical, and biographical dimensions of anger, because these manifestations appear far removed from the individual personalities of perpetrators. I am making an argument for using the sociological imagination to unravel the historical, psychic, and biographical complexities of familicide and to contribute to discussions about intimate partner violence and murder in general.

THE CRUCIAL IMPORTANCE OF SHAME

Reporting a therapeutic exchange between a man who had assaulted his wife and a counselor, David Adams notes the counselor's telling the client, "A lot of people feel insecure but they are not violent."[46] Adams goes on to point out the dangers in explaining men's violence in terms of intrapsychic problems including "poor impulse control, low frustration tolerance, fear of intimacy, fear of abandonment, dependency, underlying depression, and impaired ego functioning resulting from developmental trauma."[47] Adams adds, "Implicit in this approach is the notion that men who batter have a very fragile sense of self."[48] Adams rightly alludes to the dangers of dwelling upon intrapsychic phenomena. In concert with Adams's reservations, it is essential to see the shame and humiliated fury of the livid coercive hearts as socially and historically situated phenomena, not as intrapsychic manifestations of insecurity or low –self-esteem. Shame circulates socially. In the modern era, it is the emotion of social disconnection. In premodern times, shame was more openly acknowledged; the stuff of public rituals, if you will. In modernity, shame becomes much more subterranean, subtler, a repressive influence that brings social actors into interaction with others much more warily. For these reasons we cannot see shame as intrapsychic. Interpretations that see shame in individualizing terms are indeed inaccurate, misleading, and counterproductive.

Rather than ascertaining whether a would-be perpetrator of familicide suffers from low self-esteem or personal insecurity, it is much more useful to identify his or her level of shame and degree of social engagement and integration. This means we cannot treat shame and social disconnection as separate concepts. Rather, these aspects of the lives of perpetrators commingle and are continuous with the ebb and flow of power and emotion through the social body.

Nevertheless, the social circulation of shame and the responses to its more intense manifestations are clearly gendered. As we saw, the intensification of mothering in modernity, something that varies considerably by class, race, and ethnicity, leads to the development of a more relational orientation among women than among men. Women seem to be under less pressure to individuate than men, although this is clearly changing.

It is also the case that women are not socialized to use violence to solve problems to anything like the same degree as men, although working class girls and women are likely to feel less constrained about using violence than their middle or upper class peers, who may have other resources at their disposal. As I argued, women's emotional capital, their ability to entertain and express a wider array of emotions than men, provides them with a variety of ways to solve highly threatening problems other than through the commission of interpersonal violence and homicide. These observations help explain why we see far fewer women committing familicide. However, the fact that women do commit familicide reminds us that these differences are questions of degree, not kind. Therefore, we might expect the ratio of men to women committing familicide to change as the power relations of gender ebb and flow, women individuate more, and men spend more time parenting children.

COMPLEX PERSONHOOD

Modernity slowly but surely produces more complex forms of personhood. As people perform increasingly specialized jobs, meet a greater diversity of peers, move through a greater range of intimate relationships, and simply lead longer lives, they accumulate a range of experiences quite different from those of their premodern ancestors. The flexibility of modern social relationships provides people with enormous emotional opportunities. Likewise, as Elias argues, the increasingly longer chains and networks of interdependencies require an awareness of others well beyond the bounds of what was previously necessary in premodern times. Such an awareness can and often does increase trust among peoples far afield, people who in premodern times not only would not have known each other, but who would not have known of each other's existence.

None of these observations ought be taken as a denial of the existence of modern alienation and anomie. Clearly, these are real and destructive historical forces that can exact an enormous toll. However, we have to balance these deleterious effects against the growing peace and security of everyday social life and the psychological controls that emerge in modern times. These seeming counter-tendencies—the depressing and rage-inducing possibilities of alienation and anomie and the liberating potential of romantic love and the garnering of some control over strong emotional urges—mean that increasing social differentiation feeds ever-more-complex forms of personhood.

From the vantage point of history, I suggest the notion of modern complex personhood is inconsistent with the argument that the livid coercive heart actually controls his spouse or partner. Among modern people in general, the livid coercive hearts are among the least likely to have acquired control over their own powerful emotions, let alone the emotional styles and behavior of others. Many sought control or influence over their spouses or partners, but to suggest that they realized it is a quantum leap that, from my perspective, does not agree with the archival evidence.

Bearing in mind the endless nuances of complex personhood in the lives of the familicidal hearts, I now discuss the phenomenon of risk and risk-assessment in the field of intimate partner violence and homicide. It is more than just difficult to predict risk of future violence or death in tyrannical and abusive relationships: it is impossible. Indeed, I want to suggest that our attempts to do so reflect the objectivist posturing of modern science and a presumption that we might improve victim safety and security by using expert knowledge to calculate the risks they face.

HAUNTING AND RISK

Premodern societies changed slowly compared with their modern and late-modern counterparts. People in premodern cultures used their historic connections with tradition, ritual, ceremony, and their relatives and communities as relatively stable frames for their own lives, providing them with a sense of direction and inevitability. Using scientific and expert technical knowledge as a touchstone, modern people seek a sense of direction and control through planning the future. Without the ties and predictabilities of traditional influences, modern people also enjoy a greater array of choices. Ironically, the process of choosing a path through these choices is also a source of anxiety. As Anthony Giddens observes, "Modernity is a risk culture. . . . Under conditions of modernity, the future is continually drawn into the present by means of the reflexive organization of knowledge environments."[49]

In late-modern culture, the calculation of risk is central to the workings of what David Garland calls "the culture of control."[50] The vast apparatuses of many modern criminal justice systems have become increasingly concerned with security and protection. The idea that we can calculate risk and use this knowledge to identify and triage out certain offenders is one important aspect of these bureaucratic developments.

The use of scientific research to feed the calculation of risk is particularly pronounced in the field of intimate-partner violence. The risk literature in this field identifies the importance of various permutations and combinations of case markers, such as a prior and escalating history of domestic violence (including threats to kill, attempts to strangle, forced sex, use or attempted use of a weapon, presence of a handgun in the home), a pending separation or divorce, obsessive attempts to control the victim, perpetrator unemployment, the presence of stepchildren in the home, excessive and habitual consumption of alcohol by the perpetrator, perpetrator suicidal behavior in conjunction with perpetrator attempts to control, and so on.[51]

We saw many of these case characteristics among the livid coercive familicides, although I have not treated these characteristics with any rigor or offered them up in the form of an explanatory matrix. Clearly, the case characteristics that evidence tyranny and abusiveness are remarkably important. Indeed, the fact that so-called civilizations continue to ignore them or respond ineffectively to them is, as Evan Stark points out, an affront to democratic principles and the legitimacy and credibility of the rule of law. My objection is not to the identification of these case characteristics or to the highlighting of their destructiveness. Rather, it is to their being reified and plugged into a scientific formula that then spews out a risk-assessment score. Such crude practices strike me as a denial of complex personhood and a profound misunderstanding of the continuities and complexities of figurations of feelings, familial atmospheres of feeling, and emotional styles. These continuities and complexities defy abstraction and invite analyses that at least recognize the haunting links between the visceral, the psychological, the social, and the historical.

The reluctance by some to explore emotion reflects a suspicion or outright rejection of many things psychological and psychiatric. It is as if these approaches had little to offer, or worse still, were taboo because they contributed in some way to blaming victims for their own demise. To the extent that psychological and psychiatric approaches focus on the individual, these concerns strike me as well founded. However, many have thrown the baby out with the bathwater. As I have tried to argue, the task is not to dismiss psychological and psychiatric contributions, but rather to reframe human behavior socially and historically.

With these ideas in mind, I recap three aspects of my archival analysis that speak somewhat to the current debates about risk. I do not offer these insights as a means of improving risk assessments in cases of domestic violence and intimate terrorism, and readers should not take my remarks as a tacit approval of these dubious and imperialistic predictive practices.

First, I suggest that we gather information about the levels of shame and humiliated fury of perpetrators of intimate violence and tyranny. Second, and in a related vein, I recommend that we explore the degree to which perpetrators of intimate partner violence and tyranny are socially isolated or suffer a diminished or nominal sense of social belonging. Third, I suggest that we explicitly acknowledge that we cannot predict intimate partner homicide from among the large number of cases of intimate-partner violence. I do not urge such an acknowledgment because of the problem of missing data that muddies the waters in terms of building risk models, although this strikes me as a good reason for risk assessors to exercise a little statistical humility. Neither do I suggest that we jettison risk-assessment and management because we have yet to validate the various instruments. Recent work by Carolyn Hoyle addresses this specific matter. Hoyle concludes:

> Risk assessment and risk management for victims of intimate abuse are in their infancy. The confusing plethora of assessment tools is in itself indicative that many questions and much doubt remain as to the most reliable indicators of likely repeat victimization in cases where victims

or others have complained to the police. Absent thorough and rigorous evaluation of their effectiveness, the jury is still out.[52]

My position is a little different than Hoyle's. For me, risk assessment and its scientific logic is part of the problem, not part of a potential solution. My concern, at least in cases of familicide, is linked to the haunting presence of the inexplicable. Essentially, my exploratory and speculative analysis of the origins of familicide identifies what appear to be the *necessary* emotional and sociohistorical conditions for the appearance of this alarmingly uncanny form of mass interpersonal murder. However, I have been at pains not to infer or specify the *sufficient* conditions because it is simply not possible to know them. Arguing for the haunting presence of the inexplicable in assessing and managing risk in cases of intimate-partner violence provides a check on the modern scientific tendency to colonize the future, to draw it into the present, and to allegedly gain some control over it. These tendencies are understandable given the existentialist angst of modern life. However, when we are dealing with something as nebulous as human emotion and something as precious as victims' lives, it is perhaps wiser to acknowledge the inherent difficulties in predicting human behavior.

Whatever caveats risk assessors write into their models, plugging risk markers into a formula and supposedly deriving an understanding of the potential future of victims is an exercise in scientific pretension. In a very real sense, such practices are tantamount to playing dice with the universe and victims' lives at the same time as societies fail to address the social and historical roots of these tragedies. I suggest we cannot just ask people questions in a closed-ended manner and log their responses. These kinds of interactions with victims of domestic violence limit responses, box them, and parlay them into the categories of the scientific language of cause and effect. Such practices, I contend, are a form of imperial inquiry that parallels and mirrors batterer's attempts to control the lives of victims. In this regard, risk assessors and batterers have something in common. Neither controls the lives and futures of victims, as much as they might like to do so. Like batterers, risk assessors purport to care, claim an expertise in the lives of those seek to regulate. Curiously, in risk-assessment practices we also see the workings of power; indeed, power and the attempt to control.

CLOSING THOUGHTS ON CULTURAL CHANGE

We apparently find no familicides among more egalitarian relationships where men and women live as spouses/partners and parents in atmospheres of emotional give-and-take. Neither do we find familicide among families with same-sex adult partners. Where the archival material is sufficiently rich to explore these matters, the livid coercive familicide cases evinced unequal intimate relationships with a traditional sexual divisions of labor, with women being primarily responsible for child care, emotional nurturance, and homemaking, and men assuming prime responsibilities as breadwinners. Among civil reputable hearts we find similar sexual divisions of labor, mostly in a Caucasian middle class milieu. My findings suggest that the relationship between men's power over women or indeed sexual inequality in general, and the commission of familicide is *complex.*

The empirical evidence does not support the drawing of an arrow directly from men's power or from the domain of sexual inequality to mass interpersonal killing. Neither does it support an interpretation that posits familicide as an epiphenomenon of gender power differentials or sexual inequality. Rather, the power relations of modern gender regimes appear to exert a *contextual* and *indirect influence* on the commission of familicide. Power operates through dominant modern notions of masculinity and femininity. The familicidal hearts, nearly all men but a few women, developed grave and homicidal concerns about not living up to modern gendered standards about what men or women ought be, have, and do. In this way of thinking, power is *contested and relational*, taking the form of struggles rather than mere impositions.

The livid coercive hearts were desperate to hold on to their spouse or partners and their nuclear families. The civil reputable hearts lived in established nuclear family units, usually of long standing. Civil reputable men had successfully performed as sole providers, the women as wives and mothers. The men were soft patriarchs. They enjoyed the entitlements and privileges that accompanied such a position but they also felt overwhelmed by their responsibilities, especially when things started to go awry. The women performed their gendered callings as relatively well-to-do and esteemed wives and mothers who provided for the emotional nurturance of family members. As with the men, the female civil reputable hearts appear to have felt overwhelmed by their gender calling, especially in the face of what must have appeared as the insurmountable challenges of illness, the threat of destitution, and particularly their husband's moving on to another woman. In a nutshell, the vast majority of the familicidal hearts experienced acute shame at failing to live up to the imperatives of their gendered callings as providers, lovers, fathers, husbands, wives, mothers, or partners.

The fact that familicides occur only within modern figurations of feeling does not mean that modern intimate relationships are somehow suspect or pathological. As many researchers contend, modernity is alive with emotional possibilities and opportunities for changing relationships between spouses and intimate partners, parents and children, and between friends.[53] This relative democratization in modern gender relations means that power is contested rather than simply imposed.

The rise of romantic love as the basis for marriage marked a significant departure from the premodern strategic marriage designed to blend traditions, skills, possessions, property, and lineages. These developments commingled with the proliferation of individualism. Choosing a spouse on the basis of their emotional compatibility, their sexual attractiveness, and other highly personal and idiosyncratic qualities is in many ways the epitome of individual choice. For Giddens, the emergence of romantic love as the basis for marriage foreshadowed the rise of what he refers to as "pure relationships." He notes, "Romantic love presumes that a durable emotional tie can be established with the other on the basis of qualities intrinsic to that tie itself. It is the harbinger of the pure relationship, although it also stands in tension with it."[54] A "pure relationship" refers to "a situation where a social relation is entered into for its own sake, for what can be derived by each person from a sustained association with another; and which is continued only in so far as it is thought by both parties to deliver enough satisfactions for each individual to stay within it."[55] He continues, "In the pure relationship, trust has no external supports, and has to be developed on the basis of intimacy."[56]

Compared with selecting a marriage partner because of kinship and community pressure, modern romantic love was in many ways liberating and more egalitarian than premodern arrangements underpinned by much deeper forms of gender inequality. However, as Giddens points out, "romantic love is thoroughly skewed in terms of power. For women, dreams of romantic love have all too often led to grim domestic subjection."[57] Giddens contrasts romantic love with "confluent love." Confluent love "presumes equality in emotional give and take,"[58] something that romantic partners in the modern era engaged in sparingly, with most of the emotional work being left to women. Indeed, as I showed in the last chapter, nineteenth-century prescriptions for self-made manhood required a disguised reserve and the suppression of feelings. With confluent love, partners communicate and negotiate the emotional aspects of their relationship. Indeed, this reflexive negotiation assumes pride of place over the partners themselves. Giddens sees the rise of confluent love as one of the potentially liberating forces of modernity and particularly late-modernity, mirroring in many ways the extension of democracy in the public arena. Confluent love is therefore of relatively recent origin, does not presume either heterosexual or monogamous relationships, and is linked to the uncoupling of reproduction and sexuality.

We see growing efforts to engineer relationships to maximize the yield to the individual partners, regardless of whether the partners are married or cohabiting. Confluent love can, of course, take place within the formal institution of state-sanctioned marriage. Indeed, in spite of the de facto recognition of various rights for unmarried couples and same-sex couples and the greatly increased late-modern acceptance of premarital sex, singlehood (people choosing to live alone), childlessness, divorce, and out-of-wedlock child-rearing, it is striking that the research on marriage shows spouses seeking much more fulfillment than in previous generations. Stephanie Coontz summarizes the developments nicely:

> Even as divorce and nonmarriage have increased, our standards for
> what constitutes a "good" marriage have risen steadily. The percentage

of people who believe it is okay to cheat, lie, or keep secrets in a marriage has fallen over the past forty years. Many couples work hard to enrich their relationship and deepen their intimacy, with a dedication that would astonish most couples of the past. Marriage as a relationship between two individuals is taken more seriously and comes with higher emotional expectations than ever before.[59]

Coontz also notes that "nearly half of the five hundred largest companies in America now extend benefits to unmarried partners who live together."[60] In other late-modern societies (for example, France and Canada), Coontz informs us, "An individual can establish a legally recognized care-giving or resource-pooling relationship with any other person and receive many legal and financial benefits that used to be reserved for married couples. Two sexual partners can take advantage of this arrangement. So can two sisters, two army buddies, or a celibate priest and his housekeeper."[61]

These encouraging shifts toward confluent love are emblematic of broader changes in the cultivation of late-modern identities. If as some commentators suggest, sexual inequality is diminishing and women's economic and political opportunities are increasing, then we might encourage a concomitant increase in men's emotional capital to the point that they not only increasingly engage in emotional give-and-take, but to a degree that diminishes their feelings of shame and humiliated fury in relation to their performance of masculinity. Such cultural shifts, changes if you will in late-modern figurations of feeling, may go some considerable way toward changing the emotional styles of men and women. From my understanding of what lies at the root of familicide, such changes would also go some way toward reducing the necessary conditions for the commission of these mass interpersonal killings.

Given that men are the principal perpetrators of familicide and other forms of injurious and tyrannical intimate abuse and murder, any changes we implement must recognize the complexity of men's social lives. We cannot simply see men as oppressors and exploiters of women. It is clear that the vast majority of men are exploited under conditions of modern capitalism, that men struggle to provide for their families and are deeply and often adversely affected by the imperatives of hegemonic masculinity. We cannot insist on men's contributing more to the emotional ebb and flow of intimate relationships without doing something to recognize and change the gendered prescriptions they negotiate in society.

These changes will require slow but sure transformations in the way gender is performed by men and women. Any policies that would enhance confluent love would be desirable in this regard. In particular, we need to find a way to bridge the gaps between the emotional styles of men and women, thus undermining some of the intense imperatives of the gender regime.

It lies beyond the scope of my modest contribution to explore policies that might encourage such shifts, although the full realization of equal rights, a national child-care system, affordable housing, and an increase in the availability of meaningful and well-paid labor and more come to mind. It is preferable that we tackle the problem of familicide, intimate partner violence, and homicide through encouraging cultural change rather than through more punitive approaches based on increased criminal justice interventions. Intimate partner violence is only the presenting problem, and punitive responses to violence, abuse, and tyranny do not get at the emotional origins of such damaging behavior.

I have already noted my reservations about the notion of coercive control, a key analytical concept in the field of intimate partner violence and tyranny. I also have major concerns about suggestions such as those voiced recently by Evan Stark, that we criminalize coercive control. He opines, "In criminalizing coercive control, we mark as unacceptable in modern democratic societies a particularly noxious means of exploiting the discriminatory effects of sexual inequality in personal life."[62] Further penalizing those who commit such malevolent behavior without addressing its social, economic, and political generation runs the risk of merely perpetuating the cycle of shame. This is not to say that society ought not provide protection to victims or hold perpetrators accountable. However, to the extent that our interventions fail to identify and move toward the elimination of people's shame and rage concerning their intimate relationships, we will continue to witness familicide from time to time. The point, then, is to change culture and the figurations of feeling that feed it and are transformed by culture.

In many ways, American culture, honed out of the white heat of individual responsibility, represents the most acutely individuated of all societies. It is here that the cult of the individual sometimes assumes quite remarkable proportions. At the same time, it is in the United States, the rightful original home of familicide, that we see less willingness to recognize the importance of community, of caring for others, of socialized medicine, and of plowing significant proportions of gross domestic product back into communities to help those left behind. Rather, we see enormous expenditures on the criminal justice juggernaut and incarceration, and an abject failure to connect individual malevolence and pathology to social, economic, and political arrangements. The fact that the anti–domestic violence movement has aligned itself so closely with the criminal-justice arm of the state ought be grave cause for concern. The language of batterer-intervention programs, mandatory arrest, coordinated community responses, and so on, reflect an overzealous acknowledgment that violence, abuse, and tyranny are the problems rather than the social, political, and economic conditions that generate them.

I contend we need a long-term vision that recognizes the importance of emotional styles, familial atmospheres of feeling, and figurations of feeling, and that addresses the unsustainable levels of hyper-individuality that have come to characterize modern life. We can lock up offenders for as long as we like, but until we address the reasons for their anger, fear, anxiety, and shame, we will not move toward more egalitarian intimate relationships. Neither are we likely to see the disappearance of the familicidal heart.

NOTES

1. Appendix III reveals a considerable increase in the last two decades.

2. Lynd, 1958: 16.

3. Evan Stark argues: "In the United States, even where both partners work, the man can expect to average approximately $50,000 a year during his prime years of employment, whereas the woman can expect only $18,000. This gap is more than sufficient to support the differences in status that are exploited in coercive control." Unfortunately, Stark provides no statistical evidence to match the gendered income differentials to the social patterning of coercive control. See Stark, 2007: 190. An alternative and controversial opinion regarding gendered income disparities comes from Warren Farrell (2005), who essentially argues that men earn more than women because they are prepared to work in dangerous and dirty jobs that provide higher wages. Farrell contends that women and men with the same experience and qualifications, performing the same jobs, for equal numbers of hours per week and in the same working conditions, earn the same money.

4. We must not underestimate the way social and economic constraints prevent women from participating in both family and public life on a par with men. Many of these impediments are linked to women's disproportionate responsibilities as parents, nurturers, and household workers. Simply put, gender inequality is alive and well. The intricate mapping of the gender regime lies well beyond the scope of my rather specialized inquiry and would require the analysis of a large, specialized, and contentious literature. For a range of opinions, see Thistle, 2000; Farrell, 2005; Walby, 1997; Fuchs Epstein, 2007.

5. Beck-Gernsheim and Beck, 1995.

6. Stark (2007) estimates that 8–10 million women live under regimes of coercive control. Summarizing survey research, Dutton estimates that about 3 percent of all men in the general population qualify as patriarchal terrorists. See Dutton, 2006: 123, and footnote 66.

7. Goldberg, 1976.

8. Farrell, 1993: 30.

9. Farrell, 1993: 30.

10. Farrell, 1993: 37.

11. Brody, 1999: 56.

12. Giddens, 1992: 130.

13. Cited in Giddens, 1992: 117.

14. Cited in Dobash and Dobash, 1979: 73. Italics in the original.

15. Pence and Shepard 1990: 285, quoting Pence, 1985: 2. Italics mine.

16. Dobash and Dobash, 1998: 153.

17. Dobash and Dobash, 1998: 154, citing case 038.

18. Dobash and Dobash, 1998: 154, citing case 006.

19. Dobash and Dobash, 1998: 154, citing case 005.

20. Dobash and Dobash, 1998: 154, citing case 005.

21. Dobash and Dobash, 1998: 155, citing case 091.

22. Dobash and Dobash, 1998: 164.

23. I am not referring here to the possibility that he is ashamed of his own

violence. Rather, I reference a preexisting shame associated with his sense of his own masculinity as compromised, not living up to the prescriptions of modern standards of self-made manhood. The Dobashes appear imprecise on this matter, addressing it by writing, "some of the men voiced a sense of shame, but most did not" (Dobash and Dobash, 1998: 163). It is not clear whether this sense of shame referred to the men's use of violence or to some other transgression or failing on their part.

24. Dobash and Dobash, 1998: 168.

25. Denzin (1984) makes a similar point.

26. Scott, 1985: 284.

27. My current position on the notion of control departs from that in my earlier writing. In *Understanding Domestic Homicide*, I argued that men used violence against women "to establish control or to reassert control that they felt was ebbing away" (Websdale, 1999: 207). At another point I argued, "Batterers' assertion of power and control is often intensified by their perceptions that they have failed to gather the desired material and status trappings required by a dominant value system that celebrates individual achievement" (Websdale, 1999: 208). At still another point, I interpreted intimate partner homicide in terms of male perpetrators' sensing "they are losing control, face, or both" (Websdale, 1999: 207). As a result of my analysis of the familicide archive, my focus is now trained upon the importance of men losing face, or what I have now interpreted as their humiliated fury, rather than men losing control over women.

28. Pence and Shepard, 1990: 289.

29. Stark, 2007: 15.

30. Scott, 1990: 109.

31. Scott, 1990: 110.

32. Scott, 1990: 81.

33. Lukes, 2005: 124.

34. Namnyak et al., 2008

35. Lukes, 2005: 131.

36. Ferraro, 2006.

37. For a succinct and accessible critique of the battered woman syndrome, see Dutton, 1997.

38. See for example, Stearns and Stearns, 1986. Stephanie Shields concurs with Stearns and Stearns about the central importance of Americans' preoccupation with anger in modern emotional life. Indeed, for Shields, anger and romantic love emerge as central themes in emotional history. However, Shields argues, "The Stearns overstate the extent to which the suppression or elimination of anger stands as an ideal. Instead, the goal seems to be one of achieving an idealized state of focused and controlled experience and expression" (Shields, 2002: 145).

39. Dobash and Dobash, 1998: 155. Italics mine.

40. For a helpful summary of these studies, see Dutton, 2006: 305–306.

41. Dutton, 1995: 103.

42. Gaylin, 1984: 74.

43. I am indebted to one of the five reviewers for helping me clarify the relationship between anger and other emotions among the livid coercive hearts.

44. Ehrenreich, 1983: 133.

45. Ehrenreich, 1983: 133.

46. Adams, 1990: 176.

47. Adams, 1990: 178.

48. Adams, 1990: 179.
49. Giddens, 1991: 3.
50. Garland, 2001
51. See, for example, Campbell, 2003.
52. Hoyle, 2008: 335.
53. See, for example Giddens, 1992.
54. Giddens, 1992: 2.
55. Giddens, 1992: 58.
56. Giddens, 1992: 138.
57. Giddens, 1992: 62.
58. Giddens, 1992: 62.
59. Coontz, 2005: 278.
60. Coontz, 2005: 279.
61. Coontz, 2005: 279.
62. Stark, 2007: 384.

APPENDIX I

The Occupational Backgrounds
of the Livid Coercive
and Civil Reputable Hearts

Percentages were derived from the number of cases with discernible employment statuses (i.e., 67 of the livid coercive offenders; 44 of the civil reputable offenders).

Category of Employment	Livid Coercive Offenders n = 77	Civil Reputable Offenders n = 47
White collar/technical worker	8 (12%)	14 (32%)
Blue collar/manual worker/ service worker	43 (64%)	5 (11%)
Professional (e.g. doctor, lawyer)	4 (6%)	5 (11%)
Independently wealthy	1 (1%)	3 (7%)
Homemaker/unpaid labor	3 (4%)	6 (14%)
Independent farmer	0	3 (7%)
Public servant	3 (4%)	4 (9%)
Military	4 (6%)	0
Independent small businessman	0	5 (11%)
Other	1 (1%)	0
Missing	10	3

APPENDIX II

The Racial/Ethnic Backgrounds of the Livid Coercive and Civil Reputable Hearts

Percentages were derived from the number of cases with discernible racial/ethnic identities (i.e., 67 of the livid coercive offenders; 39 of the civil reputable offenders).

Race	Livid Coercive Offenders n = 77	Civil Reputable Offenders n = 47
Caucasian[1]	40 (59.7%)	33 (84.6%)
African/African-American	11 (16.4%)	0
Asian/Asian-American[2]	3 (4.5%)	4 (10.3%)
Latino	11 (16.4%)	1 (2.6%)
Native American/Indian	1 (1.5%)	0
Middle Eastern	1 (1.5%)	1 (2.6%)
Missing	10	8

1 Caucasian includes perpetrators from Europe, New Zealand, and one perpetrator from South Africa of Caucasian descent.

2 This includes Southeast Asian, Asian-Pacific Islander, Indian Sub-continent, and all other parts of Asia except the Middle East.

APPENDIX III
Rates of Familicide

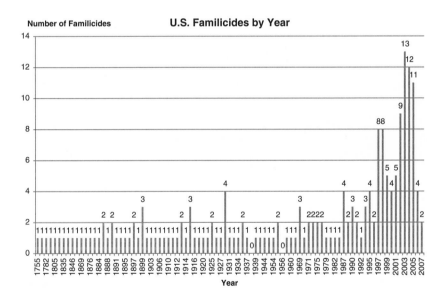

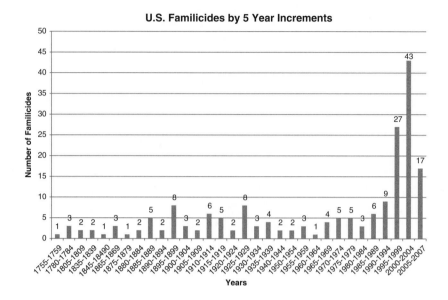

U.S. Familicides by 5 Year Increments

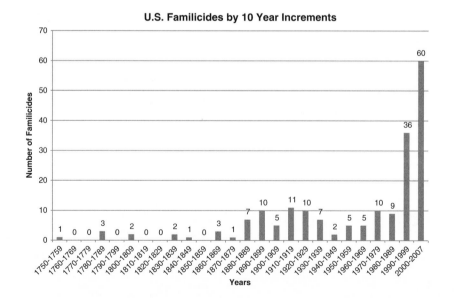

U.S. Familicides by 10 Year Increments

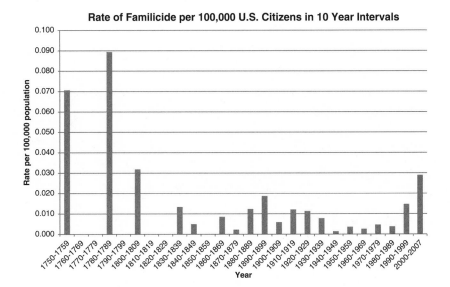

Rate of Familicide per 100,000 U.S. Citizens in 10 Year Intervals

APPENDIX IV
Survey Instrument: Male Perpetrators

PERPETRATOR'S BACKGROUND

1. How old was the perpetrator?

2. a. The perpetrator's childhood: H = Happy__ A = Abused__
      SA = Sexually Abused__ U = Unstable/troubled__
      M = Missing__ D = Difficult__ E = Educational Difficulties__
   b. Was there evidence of disrupted bonding in childhood? Y__
      N__ NA__ Missing__
   c. If yes, when? 0–5__ 6+__ NA__ Missing__
   d. Sexual exposure during childhood? Y__ N__ NA__ Missing__
   e. Itinerant childhood (moved at least three times before 10 yrs.
      old)? Y__ N__ NA__ Missing__

3. The perpetrator's birth: A = Adopted__ BP = Biological parents__ FP
   = Foster parents or Ward of state__ Missing__ F = Family other than
   Bio. Parents__

4. a. Was the perpetrator socially and/or emotionally disengaged/
      detached (a loner)? Y__ N__ NA__ Missing__
   b. Was the perpetrator acutely secretive (more than an average
      person)? Y__ N__ NA__ Missing__

PERPETRATOR'S CURRENT FAMILY

5. Mothering: T = Traditional stay-at-home mother__ WWM = Wage
   working mother__ Missing__ S = school__

6. a. Family atmosphere: H = Harmonious___ C = Conflictual___
   DV = Prior DV___ Missing___
   b. How did the offender respond to social authorities (including
   police, psychologists, boss, etc)? B = Belligerent___
   R = Resistant___ O = Outwardly compliant___ T = Seemingly
   totally compliant___ Missing___

7. Gendered division of labor? Y___ N___ NA___ Missing___

8. Money management: MMM = Mother managed money___ FMM =
   Father managed money___ DM = Democratic or mixed money
   management___ Missing___

9. Discipline of children: PM = Primarily mother___ PF = Primarily
   father___ Missing___ Mixed___

10. Family decision-making: FD = Father dominated___ MD = Mother
    dominated___ M = Mixed___ Missing___

11. Loving family? Y___ N___ NA___ Missing___

12. Were loving notes from the perpetrator to the victim left with the
    bodies? Y___ N___ NA___ Missing___

13. Were loving notes from the victim to the perpetrator left with the
    bodies? Y___ N___ NA___ Missing___

14. Was a suicide note left with the bodies or elsewhere? Y___ N___ NA___
    Missing___

15. a. Was there a change in familial relationships just before the
    killings? Y___ N___ NA___ Missing___
    b. Was another person added to the household? Y___ N___ NA___
    Missing___

SEXUAL EVENTS/HISTORY

16. a. Sexual jealousy directed at partner? Y___ N___ NA___ Missing___
    b. Did the victim have another sexual partner, including prostitute
    (real or perceived)? Y___ N___ NA___ Missing___

17. Did perpetrator have another sexual partner, including prostitute?
    Y___ N___ NA___ Missing___

18. Did the perpetrator's partner know of his lover? Y___ N___ NA___
    Missing___

19. Did the perpetrator have intimate sexual relationship with the
    victim? Y___ N___ NA___ Missing___

MENTAL HISTORY/STATUS/ISSUES

20. Was the perpetrator under the influence of illegal drugs or alcohol?
Y__ N__ NA__ Missing__

21. a. Was there a community assessment of the perpetrator having
a history of mental illness? Y__ N__ NA__ Missing__
b. Was there a clinical diagnosis of mental illness? Y__ N__ NA__
Missing__
c. Was the perpetrator diagnosed with a personality disorder? Y__
N__ NA__ Missing__

22. a. Was perpetrator mentally ill at the time of the killings? Y__ N__
NA__ Missing__
b. Is there reason to suspect the perpetrator was mentally ill at the
time of the killings? Y N NA Missing

23. Did the perpetrator plead not guilty by reason of insanity? Y__ N__
NA__ Missing__

24. Did perpetrator suffer from depression? Y__ N__ NA__ Missing__

25. Was perpetrator clinically depressed at time of killings? Y__ N__
NA__ Missing__

26. Was perpetrator psychotically depressed at the time of the killings?
Y__ N__ NA__ Missing__

27. Was perpetrator taking medication for mental illness at time of
killings? Y__ N__ NA__ Missing__

28. Was perpetrator taking medication for depression at time of the
killings? Y__ N__ NA__ Missing__

29. Had the perpetrator ever attempted to commit suicide before the
killings? Y__ N__ NA__ Missing__

30. Did the perpetrator attempt to commit suicide immediately after
the killings? Y__ N__ NA__ Missing__

31. Did perpetrator attempt to commit suicide after the killings (but not
immediately after the killings)? Y__ N__ NA__ Missing__

32. Had the perpetrator ever threatened to commit suicide before the
killings? Y__ N__ NA__ Missing__

33. Did the perpetrator kill the family pet in the familicidal episode?
Y__ N__ NA__ Missing__

34. Did the perpetrator kill any other animals in the familicidal episode?
Y__ N__ NA__ Missing__

35. Was there any history of the perpetrator abusing animals? Y__ N__
NA__ Missing__

36. Did the perpetrator have a history of delusional behavior? Y__ N__ NA__ Missing__

37. Was the perpetrator ever diagnosed with schizophrenia? Y__ N__ NA__ Missing__

38. Was there evidence of prior planning before the killings? Y__ N__ NA__ Missing__

39. Was there evidence of considerable long-term planning? Y__ N__ NA__ Missing__

40. Was there evidence of a prior inner struggle before the killings? Y__ N__ NA__ Missing__

41. Was there evidence of a long-term inner struggle over the decision to kill before the killings? Y__ N__ NA__ Missing__

42. Were the killings organized or disorganized? O = Organized__ D = Disorganized__

DOMESTIC VIOLENCE AND/OR ABUSIVE BEHAVIOR

43. a. Was there a history of physical/sexual violence in the family? Y__ N__ NA__ Missing__
    b. Was there evidence of DV in a previous relationship? Y__ N__ NA__ Missing__
    c. Had he previously killed a family member? Y__ N__ NA__ Missing__

44. Was there an official record of domestic violence in the family? Y__ N__ NA__ Missing__

45. Was the perpetrator the principal violent aggressor? Y__ N__ NA__ Missing__

46. Was the perpetrator typically or always the victim of the domestic violence? Y__ N__ NA__ Missing__

47. Was there a history of emotional abuse? Y__ N__ NA__ Missing__

48. Was the perpetrator the prime instigator of the emotional abuse? Y__ N__ NA__ Missing__

49. Was the perpetrator typically or always the victim of the emotional abuse? Y__ N__ NA__ Missing__

50. a. Was there a history of threatening behavior (such as threatening to kill his partner)? Y__ N__ NA__ Missing__
    b. Was there a history of threatening behavior toward others? Y__ N__ NA__ Missing__

51. Was the perpetrator the principal initiator of threatening behavior? Y__ N__ NA__ Missing__

52. Was the perpetrator typically or always the object of the threatening behavior? Y__ N__ NA__ Missing__

53. a. Was the perpetrator controlling? Y__ N__ NA__ Missing__
    b. Was the perpetrator striving to control the victim? Y__ N__ NA__ Missing__
    c. Was his control ebbing? Y__ N__ NA__ Missing__

54. Did killer appear to feel entitled to kill his/her family? Y__ N__ NA__ Missing__

55. a. Did the victim fear for her life? Y__ N__ NA__ Missing__
    b. Was the perpetrator stalking the victim? Y__ N__ NA__ Missing__
    c. Did the perpetrator intimidate the victim? Y__ N__ NA__ Missing__
    d. Did the victim feel entrapped? Y__ N__ NA__ Missing__
    e. Did the perpetrator degrade the victim or deny her self-respect? Y__ N__ NA__ Missing__
    f. Did the perpetrator survey the victim's life? Y__ N__ NA__ Missing__
    g. Did he isolate her? Y__ N__ NA__ Missing__

SEPARATION

56. Were the intimate partners estranged within the household? Y__ N__ NA__ Missing__

57. a. Was the victim moving in a direction away from the perpetrator? Y__ N__ NA__ Missing__
    b. Was a restraining order in place for the adult victim? Y__ N__ NA__ Missing__
    c. Was a restraining order in place for the children? Y__ N__ NA__ Missing__
    d. Had the restraining order been served on the perpetrator by the time of the killings? Y__ N__ NA__ Missing__

58. a. Had the parties physically separated? Y__ N__ NA__ Missing__
    b. Were the parties already divorced? Up to 1 mo. __ Up to 1 yr. __ Up to 5 yrs. __ Over 5 yrs. __ N__ NA__ Missing__ Y (unknown amount of time) __
    c. Had the parties been married at least twice to the same person? Y__ N__ NA__ Missing__
    d. Had the parties already divorced, but reconciled? Y__ N__ NA__ Missing__

59. Was there a separation about to occur? Y__ N__ NA__ Missing__

60. Had the separation been communicated to the perpetrator? Y__ N__ NA__ Missing__

61. Had the separation been communicated to family and friends? Y__ N__ NA__ Missing__

62. Was a divorce pending? Y__ N__ NA__ Missing__

63. Had the impending divorce been communicated to the perpetrator? Y__ N__ NA__ Missing__

64. Had the impending divorce been communicated to family and friends? Y__ N__ NA__ Missing__

65. Was there a child-custody battle occurring? Y__ N__ NA__ Missing__

SHAME, ALTRUISM, AND ECONOMICS

66. Was there evidence of shame in the perpetrator's life? Y__ N__ NA__ Missing__

67. Was there evidence of a threat of failure? Y__ N__ NA__ Missing__

68. a. Was there evidence of a threat of poverty? Y__ N__ NA__ Missing__
    b. What was the perpetrator's economic status? White-collar/ technical worker__ Manual/service worker__ Professional (doctors, etc.) __ Wealthy (major employers, etc.) __ Homemaker/unpaid labor__ Other__ Missing__ Independent__ Farmer__ Public__ Servant__ Military__
    c. Was he unemployed? Long-term__ Recently__ Pending__ Y (don't know how long) __ N__ NA__ Missing__ Sporadically employed__
    d. Was he retired? Y__ N__ NA__ Missing__
    e. Second occupation? White-collar/technical worker__ Manual/service worker__ Professional (doctors, etc.) __ Wealthy (major employers, etc.) __ Homemaker/unpaid labor__ Other__ Missing__ Independent__ Farmer__ Public Servant__ Military__ N__
    f. Did he serve in the military? In the past 5 yrs__ 5–10 yrs__ 10+ years ago__ Yes, but unknown when__ Never__ Missing__

69. a. Was the family facing financial ruin, foreclosure, or bankruptcy? Y__ N__ NA__ Missing__
    b. Did the family have an acute amount of debt causing stress? Y__ N__ NA__ Missing__

c. Was the family having serious financial difficulties? Y__ N__ NA__ Missing__

70. Was the killer attempting to protect his family by killing them? Y__ N__ NA__ Missing__

PHYSICAL PROBLEMS

71. Did the perpetrator suffer from any physical illness? Y__ N__ NA__ Missing__

72. Did the perpetrator suffer from any terminal illness? Y__ N__ NA__ Missing__

73. Did the perpetrator's partner suffer from any physical illness? Y__ N__ NA__ Missing__

74. Did the perpetrator's partner suffer from any terminal illness? Y__ N__ NA__ Missing__

75. Did the children suffer from any physical illness? Y__ N__ NA__ Missing__

76. Did the children suffer from any terminal illness? Y__ N__ NA__ Missing__

77. Did the children have any special needs that caused great distress? Y__ N__ NA__ Missing__

RELIGION

78. Was the family actively religious? Y__ N__ NA__ Missing__

79. a. Did the family attend church at the time of the killing? Y__ N__ NA__ Missing__
    b. Did the family attend church for a significant portion of their lives? Y__ N__ NA__ Missing__

80. Did the family experience a shift in their religious beliefs in the weeks and months before the killings? Y__ N__ NA__ Missing__

81. a. Was the family a member of a religious institution (church, synagogue, other) at the time of the killings? Y__ N__ NA__ Missing__
    b. Was the family a member of a religious institution (church, synagogue, other) for a significant portion of their lives? Y__ N__ NA__ Missing__

82. Was the adult victim actively religious? Y__ N__ NA__ Missing__

83. a. Did the adult victim attend church at the time of the killings? Y__ N__ NA__ Missing__
    b. Did the adult victim attend church for a significant portion of their life? Y__ N__ NA__ Missing__

84. Did the adult victim experience a shift in religious beliefs in the weeks and months before the killings? Y__ N__ NA__ Missing__

85. a. Was the adult victim a member of a religious institution (church, synagogue, other) at the time of the killings? Y__ N__ NA__ Missing__
    b. Was the adult victim a member of a religious institution (church, synagogue, other) for a significant portion of their life? Y__ N__ NA__ Missing__

86. Was the perpetrator actively religious? Y__ N__ NA__ Missing__

87. a. Did the perpetrator attend church at the time of the killings? Y__ N__ NA__ Missing__
    b. Did the perpetrator attend church for a significant portion of their life? Y__ N__ NA__ Missing__

88. Did the perpetrator experience a shift in religious beliefs in the weeks and months before the killings? Y__ N__ NA__ Missing__

89. a. Was the perpetrator a member of a religious institution (church, synagogue, other) at the time of the killings? Y__ N__ NA__ Missing__
    b. Was the perpetrator a member of a religious institution (church, synagogue, other) for a significant portion of their life? Y__ N__ NA__ Missing__

90. a. Did religious beliefs play some role in the killings? Y__ N__ NA__ Missing__
    b. Was there a sense of transcendence ("going to a better place")? Y__ N__ NA__ Missing__

91. Did God or some other deity "compel" the killings? Y__ N__ NA__ Missing__

92. Did other spirits or beings "compel" the killings? Y__ N__ NA__ Missing__

OTHER AGENCY INVOLVEMENT

93. Had law enforcement been called to the case before? Y__ N__ NA__ Missing__

94. Did Child Protective Services (CPS) or a similar agency have contact with the family prior to the killings? Y__ N__ NA__ Missing__

95. Did a social worker have contact with the family prior to the killings? Y__ N__ NA__ Missing__

96. Did public health officials have contact with the family prior to the killings? Y__ N__ NA__ Missing__

97. Did a mental health worker have contact with the family prior to the killings? Y__ N__ NA__ Missing__

98. Did a domestic violence service provider/advocate have contact with the family prior to the killings? Y__ N__ NA__ Missing__

99. Had the district attorney or other prosecuting agency have contact with the family prior to the killings? Y__ N__ NA__ Missing__

100. Did someone from probation/parole have contact with the family prior to the killings? Y__ N__ NA__ Missing__

101. Had any other agency come into contact with the family prior to the killings? Y__ N__ NA__ Missing__. If so, please list:

_____

RACE

102. Perpetrator's race: C = Caucasian__ AFR = African American__ ASI = Southeast Asian American__ L = Latino__ O = Other__ (please specify) __ Missing__

103. Adult victim's race: C = Caucasian__ AFR = African American__ ASI = Southeast Asian American__ L = Latino__ O = Other (please specify)__ Missing__

METHOD

104. Primary method for the killing: F = Firearm__ K = Knife/sharp instrument__ S = Strangulation__ P = Poison__ B = Blunt instrument__ A = Arson__ M = Motor vehicle__ O = Other (please specify) __ Missing__

105. Secondary method of killing: F = Firearm__ K = Knife/sharp instrument__ S = Strangulation__ P = Poison__ B = Blunt instrument__ A = Arson__ M = Motor vehicle__ O = Other (please specify) __ NA__ Missing__

106. More than two methods (If yes, please explain)? Y__ N__ N__ A__

RELATIONSHIP LENGTH (IN YEARS: 1, 4.5, 3.25, E.G.)

107. a. Length of time in relationship continuously: __
     b. Length of time married: __

108. Length of time in relationship intermittently: __

109. Age difference between the perpetrator and adult victim: __

110. Age of the youngest child: __

111. Number of children in the household: __

112. Did the perpetrator start a fire? Y__ N__ NA__ Missing__

REFERENCES

Adams, D., 1990. Treatment models of men who batter: A profeminist analysis. In Yllo, K., and Bograd, M. (Eds.), *Feminist perspectives on wife abuse* (pp. 176–199). Newbury Park, CA: Sage.

Adams, D., 2007. *Why do they kill? Men who murder their intimate partners.* Nashville, TN: Vanderbilt University Press.

Alder, C., 1991. Socioeconomic determinants and masculinity. In Chappell, D., Grabosky, P., and Strang, H. (Eds.), *Australian violence: Contemporary perspectives* (pp. 161–176). Canberra: Australian Institute of Criminology.

Alder, C., and Polk, K., 2001. *Child victims of homicide.* Cambridge, U.K.: Cambridge University Press.

Adler, J., 1997. My mother-in-law is to blame, but I'll walk on her neck yet. *Journal of Social History, 31,* 253–276.

Allatt. P., 1993. Becoming privileged: The role of family processes. In Bates, I., and Riseborough, G. (Eds.), *Youth and inequality.* Buckingham, UK: Open University Press.

Alvarez, A., and Bachman, R., 2008. *Violence: The enduring problem.* Thousand Oaks, CA: Sage.

American Psychological Association., 2007. *APA Dictionary of Psychology.* Washington, D.C.

Anderson, E., 1999. *Code of the street: Decency, violence, and the moral life of the inner city.* New York: W. W. Norton.

Archer, J. E., 2003. Researching violence in the past: Quantifiable and qualitative evidence. In Lee, R. M., and Stanko, E. A. (Eds.), *Researching violence: Essays on methodology and measurement* (pp. 15–29). London: Routledge.

Arendt, H., 1970. *On violence.* London: Allen Lane.

Armstrong, T. (Ed)., 1996. The Gray family murders. In *The history of Oakdale Township, vol. 2* (pp. 83–115). Oakdale, Minnesota: Oakdale Lake Elmo Historical Society.

Baker, N. W., Gregware, P., and Cassidy, M. A., 1999. Family killing fields: Honor rationales in the murder of women. *Violence against women, 5*(2), 164–184.

Barnes, E., 2002. Loving with a vengeance. In Shamir, M., and Travis, J. (Eds.), *Boys don't cry: Rethinking narratives of masculinity and emotion in the U.S.* (pp. 44–63). New York: Columbia University Press.

Barrett, M., and McIntosh, M., 1982. *The anti-social family.* London: Verso.

Bauman, Z., 1990. *Thinking sociologically.* Oxford, U.K.: Basil Blackwell.

Bean, C., 1992. *Women murdered by the men they loved.* Binghamton, New York: Haworth Press.

Beck, E. M., and Tolnay, S. E., 1990. The killing fields of the Deep South: The market for cotton and the lynching of blacks, 1882–1930. *American Sociological Review, 55*, 526–539.

Becker, M. B. Changing patterns of violence and justice in fourteenth- and fifteenth-century Florence. *Comparative Studies in Society and History*, xviii: 281–296.

Beck-Gernsheim, E., and Beck, U., 1995. *The normal chaos of love*. Cambridge, U.K.: Polity Press.

Bellah, R., 1996. *Habits of the heart: Individualism and commitment in American Life*. Berkeley, CA: University of California Press.

Benford, T. B., and Johnson, J. P., 2000. *Righteous carnage: The List murders*. New York: toExcel.

Benjamin, J., 1988. *The bonds of love: Psychoanalysis, feminism, and the problem of domination*. New York: Pantheon.

Bloch, M., 1961. *Feudal society. Vol. 2: Social classes and political organizations*. Chicago: University of Chicago Press.

Bourdieu, P., 2001. *Masculine domination*. Stanford, CA: Stanford University Press.

Bourdieu, P., 2005. Habitus. In Hillier, J., and Rooksby, E. (Eds.), *Habitus: A sense of place, 2nd ed.* (pp. 43–49). Aldershot, U.K.: Ashgate.

Bradley, H., 1999. The seductions of the archive: Voices lost and found. *History of the human sciences, 12*(2), 107–122.

Braithwaite, J. *Crime, shame and reintegration*. Cambridge, U.K.: Cambridge University Press.

Brody, L., 1999. *Gender, emotion, and the family*. Cambridge, MA: Harvard University Press.

Brookman, F., 2005. *Understanding homicide*. Thousand Oaks, CA: Sage.

Bruch, H. 1967. Mass murder: The Wagner case. *American Journal of Psychiatry, 124*(5), 693–698.

Campbell, A., 1993. *Men, women and aggression*. New York: Basic Books.

Campbell, J., et al., 2007. Intimate partner homicide: Review and implications of research and policy. *Trauma, violence and abuse, 8*, 246–269.

Centerwall, B. S., 1984. Race, socioeconomic status and domestic homicide: Atlanta, 1971–1972. *American Journal of Public Health, 74*, 813–815.

Centerwall, B. S., 1995. Race, socioeconomic status, and domestic homicide. *Journal of the American Medical Association, 273*(22), 1755–1758.

Chodorow, N., 1978. *The reproduction of mothering*. Berkeley, CA: University of California Press.

Chodorow, N., 1998. The enemy outside. *Journal for the Psychoanalysis of Culture and Society, 3*(1), 25–38.

Chodorow, N., 1999. *The power of feelings*. New Haven, CT: Yale University Press.

Chused, R., 1984. The Oregon donation land act of 1850 and 19th-century federal married women's property law. *Law and History Review, 2*(1), 44–78.

Cleary, M., 2005. Mothering under the microscope: Gender bias in law and medicine and the problem of Munchausen syndrome by proxy. *Thomas M. Cooley Journal of Practical and Clinical Law, 7*(3), 183–250.

Cohen, D. A., 1995. Homicidal compulsion and the conditions of freedom: The social and psychological origins of familicide. *Journal of Social History, 28*(4), 725–764.

Collins, R., 2008. *Violence: A micro-sociological theory.* Princeton, NJ: Princeton University Press.

Colman, A. M., 2006. *Oxford dictionary of psychology.* New York: Oxford University Press.

Connell, R. W., 1987. *Gender and power.* Sydney, Australia: Allen and Unwin.

Connell, R. W., 1995. *Masculinities.* Berkeley, CA: University of California Press.

Connell, R. W., and Messerschmidt, J., 2005. Hegemonic masculinity: Rethinking the concept. *Gender and Society, 19,* 829–859.

Cooley, C. H., 2006. *Human nature and the social order.* London: Transaction Publishers.

Coontz, S., 2005. *Marriage, a history: How love conquered marriage.* New York: Penguin.

Cott, N., 1976. Eighteenth-century family and social life revealed in Massachusetts divorce records. *Journal of Social History, 10,* 20–43.

Cowan, J. 1835. *The life and confession of John W. Cowan.* Cincinnati, OH: Kendall and Henry.

Damasio, A., 1994. *Descartes' error: Emotion, reason, and the human brain.* New York: Penguin.

Davis, K., 1936. Jealousy and sexual property. *Social Forces, 14,* 395–405.

DeMause, L. (Ed.), 1974. *The history of childhood.* New York: The Psychohistory Press.

D'Emilio, J., and Freeman, E. B., 1997. *Intimate matters: A history of sexuality in America.* Chicago: University of Chicago Press.

De Becker, G., 1997. *The gift of fear.* New York: Random House.

Degler, C., 1981. *At odds: Women and the family in America from the Revolution to the present.* New York: Oxford University Press.

Demos, J., 1970. *A little commonwealth: Family life in Plymouth Colony.* New York: Oxford University Press.

Denzin, N., 1984. Toward a phenomenology of domestic, family violence. *American Journal of Sociology, 90*(3), 483–513.

Dill, B., 1988. Our mothers' grief: Racial ethnic women and the maintenance of families. *Journal of Family History, 13*(4), 415–431.

Dobash, R. E., et al., 2007. Lethal and nonlethal violence against an intimate partner. *Violence Against Women, 13*(4), 329–353.

Dobash, R. E., and Dobash, R., 1979. *Violence against wives.* New York: Free Press.

Dobash, R. E., and Dobash, R., 1998. Violent men and violent contexts. In Dobash, R. E., and Dobash, R. P. (Eds.), *Rethinking violence against women* (pp. 141–168). Thousand Oaks, CA: Sage.

Durkheim, E., 1952. *Suicide.* London: Routledge and Kegan Paul.

Durkheim, E., 1993. The normal and the pathological. In Kelly, D. H. (Ed.), *Deviant behavior: A text reader in the sociology of deviance,* 4ᵗʰ ed. (pp. 61–65). Los Angeles: California State University.

Dutton, D., 1995. *The batterer.* New York: Basic Books.

Dutton, D., 2006. *Rethinking domestic violence.* Vancouver, BC: UBC Press.

Dutton, M. A., 1997. Critique of the "battered woman syndrome" model. VAWNET Applied Research Forum. National Resource Center on Domestic Violence.

Dutton, M. A., and Goodman, L., 2005. Coercion in intimate partner violence: Toward a new conceptualization. *Sex Roles: A Journal of Research, 52,* 11–12, 743–756.

Duwe, G., 2000. Body count journalism: The presentation of mass murder in the news media. *Homicide Studies*, *4*, 364–399.

Duwe, G., 2004. The patterns and prevalence of mass murder in twentieth-century America. *Justice Quarterly*, *21*, 729–762.

Duwe, G., 2005. A circle of distortion: The social construction of mass murder in the United States. *Western Criminology Review*, *6*(1), available at http://wer.sonoma.edu/v6n/duwe.htm.

Eagleton, T., 2000. *The idea of culture*. Oxford. Blackwell.

Edes, P. 1818. *Horrid murder: Sketches of the life of Captain James Purrinton*. Boston: Printed for Nathaniel Coverly.

Ehrenreich, B., 1983. *The hearts of men*. New York: Anchor.

Eisner, M., 2001. Modernization, self-control and lethal violence. *British Journal of Criminology*, *41*, 618–638.

Elias, N., 1994. *The civilizing process*. Oxford, U.K.: Blackwell.

Epstein, F. C., 2007. Great divides: The cultural, cognitive and social bases of the global subordination of women. *American Sociological Review*, *72*, 1–22.

Evans, D., 2001. *Emotion: A very short introduction*. Oxford, U.K.: Oxford University Press.

Ewing, C., 1997. *Fatal families: The dynamics of intrafamilial homicide*. Thousand Oaks, CA: Sage.

Faludi, S., 1999. *Stiffed: The betrayal of the American man*. New York: Harper Collins.

Farrell. W., 1993. *The myth of male power*. New York: Simon and Schuster.

Farrell, W., 2005. *Why men earn more*. New York: American Management Association.

Ferraro, K., 2006. *Neither angels nor demons: Women, crime and victimization*. Boston: Northeastern University Press.

Fitzgerald, N. K., 1971. Towards an American Abraham: Multiple parricide and the rejection of revelation in the early national period. Master's thesis, Brown University, Providence, RI.

Fletcher, J., 1997. *Violence and civilization: An introduction to the work of Norbert Elias*. Cambridge, U.K.: Polity.

Fliegelman, J., 1982. *Prodigals and pilgrims: The American revolution against patriarchal authority, 1750–1800*. Cambridge, MA: Harvard University Press.

Fontaine, S., 1978. The civilizing process revisited: An interview with Norbert Elias. *Theory and Society*, *5*(2), 243–253.

Ford, D., 1991. Prosecution as a victim power resource: A note on empowering women in violent conjugal relationships. *Law and Society Review*, *25*(2), 313–334.

Foucault, M. (Ed.), 1975. *I, Pierre Riviere, having slaughtered my mother, my sister, and my brother: A case of parricide in the 19th century*. Lincoln, NE: University of Nebraska Press.

Fox, J. A., and Levin, J., 2005. *Extreme killing: Understanding serial and mass murder*. Thousand Oaks, CA: Sage.

Freud, S., 1923. *The ego and the id*. New York: Hogarth Press.

Freud, S., 2005. *Civilization and its discontents*. New York: Norton.

Fromm, E., 1973. *The anatomy of human destructiveness*. New York: Henry Holt and Company.

Gap Min, P. (Ed.), 2006. *Asian Americans: Contemporary trends and issues, 2nd ed.* Thousand Oaks, CA: Pine Forge Press.

Garland, D., 1990. *Punishment and modern society*. Chicago: University of Chicago Press.

Garland, D., 2001. *The culture of control: Crime and social order in contemporary society*. Chicago: University of Chicago Press.

Gaylin, W., 1989. *The rage within: Anger in modern life*. New York: Penguin.

Geertz, C., 1973. *The interpretation of cultures: Selected essays*. New York: Basic Books.

Giddens, A., 1979. *Central problems in social theory*. London: MacMillan.

Giddens, A., 1990. *The consequences of modernity*. Stanford, CA: Stanford University Press.

Giddens, A., 1991. *Modernity and self-identity: Self and society in the late modern age*. Stanford, CA: Stanford University Press.

Giddens, A., 1992. *The transformation of intimacy: Sexuality, love and eroticism in modern societies*. Stanford, CA: Stanford University Press.

Gill, A., 2009. Honor killings and the quest for justice in black and minority ethnic communities in the United Kingdom. *Criminal Justice Policy Review*, Jan. 2009, 1–20.

Gilligan, J., 1997. *Violence: Reflections on a national epidemic*. New York: Vintage Books.

Gilligan, J., 2003. Shame, guilt, and violence. *Social Research*, 70(44), 1149–1180.

Ginat, J., 1981. Comment. *Current Anthropology*, 22(2), 153.

Given, J. B., 1977. *Society and homicide in thirteenth-century England*. Stanford, CA: Stanford University Press.

Goetting, A., 1999. *Getting out: Life stories of women who left abusive men*. New York: Columbia University Press.

Goffman, E., 1959. *The presentation of self in everyday life*. New York: Doubleday.

Goffman, E., 1963. *Behavior in public places*. New York: Free Press.

Goldberg, H., 1976. *The hazards of being male*. New York: Signet.

Goleman, D., 1995. *Emotional intelligence*. New York: Bantam.

Goodman, L. A., Dutton, M. A., Weinfurt, K., and Cook, S., 2003. The intimate partner violence strategies index: Development and application. *Violence and Victims*, 9(2), 163–186.

Gordon, A., 1997. *Ghostly matters: Haunting and the sociological imagination*. Minneapolis, MN: University of Minnesota Press.

Goudsblom, J., and Mennell, S. (Eds.), 1998. *The Norbert Elias reader*. Oxford, U.K.: Blackwell.

Gould, S. J., 1997. Evolution: The pleasures of pluralism. *New York Review of Books*, xliv (11 June 1997), 47–52.

Gresswell, D. M., and Hollin, C. R., 1992. Towards a new methodology for making sense of case material: An illustrative case involving attempted multiple murder. *Criminal Behavior and Mental Health*, 2, 329–341.

Greven, P. J., 1978. *Family structure in seventeenth-century Andover, Massachusetts*. New York: St. Martin's Press.

Gross, B., 2008. Caretaker cruelty: Munchausen's and beyond. *The Forensic Examiner*, 17(2), P54-57.

Gurr, T. R., 1981. Historical trends in violent crime: A critical review of the evidence. *Crime and Justice: An Annual Review of Research*, 3, 295–353.

Gutman, H., 1976. *The black family in slavery and freedom, 1750–1925*. New York: Pantheon.

Guttmacher, M., 1960. *The mind of the murderer.* New York: Farrar, Straus and Cudahy.

Hair, P. E. H., 1971. Deaths from violence in Britain: A tentative secular survey. *Population Studies, xxv,* 5–24.

Halttunen, K., 1998. *Murder most foul: The killer and the American gothic imagination.* Cambridge, MA: Harvard University Press.

Hammer, C. I., 1978. Patterns of homicide in a medieval university town: Fourteenth-century Oxford. *Past and Present, 78,* 3–23.

Hanawalt, B. A., 1979. *Crime and conflict in English communities 1300–1348.* Cambridge, MA: Harvard University Press.

Hart, B., 1988. Beyond the duty to warn: A therapist's duty to protect battered women and children. In Yllo, K., and Bograd, M. (Eds.), *Feminist perspectives on wife abuse* (pp. 234–247). Newbury Park, CA: Sage.

Haskell, T. J., 1985. *Capitalism and the origins of humanitarian sensibility.* i, *90,* 339–361, 547–566.

Hemphill, C. D., 1998. "Class, gender, and the regulation of emotional expression." In Stearns, P. N., and Lewis, J. (Eds.), *An emotional history of the United States.* New York: New York University Press.

Hirose, S., 1979. Depression and homicide: A psychiatric and forensic study of four cases. *Acta Psychiatrica Scandinavia, 59,* 211–217.

Hochschild, A. R., 1983. *The managed heart: Commercialization of human feeling.* Berkeley, CA: University of California Press.

Hoyle, C., 2008. Will she be safe? A critical analysis of risk assessment in domestic violence cases. *Children and Youth Services Review, 30,* 323–337.

Huizinga, J., 1999. *The waning of the Middle Ages.* New York: Dover.

Hunnisett, R. F., 1961. *The medieval coroner.* Cambridge: Cambridge University Press.

Illouz, Eva., 2007. *Cold intimacies: The making of emotional capitalism. Cambridge. Polity.*

Johnson, C. H., 2005. *Come with Daddy: Child murder-suicide after family breakdown.* Crawley, Western Australia: University of Western Australia Press.

Johnson, M. M., 1988. *Strong mothers, weak wives.* Berkeley, CA: University of California Press.

Johnson, M. P., 1995. Patriarchal terrorism and common couple violence: Two forms of violence against women. *Journal of Marriage and the Family, 57,* 283–294.

Johnson, M. P., 2006. Conflict and control: Gender symmetry and asymmetry in domestic violence. *Violence Against Women, 12*(11), 1003–1018.

Johnson, M. P., 2008. *A typology of domestic violence.* Boston: Northeastern University Press.

Jones, A., 1980. *Women who kill.* New York: Holt, Rinehart and Winston.

Jones, J., 1985. *Labor of love, labor of sorrow.* New York: Basic Books.

Kagan, J., 2007. *What is emotion?.* New Haven: Yale University Press.

Kane, A., 2001. Finding emotion in social movement practices. In Goodwin, J., Jasper, J. M., and Polletta, F., *Passionate politics: Emotions and social movements* (pp. 251–266). Chicago. University of Chicago Press.

Katz, J., 1988. *Seductions of crime: Moral and sensual attractions in doing evil.* New York: Basic Books.

Kaufman, G., 1996. *The psychology of shame.* New York: Springer.

Keetley, D., 2006. Homicidal envy. *Early American Literature, 41*(2), 273–304.

Kelly, L., 1988. *Surviving sexual violence*. Cambridge, U.K.: Polity Press.

Kierkegaard, S., 1957. *The concept of dread*. Princeton, NJ: Princeton University Press.

Kimmel, M., 2006. *Manhood in America: A cultural history*. New York: Oxford University Press.

Kressel, G., 1981. Sororicide/filiacide: Homicide for family honour. *Current Anthropology*, 22(2), 141–158.

Kumar, K., 1978. *Prophecy and progress: The sociology of industrial and post-industrial life*. Harmondsworth, U.K.: Penguin.

Laroche, D., 2005. *Aspects of the context and consequences of domestic violence— Situational couple violence and intimate terrorism in Canada in 1999*. Government of Quebec, Canada.

Lasch, C., 1979. *Haven in a heartless world*. New York: Basic Books.

Lasch, C., 1985. Review: Historical sociology and the myth of maturity: Norbert Elias's "very simple formula". *Theory and Society*, 14(5), 705–720.

Lee, R. M., and Stanko, E. A., 2003. *Researching violence: Essays on methodology and measurement*. London: Routledge.

Leonard, I. M., and Leonard, C. C., 2003. The historiography of American violence. *Homicide Studies*, 7(2), 99–153.

Levin, J., and Fox, J. A., 1985. *Mass murder: America's growing menace*. New York: Plenum.

Lewis, H. B., 1971. *Shame and guilt in neurosis*. New York: International Universities Press.

Leyton, E., 2005. *Hunting humans: The rise of the modern multiple murderer*. Toronto, Ontario, Canada: McClelland and Stewart.

Lindsay, P., 1958. *The mainspring of murder*. London: John Long.

List, J. (with Austin Goodrich), 2006. *Collateral damage: The John List story*. New York: iUniverse Incorporated.

Lombard, A. S., 2003. *Making manhood: Growing up male in colonial New England*. Cambridge, MA: Harvard University Press.

Luckenbill, D., 1977. Criminal homicide as a situated transaction. *Social Problems*, 25, 2: 176-186.

Lukes, S., 2005. *Power: A radical view, 2nd ed.* New York: Palgrave.

Lynd, H., 1958. *On shame and the search for identity*. New York: Harcourt, Brace and World.

Lystra, K. *Searching the heart: Women, men and romantic love in nineteenth-century America*. New York: Oxford University Press.

MacDonald, J., 1961. *The murderer and his victim*. Springfield, IL: Charles Thomas Publishers.

MacDonald, M., and Murphy, T., 1993. *Sleepless souls: Suicide in early modern England*. Oxford, U.K.: Clarendon Press.

MacFarlane, A., 1978. *The origins of English individualism*. Oxford, U.K.: Basil Blackwell.

MacFarlane, A., 1979. Review of Lawrence Stone, 1977. Family, sex and marriage in England, 1500–1800. *History and Theory*, 18, 103–126.

McManners, J., 1981. *Death and the Enlightenment*. New York: Oxford University Press.

Malmquist, C. P., 1980. Psychiatric aspects of familicide. *Bulletin of the American Academy of Psychiatry and Law*, 13, 221–231.

Marietta, J. D., and Rowe, G. S., 1999. Violent crime, victims, and society in Pennsylvania, 1682–1800. *Pennsylvania History*, 66, 24–54.

Marx, K., and Engels, F., 1970. *Selected works.* New York: International Publishers.

Masaki, B., and Wong, L., 1997. Domestic violence in the Asian community. In Lee, E. (Ed.), *Working with Asian Americans: A guide for clinicians* (pp. 439–451). New York: Guilford Press.

McLellan, F., 2006. Mental health and justice: The case of Andrea Yates. *The Lancet*, 122/2006, *368*(9551), 1951–1954.

McDade, T., 1961. *The annals of murder.* Norman, OK: University of Oklahoma Press.

McDonald, B. D., 1986. Domestic violence in colonial Massachusetts. *Historical Journal of Massachusetts, 14*(1), 53–64.

Mead, G. H., 1967. *Mind, self, and society.* Chicago: University of Chicago Press.

Mead, M., 1998. Jealousy: Primitive and civilized. In Clanton, G., and Smith, L. G. (Eds.), *Jealousy, 3rd ed.* (pp. 115–126). New York: University Press of America.

Meloy, J. R., 1997. *Violent attachments.* Northvale, NJ: Jason Aronson.

Meyer, C., and Oberman, M., 2001. *Mothers who kill their children.* New York: New York University Press.

Mills, C. W., 1959. *The sociological imagination.* New York: Oxford University Press.

Mills, L. G., 2008. Shame and intimate abuse: The critical missing link between cause and cure. *Children and Youth Services Review, 30*, 631–638.

Mintz, S., and Kellogg, S., 1988. *Domestic revolutions: A social history of American family life.* New York: Free Press.

Mitchell, S. M., 1805. *A narrative of the life of William Beadle, 4th ed.* Greenfield, CT:

Monkkonen, E., 2000. *Murder in New York City.* Berkeley, CA: University of California Press.

Morrison, A. P., 1989. *Shame: The underside of narcissism.* Hillsdale, NJ: The Analytic Press.

Motz, A., 2001. *The psychology of female violence: Crimes against the body.* Hove, UK: Brunner-Routledge.

Mowat, R. R., 1966. *Morbid jealousy and murder.* London: Tavistock.

Namnyak, N., et al., 2008. "Stockholm syndrome": Psychiatric diagnosis or urban myth?. *Acta Psychiatrica Scandinavia, 117*, 4–11.

Nesca, M., and Kincel, R., 2000. Catathymic violence in a case of triple homicide. *American Journal of Forensic Psychiatry, 21*(2), 43–55.

Norton, M. B., 1980. *Liberty's daughters: The Revolutionary experience of American women, 1750–1800.* Boston: Little, Brown.

Nowotny, H., 1981. Women in public life in Austria. In Fuchs-Epstein, C., and Coser, R. L. (Eds.), *Access to power: Cross-national studies of women and elites.* London: George Allen and Unwin.

Pascal, B., 1995. *Pensées and other writings.* Oxford. Oxford University Press.

Patel, S., and Gadit, A. M., 2008. Karo-Kari: A form of honour killing in Pakistan. *Transcultural Psychiatry, 45*, 683–694.

Paulozzi, L., Saltzman, L., Thompson, M., and Holmgreen, P., 2001. Surveillance for homicide among intimate partners—United States, 1981–1998. *Mortality and Morbidity Weekly Reports*, Oct. 12, 1–16.

Pence, E., 1985. *Criminal justice response to domestic assault cases: A guide for policy development.* Duluth, MN: Domestic Abuse Intervention Project.

Pence, E., 1999. Some thoughts on philosophy. In Shepard, M., and Pence, E. (Eds.). *Coordinating community responses to domestic violence: Lessons from Duluth and beyond* (pp. 25–40). Thousand Oaks, CA: Sage.

Pence, E., and Shepard, M., 1990. Integrating feminist theory and practice: The challenge of the battered women's movement. In Yllo, K., and Bograd, M. (Eds.), *Feminist perspectives on wife abuse* (pp. 282–298). Newbury Park, CA: Sage.

Pinker, S., 2007. A history of violence: We are getting nicer every day. *The New Republic*, Mar. 19, 18–21.

Pleck, E., 1987. *Domestic tyranny*. New York and London: Oxford University Press.

Polanyi, K., 2001. *The great transformation: The political and economic origins of our time*. Boston: Beacon Press.

Polk, K., 1994. *When men kill*. Cambridge, U.K.: Cambridge University Press.

Polk, K., 1998. Violence, masculinity and evolution: A comment on Wilson and Daly. *Theoretical Criminology*, *2*(4), 461–469.

Raitt, F. E., and Zeedyk, S., 2004. Mothers on trial: Discourses of cot death and Munchausen's syndrome by proxy. *Feminist Legal Studies*, *12*(3), 257–278.

Raven, B. H., 1992. A power/interaction model of interpersonal influence: French and Raven thirty years later. *Journal of Social Behavior and Personality*, *7*(2), 217–244.

Raven, B. H., 1993. The bases of power: Origins and recent developments. *Journal of Social Psychology*, *49*(4), 227–251.

Reichard, S., and Tillman, C., 1950. Murder and suicide as defenses against schizophrenic psychosis. *Clinical Psychopathology*, *11*(4), 149–163.

Roth, R., 1999. Spousal murder in northern New England, 1776–1865. In Daniels, C., and Kennedy, M. V. (Eds.), *Over the threshold: Intimate violence in early America* (pp. 65–93). New York: Oxford University Press.

Rothman, E. K., 1987. *Hands and hearts: A history of courtship in America*. Cambridge, MA: Harvard University Press.

Rotundo, E. A., 1987. Patriarchs and participants: A historical perspective on fatherhood. In Kaufman, M. (Ed.), *Beyond patriarchy: Essays by men on pleasure, power, and change* (pp. 64–70). New York: Oxford University Press.

Rotundo, E. A., 1993. *American manhood: Transformations in masculinity from the Revolution to the modern era*. New York: Basic Books.

Sartre, J. P., 1939. *The emotions: Outline of a theory*. New York: Philosophical Library.

Scheff, T., 2004. Elias, Freud and Goffman: Shame as the master emotion. In Loyal, S., and Quilley, S. (Eds.), *The sociology of Norbert Elias* (pp. 229–242). Cambridge, U.K.: Cambridge University Press.

Scheff, T., and S. Retzinger., 2001. *Emotions and violence: Shame and rage in destructive conflicts*. Lincoln, NE: iUniverse, Inc.

Schlesinger, L. B., 2000. Familicide, depression and catathymic process. *Journal of Forensic Science*, *45*(1), 200–203.

Scott, J. C., 1985. *Weapons of the weak*. New Haven, CT: Yale University Press.

Scott, J. C., 1990. *Domination and the arts of resistance*. New Haven, CT: Yale University Press.

Shamir, M., and Travis, J., 2002. *Boys don't cry: Rethinking narratives of masculinity and emotion in the U. S.* New York: Columbia University Press.

Sharkey, J., 1990. *Death sentence: The inside story of the John List murders*. New York: Signet.

Sharpe, J. A., 1981. Domestic homicide in early modern England. *The Historical Journal*, 24(1), 29–48.

Sharpe, J. A., 1999. *Crime in early modern England*. London: Longman.

Sharratt, B., 1989. In whose voice? The drama of Raymond Williams. In Eagleton, T. (Ed.), *Raymond Williams: Critical perspectives* (pp. 130–149). Boston: Northeastern University Press.

Shields, S. A., 2002. *Speaking from the heart: Gender and the social meaning of emotion*. Cambridge, U.K.: Cambridge University Press.

Smith, D. S., and Hindus, M. S., 1975. Premarital pregnancy in America 1640–1971, An overview and interpretation. *Journal of Interdisciplinary History*, 5(4), 537–570.

Smithey, M., 1997. Infant homicide. *Deviant Behavior*, 18, 255–272.

Spelman, E., 1988. *Inessential woman: Problems of exclusion in feminist thought*. Boston: Beacon Press.

Stanko, E., 1990. *Everyday violence*. London: Pandora.

Stark, Evan., 2007. *Coercive control: How men entrap women in personal life*. New York: Oxford University Press.

Stearns, C. Z., and Stearns, P. N., 1986. *Anger: The struggle for emotional control in America's history*. Chicago: Chicago University Press.

Stearns, P., 1989. *Jealousy: The evolution of an emotion in American history*. New York: New York University Press.

Stone, L., 1977. *The family, sex and marriage in England, 1500–1800*. New York: Penguin.

Stone, L., 1983. Interpersonal violence in English society, 1300–1980. *Past and Present*, 101, 22–33.

Sudarkasa, N., 1981. Interpreting the African heritage in Afro-American family organization. In McAdoo, P. H. (Ed.), *Black families* (pp. 37–53). Beverly Hills, CA: Sage.

Sullivan, J., 1990. Slaying suspect saw two choices, doctor testifies. *New York Times*, April 7, 1990.

Taylor, H., 1998. Rationing crime: The political economy of criminal statistics since the 1850s. *Economic History Review*, 51(3), 569–90.

Thistle, S., 2000. The trouble with modernity: Gender and the remaking of social theory. *Sociological Theory*, 18(2), 275–288.

Thomas, H. E., 1995. Experiencing a shame response as a precursor to violence. *Bulletin of the American Academy of Psychiatry and Law*, 23(4), 587–593.

Thompson, E. P., 1977. Review of *Family, sex and marriage in England, 1500–1800*, by Lawrence Stone (1977). *New Society*, 8 September, 1977.

Toolis, K., 2002. Family man. *The Guardian*, July 13, 2002.

Trumbach, R., 1978. The rise of the egalitarian family. Academic Press. New York.

Trumbach, R., 1979. Europe and its families. *Journal of Social History*, 13(1), 136–143.

Turner, J. H., and Stets, J. E., 2005. *The sociology of emotions*. Cambridge, U.K.: Cambridge University Press.

Ulrich, L. T., 1990. *A mid wife's tale: The life of Martha Ballard, based on her diary, 1785–1812*. New York: Vintage.

Van Krieken, R., 1989. Violence, self-discipline and modernity: Beyond the civilizing process. *Sociological Review*, 37, 193–218.

Walby, S., 1997. *Gender transformations*. New York: Routledge.

Wallace, A., 1986. *Homicide: The social reality*. Sydney, NSW: Bureau of Crime Statistics and Research.

Wang, K., 1996. Battered Asian American women: Community responses from the battered women's movement and the Asian American community. *Asian Law Journal, 3*, 151–185.

Weber, M., 1930. *The Protestant ethic and the spirit of capitalism*. London: Allen and Unwin.

Websdale, N., 1999. *Understanding domestic homicide*. Boston: Northeastern University Press.

Websdale, N., 2001. *Policing the poor: From slave plantation to public housing*. Boston: Northeastern University Press.

Websdale. N., and Alvarez, A., 1998. Forensic journalism as patriarchal ideology: The media construction of domestic homicide-suicide events. In Hale, D., and Bailey, F. (Eds.), *Popular culture, crime and justice* (pp. 123–141). Wadsworth.

Wertham, F., 1937. The catathymic crisis: A clinical entity. *Archives of Neurology and Psychiatry, 37*, 974–977.

West Berkshire Safer Communities Partnership, 2008. A domestic homicide review into the deaths of Julia and William Pemberton. November, 2008.

West, D. J., 1967. *Murder followed by suicide: An inquiry carried out for the Institute of Criminology, Cambridge*. Cambridge, MA: Harvard University Press.

Wilcox, B., 2004. *Soft patriarchs, new men: How Christianity shapes fathers and husbands*. Chicago, Illinois: University of Chicago Press.

Williams, D. E., 2003. Writing under the influence: An examination of Wieland's "well authenticated facts" and the depiction of murderous fathers in post-Revolutionary print culture. *Eighteenth-Century Fiction, 15*, 3–4, and 643–668.

Williams, R., 1961. *The long revolution*. London: Chatto and Windus.

Williams, R., 1977. *Marxism and literature*. Oxford, U.K.: Oxford University Press.

Williams, R., 1994. The analysis of culture. In Storey, J. (Ed.), *Cultural theory and popular culture* (pp. 56–64). New York: Harvester Wheatsheaf.

Wilson, M. I., and Daly, M., 1988. *Homicide*. New York: Aldine de Gruyter.

Wilson, M. I., and Daly, M., 1998. Lethal and nonlethal violence against wives and the evolutionary psychology of male sexual proprietariness. In Dobash, R. E., and Dobash, R. P. (Eds.), *Rethinking violence against women* (pp., 199–230). Thousand Oaks, California: Sage.

Wilson, M., Daly, M., and Daniele, A., 1995. Familicide: The killing of spouse and children. *Aggressive Behavior, 21*, 275–291.

Wolfgang, M. E., 1958. *Patterns of criminal homicide*. Philadelphia: University of Pennsylvania Press.

Woloch, N., 1994. *Women and the American experience, 2nd ed.* New York: Knopf.

Wrong, D., 1961. The oversocialized conception of man in modern sociology. *American Sociological Review*, 26, 2, 183–193.

Yin, S., 2006. Elderly white men afflicted by high suicide rates. August, 2006. Washington D.C.: Population Reference Bureau. Available at: http://www.prb.org/Article/2006/ElderlyWhiteMenAfflictedbyHighSuicideRates.aspx.

Zaretsky, E., 2004. *Secrets of the soul: A social and cultural history of psychoanalysis*. New York: Vintage.

Zinn, H., 2003. *A people's history of the United States*. New York: Harper Collins.

INDEX

Accusatory perpetrators, 19–20
Adams, David, 128, 273
Adultery. *See* Honor killings; Jealousy
Affective individualism, 14–17, 112–13
African Americans, 114, 115, 248, 258
    first recorded familicide among,
        114–15
    slavery and, 15–16
Alcohol abuse, 221. *See also* Drug abuse
Alder, Christine, 3, 24–25
Ali, Ibrahim (pseudonym), 178*t*, 187,
        202, 225
Alienation, 38–40, 220, 222, 224.
        See also Emotional isolation
Allatt, Patricia, 31
Allen, Benjamin (pseudonym), 181, 188,
        194, 195, 197, 225
Allen, Patricia (pseudonym), 178*t*, 181–82,
        185–86, 188, 193–97, 225–26
Altruism, sense of, 205–7, 212, 213,
        295–96
Altruistic familicide, 232
Alvarez, Alex, 184
Anderson, Elijah, 38
Anger. *See also* Rage, anger and
    centrality of, 271–73
    controlling, 237–39
    defined, 237
Angry perpetrators, 19–20
Anomie, 16, 220
Anxieties, 220–26. *See also* Emotional
        suffering
Arendt, Hannah, 33
Asian Americans, 16

Attachment problems, 31, 172. *See also*
        Pyrrhic victories

Baines, Priscilla (pseudonym), 178*t*,
        184–85
Ballard, Martha, 103–5
Barak, Danny, 184–85
Battered women. *See also* Intimate-partner
        violence; Victims
    "giving up," 29
    perceptiveness about their
        situations, 6
Batterers
    psychopathology, 31
Battering, 3. *See also specific topics*
    anger and, 271–73. *See also* Anger
    causes, 264–66
    control and, 267–70, 283n27. *See also*
        Control
    defined, 3–4
    power and, 263–67, 283n27. *See also*
        Power
Beadle, Lydia, 98–100
Beadle, William, 102, 127, 189
    act of familicide, 101
    emotional inflexibility, 223
    killing with care, 223
    overview, 88*t*, 98–101
    planning and preparation, 99–101
    religious beliefs, 97, 99–102
    shame and humiliation, 98
    Stephen Mitchell on, 98–101
    writings, 98–100, 102
Bean, Constance, 3

314 INDEX

Beckenbauer, Gerd (pseudonym), 129,
147–51, 153, 158, 160
Beckenbauer, Jenny (pseudonym), 149
Beckenbauer, Misook (pseudonym), 137,
158, 174n23
act of familicide, 147, 149
background, 147–50
as batterer, 148, 150, 152
compared with Mandy Miller
(pseudonym), 227, 228
impression management, 158
livid coercive heart, 129–30, 249
overview, 126t, 147
pride and shame, 150, 158
psychiatric problems, 160
depression, 148, 150
relationship with Gerd, 147–51, 153,
158
controlling and obsessive behavior,
147–51
self-blame, 148
self-destructive behavior, 148, 160
social attachments, 130
Benjamin, Jessica, 256n113
Biological factors, 27
Bloch, Marc, 117
Bluster, 125, 158, 159, 266–67
Body language, changes in, 165
Bostrum, Larry, 4–5
Bostrum, Shirley, 4–5
Bowlby, John, 31
Brandley, Lillian, 178t, 184
Brockden Brown, Charles, 102
Brody, Leslie, 263
Bronski, Kenny (pseudonym), 187, 200,
208
overview, 178t
as responsible and respectable citizen,
183–84
shame and humiliation, 204, 207, 208,
229
suicide note, 207
Bronski, Sara (pseudonym), 183
Brookman, Fiona, 24, 25, 27
Burland, William, 88t, 90

Camacho, Oscar (pseudonym), 156,
171–73
act of familicide, 131
anxiety, 225
as career criminal, 131
children, 131
employment, 173
overview, 126t, 130
powerlessness, 132

relationship with Carmella Sifuentes,
131, 139, 145
religion, spirituality, and, 132, 171
sexual abuse of Carmella's daughters,
146–47
Websdale's interview with, 130–32,
139, 145, 171
Campbell, Anne, 3
Campbell, Jacqueline, 4
Campbell, Mr., 76, 77, 79, 80
Capitalism, 223, 245. *See also* Modern era;
Social and historical contexts of
mass killings
Carbon, Susan, 2
Care, killing with, 212–13
Casual brutality, 115–16
Catathymic homicide, 172
Chesterfield, Lord, 218
Child abuse
fatal, 24–25
sexual abuse, 146–47
Children, obsessive attempts to control,
145–46
Chodorow, Nancy, 246–50, 256n112,
257n119, 257n123
Civilizing Process, The (Elias), 41.
See also Elias, Norbert
Civil reputability, basis of, 225
Civil reputable hearts, 21, 176, 177,
238–40, 245. *See also*
Emotional continuum
fitting into the social order, 177, 179
early socialization, 179–82
impression management, 186–89
responsible and respectable citizens,
103, 182–86
latent discontent, 189
acute emotional isolation, 189–95
anger and rage, 195–96, 238–40
emotional suffering, 196–201
vs. livid coercive hearts., 44, 58n201,
176–77, 186, 250, 278, 286
occupational backgrounds, 46, 285
pathways to familicide, 201
ignominy, 201–5
killing with care, 212–13
motives and beliefs, 205–8
planning and preparation,
208–12
racial/ethnic backgrounds, 286
Clanton, Marge (pseudonym),
138, 146, 158, 167, 168
Clanton, Peggy (pseudonym), 146,
167–68
Clark, Bob. *See* List, John Emil

Cobbe, Frances Power, 264
Coercive control, 27–28, 30, 56n106,
        129, 269, 281
    criminalizing, 281
    defined, 27, 267
    Evan Stark on, 27, 28, 55n106, 151,
        152, 175n39, 267–68, 281, 282n3
    resisting, 28–29
Cohen, Daniel, 94–95, 97
Cold intimacies, 223
Coleman, Mary, 145
Collins, Randall, 36, 38
Colonial America, 1st appearance of
        familicide in, 19
Communal manhood, 219
Complex personhood, 28
Confluent love, 279
Connecticut Fatality Review Team
        Initiative, 4
Connell, Robert W., 36, 250–51
Conspicuous consumption, 187, 202
Contradictory/intermediate hearts, 44–45.
        See also Emotional continuum
Control, 20, 25, 160, 244, 267–70. See
        also Intimate-partner violence;
        Power; Sexual proprietariness
    ability/potential to vs. attempts to, 28
    bidirectional, 163
    culture of, 275
    obsessive attempts to, 140, 142,
        145–48, 150, 151
    terminology, 55n106, 269
Controlling emotion in the modern era,
        217–20, 222–23, 237–39
Cooley, Charles Horton, 64
Coontz, Stephanie, 279–80
Cooper, Daniel, 76–78, 80
Cooper, Emma, 68t, 76–83
Cooper, Florence, 77–79
Cooper, Fred, 77–78
Cott, Nancy, 113
Cowan, John W., 106, 110–15, 127, 128
    act of familicide, 106, 110
    childhood, 107–8, 127–28
    livid coercive masculinity, 111, 127
    overview, 88t
    relationship with Mary, 108–10, 113
        jealousy, 109–10, 113–14, 122n136,
        128
    shame and humiliation, 111, 128
Cowan, Mary Sinclair, 106–10, 113
Cultural change, 277–82. See also
        Familicide, history; Social and
        historical contexts of mass killings
Curtis, Mary, 178t, 184, 207–8

Daly, Martin, 7, 19–20, 25–27,
        55n92
Damasio, Antonio R., 61–62
Daniele, A., 19–20
Death review. See Fatality review
        teams; Wide-angled lens
        death review
De Becker, Gary, 165
Deep acting, 222
Degler, Carl, 113
Deism, 94, 97, 101–2. See also
        Religion
Denzin, Norman, 37–38
Dependency, 20, 243–44, 247.
        See also Interdependencies
Depression, 20, 25, 159–60, 237–40,
        255n85. See also Emotional
        suffering
    postpartum, 193
Despondent offenders, 20
Detachment, 21
Divorces and separations, 227
Dobash, Rebecca, 265, 266, 271
Dobash, Russell, 265, 266, 271
Domestic Abuse Intervention Project
        (DAIP), 264, 267
Domestic violence. See Battering;
        Intimate-partner violence;
        Intimate terrorism
Drives, 41–43
Drug abuse, 107, 221
Dutton, Donald, 30–32, 34, 163,
        244, 272
Dutton, Mary Ann, 28–29
Duwe, G., 53n47

Eckinger, Bertha, 252n32
Eckles, Paul (pseudonym), 192
Economic factors. See
        Socioeconomic class
Edes, Peter, 103–6
Ehrenreich, Barbara, 262, 272
Eisner, Manuel, 117, 235
Elias, Norbert, 75
    on civilizing process and
        modernization, 13–14, 41, 43,
        233–37
    on drives, 41–43
    family, socialization of children, and,
        239, 247
    on figurations, 46, 62, 64, 66
    gender differences and, 247
    on interdependencies, 14, 41,
        42, 62, 65, 66, 235, 238,
        259, 274

Elias, Norbert *(cont.)*
    psychoanalysis and, 42–43, 62, 75
    on shame and other emotions, 41, 64,
        220, 233–35
    societal factors and, 13–14, 41, 53n27,
        238, 259
Emotional abuse, 128–29
Emotional capital, 31
Emotional continuum, 41–46, 47*t*, 47*f*
Emotional drives. *See* Drives
Emotional habitus, 70
Emotional isolation, acute, 189–95
Emotional styles, 61, 245
    the mélange of visceral,
        psychological, social, and
        historical energies, 61–65
    modernity, familicide, and, 240–51
Emotional suffering, 196–201
Emotion(s), 36–41, 163. *See also*
        Controlling emotion in the
        modern era
    role of, 270–71
    visceral experience of, 36
England
    during early modern period, 92, 93,
        112
    during medieval period, 89–92
Entitlement to kill, 20, 206, 250, 251
Erasmus, 234
Ewing, Charles, 20

Factitious disorder, 215n48
Faludi, Susan, 34–35, 244
Familicidal hearts, 10, 12. *See also
    specific topics*
    classification, 47*f*, 47*t*
    defined, 1
    necessary *vs.* sufficient conditions for
        the rise of, 251
    overview, 46–49
    terminology, 68, 70
Familicide. *See also specific topics*
    the act of, 171–73
    definitions, 1, 7
    historical emergence, 18–19
    history, 87
        early modern period, 92–94
        medieval period, 89–92
        modern era, 94–118. *See also*
        Modern life
    overview, 46–49
    prevalence, 117, 118n10, 119n25,
        258, 259, 287–89. *See also*
        Familicide, history
    research into family killing and, 19–27

terminology, 8
    types of perpetrators, 19–20
Familicide archive, 1, 10–11
Family, historical perspective on the, 14,
    154–55
*Family, Sex and Marriage in England
    1500-1800* (Lawrence Stone), 112
Family annihilation, 258
Farrell, Warren, 262, 282n3
Fatality review teams, 2–4, 6–7, 10
Fear, 237. *See also* Victims, perceptual
    acuity
Feelings. *See* Emotion(s); Figurations of
    feelings
Female perpetrators. *See* Women
    perpetrators
Feminists, 3
Ferraro, Kathleen, 29, 165, 269
Figurations of feelings, 46, 48, 62, 65–67
Filicide-suicide, 24–25. *See also* Infanticide
Fletcher, Jonathan, 41, 236
Ford, David, 162
"Forensic journalism," 184
Formani, Heather, 263
Foucault, Michel, 39, 57n180
Freud, Sigmund, 41, 42, 58n191, 63,
    81–82, 83n13, 145
Fromm, Erich, 132, 242

Gadit, A. M., 255n92
Garland, David, 9, 275
Gaylin, William, 272
Geertz, Clifford, 9–10
Gender differences, 19, 24, 26. *See also
    under* Stark, Evan; Women
    Chodorow on, 246–50, 256n112
    power and, 263–67
    suicide and, 55n91
    in violent behavior, 147, 151–53
Gender regimes, modern, 261–63
Gender relations, 3–4. *See also
    specific topics*
Ghostly Matters (Gordon), 28
Ghostly presence of modern era figura-
    tions of feelings, 48. *See also*
    Figurations of feelings
Ghosts, language of, 60, 70, 75, 81, 82,
    84n47
Giddens, Anthony, 217, 220, 221, 263,
    275, 279
Gill, Aisha, 241
Gilligan, James, 33–34, 38, 170, 242, 243
Given, James, 91–92, 119n22
"Giving up" (battered women), 29
Goetting, Ann, 3

Goffman, Erving, 27, 43, 63, 155, 217, 222
Goldberg, Herb, 262
Goleman, Daniel, 237, 252n18
Goodman, Lisa, 28–29
Gordon, Avery, 28, 60, 75, 80–82, 111, 151
Gothic narratives, 94–95, 98, 102
Graham, Jack (pseudonym), 71
Grief, 220–21
Gurr, Ted, 116, 117, 124n179
Guttmacher, Manfred, 230–31

Halttunen, Karen, 93–94
Hammer, Carl, 90, 91
Hanawalt, Barbara, 89, 91, 119n22, 254n59
Harris, Brian, 199–200
Hart, Barbara, 2, 109
Hassler, Robin, 2
Haunted hearts, 83. See also Cooper, Emma; Mason, Owen; Shell, Lonnie
    and uncanny acts, 67–71
Haunting, 60, 69–70, 79, 82, 98, 251
    concept and nature of, 75, 80–81
    language of, 23, 48
    and risk, 261, 275–77
    uncanny acts and, 81–82, 251
Heady, Esther, 77–78
"Heart," meanings of the word, 70
Hemphill, C. Dallett, 218
Hester, Malcolm (pseudonym), 137, 153–54
    abuse of Shirley and her children, 146–47, 153–54, 159
    ignominy, 169–70
    impression management, 158–59
    inability to work, 169, 170, 173
    overview, 126t
    Shirley Malcolm's fear of, 165–66
    suicide note to father, 169–70
Hester, Shirley (pseudonym), 146–47, 153–54, 165–66, 170
Hicks, Roy (pseudonym), 188, 193–94
Hochschild, Arlie, 222
Hofford, Merry, 2
Holcombe, Billy (pseudonym), 185, 197, 198, 212
Holcombe, Heather (pseudonym), 178t, 185, 193, 196–98, 212, 225
Homicide
    multiple. See Multicide

research into, 19–27
Homicide-suicide, 20. See also Filicide-suicide
    gender differences in, 55n91
Honor killings, 240–42, 245. See also Karo-Kari
Hoyle, Carolyn, 276–77
Huizinga, Johan, 124n180, 217–18
Humiliated fury, 140
Humiliation, 24, 38, 201, 226–27. See also Ignominy; Shame
Hunnisett, R. F., 90, 91
Hysteria, 83n13

Ignominy, 127, 167–70, 201–5
    defined, 167
    state of, 167
Illouz, Eva, 223
Implements of civilization, 234
Impression management, 63, 155–59, 186–89. See also Civil reputable hearts, fitting into the social order
Individualism. See Affective individualism
Individuality of partner, failure to recognize, 20
Infanticide, 24, 79–80. See also Cooper, Emma; Filicide-suicide
Insanity. See also Psychosis; Schizophrenia
    temporary, 225–26, 253n34. See also Allen, Patricia; Cooper, Emma; Curtis, Mary
Insanity defense, 73–75, 79, 253n34. See also Allen, Patricia
Instincts. See Drives
Interdependencies, 70, 80, 197, 259. See also Dependency; Figurations of feelings
    Norbert Elias on, 14, 41, 42, 62, 65, 66, 235, 238, 259, 274
Intimacy, 141, 195, 223. See also under Livid coercive hearts; Pyrrhic victories
Intimate-partner violence, 111–12, 142, 151–53. See also Battered women; specific topics
    control, emotional capital, and, 27–36
    female-perpetrated, 151–53. See also Women perpetrators
    prevalence, 152–53
    psychodynamics, 31
    terminology, 55n106
Intimate terrorism, 55n106, 129, 151–52, 174n32

Jacobs, Charmaine, 191
Jealousy, sexual, 141–45, 147–50
  of Daniel Kannon, 115
  Dawn Keetley on, 114
  delusions of infidelity, paranoia, and, 144
  gender differences and, 25
  of John Cowan, 109–10, 113–14, 122n136, 128
  of Marcus Sims (pseudonym), 142–44
  of Matthew Womble, 106
  prevalence as motive for familicide, 25
  research on, 122n136
  sociological factors and, 116
Johnson, Byron, 2
Johnson, Michael, 55n106, 129, 151–52
Johnson, Ruby (pseudonym), 145
Jones, Ann, 253n34

Kannon, Daniel, 88t, 114–15
Karo-Kari, 241, 255n92
Katz, Jack, 38
Kaufman, G., 103
Keane, Norman (pseudonym), 68, 69, 159, 164, 169
Kearley, Angela (pseudonym), 181–82, 196–97
Keetley, Dawn, 113, 114, 115
Kincel, Rudolph, 20–22
Kraepelin, Emil, 144
Kressel, Gideon, 240

Langdon, Bill (pseudonym), 138, 146, 153
  abuse of Marge Clanton and her daughter, 146
  act of familicide, 166
  child abuse, 137
  ignominy, 167–68
  impression management, 158
  overview, 126t
Laroche, Denis, 152–53, 174n32
Lasch, Christopher, 236
Latin Americans, 16
Le Bere, Emma, 88t, 89–90
Leland, James, 106
Lessing, Georgina (pseudonym), 137, 141, 160, 161
Lewis, Helen Block, 233
Leyton, Elliot, 23, 204
Lindsay, Philip, 23
List, Alma, 180–81
List, Helen Taylor, 190, 196, 202
List, John Emil, 60, 180, 183
  anger and rage, 196

as "Bob Clark," 190–91
  early socialization, 180–81, 213n7
  emotional alienation, 190–91
  motives and beliefs, 206–7
  overview, 178t
  planning and preparation, 210–11
  psychiatric problems, 200–201
  shame, 186, 187, 202–3
  unemployment and financial problems, 186–87, 202–3
List, John Frederick, 180–81
Livid coercion, 269
  cases of, 126t, 128–30. *See also specific cases*
  jealousy, obsessive attempts to control, and, 140–54
  shame and, 40
Livid coercive hearts, 125, 127, 129, 138, 154–55, 243, 244. *See also* Emotional continuum; *specific topics*
  vs. civil reputable hearts, 44, 58n201, 176–77, 186, 250, 278, 286
  depression, 159–60
  early socialization, 130–38, 141
  the final act, 171–73
  ignominy, 167–70
  impression management and bluster, 156–59
  occupational backgrounds, 46, 285
  planning and preparation in the midst of humiliated fury, 170–71
  Pyrrhic victories, 154–56
  racial/ethnic backgrounds, 286
  in search of intimacy, 138–54
Livid coercive masculinity. *See* Cowan, John
Longo, Christian, 45, 49
Loss, 220–21
Love, romantic *vs.* confluent, 279. *See also* Romance
Lukes, Steven, 268, 269
Lynd, Helen, 261

"Male revolt," 262
Malloy, Meredith, 146
Marietta, J. D., 96
Marriage, 279–80
  romance as basis for, 112, 113, 278–79
Marx, Karl, 17–18
Masculine possibilities, different, 272
Masculine pride, 25, 219
Masculinity, 266
  hegemonic, 250–51

Mason, Nancy (pseudonym), 68, 69, 164,
168–71
Mason, Owen (pseudonym), 68–69, 137,
153, 169, 172
bluster, 159
depression, 160
financial problems, 173
ignominy, 168, 169
Nancy's fear of, 164–65, 168
overview, 68*t*, 126*t*
planning to kill Nancy, 169–71
Mason, Peter (pseudonym), 170–71
Mass murder, 22–23
McDonald, Brenda, 93
McDonald, John, 230
McFarlane, Alan, 123n157
Mead, George Herbert, 64
Medieval period, 89–92
Meloy, J. Reid, 172
Mental illness, 196, 197. *See also* Insanity;
Psychosis
Messner, Steven, 24
Meyer, Cheryl, 79–80
Miller, Andrew (pseudonym), 185,
211–12, 227–28, 270
Miller, Delores, 190–91
Miller, Mandy (pseudonym), 179*t*, 185,
205, 211–13, 227–28, 270, 271
Mills, C. Wright, 13, 37
Mills, Linda, 31
Mindham, Phoebe (pseudonym), 148–49
Mitchell, Stephen Mix, 98–101
Mochrie, Catherine, 182, 186, 209
Mochrie, Robert, 186, 187
emotional isolation, 191, 224–25
emotional suffering, 198–99
financial problems, 199, 202, 229
gender dynamics and, 249
killing with care, 213, 223–24
motives and beliefs, 206
overview, 179*t*
planning and preparation, 208–9
as responsible and respectable citizen,
182
Modern era, 94–118
controlling emotion in, 217–20,
222–23, 237–39
Modern era figurations of feelings, 46, 48.
See also Figurations of feelings
Modernity, 275
emotional styles and familicide in,
240–51
Modern life. *See also* Modernity
linking emotional, social, and historical
landscapes, 13–18

Modern period, early, 92–94
Monomania, 39
Montana Death Review Initiative, 5
Motson, Paul, 180, 187–88
early socialization, 180
impression management, 187–88
medications for emotional suffering,
199
motives and beliefs, 206–7
overview, 179*t*
planning and preparation, 210
as responsible and respectable citizen,
183
termination of employment, 201–2
Motz, A., 24
Mowat, R. R., 144
Mullane, Frank, 5
Multicide, 1, 19, 23. *See also specific topics*
Murphy, Terence, 93
Myrack, John, 88*t*, 96–97

Narcissism, 20, 21, 205–7. *See also*
Entitlement to kill
National Domestic Violence Fatality
Review Initiative (NDVFRI), 2–3,
7, 12
Nature *vs.* nurture. *See* Biological factors
Negotiation of abusive relationships, 28
Neonaticide, 24
Nesca, Marc, 20–22, 171
Neurosis, 85n52
Normlessness, 16
Nowotny, Helga, 31

Oberman, Michelle, 80
Obsessive attempts to control, 140, 142,
145–48, 150, 151. *See also* Control
Occupational backgrounds, 46, 182, 227,
285
Office on Violence Against Women
(OVW), 3. *See also* Violence
Against Women Office
Oliver, Rebecca, 106
Oxley, Bertha (pseudonym), 134
Oxley, Bill (pseudonym), 134–36
Oxley, Bonnie (pseudonym), 134–39,
141, 145, 160–62, 166
Oxley, Connie (pseudonym), 134–36,
160, 161
Oxley, Kevin (pseudonym), 144, 145, 161
act of familicide, 166
anxieties, 221
childhood, 134–36, 141, 221
depression, 159
drug abuse, 159, 221

Oxley, Kevin (pseudonym) *(cont.)*
  employment, 173
  overview, 126*t*, 134
  personality, 136
  rage, 141
  relationship with Bonnie, 138, 160–62
    jealousy, 141, 145

Paranoia, 144. *See also* Jealousy
Paraphilias. *See* Sexual deviance
Passionate manhood, 219
Patel, S., 255n92
Patriarchal terrorism, 55n106
Pemberton, Julie, 5
Pemberton, Will, 5
Pence, Ellen, 34, 267, 268
Personality characteristics that predispose
    men to familicide, 20. *See also*
    specific traits
Personhood, complex, 274–75
Pilau, Andrea, 136
Planning and preparation, 208–12
  in the midst of humiliated fury, 170–71
Pleck, Elizabeth, 89, 115
Polk, Kenneth, 24–26, 256n100
Possessive individualism, 112
Postpartum depression and psychosis,
    193. *See also* Cooper, Emma
Posttraumatic stress disorder (PTSD),
    200–201
Power, 23, 263–67. *See also* Control
  as contested and relational, 278
  expression of naked, 27
  feelings *vs.* perceptions of, 33
  in intimate relationships, 28
  men, women, and, 3–4, 32–35
  outcomes of, 28
  personal sense of, 221
  social, 33
  violence and, 33, 34
Power and Control Wheel, 34–35
Pregnancy(ies), 24, 113, 115, 120n52,
    154, 169, 187, 190
Premonitions of familicide. *See* Victims,
    perceptual acuity
Pride. *See* Masculine pride; Shame
Psychic scarcity, 132
Psychoanalysis, 42–43, 58n191, 62, 75.
    See also Freud
Psychosis, 45, 85n52, 89, 98, 214n45.
    See also Insanity; Schizophrenia
  postpartum, 193
Purrinton, Betsy, 104, 105
Purrinton, James, 88*t*, 103–6, 189
Pyrrhic victories, 125, 127, 154–56

Race/ethnicity, 114, 248
  and livid coercive and civil reputable
    hearts, 58n201, 286
Rage, 23, 140, 141
  anger and, 195–96, 237–40
  shame, humiliation, and, 38. *See also*
    Humiliation; Shame
Reality testing, 82
Reason, suspension of. *See* Cooper, Emma
Religion, 102, 103, 202. *See also* Deism
  James Purrinton and, 105–6
  James Yates and, 97–98
  Lonnie Shell (pseudonym) and, 72
  Matthew Womble and, 106
  suicide and, 93–94
Retzinger, Suzanne, 38–39, 229
Review teams. *See* Fatality review teams
Riviere, Pierre, 39–40
Road rage, 140
Romance
  as basis for marriage, 112, 113, 278–79
  lure of, 138–40
Ronaldo, Ben (pseudonym), 144–45,
    162–63
  childhood, 136–37
  drug abuse, 137, 159
  employment, 169, 173
  humiliated fury, 140
  ignominy, 169
  overview, 126*t*, 136
  psychiatric problems, 159–60
  rage, 140
  relationship with Laurie, 139, 159,
    162, 163
    jealousy, 144–45, 162, 169
  suicidality, 159
Ronaldo, Donny (pseudonym), 136
Ronaldo, Laurie (pseudonym), 136, 137,
    140, 144–45, 162, 163, 169
Rosenfeld, Richard, 24
Roth, Randolph, 92, 94, 111, 116
Rotundo, Anthony, 219
Rowe, G. S., 96

Sadism, 132, 154
Sartre, Jean-Paul, 32
Saving face. *See* Shame
Scheff, Thomas, 38–39, 229
Schizophrenia, 22, 45
Schlesinger, Louis, 22
Scholes, Fred (pseudonym), 143
Scott, James, 267, 268
Self, sense of, 20, 64, 222–23
Self-blame, 148
Self-identity, threats to, 22. *See also* Shame

Serial killers, 195
Sexual deviance, 72–73, 84nn50–51, 146
Sexuality, 72–73
Sexual proprietariness, 25–26. *See also* Jealousy
Shame, 24, 38–40, 226–37, 244. *See also* Emotional suffering; Honor killings; Ignominy; Impression management
  Freud on, 63
  gender and, 31
  importance, 233, 273–74
  James Gilligan on, 242, 243
  as master emotion, 38–39
  Norbert Elias on, 64, 220, 233–35
Sharpe, J. A., 92, 93, 118n3
Shell, Lonnie (pseudonym), 68t, 71–75, 225
Shell, Sybil (pseudonym), 72, 73
Shepard, M., 267
Shields, Stephanie, 283n38
Sifuentes, Carmella (pseudonym), 130, 131, 138, 145–47
Sims, Alex (pseudonym), 142
Sims, Gloria (pseudonym). *See also under* Sims, Marcus, Sr.
  fear of being killed, 142, 164, 166–67
  maneuverability, resistance, and agency, 163–64
  separation, 142, 143, 157, 163–64
Sims, Janine (pseudonym), 141–42, 145, 146, 157, 242–43
Sims, Marcus, Jr. (pseudonym), 145–46
Sims, Marcus, Sr. (pseudonym)
  act of familicide, 132–33, 142, 171, 270
  childhood, 133–34
  ignominy, 171
  impression management, 157
  inability to hold down job, 173
  livid coercion, 141–46
  masculinity and, 171, 249, 270, 271
  overview, 126t, 132–33
  poetry, 139, 143–44, 157, 228
  relationship with Gloria, 139, 142, 143, 157, 163, 164, 270, 271
    jealousy, 142–44, 157
  relationship with Janine, 141–42, 145, 146, 157
  shame and need to reclaim pride, 144, 157, 228, 242, 249, 270
Situational couple violence, 152
Slavery, 15–16

"Snapping," 49, 169
Social and historical contexts of mass killings, 22–26, 95–96. *See also* Anxieties; Elias, Norbert; Familicide, history
Social disconnection, 224. *See also* Alienation
Socialization, early
  civil reputable hearts and, 179–82
  livid coercive hearts and, 130–38, 141
Social order. *See* Civil reputable hearts, fitting into the social order; Impression management
Social stigma, fear of, 24
Socioeconomic class, 26
Sociological imagination, 13
Sociology *vs.* psychology, 32
Spelman, Elizabeth, 247–48, 256n119
Spencer, Katrina (pseudonym), 146, 158, 166, 168, 168
Stark, Evan
  on coercive control, 27, 28, 55n106, 151, 152, 175n39, 267–68, 281, 282n3
  vs. David Dutton, 32
  on gender differences and gender relations, 27–28, 32, 55n106, 151, 152, 267–68, 282n3
Stearns, Peter N., 109, 116, 283n38
Stets, Jan, 36
Stone, Lawrence, 112, 115–16, 122n157
Structure of feeling, 62, 65–66. *See also* Figurations of feelings
Suicide, 20, 55n91
  following homicide. *See* Filicide-suicide; Homicide-suicide
  secularization of, 93–94
Surface acting, 222
Survey instrument for male perpetrators, 290–99

Talbie, Dorothy, 88t, 93
Talbie, Womble, 88t
"Tantrum," 238
Taylor, Howard, 53n23
Thick description, 10
Toolis, Kevin, 191, 199, 209
Town, Michael, 2
Triggering mechanisms, 74. *See also* Ignominy
Trunbach, Randolph, 112–13
Trust in the world, 221
Turner, Jonathan, 36

Ulrich, Laurel Thatcher, 103–5
Uncanny acts, 82, 259. *See also*
    Cooper, Daniel; Shell, Lonnie
    (pseudonym)
Uncanny feelings and experiences,
    81–82
Unconscious mind, 42, 58n191, 111
Understanding Domestic Homicide
    (Websdale), 283n27
Unworthiness, feeling of, 24. *See also*
    Shame

Victims. *See also* Battered women
  fearing for their lives, 152–54
  maneuverability, resistance, and agency,
    156, 160–64
  perceptual acuity, 164–67
Violence Against Women Office (VAWO),
    2. *See also* Office on Violence
    Against Women (OVW)

Wagner, 179*t*, 180, 183, 203–4, 207, 232
Wallace, Alison, 4
Wertham, F., 171
West, D. J., 232
White, Nancy (pseudonym), 179*t*, 185,
    192–93, 205
Wide-angled lens death review, 5, 6
Wilczynski, Ania, 226

Williams, Raymond, 65–67, 70
Willie W., 230–32
Wilson, Margo I., 7, 19–20, 25–27,
    55n92
Windley, Fanny, 253n34
Wolfgang, Marvin, 26, 55n91
Womble, Matthew, 106, 110
Women. *See also* Gender differences;
    Victims
  "fully regulated," 28
Women perpetrators, 47*t*, 47*f*, 250,
    278. *See also* Insanity, temporary;
    Intimate-partner violence,
    female-perpetrated
  absence of criminal background, 204
  anxieties, 225
  husband's standing in community, 182,
    184, 250
  ignominy, 202
  power, gender, and, 263–64
  reasons for killing, 250, 278
  socioeconomic and occupational
    backgrounds, 46, 182, 227
Wu, Kevin (pseudonym), 179*t*, 187, 200,
    202, 206, 213

Yates, James, 88*t*, 97–98

Zaretsky, E., n191, 83n13